Internationalisation of Higher Education and Global Mobility

Internationalisation of Higher Education and Global Mobility

Edited by
Bernhard Streitwieser

Oxford Studies in Comparative Education
Series Editor: David Phillips

SYMPOSIUM
BOOKS

Symposium Books
PO Box 204, Didcot, Oxford OX11 9ZQ, United Kingdom
www.symposium-books.co.uk

Published in the United Kingdom, 2014

ISBN 978-1-873927-42-7

This publication is also available on a subscription basis
as Volume 23 Number 2 of *Oxford Studies in Comparative Education*
(ISSN 0961-2149)

Printed and bound in the United Kingdom by Hobbs the Printers, Southampton
www.hobbs.uk.com

Contents

Foreword

SIMON MARGINSON

Notwithstanding cross-border tensions and one-way imperial projects, and the fact the world continues to be ordered as a zero-sum configuration of nation-states, processes of globalisation seem to be unstoppable. We are moving closer towards a single world society, a momentous historical development. Global mobility of persons is ever growing. Ideas move synchronously from one institution to the next. For the globally connected elite in the major cities, a world society already exists. More broadly, half of the world's population is now engaged in mobile phone networks, a technical precondition for universal society. One polity is much further off. Globalisation is uneven. Some nations and cities are more engaged than others. But none can remain outside the process.

Nowhere are global convergence and partial integration more apparent than in higher education and knowledge. A single system of networked research universities has emerged, subject to global mapping, comparison and ranking, though other parts of education are more solely localised and mostly remain decoupled from global circuits. Research universities remain embedded in localities while subject at the same time to both national policy, financing and regulation, and also global linkages, movements and comparisons.

It is sometimes suggested that globalisation may have peaked and a more separated higher education world may reassert, but this is wishful nostalgia. Consider what have been the major developments affecting national education systems in the last decade or so. There have been four such developments; and all are changes occurring at the global level: through global comparisons, or global systems, or shifts in the global balance of power in education and science.

First, there is the growing impact on policy and practice in secondary schooling, of the Organisation for Economic Cooperation and Development's Programme for International Student Assessments (PISA) of the educational achievement of 15-year-olds, which has become the principal performance indicator for school-level education bureaucrats and ministers. Not all countries are focused on lifting their PISA scores, but many are. Some such as South Korea have implemented major programs focused specifically on lifting reading, science or mathematics achievement. There is intense international interest in systems such as Finland, Korea and Shanghai that are doing especially well in PISA. This is leading to a spate of policy borrowing.

Second, there is the rise and rise of university rankings, especially research rankings. Global university rankings were a minor item when the first Shanghai Jiao Tong University top 500 league table was issued in 2003. They have ballooned in importance and are now front-page news in many countries. Research persistently shows that, despite the shortcomings of this form of cross-border comparison, rankings are highly influential with families and students in decisions about international education. They also affect the esteem (and often the revenue) given to universities by governments, industry and philanthropy, and shape patterns in the cross-border movements of academic faculty. Global rankings inexorably push governments and universities alike towards the model of the comprehensive Anglo-American science university that makes up the ranking template. They drive mergers designed to secure critical mass and offshore recruitment designed to lift citation rates. University ranking has become perhaps the chief performance indicator for ministers of higher education, and university presidents/rectors/vice-chancellors.

Third, there is the advent of Mass Open Online Course (MOOC) programs in September 2011 at Stanford University. Through the for-profit corporations Coursera and Udacity at Stanford, and edX run by MIT and Harvard, MOOC offerings and enrolments have grown extraordinarily rapidly. It is already apparent that this is a major game-changer in worldwide higher education. MOOCS offer programs from global brand universities that feature leading world experts. Students' work is assessed using multiple-choice online software, and the minority of students who complete the program successfully receive certification at its end. MOOCS also provide scope for social networking between students. As a free platform with user-navigated content and social interaction, they are perfectly attuned to the Web, unlike other online prototypes that tend to replicate the bricks and mortar university in a virtual form. As free and certified programs from prestigious universities, they are an attractive alternative to any program in any mode that charges tuition fees. MOOCs may radically reduce the average cost of teaching, lower the number of academic faculty in many countries and weaken the position of universities that are prestigious at national level but left in the shade by the global giants. MOOCs also promise to further increase the global power and authority of the leading US universities, thus compounding the normalising effects of rankings. Both trends push us in the direction of greater global standardisation.

Finally, consider the growing weight of higher education and science in East Asia and Singapore. There used to be two major zones in worldwide higher education and science: North America, and Western Europe and the United Kingdom (UK). After 1970 Japan was added as the outrider. Now there are three such zones. Already the Post-Confucian systems in East Asia – China, Hong Kong SAR, Taiwan, South Korea and of course Japan – invest as much in R&D as do the whole of Europe and the UK. Published journal papers are increasing by 17% a year in China and already the total paper output in that country is half the level of the United States. Quality (as measured by citation rates) lags behind quantity but is improving rapidly. Already China produces more than 10% of the world's most-cited top 1% papers in both engineering and chemistry. Science output in Korea, Singapore and Taiwan is also growing rapidly. World-class universities are advancing in all these systems. These outputs reflect the investments of five to ten years ago and, given that funding of the leading universities continues to increase, the rise of Asian science will continue. In turn this ensures that universities in the East will attract ever more talent from all over the world. In a radical transformation of the Atlantic and European domination of the last three centuries, in future much of the world's knowledge will come from East Asia. The rise of higher education in East Asia, amid dynamic modernising economies, is leading to a more plural world in which the cultural mix will be more diverse. MOOCs and rankings assert American domination. This process of pluralisation is working in the opposite direction. There are also signs that universities in parts of western Europe are becoming stronger in relative terms.

These are the four headline developments – PISA comparisons, global university rankings, MOOCs and the rise of new higher education powers – but there are many more signs of internationalisation and globalisation discussed in this book. Mobility and knowledge convergence affect universities and their personnel everywhere. All non-English-speaking nations are caught up in the new hegemony of English-language science and of the American models of universities and systems. All face the same tensions between global pluralisation and standardisation, tensions that are differently (and differentially) manifest in every national and local case.

Internationalisation of Higher Education and Global Mobility is a fine collection that provides an unparalleled insight into these different aspects of globalisation in higher education. The book tracks the main trends through different spatial lenses: in terms of the world as a whole, in terms of the main regions and particular national and institutional sites, and in terms of the implications for cross-border relations of power and for social inclusion. Several chapters also rework our conventional tools of interpretation, particularly in relation to mobility of persons and of educational institutions and programs. The chapters in this book will deepen the scholarship of international higher education and guide us towards stronger empirical research projects in future.

INTRODUCTION

Internationalisation of Higher Education and Global Mobility

BERNHARD STREITWIESER

In recent decades the production of scholarship on internationalisation in higher education has grown exponentially. Continuous and rapid developments in the global higher education landscape have posed new questions, presented greater challenges and opened up new opportunities that invite scholarly observers, policy makers, practitioners, and critics and champions of international education [1] alike to respond, to share their knowledge and to propose innovative solutions.

This book brings together the voices of many of the leading experts in international higher education today to share their reflections on many of these critical questions and, in some cases, to offer their predictions about what we might expect in the future. In this 'revolutionary' and 'tumultuous' time of change in higher education (Knight, 2008; Altbach et al, 2012), students who participate in international educational exchange, practitioners who structure and manage their sojourns abroad, and scholars who provide analysis are confronted with myriad new opportunities for deeper reflection and even more active engagement than ever before (Kandeko & Weyers, 2013).

With the acceleration of trends driven today by globalisation and its impact on higher education, scholars have a wide range of issues with which to contend. These include a continued pattern in the twenty-first century of massification of higher education participation; increased information sharing through internet technology and expanded means of travel; greater movement of students and professionals worldwide through an ever-changing matrix of sending and receiving countries and the shifting push and pull factors that drive them; challenges to traditional public education through new, private niche providers; rapidly developing massive open online courses and other experiments; and an ongoing race for new partnerships and learning collaborations through any variety of cross-border configurations, among many other trends.

Where mobility [2] as part of this larger process of internationalisation is concerned, we must not only marvel at the often anecdotally understood and assumed benefits of educational exchange but, as Jane Knight (2012) warns us, also be vigilant of the unintended consequences and their implications. Indeed, each of the trends we observe in internationalisation also incorporates vexing challenges related to ensuring access to educational opportunity and improving the overall quality of the experience in a time of seemingly always greater competition among, and often division between, any variety of stakeholders. These constituencies include national and local governments, private and public institutions, wealthy and needy students, secure and temporary faculty, highly ranked and poorly positioned institutions, and geographic centres and peripheral followers, to name just a few of the appositions. With the belief that educational mobility through its participants can also expand national and cultural identity elsewhere, and thus serve an important fourth role of foreign policy alongside diplomatic, military and commercial dimensions – as Philip Coombs argued in 1964 and Hickling-Hudson and Arnove note in their chapter in this book – our dual role as observers of and participants in higher education internationalisation today presents us with both great opportunities and heightened risks.

The sum of the articles and the corresponding structure of this book moves from, first, a global, supranational perspective on the wide scope of issues related to internationalisation and mobility as they affect higher education systems. In the second part of the book each chapter focuses on a specific geographic region and examines more closely some of the issues at play in Europe, the Middle East, the United States, Africa, Asia and Latin America. Finally, the third part of the book offers profiles of some of the individual institutions, practitioners and participants who are involved in shaping mobility through their everyday work.

Part 1 of the book provides a current big picture perspective of many of the main trends that are affecting student and staff mobility today. In the first chapter, Rahul Choudaha and Hans De Wit take the events of September 11th and the start of the financial crisis of 2008 as their jumping-off point to provide a comparative analysis of mobility in terms of global competition for top talent, types of mobile students, issues related to language and levels and areas of study, and an assessment of the direction they see mobility taking in the future.

In the second chapter, Darla Deardorff presents an argument for why she sees traditional ways of engaging in mobility as no longer adequate today, given global migration flows and the increasing divides between those with access to education, technology for distance learning and mobility programmes and those without it. Deardorff questions what higher education's fundamental responsibilities in internationalisation in essence are. Through that critique she advocates that we look more deeply at the rationales and reasons that underlie the institutional push for increased mobility, lest we lose sight of still critical and unresolved issues fundamentally related to access, equity, and assessment of value and quality.

In the third chapter, Jane Knight introduces a framework for understanding the controversial development of cross-border education and its gradual shift over time from a cooperative undertaking, to one characterised by partnerships, to one now commercialised and highly competitive. The 'three generations of crossborder education' show a transition from the movement of students, faculty and scholars, to the establishment of twinning arrangements, branch campuses and distance learning, to most recently the creation of education hubs – 'a concerted and planned effort by a country (or zone, city) to build a critical mass of education/knowledge actors and strengthen its efforts to exert more influence in the new marketplace of education'.

The fourth chapter, by Angeline Barrett, Michael Crossley and Peter Titanji Fon, examines internationalisation in higher education from the perspective of North–South cross-cultural collaborations and research capacity building. The discussion is based on the authors' experience in a partnership between the University of Buea in Cameroon and the University of Bristol in the United Kingdom (UK) and their joint projects aimed at strengthening the teaching and learning of research methods within doctoral programmes. The authors conclude that, while much of the existing literature on the internationalisation of higher education has focused on teaching and learning, the implications of internationalisation on research have yet to be better understood.

Finally, the fifth chapter in Part 1, by Joan Dassin, Juergen Enders and Andrea Kottmann, offers a comprehensive review of the relationship between educational opportunity and broader social justice issues in developing countries. The authors ask how educational opportunity, especially for international study at the graduate level, can have a more lasting impact on reversing discrimination and stigmatisation and refocus mobility from an undertaking that benefits only a select few to one that offers opportunity to a broader spectrum of deserving individuals. The authors contend that expansion and diversification are not by themselves democratising trends but rather that access to higher education and global mobility today are still deeply stratified by gender, class, race, ethnicity, rural versus urban location, and cost. Using the Ford Foundation's International Fellowship Program as their case, the authors illustrate how mobility programmes that include students who otherwise lack systematic access to higher education can operate successfully in a wide variety of international settings and educational systems when afforded the opportunity. Perhaps most importantly, their study counters the argument that social inclusion lowers academic standards in highly competitive graduate programmes.

In the second part of the book, we turn to region-specific studies that address aspects of internationalisation and mobility in Europe, the Middle East, the United States, Africa, Asia and Latin America. In chapter six, the first chapter in Part 2, Bernd Waechter examines recent trends in student mobility across Europe utilising the comparable joint international database collections of the UNESCO, OECD and EUROSTAT (UOE). Elaborating on his work on the landmark study *Mapping Mobility,* Waechter discusses the patterns of student mobility into, out of and between the countries of the Europe 32 Region.

For the seventh chapter we stay in Europe but turn to a detailed discussion of the Erasmus Mobility Programme. Thomas Norgaard frames his discussion of the Erasmus programme with an initial tribute to Dr Sofia Corradi, known as 'Mama Erasmus', an activist who spent more than two decades pushing for change within the Italian university system and promoting a wider 'culture of student mobility' more generally throughout Europe. After articulating his philosophical interpretation of Corradi's educational vision for Erasmus, Norgaard unpacks the design and institutional realities of the Programme in view of Corradi's early vision and goes on to critique its manifestation in practice today.

In the eighth chapter, Justin Powell comparatively profiles the internationalisation strategies of two recently established institutions, one in Europe and the other in the Middle East. Profiling the University of Luxembourg and Qatar University, two hyper-diverse and well-funded yet distinctly different national institutions confronting similar global issues today, Powell shows how both institutions reflect the ethnically and linguistically diverse countries in which they reside but at the same time promote ambitions that stretch far beyond their borders. In each case, these universities have adeptly managed to become global players through carefully planned strategies that are characterised by heavy investment in select, high-potential multidisciplinary research fields and the establishment of cutting-edge facilities, the development of high-level multicultural networks of faculty, staff and students, active engagement in cross-border mobility, and the development of undergraduate and graduate programmes that train local elites and also draw in new international talent.

In the ninth chapter, Anthony Welch takes us to South East Asia and a profile of contemporary Islamic higher education in a region he argues has so far been less well represented in the scholarship on higher education. His study examines the flowering of Islamic scholarly centres, the growth of international mobility of staff and students in the region, and efforts to recruit large numbers of students from the Gulf States and the broader Arab world. Welch's discussion shows how these efforts have begun to slowly reverse traditional paths of mobility and how pan-Islamic student and staff exchanges, joint programmes and more flexible curricula may help eventually restore the ancient leading centres of Islamic learning as the magnets for scholars and students and contributors to knowledge they once were.

In the tenth chapter, Jon Powell and Cynthia Miller-Idriss examine the role of area study centres run by US universities in the advancement of academic staff mobility abroad. Their study draws on interview data from a long-term, mixed-methods investigation of area studies centres conducted at eight American universities that are heavily involved in the formal exchange of students and scholars. Through closely analysing the activities of these centres and sharing the perspectives of the personnel who work there, the authors provide an insightful analysis of the specific mechanics underlying how mobility is organised and facilitated.

In the eleventh chapter, Rose Amazan takes us to Africa and an examination of the international skilled migration patterns of Ethiopia's diaspora. Noting some countries' recent successes in counteracting the flight of skilled personnel, such as India and China, Amazan takes stock of Ethiopia's efforts in this regard. Her analysis shows how mobilising Ethiopia's skilled diaspora could make a valuable contribution to the country's national development and reap the necessary social and economic benefits. More broadly, Amazan's chapter sheds light on the economic, social, cultural and political manifestations of the push and pull of globalisation and promoting educational dialogue across the North and South.

In the twelfth chapter, Juergen Henze provides an expansive picture of developments in Chinese state-controlled internationalisation in higher education and regional and institutional variations in strategy and policy outcomes. His analysis characterises internationalisation in China as an interrelated space of a worldwide process concurrently inwardly driven and outwardly shaping the internationalisation space in parts of the Western world. Drawing on domestic and international scholarly discussions of Chinese higher education, Henze expands Jane Knight's oft-cited definition of internationalisation [3] by introducing the term *reflexive internationalisation* – 'the enlightened analysis of processes, structures, interrelatedness (dependencies) of intended action within the frame of global internationalisation and its critical reflexive analysis [as well as] various kinds of reach-out "influences" of internationalisation strategies in cross-national and cross-cultural perspectives'.

The last chapter in Part 2, by Anne Hickling-Hudson and Robert Arnove, takes us to Latin America and the Caribbean and a study of how Cuban internationalism in higher education promotes and facilitates mobility. Particularly salient in their analysis is the contrast they draw between the philosophy driving Cuba's mobility efforts – solidarity with other developing countries, provision of mutual support, and assistance based on need and capability – and many current sending and receiving countries, where market principles and the profit motive generally determine the agenda (with some important exceptions in Europe). The paper examines numerous political and social considerations behind Cuba's role as a regional and international 'hub' for higher education today.

Finally, the chapters in Part 3 highlight issues related to ways that students and administrators engage in mobility. To provide a general framework for this discussion some initial, broad statistics are helpful. Over the past 50 years the number of students who study outside their home countries had expanded from less than a quarter of a million to over 4.1 million by 2010 (Organisation for Economic Cooperation and Development, 2012) among the 165 million students worldwide who participate in formal higher education (UNESCO, 2013). Although these numbers mirror general massification trends within global tertiary enrolment as they have increased over more than a century (Schofer & Meyer, 2005), some scholars estimate that participation in international education will expand even more rapidly in the future, perhaps reaching 7.2 million by 2025 (Boehm et al, 2002, p. 3).

In terms of voluntary study abroad or what is referred to as 'horizontal or temporary mobility' (Rivza & Teichler, 2007), the popularity of education abroad programming has undoubtedly been driven by the ubiquitous public rhetoric around globalisation and the conviction that building intercultural competence reaps undeniable professional dividends. However, the numbers of students who engage in study abroad remain remarkably low in many countries because of the costs associated, among other factors. Many of those who participate in study abroad still represent a socio-economic elite despite some governmental and institutional efforts to increase opportunity. In the USA, for example, still only 1-2% of college and university students studied abroad in the 2010-11 academic year (Institute of International Education Open Doors, 2012). By contrast, in Europe, although with enormous variation between countries, the participation rate of students participating in study abroad within the framework of the Erasmus Mobility Programme averages closer to 10%. As a taxpayer-funded initiative established in 1987 and today the largest exchange programme in the world (Mitchell, 2012), Erasmus has offered over 3 million students of all socio-economic levels competitive grants to gain international study or work experience in more than 33 European countries for a semester or a year.

In this last part of the book, Ogden, Streitwieser and Crawford in Chapter 14 critique some of the programming components of US study abroad that have traditionally been lauded as intercultural spaces for transformative student learning. Their argument challenges long-held assumptions about the ability of these 'meeting grounds' to deliver on their promises and examines how these learning spaces have changed over time in response to globalisation and the internationalisation of higher education. Using the concepts of *positionality*, *reciprocity* and *intentionality* to suggest new approaches to facilitating student learning, to promoting sustainable community engagement, and to enhancing programme design and ongoing assessment, they contend that many untested claims and long-held assumptions about study abroad's impact on learning stand to be challenged.

In Chapter 15, Streitwieser and Van Winkle examine the European Erasmus Mobility Programme and one of its key goals: developing in participants a strengthened sense of European identity. While scholars currently debate whether greater European-mindedness is a hallmark of students who self-select into the programme or is a result of the experience of studying abroad within Europe, Streitwieser and Van Winkle pre-empt this debate by addressing the more fundamental question of how Erasmus participants interpret the notion of citizenship identity to begin with and whether or not they believe participating in Erasmus can even play an important role in their identity development.

Chapter 16, by Jos Beelen, explores the role of incoming student mobility for Internationalisation at Home in the context of higher education in the UK, the Netherlands and Australia. Beelen argues that in the aim to internationalise the curriculum for all students, priority often ends up being given to accommodating international students and causing home students to become marginalised. He advocates that developing new forms of mobility that combine physical with virtual and outgoing with incoming mobility would better serve to provide the international experience for all students that traditional incoming mobility currently fails to deliver.

The last chapter in the book, by Loberg and Rust, return us to the US context and the question of what factors lead to high participation rates in international education. Based on interviews with professionals who work at or collaborate with institutions successfully sending many students abroad each year, the authors explore the strategies that account for success in overcoming perceived barriers to participation. They conclude that faculty support more than increased funding to aggressive marketing is the most important influencing factor in a student's decision of whether or not to study abroad.

The essays in this book were selected to further advance a discussion I initiated as the guest editor for a special issue of the online journal *Research in International and Comparative Education*, in January 2012 (volume 7). While the essays in that publication examined a range of the issues related to the study of mobility in Comparative Education scholarship, the essays in this book have aimed to further expand the study of mobility by situating it more broadly within the phenomenon of the internationalisation of higher education today. It is my hope that the discussions in this book will make a valuable contribution to expanding the scope of research in the field of Comparative and International Education and ultimately facilitate further theory development and policy formation as we witness the continuing and dynamic processes of internationalisation of higher education and global mobility.

Notes

[1] See the Forum on Education Abroad's *Education Abroad Glossary* for a detailed description of the concept of 'international education' (http://www.forumea.org/UnderstandingtheUSEducationalSystem.cfm).

[2] The discussions presented in this book understand the term 'mobility' to cover more than just the notion of student study abroad but also include staff

exchange and forced mobility through migration. For discussion of various types of 'mobilities' see Teichler et al (2011).

[3] 'The process of integrating an international, intercultural or global dimension into the purpose, functions or delivery of postsecondary education' (Knight, 2008, p. 21).

References

Altbach, P., Reisberg, L. & Rumbley, L.E. (2009) *Trends in Global Higher Education: tracking an academic revolution. Executive Summary*. A Report Prepared for the UNESCO 2009 World Conference on Higher Education. Paris: UNESCO.

Boehm, A., Davis, D., Meares, D. & Pearce D. (2002) *The Global Student Mobility 2025 Report: forecasts of the global demand for international education*. Canberra: IDP.

Coombs, P. (1964) *Fourth Dimension of Foreign Policy: educational and cultural affairs*. New York: Harper & Row.

Institute of International Education (2012) Opendoors 20/12 'Fast Facts'. New York: IIE. http://www.iie.org/opendoors

Kandeko, C.B. & Weyers, M. (2013) *The Global Student Experience: an international and comparative analysis*. Oxford: Routledge.

Knight, J. (2003) Updated Internationalization Definition, *International Higher Education*, 33, 2-3.

Knight, J. (2008) *Higher Education in Turmoil: the changing world of internationalization*. Rotterdam: Sense.

Knight, J. (2012) Student Mobility and Internationalization: trends and tribulations, *Research in International and Comparative Education*, 7(1), 20-33.

Mitchell, K. (2012) Student Mobility and European Identity: Erasmus study as a civic experience, *Journal of Contemporary European Research*, 8(4), 490-518.

Organisation for Economic Cooperation and Development (2012) *Education at a Glance 2012*. Paris: OECD.

Rivza, B. & Teichler, U. (2007) The Changing Role of Student Mobility, *Higher Education Policy*, 20, 457-475.

Schofer, E. & Meyer, J.W. (2005) The Worldwide Expansion of Higher Education in the Twentieth Century, *American Sociological Review*, 70(6), 898-920.

Teichler, U., Ferencz, I. & Wächter, B. (Eds) (2011) *Mapping Mobility in European Higher Education. Volume I: Overview and Trends*. Bonn: DAAD.

UNESCO (2013) Global Flow of Tertiary-Level Students. http://www.uis.unesco.org/Education/Pages/international-student-flow-viz.aspx (accessed 29 August 2013).

CHAPTER 1

Challenges and Opportunities for Global Student Mobility in the Future: a comparative and critical analysis

RAHUL CHOUDAHA & HANS DE WIT

ABSTRACT The pace, directions and outcomes of international student mobility are significantly influenced by a complex interplay of multiple push and pull variables. While outward mobility of international students has grown at a steady pace, it masks the changing nature of the growth and external factors that influenced it. The changing context of the global knowledge economy has transformed and continues to transform the nature of student mobility. The focus of this chapter is to discuss the future of global student mobility with a comparative and critical perspective. First, comparative analysis of mobility from key source countries and to key destination countries is discussed, with an emphasis on the role of economic environment, immigration policies and demographic shifts. In addition, the relationship between international student recruitment and skilled migrants is presented. Second, a critical analysis of the role of mobility in the larger framework of internationalisation is presented, addressing topics such as types of mobile students, the language factor, mobility by level and area of study, and other factors (reputation, costs, cross-border delivery) as well as study abroad as part of the home degree. Finally, we conclude with future directions of student mobility.

Introduction

History tells us that the changes in external and internal environment play an extremely important role in the process of internationalisation of higher education (De Wit & Merkx, 2012). Specifically, the pace, directions and outcomes of international student mobility are significantly influenced by a complex interplay of multiple push and pull variables: mutual understanding (political, social and cultural factors), revenue earning (economic factor), skill migration (economic factor) and capacity building (educational factors). (For an overview of push and pull variables see Agarwal et al, 2008, p. 241.) While some variables have hindered mobility, many more have enabled it to offer a consistent growth in numbers over the decades. The first decade of the twenty-first century has seen the number of globally mobile students nearly double from 2.1 million in 2000 to 4.1 million in 2010, growing at an average annual rate of 7.2% (Organisation for Economic Cooperation and Development [OECD], 2012).

> Europe is the preferred destination for students studying outside
> their country, with 41% of all international students. North
> America has 21% of all international students. Nevertheless, the
> fastest growing regions of destination are Latin America and the
> Caribbean, Oceania and Asia, mirroring the internationalisation of
> universities in an increasing set of countries. (OECD, 2012,
> p. 361)

While this growth indicates the aspirations and desires of international students to go abroad, it masks the changing nature of the growth and external factors that have influenced it. The twenty-first century has been marked by two major external factors: the tragic event of the 9/11 terrorist attack and its geopolitical and economic impact, and the global financial crisis of 2008 and its further impact on the world economy and the euro, which changed the dynamics between source and destination countries. The far-reaching effects of these two unpredictable events, together with the changing context of the global knowledge economy in which emerging economies in Asia, Africa and Latin America are taking a more prominent place, have transformed and continue to transform the nature of student mobility.

The focus of this chapter is to discuss the future of global student mobility with a comparative and critical perspective. First, comparative analysis of mobility from key source countries and to key destination countries is discussed, with an emphasis on the role of economic environment, immigration policies and demographic shifts. In addition, the relationship between international student recruitment and skilled migrants is presented. Second, a critical analysis of the role of mobility in the larger framework of internationalisation is presented, addressing topics such as types of mobile students, the language factor, mobility by level and area of study, and other factors (reputation, costs, cross-border delivery) as well as study abroad as part of the home degree. Finally, we conclude with future directions of student mobility.

A Comparative Analysis of Mobility

Much has been written about the growth of international student mobility and key sending and receiving countries. Very little, however, has been analysed to uncover why and how patterns have changed. This section thus examines the changing nature of mobility with an emphasis on what has changed and why.

In the last decade, the dominance of the three leading destinations has remained relatively steady (OECD, 2012). In 2000, 39% of globally mobile students were enrolled either in the USA (23%), the United Kingdom (UK) (11%) or Australia (5%). This aggregate share declined slightly to 37% in 2010, with the USA hosting 17%, the UK 13% and Australia 7%. The drop in aggregate portion was driven by the USA's loss of 6%, which was redistributed between Australia and the UK. This means that if the USA were to have maintained its share of the student mobility market of 23%, it would have needed to have enrolled nearly 250,000 additional students than it did by 2010.

The USA's market share slid owing primarily to a combination of two simultaneous factors: stricter immigration policies in the USA after 9/11 that raised entry barriers for international students, and a more welcoming stance adopted by Australia and the UK. The repercussions of 9/11 were that of tightened entry and monitoring of international students through the Student and Exchange Visitor Information System, which ultimately hurt the USA's image overseas. In 2005-06, international student enrolment in the USA hit an all-time low post-9/11 of 565,000 – a decrease of 21,500 from 2002-03 figures (Institute of International Education, 2012).

On the other hand, both Australia and the UK lowered barriers for international students by offering an attractive package of lower cost, future immigration potential and welcoming outreach. Their immigration policies offered easier post-study employment and permanent residency pathways. Moreover, national-level marketing along with aggressive use of commission-based agents resulted in Australian and British universities attracting more international students. In contrast, post-education employment became very difficult in the USA not only in terms of obtaining work permit but also owing to sheer decline in job availability. As a result, within a decade, Australia and the UK added nearly 165,000 and 310,000 foreign students, respectively (OECD, 2012).

In other words, the post-9/11 scenario made the USA less attractive, but it did not curtail the aspirations of globally mobile students, and hence, the USA's loss in share became the UK's and Australia's gain. Growth of international student enrolment in these latter two countries would have continued if it had not been for the global financial crisis of 2008. The unforeseen ramifications of the financial recession took policy-makers and higher education institutions by surprise. It further exposed two critical issues regarding international student enrolment in Australia and the UK: the high proportion of foreign students as compared with domestic students, and concerns related to quality and intentions of some international students owing to increasing cases of visa abuse and its relationship to aggressive recruitment practices. Australia and the UK tightened up their visa policies in response to these challenges, which in turn sent discouraging messages to prospective international students and put the brakes on growth in international student enrolment.

In 2010, foreign students represented 21% and 16% of higher education enrolment in Australia and the UK, respectively, compared to less than 4% in the USA (OECD, 2012). This indicates a higher dependence of Australia and the UK on foreign students than the USA. This dependence also has direct financial implications for universities; for example, the UK has projected to lose £2-3 billion per year in economic contributions of international students (Cavanagh & Glennie, 2012).

Aside from the aforementioned two global events, other major external influences on student mobility are demographic shifts and economic growth. The effects can be seen from the perspective of key source countries. Contrary to the top three destination countries maintaining their market share and rank order, the major senders of international students have considerably changed over the last decade. In 2000, the top three source countries of foreign students enrolled in OECD countries were China (7%), Japan (5%) and Korea (4%) – forming 16% of all mobile students. In comparison, China (19%), India (7%) and Korea (5%) have become the top source countries, representing nearly 31% of all foreign student enrolment in 2010 in OECD countries.

This shift reflects changes related to demographics and economy in key sending countries. Within the last 10 years, Japan's and Korea's population of those aged under 25 has declined from 27% to 24% and 38% to 30%, respectively (World Bank, 2011). Even China and India – the countries with the largest population – have experienced similar declines in the proportion of this age group from 41% to 35% and 53% to 48%, respectively. However, in absolute terms, China and India have more than one billion people in this age bracket as compared to nearly 45 million between Japan and Korea.

Demographics are one explanation for the shift in key source countries, but another is economic growth. China and India saw dramatic growth in GDP per capita in terms of purchasing power parity from 2000 to 2010. Within this time frame, China and India grew by 220% and 120%, whereas Korea and Japan rose by 67% and 31%, respectively (World Bank, 2011). Even more interesting is growth in high-net worth individuals (HNIs) with investible assets of US$1 million or more. China experienced growth in the number of HNIs from 320,000 in 2005 to 562,000 in 2011 as compared with India from 83,000 to 126,000 in the same period (Cap Gemini, 2012). The confluence of economic growth, a large youth population and expanded access to education has fuelled the demand for global mobility.

The increasing ability of prospective students in rapidly developing countries like China and India to afford higher education overseas has collided with Australian and British institutions' increasing fiscal dependency on international students. More recently, discussions about the use of commission-based agents has gained momentum in the USA as many budget-constrained public institutions are looking to recruit international students more aggressively. Today, the rationale for international student recruitment has unfortunately shifted from attracting diverse talent to seeking additional sources of revenue. As a result (of the financially driven model) universities are increasingly over-relying on select countries, which not only compromises in-class and on-campus diversity but also poses financial risks. These issues highlight the importance of identifying and cultivating new source countries for recruiting international students (Choudaha & Kono, 2012).

Increasing the Stay Rate: global competition for top talents

In addition to the above-described picture of the dynamics of student mobility for key source and destination countries, we observe related demographic and economic factors on a global scale. Northern America, Europe, Australia and Japan face a demographic challenge. For the OECD, 'over the next couple of decades nothing will impact on [member] economies more profoundly than demographic trends, and chief among them, ageing' (Cotis, in Hawthorne, 2012, p. 420). The knowledge economies of the OECD member countries require highly skilled people who, owing to ageing and also to less interest by their own youth in the hard sciences, will not be sufficiently available, and so skilled immigrants are needed to fill the gaps. A recent report entitled *The World at Work: jobs, pay, and skills for 3.5 billion people* speaks of a 'mismatch between jobs and graduates' (McKinsey, 2012). The study claims that although there is global unemployment for 75 million young people, 39% of employers indicate they have difficulties filling vacancies for skilled labour.

The pattern of low-skilled immigration from the so-called South to the North of the past century has been replaced by a need for high-skilled migrants. At the same time, the emerging societies in Asia, Africa and Latin America also need more skilled labour to develop their economies, resulting in global competition for top talents. Several countries over recent decades have made it more attractive for highly skilled people to come and work, while at the same time restricting immigration of lower skilled people. These efforts have included:

– post-study 'job-search' schemes that allow international students to stay in the country after graduation for the purposes of job seeking;
– the general streamlining of procedures for obtaining student visas and highly skilled work permits;
– amended naturalisation and permanent residency laws that take years of residence as an international student into account when

assessing eligibility for acquiring citizenship/long-term residence status;
– the easing of work restrictions during the study and post-study periods;
– new visa categories specifically designed to attract and retain international students;
– privileges for international graduates when accessing certain visa schemes, e.g. lower minimum income requirements and the waiver of labour market tests (priority examination). (Sykes, 2012, p. 9)

A clear example is Canada, where immigration of skilled labour has received much support from federal and state governments. At the same time,

by the early 2000s, skilled class entering immigrants (to Canada) were actually more likely to enter low-income and be in chronic low income than their family class counterparts, and the small advantage that the university educated entering immigrants had over, say, the high school educated in the early 1990s had largely disappeared by 2000, as the number of highly educated rose. What did change was the face of the chronically poor immigrant: by the late 1990s one-half were in the skilled economic class, and 41% had degrees (up from 13% in the early 1990s). (Pico et al, 2007 cited by Hawthorne, 2012, p. 420)

Countries increasingly understand that immigration of skilled people is not always effective, and for that reason '[I]nternational students have come into the spotlight as an attractive group of prospective skilled immigrants' (Sykes, 2012, p. 8). Where in the past, these countries would have an open mind to receiving international students in general and even subsidised their education, one can observe in several countries, in particular in Europe, a shift towards more controlled immigration of international students and measures to increase their stay rate. The Netherlands, Denmark and Sweden are clear examples of such policies. Over the past decade they have on the one hand introduced full cost fees for non-EU students and at the same time developed scholarship schemes to selectively target talent and create opportunities for students to stay after graduation. The Danish Minister of Science, Helge Sander, formulated this policy in the following way:

We feared that with free education also for students coming to Denmark from outside Europe, the Danish universities would risk being flooded by non-EU/EEA citizens and that this would put a massive strain on the state educational expenses ... But although Denmark introduced tuition fees, we secured the opportunity of studying for free in Denmark for highly qualified students by introducing a scholarship scheme. Through the funding for this scheme, the Danish state can control expenses associated with educating foreign students in Denmark. (University World News, no. 108, 24 January 2010)

The percentage of international students who stay after their graduation in the country of study, the so-called 'stay rate', is on average 25% for OECD countries (Sykes, 2012, pp. 10-11) whereas the regional and local alumni retention rates in general are 60% for all graduates and 70% for Master's and doctoral graduates. Hawthorne (2008, 2010, 2012) and the OECD (2011) warn that an increase in the stay rate is not a guaranteed solution to the needs of national economies, both in quantitative and qualitative terms, but governments still make increasingly more efforts to stimulate the stay rate of top talents. The benefits are clear:

> They confront few of the barriers experienced by foreign-trained professionals, in terms of host-country language ability, qualification recognition, or acculturation. Their productive lives will be longer, given their youth at point of enrolment. They present a palatable option for countries with ambivalent views on migration, in a context where demographic contraction is fuelling demand. ... For many students, international education has become Stage 1 of a global career trajectory. Following graduation, they will address workforce undersupply and maldistribution, including the mismatch between the skills set of domestic workers and the needs of the knowledge economy. While their scale of longterm retention is unclear, former students will compensate for out-migration from host countries. ... It is important to note that international students are becoming highly informed consumers, seeking the optimal global package. (Hawthorne, 2012, p. 432)

The obstacles are clear as well, as international students are increasingly becoming calculating consumers who explore the best options in their home country and their country of study, as well as in other countries. Lack of integration, discrimination and lack of support are important push factors driving international students away after graduation.

The study *Mobile Talent? The Staying Intentions of International Students in Five EU Countries* (Sykes, 2012) summarised the results of an online survey among international students in Germany, the Netherlands, the UK, France and Sweden. Almost two out of three international students expressed the intention to stay after their graduation for a shorter or longer period to work. The reality, though, is that only one in four do so, with slightly more – one in three – in France, which probably can be explained by the fact that international students in France have a stronger relation to French language and culture than international students have for other destination countries. The study states:

> Although international students do possess a number of qualities that make them an attractive group of skilled migrants, they still require services and support to guarantee their integration. Emerging research findings and the results of this report indicate that simply studying in a country is not sufficient to overcome many of the difficulties migrants face, such as gaps in language proficiency, acculturation, visa insecurity and concerns about family migration and discrimination. (Sykes, 2012, p. 7)

A recent Dutch study (Sociaal Economische Raad, 2013) confirms that three themes are the most crucial in increasing the stay rate of international students in the Netherlands: the need for better preparation for the Dutch labour market during the period of study; Dutch language, culture and social life; and better facilities, in particular accommodation.

A study by the European Migration Network on the immigration of international students to the EU shows that in recent years member states have given more attention to policies and practices for attracting international students to the EU. At the same time, differences still exist, 'particularly in relation to access to the labour market during and after completion of studies, but also in relation to the benefits provided to international students when accessing the labour market and during their stay in general' (European Migration Network, 2013, p. 8).

In summary, we notice that international student mobility patterns are an outcome of a complex interplay of external and internal and push and pull variables. These include variables like 9/11, the global financial crisis, demographic factors and the development of the global knowledge economy. As a result of the increasing pace of globalisation, the complexity and intensity of external variables will also continue to increase and hence predicting the future of mobility will become more and more difficult. Despite this limitation, it is safe to predict that overall mobility will continue to grow while the relationship between key sources and countries may significantly alter with any major external event like the outcome of the eurozone crisis.

This section contextualised student mobility from a comparative perspective and the following section highlights its relationship in the larger framework of internationalisation of higher education from a critical and contextual perspective.

Critical Analysis of Mobility

As stated before, several push and pull factors play a role in the mobility of international students. We look at some of them here: types of internationally mobile students, the language factor, level and area of study, the reputation factor, the cost factor, and cross-border delivery.

Types of Mobile Students

A recent study from World Education Services, *Not All International Students Are the Same: Understanding Segments, Mapping Behavior* (Choudaha et al, 2012), highlights that international students differ in terms of their academic preparedness and financial resources, which translates into different needs of students. Thus, lumping all international students into one category does a disservice to them and causes institutional practices and national polices to be misguided. It identifies four types of US-bound international students: *Strivers* (30%), *Strugglers* (21%), *Explorers* (25%) and *Highfliers* (24%).

Strivers (30%) are the largest segment of the overall US-bound international student population. Almost two-thirds of this segment (63%) were employed full time or part time during the application process, presumably because they need to support themselves.

Of all the segments, they are the most likely to select information on financial aid opportunities among their top three information needs (45%). Financial challenges do not deter these highly prepared students from pursuing their academic dreams: 67% plan to attend a top-tier US school.

Strugglers (21%) make up about one-fifth of all US-bound international students. They have limited financial resources and need additional preparation to do well in an American classroom: 40% of them plan to take an English as a Second Language programme in the future.

They are also relatively less selective about where they obtain their education. Only 33% of them selected information about a school's reputation among their top three information needs. *Strugglers* were found to be particularly likely to use agent services such as essay, résumé or personal statement editing.

Explorers (25%) are very keen on studying abroad, but their interests are not exclusively academic. Compared with the other segments, they are the most interested in the personal and experiential aspects of studying in the United States, with 19% of this segment reporting that information on student services was in their top three information needs during the college search.

Explorers are not fully prepared to tackle the academic challenges of the best American institutions and are the most likely to plan to attend a second-tier institution (33%). They are also the most likely to use the services of an education agent (24%).

Highfliers (24%) are academically well-prepared students who have the means to attend more expensive programmes without expecting any financial aid from the institution. They seek a US higher education primarily for its prestige: almost half of the respondents in this segment (46%) reported that the school's reputation is among their top three information needs.

Highfliers, along with *Explorers*, form the emerging segment driven by the expanding wealthy classes in countries like China and India.

One can also distinguish between 'global' and 'glocal' international students. Global students, in particular *Highfliers* and *Strugglers*, are those who want to study abroad owing to their strong desire for achievement or emigration, respectively. 'Global' students are different, as they would like to earn the social prestige and career edge offered by foreign education without having to go very far from home, and hence are more likely to look for transnational offerings at home (Choudaha, 2013).

Although, there is no parallel analysis available for the types of international students headed to Europe or other regions, one can assume that the picture will not conceptually differ from the US context. One can also assume that *Strivers* and *Highfliers* more likely first attempt to go to the top institutions in the USA or the UK, given the reputation of their higher education system and their positions in the international rankings, which influence student perceptions. With the exception of the UK, transnational offerings by European institutions of higher education are still limited and do not provide sufficient options.

Language

An increasing number of universities around the world move from teaching in their home language to teaching in English so as to attract more international students. In general, as the OECD observes, 'countries whose language is widely spoken and read such as English, French, German, Russian and Spanish, are therefore leading destinations of foreign students, both in absolute and relative terms' (OECD, 2011, p. 323).

However, it would be too easy to state that language is the solution for attracting international students. Two articles address this. Bradford (2012) highlights linguistic concerns: 'the quality of teaching and learning that occurs when instructors and/or students are working in a non-native language'; cultural challenges: 'lack of intercultural knowledge important for developing internationalized curricula, adopting more inclusive practices, and promoting reciprocal cultural understanding'; and structural challenges: 'in addition to finding faculty to teach in the programs, any institution adopting English-medium instruction must also extend its administration and support services to cater to a new heterogeneous student and faculty body in English' (pp. 8-9). Likewise, Labi (2011) cites Associate Professor Karen Lauridsen at the Aarhus School of Business and Social Sciences, stating that 'it has become apparent that teaching difficulties are not simply a question of language but are rooted in profound cultural differences'. And she continues that even universities in Britain 'need to address the fact that they can't just teach in English the way they teach native speakers'.

The issue of teaching in English has become a serious academic quality concern for all universities, whatever their mother language is. A more diverse faculty and student population in the classroom demands that universities address these academic issues related to teaching in English.

Teaching in English is not synonymous with internationalisation but is only one of several instruments for it. If one is using that instrument one also has to address the quality concerns that are related to it. Universities should think more strategically about when, where, how and why they should transfer programmes from being taught in their mother language into English (or any other second language) (De Wit, 2012a).

Level and Area of Study

It is also important to look at how mobility is related to disciplines and the need for skilled migrants.

According to the OECD, all countries show higher incoming student mobility relative to total enrolments in advanced research programmes. 'This may be due to the attractiveness of advanced research programmes in these countries, or to a preference for recruiting international students at higher levels of education because of their potential contribution to domestic research and development, or in anticipation of recruiting these students as highly qualified immigrants' (OECD, 2012, p. 368). Likewise, in the USA, nearly one out of five international students are enrolled at doctoral level (Institute of International Education, 2012). At the same time, recent growth in enrolment driven is driven by students from China and Saudi Arabia at Bachelor level (Choudaha & Kono, 2012).

As for the areas of study, there seems to be in some countries compared to others a dominance of social sciences, business and law followed by humanities, while there is a stronger need for engineering and sciences. To give one example from Europe to illustrate the differences in success in attracting more students in those two areas: in Sweden, according to OECD figures, 34.5% study engineering and 17.2% sciences; in Finland 31.7% and 11.2%; and in Denmark 19.3% and 10.3%, while in a country of similar size and quality of education, the Netherlands, only 3.9% and 3.4% do so. In the Netherlands nearly half of the international students, 49.2%, study social sciences/economy/law (OECD, 2012, p. 375).

Given these numbers, one could argue that even though the Netherlands has seen an increase in the number of international students over the past decade, the impact in attracting talent relevant to the economy is less than in the three Scandinavian countries. This might be related to the lack of a scholarship scheme focussed on students in engineering and sciences.

Other Factors

Besides languages and levels and areas of studies, there are other push and pull factors that play a role. Reputation, as expressed in rankings by area of study, institution and by higher education systems, is increasingly becoming a pull factor, in particular for *Strivers* and *Highfliers*.

Costs of study, both tuition fees and costs of living, are another factor. As tuition fees in the USA and the UK increase and several European countries introduce full cost fees for non-EU students (e.g. Denmark, Sweden, the Netherlands), students and their families are more likely to take tuition fees in combination with costs of living into consideration.

This also includes the option of studying at a foreign university in their own country or region, and making cross-border delivery of higher education an alternative option. Although the number of branch campuses and franchise operations by foreign universities is increasing, their impact is still limited both in numbers and origins of providers (primarily the English-speaking world). Some consider the recent offer of Massive Open Online Courses (MOOCs) an alternative option for international students to access higher education at no or low cost, although its impact is still unclear (Choudaha, 2013). It is more likely to stimulate interest in degree study abroad than be an alternative to it.

Study Abroad as Part of the Home Degree

Study abroad as part of the home degree is in absolute numbers and in social, political and economic impact less a factor than the degree mobility, as described above, although its importance in Europe and North America should not be neglected. In the USA, only 1.4% of the total student population spend some time abroad, predominantly white (80.5%) undergraduate (nearly 89%) students, with Europe (54.5%) still largely the destination and only 4% going for a whole academic year (De Wit et al, 2012, p. 3). And although in absolute numbers and diversity the participation and location of study abroad over the past decade has increased, and in both national and institutional policy statements its relevance is increasingly emphasised, the percentages stay very small and the length of the experience is declining.

In Europe in 2012, the 25th anniversary of the European flagship programme, Erasmus, funded by the European Commission, was celebrated amid fears of becoming a victim of its own success due to the increased numbers but reduced funding. In 1987, 3244 students spent a part of their Erasmus study in another member country. Three million students have followed their example in the past 25 years and the number of countries has grown from 11 to 33, including non-EU member states such as Croatia, Iceland, Lichtenstein, Norway, Turkey and Switzerland. The budget of the programme for the period 2007-13 is 3.1 billion euros.

More than in numbers of mobile students, the impact of the programme has been on the internationalisation and the reform of higher education. Erasmus has paved the way for the reform of European higher education under the Bologna Process, has been a pilot for its credit point system ECTS, and was an initiator for the opening-up of EU membership to countries in Central and Eastern Europe, as it is for current aspiring candidate members. It also inspired cooperation between Europe and the rest of the world, and – unfortunately still with little success – similar initiatives in other regions. The programme has stimulated both national governments and institutions of higher education to develop European and international strategies.

Accompanying these success stories, however, is also an increased concern about the focus on numbers and percentages, which detracts from the need to concentrate on the content and the quality of the international experience. In the early years of the Erasmus programme, the enthusiasm of faculty – encountering their colleagues, learning about their curricula and teaching methods – was driving the success and the impact of the programme. Erasmus has moved away from those inspiring days and has become too much of a bureaucratic exercise, in which only numbers count. If the Erasmus programme could get back its focus on curriculum and learning outcomes, not only would it enhance the quality of the experience but it would also increase the interest of the faculty and the students, and as a result probably also the numbers (see De Wit, 2012b).

If one compares study abroad for the home degree in Europe and even the USA with other parts of the world, there is still a long way to go. In other countries such as Australia and Canada, the numbers are comparable with the USA. In Japan this is far less the case, even though recently the Japanese government initiated plans to stimulate study abroad. In Latin America, Asia and Africa, study abroad is still relatively absent. We know little about the impact of study abroad on employability, skilled migration and degree mobility, but it is generally assumed that there is an impact, and in that sense, study abroad can be seen as a major push factor in stimulating degree mobility and skilled migration in that region of the world.

Future Directions of International Student Mobility

The growth of international student mobility is not coming to an end yet, and will for several years still be dominated by current major sending and receiving countries. However, at the same time, one will see a gradual diversification in both sending and receiving countries, with global competition for students becoming more dominant and big sending countries like China, India, South Korea, Singapore, Malaysia, South Africa, Russia and Brazil also becoming receiving countries.

There will be more focus on increasing the stay rate of the best students and scholars. Scholarship programmes will increase but be more selectively focussed on top talent, whereas other students will have to pay higher tuition fees when studying abroad.

For the coming decade, teaching in English will continue to be a pull factor, although increasingly other languages, in particular Spanish, will become an alternative.

Reputation, expressed in international rankings, will also stay an important pull factor: the better the reputation of the education system of the country and/or of the individual university, the more likely international students, in particular *Strivers* and *Highfliers*, will aspire to go there.

Cross-border delivery of higher education will continue to increase and become an alternate option for international students, as costs and social factors will become more attractive. But all in all, it will remain a minor percentage within the overall offerings in higher education in the decades to come. MOOCs will increasingly become a factor in international higher education, but instead of becoming an alternative for study abroad, they will stimulate the interest of students to study in another country and to attend a university with a good reputation abroad.

Study abroad as part of the home degree will increase as well in the years to come and will become more a factor in other parts of the world than only in Europe, North America and Australia/New Zealand. This will also have a push effect on degree mobility.

To sum up, the future of global student mobility will continue to interact with a number of variables and become even more complex with the emergence of new variables like MOOCs; however, the growth momentum is expected to remain healthy.

References

Agarwal, P., Elmahdy Said, M., Sehoole, M., Sirozi, M. & De Wit, H. (2008) The Dynamics of International Student Mobility in a Global Context: summary, conclusions, and recommendations, in H. De Wit, P. Agarwal, M. Elmahdy Said, M. Sehoole & M. Sirozi (Eds) *The Dynamics of International Student Circulation in a Global Context,* pp. 233-261. Rotterdam: Sense.

Bradford, A. (2012) Adopting English-Taught Degree Programs, *International Higher Education*, 69, 8-9.

Cap Gemini (2012) *World Wealth Report*. http://www.capgemini.com/services-and-solutions/by-industry/financial-services/solutions/wealth/worldwealthreport/wwr_archive/

Cavanagh, M. & Glennie, A. (2012) *International Students and Net Migration in the UK.* London: Institute for Public Policy Research.

Choudaha, R. (2013) Know Your International Students – global or glocal? *University World News*, 27 April, Global Edition Issue 269. http://bit.ly/TNEglocal.

Choudaha, R. & Kono, Y. (2012) Beyond More of the Same: the top four emerging markets for international student recruitment. World Education News & Reviews. http://www.wes.org/ewenr/12oct/feature.htm

Choudaha, R., Orosz, K. & Chang, L. (2012) Not All International Students Are the Same: understanding segments, mapping behavior. World Education News & Reviews. http://www.wes.org/ewenr/12aug/feature.htm

De Wit, H. (2012a) Teaching in English is Not About Politics But Quality. *University World News.* http://www.universityworldnews.com/article.php?story=20121114175515819

De Wit, H. (2012b) Erasmus at 25: what is the future for international student mobility? *The Guardian*. http://www.guardian.co.uk/higher-education-network/blog/2012/may/21/erasmusprogramme

De Wit, H., Ferencz, I. & Rumbley, L.E. (2012) International Student Mobility: European and US perspectives, *Perspectives*, 1-7.

De Wit, H. & Merkx, G. (2012) The History of Internationalization of Higher Education, in D.K. Deardorff, H. De Wit, J.D. Heyl & T. Adams (Eds) *The SAGE Handbook of International* Education, pp. 43-59. Los Angeles: Sage.

European Migration Network (2013) *EMN Synthesis Report – immigration of international students to the EU*. European Migration Network Study 2012. Brussels: EMN.

Hawthorne, L. (2008) *The Impact of Economic Selection Policy on Labour Market Outcomes for Degree-Qualified Migrants in Canada and Australia*. Ottawa: Institute for Research Policy.

Hawthorne, L. (2010) How Valuable is 'Two-Step Migration'? Labour Market Outcomes for International Student Migrants to Australia, *Asia Pacific Migration Journal* (Special Edition), 19(1), 5-36.

Hawthorne, L. (2012) Designer Immigrants? International Students and Two-Step Migration, in D.K. Deardorff, H. De Wit, J.D. Heyl & T. Adams (Eds) *The SAGE Handbook of International* Education, pp. 417-435. Los Angeles: Sage.

Institute of International Education (2012) *Open Doors: report on international educational exchange* New York: Institute of International Education.

Labi, A. (2011) Europe's Push to Teach in English Creates Barriers in the Classroom, *The Chronicle of Higher Education*, 13 February. http://chronicle.com/article/Europes-Drive-to-Teach-in/126326/

McKinsey (2012) *The World at Work: jobs, pay, and skills for 3.5 billion people*. http://www.mckinsey.com/insights/mgi/research/labor_markets/the_world_at_work

Organisation for Economic Cooperation and Development (2011) *Education at a Glance 2011*. Paris: OECD.

Organisation for Economic Cooperation and Development (2012) *Education at a Glance 2012*. Paris: OECD.

Sociaal Economische Raad (2013) *Analyse t.b.v. de voorbereiding van Make it in the Netherlands! Advies over bidning van buitenlandse studenten aan Nederland*. Commissie Arbeidsmarkt- en onderwijsvraagstukken SER, 22 maart 2013. The Hague: SER.

Sykes, B. (2012) *Mobile Talent? The Staying Intentions of International Students in Five EU Countries*. Berlin: Sachverständigenrat deutscher Stiftungen für Integration und Migration.

World Bank (2011) *World Population Prospects*. http://esa.un.org/unpd/wpp/Excel-Data/population.htm

CHAPTER 2

Why Engage in Mobility?
Key Issues within Global Mobility:
the big picture

DARLA K. DEARDORFF

ABSTRACT Universities engage in mobility to what end? Mobility is more than simply moving people around the world. What are universities hoping to achieve through mobility programs? This article explores key issues surrounding global mobility including access, assessment, and balance. Research can play a key role in helping universities understand these bigger picture issues connected with internationalization of higher education.

In his book, *Start With Why: how great leaders inspire everyone to take action*, author Simon Sinek (2011) notes that while everyone knows what they do and many know how they do it, very few know 'why', which he defines beyond results to be the purpose or cause. This volume contains numerous articles about aspects of global mobility within higher education. Underlying all of the discussion on global mobility needs to be the question 'Why?' Universities engage in mobility to what end? What are universities hoping to achieve through mobility programs? The increased commercialism and commodification of education abroad programs, where the focus is more often on numbers and percentages of students being moved around and on income generated than on ensuring quality of experience, seem to indicate that this question of 'Why?' should be revisited. This chapter does that through a brief highlight of some key issues that researchers and administrators need to discuss in terms of the 'big picture' of global mobility.

In university literature on education abroad programs, standard reasons are given for students to study abroad: to gain different perspectives, to develop languages and global skills, to become global citizens, to be better prepared for the global workforce, and so on. On broader levels, rhetoric around mobility usually incorporates global competitiveness (United States) or social cohesion (Europe) (De Wit, 2011). Yet, a skeptic may point out that so much of this seems like empty rhetoric. The question remains: Why engage in global mobility? James Skelly (2009), in a chapter entitled 'Fostering Engagement', writes that international educators need to 'embed their work in a broad and compelling discourse that might provide a vision that is not exclusively focused on the state or the market, but is instead global and human centric in its orientation' (p. 22). In exploring the 'why' and the bigger picture of global mobility, a purpose may emerge that philosopher Martha Nussbaum (1997) articulated when she noted the importance of having an ability 'to see (ourselves) ... as human beings bound to all other human beings by ties of recognition and concern' (p. 10). This is similar to Nwosu's (2009) definition of the comparable concept of *Ubuntu*, an African word that situates one's identity within the larger group or, as Tutu (2011) observes, it's about one's humanity being bound up in others.

Bigger Picture Issues

One way of exploring this 'why' question is to focus on five big picture issues in looking to the future of global mobility; these issues give rise to research-related questions that can jointly be addressed through the international and comparative education fields.

1. Realistic outcomes. With a worldwide movement toward competency-based learning and outcomes-based assessment (Sanchez & Ruiz, 2008; Deardorff & van Gaalen, 2012), global mobility programs need to be realistic in what can be accomplished through a limited sojourn into another culture. As has been discussed in this volume, there are many factors that impact the successful achievement of outcomes, including appropriate preparation and interventions of challenge and support (see also Engle & Engle, 2003; Medina-López-Portillo, 2004; Hoff, 2008; Killick, 2012; Vande Berg et al, 2012). Although many global mobility programs already state clear outcomes, there remains much work and research to be done in this area. For example, outcome statements are often filled with words such as 'intercultural competence' or 'global citizenship', which have not been defined based on the existing literature and work (see Deardorff, 2009; Lewin, 2009) and more research needs to be done on effective interventions leading to specific outcomes. Further, there are explicit implications of research that may even delve into ethical implications of what such programs claim to be able to achieve. For example, given that research indicates that the development of intercultural competence is a lifelong process (Deardorff, 2006), how realistic are outcomes that purport to develop participants' intercultural competence and, moreover, actually measure and ascertain that one has achieved this? And given that each participant is at a different stage of development, how are programs designed to intervene appropriately for each of the participants? Further research is needed around these and other questions related to *realistic* outcomes of global mobility programs.

2. Impact – intercultural dialogue and building a global community. Very few studies have been done on the long-term impact of global mobility programs and the few that have been done often tend to focus on the impact on individual participants (Paige et al, 2009). In combining the 'why' question and the outcomes issue in the long term, what are the larger impacts of these programs? Specifically, how are global mobility programs building a global community? How are these programs fostering meaningful, longer term relationships (see Ogden, Streitwieser and Crawford in this volume)? And moreover, given the global discourse on intercultural dialogue within the United Nations, the Council of Europe, and beyond (Bergan & Restoueix, 2009; Besley & Peters, 2011; Besley et al, 2011), the question needs to be asked how global mobility programs are contributing to intercultural dialogue initiatives around the world and connecting to relevant world issues as raised by the Millennium Development Goals, which are as follows:

1. eradicating extreme poverty and hunger;
2. achieving universal primary education;
3. promoting gender equality and empowering women;
4. reducing child mortality rates;
5. improving maternal health;
6. combating HIV/AIDS, malaria, and other diseases;
7. ensuring environmental sustainability; and
8. developing a global partnership for development.[1]

Some mobility programs, especially those focused more specifically on research and/or community engagement (Streitwieser, 2009), no doubt align with some of these larger issues. For example, universities have typically been strong players in developing global partnerships for development, so to that end, how can mobility programs build on some of higher education's strengths in addressing these larger goals? (See Barrett, Crossley and Fon in this volume.) How do mobility programs need to change to address these global issues? How can mobility programs connect more closely to civil society groups and non-governmental organizations so as not to operate only in the proverbial 'ivory towers' of higher education – and instead, to be changed by these connections? It is time that global mobility programs begin focusing on larger impacts, beyond impact on individuals, institutional impact, or economic impact on a community and, rather, address how these programs are impacting the larger global community in terms of addressing relevant issues that face humans in this century.

3. Access. In their chapter entitled 'Bridges to the Future', Deardorff et al (2012) note the following: 'With only 10% of the world's population having access to secondary education and 1% with access to higher education, access to education is a little discussed but increasingly crucial issue within the global landscape' (p. 463). And further, given the even smaller percentages that participate in mobility programs, the question becomes: What is higher education's responsibility to the vast majority of those without access to education, and especially to mobility programs? How will higher education address the increasing divide between those who have access to education and those who do not? And further, how will global migration flows impact access issues? The access issue leads into a deeper discussion around global responsibilities of mobility programs. One response to this question could be the deeper community engagement of sojourners in their host communities. Examples of deeper community involvement include Duke University's unique DukeEngage program, designed specifically to immerse students in a community project/organization (of at least eight weeks in length) and the International Student Exchange Program's new Global Engagement Program Model, which helps students become more immersed in the local community through volunteer work, service learning for academic credit, independent study, community service, internships and/or research projects. Characteristics of such programs could include ongoing involvement (beyond a one-time 'drop in and leave'-type experience), opportunities for authentic interactions (beyond surface-level exchanges and navigational-type interactions) with focus on building lasting relationships and *mutual* involvement of hosts and sojourners toward the achievement of *common* goals (beyond accumulating experiences for a sojourner's résumé).

4. *Virtual mobility.* Another response to the previous issue of access is through virtual mobility. Given the rapidly changing technological landscape, mobility as it has traditionally been known is also in a process of change. As noted by Deardorff et al (2012), 'In recent years, more students and faculty from different parts of the world are interacting online in classrooms, projects, and assignments and learning from each other's different cultural, international, and didactic views directly and interactively in a way that physical mobility may not always accomplish' (p. 459). One successful example of this is East Carolina University, which has developed a successful first-year course called 'Global Understanding', connecting students with overseas counterparts through chat technology and videoconferencing. Edwards and Teekens (2012) observe that 'strong institutional partnerships, resource commitment on the home campus, and engaged faculty are the primary determinants of success in such arrangements' (p. 274). It also remains to be seen as to the impact of Massive Open Online Courses (MOOCs), through Massive Multiplayer Collaborative Design with online gaming, and other emerging technologies. Questions that need further research include the following: What is the effectiveness of in-country participation versus virtual participation? What types of virtual mobility are the most effective in achieving the overall course/program goals? What kinds of support and intervention need to be put in place to facilitate transformation learning through virtual mobility? It will be important for current mobility programs to envision a future in which virtual mobility plays not only a key role but one in which there's a definite 'value-added' in the actual physical mobility that may occur.

5. *Changing global landscape.* While traditional mobility programs have been between and among Western countries and the rest of the world, the changing global landscape (see De Wit and Choudaha in this volume, and also Deardorff et al, 2012) has given rise to 'other systems of higher education and research, especially in Asia and to a certain extent in Latin America ... associated with the spread of modernization' (American Council on Education, 2011, p. 15). This means that players and partners and even entire mobility programs are evolving and as they do, the global landscape itself is changing in terms of mobility. For example, national governments are now a driving force in propelling mobility forward. Take, for instance, Brazil's Science Without Borders Program, Japan's Global 30 Program or the USA's 100,000 Strong China initiative and the USA's 100,000 Strong in the Americas, launched by Barack Obama in Chile in 2011, as well as the longstanding Erasmus Programme in Europe, the US-sponsored Fulbright Program, and the United Kingdom's Chevening Programme. Future trends may include a growth in regional mobility through greater development of regional networks and increased intracontinental engagements, collaborations and reforms (Jowi, 2012). This will lead to steady growth of scholarship and research from non-Western perspectives and these fresh perspectives can help guide future developments in global mobility. As Jones and De Wit (2012) note, 'those countries with longer histories of internationalization need to learn from the varied contributions to debates and practice of other developed nations' (p. 25). This also provides an ideal area of synergistic scholarship between the respective fields of international education and comparative education.

As discussed in chapters in this book, changes in the global mobility landscape include other players as well as changes in the traditional constituency. In terms of the latter, the traditional constituency for mobility programs has been undergraduate students. Increasingly, trends toward growing numbers of primary and secondary exchanges, as well as direct degree enrollments and online interactions (as discussed in this chapter), are changing not only participant expectations in such programs, but also the very nature of postsecondary mobility programs, including an increased demand for practical experiences abroad including through internships, research, and service learning/engagement. This means that postsecondary programs must build on prior experiences of participants, whether previously abroad or within their own countries and at their own institutions, given the emphasis on internationalization at home practices (see Beelen, this volume).

While universities have been the primary actors in global mobility programs for students, those institutions are now competing with an ever-growing diversification of different experiences and education providers, including corporations, and for-profit and not-for-profit organizations. Such diversification may lead to a wider range of partnerships beyond traditional postsecondary partners. This diversification also leads to a growing number of ethical issues including those related to recruiters and agents, degree mills, and third-party providers. In addition, as mentioned here in the discussion of virtual technology, universities are now having to compete with such online venues as Khan Academy, Udacity, edX, and Coursera, among others. These changes may well result in postsecondary institutions losing their monopoly on global mobility programs. In such a rapidly diversifying landscape, the 'why' of the purpose of mobility programs may become even more quickly diluted. Throughout these and future changes, higher education institutions must stay focused on 'why' they are engaging in mobility programs.

Conclusion

Martin Luther King, Jr. once stated, 'We must learn to live together as brothers, or perish together as fools.' This profound statement sharply brings into focus the 'why' of mobility programs. Traditional ways of engaging in mobility are no longer be adequate in today's world. With looming global challenges, the major ones delineated by the Millennium Development Goals, mobility programs need to refocus attention on why they exist. This chapter has raised numerous questions which need in-depth exploration, given the issues around realistic outcomes, impact, access, virtual mobility, and the changing global landscape of higher education that have the potential to transform mobility programs. Further research, especially from comparative perspectives, can help guide future directions of such programs in addressing these challenges.

Note

[1] http://www.un.org/millenniumgoals/

References

American Council on Education (2011) *Report of the Blue Ribbon Panels on Global Engagement: strength through global leadership and engagement.* Washington, DC: Center for Internationalization and Global Engagement, American Council on Education.

Bergan, S. & Restoueix, P. (Eds) (2009) *Intercultural Dialogue on Campus.* Strasbourg: Council of Europe Publishing.

Besley, A.C. & Peters, M.A. (Eds) (2011) *Interculturalism, Education and Dialogue.* New York: Peter Lang.

Besley, A.C., Peters, M.A. & Jiang, X. (Eds) (2011) The Council of Europe's *White Paper on Intercultural Dialogue, Policy Futures in Education* (Special Issue), 9(1). http://www.wwwords.co.uk/pfie/content/pdfs/9/issue9_1.asp

De Wit, H. (2011) *Trends, Issues and Challenges in Internationalisation of Higher Education.* Amsterdam: Hogeschool van Amsterdam.

Deardorff, D.K. (2006) Identification and Assessment of Intercultural Competence as a Student Outcome of Internationalization, *Journal of Studies in International Education*, 10(3), 241-266.

Deardorff, D.K. (Ed.) (2009) *The Sage Handbook of Intercultural Competence*. Thousand Oaks: Sage.

Deardorff, D.K., De Wit, H. & Heyl, J.D. (2012) Bridges to the Future: the global landscape of international higher education, in D.K. Deardorff, H. De Wit, J.D. Heyl & T. Adams (Eds) *The Sage Handbook of International Higher Education*. Thousand Oaks: Sage.

Deardorff, D.K. & van Gaalen, A. (2012) Outcomes Assessment in the Internationalization of Higher Education, in D.K. Deardorff, H. De Wit, J.D. Heyl & T. Adams (Eds) *The Sage Handbook of International Higher Education*. Thousand Oaks: Sage.

Edwards, J. & Teekens, H. (2012) Leveraging Technology and the International Classroom for Cross-cultural Learning, in D.K. Deardorff, H. De Wit, J. Heyl & T. Adams (Eds) *The SAGE Handbook of International Higher Education*. Thousand Oaks, CA: Sage.

Engle, J. & Engle, L. (2003) Study Abroad Levels: toward a classification of program types, *Frontiers*, 9, 1-20.

Hoff, J. (2008) Growth and Transformation Outcomes in International Education, in V. Savicki (Ed.) *Developing Intercultural Competence and Transformation: theory, research and application in international education*. Sterling, VA: Stylus.

Jones, E. & De Wit, H. (2012) Globalization of Internationalization: thematic and regional reflections on a traditional concept, *AUDEM*, 3, 35-54.

Jowi, J. (2012) Re-thinking Internationalization and What it Portends for Africa, *IAH Horizons*, February/March, p. 29.

Killick, D. (2012) Seeing-Ourselves-in-the-World: developing global citizenship through international mobility and campus community, *Journal of Studies in International Education*, 16 (September), 372-389.

Lewin, R. (Ed.) (2009) *The Handbook of Practice and Research in Study Abroad: higher education and the question for global citizenship*. New York: Routledge.

Medina-López-Portillo A. (2004) Intercultural Learning Assessment: the link between program duration and the development of intercultural sensitivity, *Frontiers*, X, 179-199.

Nussbaum, M. (1997) *Cultivating Humanity: a classical defense of reform in liberal education*. Cambridge, MA: Harvard University Press.

Nwosu, P. (2009) Understanding Africans' Conceptualizations of Intercultural Competence, in D.K. Deardorff (Ed.) *The Sage Handbook of Intercultural Competence*. Thousand Oaks: Sage.

Paige, R.M., Fry, G.W., Stallman, E.M, Josic, J. & Jon, J.E. (2009) Study Abroad for Global Engagement: the long-term impact on mobility experiences, *Intercultural Education*, 20, suppl. S1-2, 29-44.

Sanchez, A. & Ruiz, M. (Eds) (2008) *Competence-Based Learning: a proposal for the assessment of generic competences*. Bilbao: University of Deusto.

Sinek, S. (2011) *Start With Why: how great leaders inspire everyone to take action.* New York: Penguin.

Skelly, J. (2009) Fostering Engagement, in R. Lewin (Ed.) *The Handbook of Practice and Research in Study Abroad: higher education and the question for global citizenship.* New York: Routledge.

Streitwieser, B. (2009) Undergraduate Research During Study Abroad: scope, meaning, and potential, in R. Lewin (Ed.) *The Handbook of Practice and Research in Study Abroad: higher education and the quest for global citizenship.* New York: Routledge.

Tutu, D. (2011) *God is Not Christian, and Other Provocations.* New York: HarperOne.

Vande Berg, M., Paige, R.M. & Lou, K. (2012) *Student Learning Abroad: what our students are learning, what they're not, and what we can do about it.* Sterling: Stylus.

CHAPTER 3

Three Generations of Crossborder Higher Education: new developments, issues and challenges[1]

JANE KNIGHT

ABSTRACT Internationalization is one of the major forces impacting and shaping higher education as it changes to meet the challenges of the twenty-first century. One aspect of internationalization which is particularly important and controversial is crossborder education. Academic mobility has moved from people (students, faculty, scholars) to program (twinning, franchise, MOOCs, virtual) and provider (branch campus, binational universities) mobility and now to the development of international education hubs. Crossborder education has gradually shifted from a development cooperation framework, to a partnership model, and now to a commercial and competitiveness model. The purpose of this chapter is to explore the rationales, scope, and scale of the three generations of crossborder education. The first part examines how the multifaceted phenomenon of crossborder education relates to internationalization in general and provides a working definition. The three generations of crossborder education are analyzed in the second part so as to provide a basic understanding of program and provider mobility and the recent positioning of countries as education hubs. Attention is given to examining the rationales and perspectives of different stakeholders – students, foreign institutions and host country institutions. The last section discusses important emerging issues, challenges, and unintended consequences related to crossborder higher education.

Introduction

Higher Education Internationalization Has Fundamentally Transformed the World of Education and Has Dramatically Changed Itself

Internationalization is one of the major forces impacting and shaping higher education as it changes to meet the challenges of the twenty-first century.

Overall, the picture of internationalization that is emerging is one of complexity, diversity, and differentiation. One aspect of internationalization which is particularly important and controversial is crossborder education.

Academic mobility has moved from people (students, faculty, scholars) to program (twinning, franchise, virtual) and provider (branch campus) mobility and now to the development of education hubs. Crossborder education has gradually shifted from a development cooperation framework, to a partnership model, and now to a commercial and competitiveness model (Knight, 2013). There is no question that the international dimension of higher education is becoming increasingly important, and at the same time more complex.

Crossborder education refers to the 'movement of people, knowledge, programs, providers, policies, ideas, curricula, projects, research and services across national or regional jurisdictional borders' (Knight, 2007, p. 24). Crossborder education is often mistakenly confused with the term *internationalization*. It is important to understand that crossborder education is only one part of the complex process of internationalization. There are two interdependent pillars of internationalization – at home or campus-based, and abroad/crossborder education. This chapter focuses on crossborder education while acknowledging the strong connection with and implications for campus-based internationalization.

Three Generations of Crossborder Education

Any study of higher education shows that academic mobility has been happening for a very long time. Scholars and knowledge have been moving around the world for centuries. But, late in the twentieth century, the movement of programs and higher education institutions across borders became more popular and numerous. No longer were there isolated incidences of foreign programs and providers resident in a small number of countries; the numbers started to grow exponentially. By the early 2000s, some countries began to develop a critical mass of foreign providers, programs, and students and the third generation in the form of education hubs, cities, and zones began to appear. The purpose of Table I is to summarize the highlights of each of the three generations. Worth noting is that these generations are not mutually exclusive. In the following sections, each generation is examined in depth so as to understand the differences and similarities among them and to raise some of the issues and challenges associated with each category.

The First Generation: people mobility

Student and scholar mobility has been occurring for as long as universities have been in existence. In fact, the concept of universe in the term *university* is proof of the global dimension. The startling change in student mobility is that the numbers have multiplied exponentially in the last 50 years.

Crossborder education	Primary focus	Description
First generation	*Student/people mobility* Movement of students to foreign country for education purposes	Full degree or for short-term study research, fieldwork, internship, exchange programs
Second generation	*Program and provider mobility* Movement of programs or institutions/companies across jurisdictional borders for delivery of education	*Program mobility* Twinning Franchised Articulated/ validated Joint/double award Online/distance *Provider mobility* Branch campus Virtual university Merger/acquisition Independent institutions
Third generation	*Education hubs* Countries attract foreign students, researchers, workers, programs, providers, R and D companies for education, training, knowledge production, innovation purposes	*Student hub* – students, programme, providers move to foreign country for education purposes *Talent hub* – students, workers move to foreign country for education and training and employment purposes *Knowledge/innovation hub* – education researchers, scholars, HEIs, R&D centres move to foreign country to produce knowledge and innovation

Table I. Three generations of crossborder education.

For example, international students in foreign countries expanded from 238,000 in the 1960s (Chen & Barnett, 2000) to 3.3 million in 2008 (Organisation for Economic Cooperation and Development, 2010). But the numbers of students, the modes of mobility (full degree abroad, exchange, internships, semester/year abroad), the destination countries, and the driving rationales have changed dramatically. It is estimated that 7.8 million students will be enrolled in foreign countries for their tertiary education by 2025 (Boehm et al, 2002). These statistics indicate that student mobility will continue to expand but new forms of crossborder education are needed to meet this demand.

The Second Generation: program and provider mobility

In the second generation of crossborder education, the programs and providers are mobile – not only the students. In the early 1990s the movement of programs and providers across borders began to increase substantially and have an impact on the numbers of students who could access foreign higher education programs and qualifications without leaving home. As Table II illustrates, there are different rationales driving the movement of academic programs and higher education providers across borders. It is informative to examine the perspectives and expectations of the students, the foreign institution providing the education (i.e. sending country higher education institution), and the host country. There are stark differences in why and how crossborder education is used by different countries and regions around the world (Altbach & Knight, 2007). This demonstrates that one model of crossborder education does not fit all countries. The local context, culture, and national priorities dictate the crossborder education approach.

Rationales and impact	Enrolled students in receiving (host) country	Institution/provider in sending country	Institution/ provider in receiving country
Increased access/ supply in home country	Ability to gain foreign qualification without leaving home. Can continue to meet family and work commitments	Attracted to unmet need for higher education and training and or invitation to establish presence in foreign country	Competition, collaboration or co-existence with foreign providers
Cost/income	Less expensive to take foreign program at home as no travel or accommodation costs. But tuition fees of quality foreign providers may be much higher than local HEIs.	Strong imperative to generate a profit for crossborder operations as well as increased profile.	Varied rationales and impacts depending on whether local institution/ provider is competing or cooperating with foreign providers. Can include development of new talent, revenue generation or increased regional profile
Selection of courses and programs	Increased access to courses/ programs in high	Tendency to offer high demand courses which	Need to offer broad selection of courses which may not have

demand by labour market	require little infrastructure or investment unless infrastructure is provided by host country	high enrolments and/or have major lab or equipment requirements
Language/cultural and safety aspects	Can have access to courses in foreign and/or indigenous language. Remain in familiar cultural and linguistic environment.	Language of instruction and relevance of curriculum to host country important issues. If foreign language used additional academic and linguistic support may be needed	Provide courses and programs according to local cultural and linguistic norms and practices but consistent with admission requirements and quality standards of home institution
Quality	Can be exposed to higher or lower quality course provision	Depending on delivery mode, quality may be at risk. Assurance of relevant and high quality courses may require significant investment	Presence of foreign providers may be a catalyst for innovation and improvement of quality in courses, management and governance.
Recognition of qualification	Foreign qualification has to be recognized for academic and employment purposes	May be difficult for academic award and for institution to be recognized in foreign country	Recognized home providers have an advantage. Foreign providers my wish to collaborate for award granting powers
Reputation and profile	Due to massive marketing campaigns international profile is often mistakenly equated with quality of provider/program	Profile and visibility are key factors for high enrolments and strategic alliances	Home (domestic) providers are challenged to distinguish between foreign providers with high/low profile and high/low quality

Table II. Stakeholder perspectives on program and provider mobility.

To understand the phenomenon of program and provider mobility, it is helpful to examine each mode of movement and the associated issues.

Program mobility. Crossborder mobility of *programs* can be described as 'the movement of individual education/training courses and programs across jurisdictional borders through face to face, distance or a combination of these modes' (Knight, 2007, p. 28). Credits towards a qualification can be awarded by the sending foreign country provider or by an affiliated domestic partner or jointly. Franchising, twinning, double/joint degrees, and various articulation models are the more popular methods of crossborder program mobility (Knight, 2007).

A critical factor in program mobility is 'who' awards the course credits or ultimate credential. As the movement of programs proliferates, there will undoubtedly be further changes to national, regional, and even international regulatory frameworks. The question of 'who grants the credits/awards' will be augmented by 'who recognizes the provider' and whether or not the program has been 'accredited or quality assured' by a bona fide body either domestically or internationally. Of central importance is whether the qualification is recognized for employment or further study in the receiving country and in other countries as well. The perceived legitimacy and recognition of the qualification at home and abroad are fundamental issues yet to be resolved.

The last decade has seen the introduction of twinning and franchise programs. The benefits of these arrangements to students, host institutions as well as the foreign providers are many and varied. However, issues related to quality of teaching, relevance of course content, admission requirements, testing and evaluation, and qualifications of teaching staff must be addressed. Double/joint/combined degree programs differ from twinning and franchise programs in that the course curriculum is jointly designed and delivered by the partner institutions. This means that foreign curriculum is not imported, instead it is jointly developed.

A joint degree program awards one joint qualification upon completion of the collaborative program requirements established by the partner institutions. The duration of the program is normally not extended and thus students have the advantage of completing a joint program in the same time period as an individual program from one of the institutions. They normally involve student mobility or professor mobility. Strategies to integrate distance and virtual education into the programs are being explored. One issue concerning joint degree certification is that many countries do not legally allow the stamps of two different institutions on the actual certificate. The risk of not being able to legally award a joint qualification is leading to the dubious practice of awarding two individual degrees for the same workload or course credits of one program. The integrity of providing two degrees for the same student workload is highly questionable and merits closer reflection.

The legal roles and responsibilities of the participating partners in terms of academic, staffing, recruitment, evaluation, financial, and administrative matters are core issues. While the movement of programs across borders has been taking place for years, it is clear that the new types of providers, partnerships, awards, and delivery modes are challenging national and international higher education policies (Verbik & Merkley, 2006).

A popular and more recent development is online program mobility in terms of Massive Open Online Courses, commonly referred to as MOOCs. While the technology for this type of program delivery has been available for several years, it is only since 2012 that we have seen major consortia like Coursera (Stanford, Princeton, Michigan and the University of Pennsylvania), edX (MIT and Harvard) and Udacity (private company) launch their platforms and new programs. Huge numbers of enrolments characterize these initiatives, for instance Coursera had one million course registrants in their first six months of operation in 2012, but it appears that fewer than 10% actually take the exams and even fewer pass them (Observatory on Borderless Higher Education, 2012b). It is still turbulent times in terms of costs, qualifications offered, proctoring of exams, and technology but this trend may be one answer to the important question of how to internationalize and increase access for those interested in lifelong learning with or without credit.

Provider mobility. Crossborder mobility of providers can be described as 'the physical or virtual movement of an education provider (institution, organization, company) across a jurisdictional border to offer education/training programs and/or services to students and other clients' (Knight, 2007, p. 29). The difference between program and provider mobility is one of scope and scale in terms of programs/services offered and the local presence (and investment) by the foreign provider. Credits and qualifications are awarded by the foreign provider (through foreign, local, or self accreditation methods) or by an affiliated domestic partner. Different forms of crossborder provider mobility include standalone branch campuses, independent institutions, virtual universities, acquisitions or mergers, study centres, and teaching sites embedded in foreign partner institutions.

The virtual and physical movement of providers to other countries raises many of the same registration, quality assurance, and recognition issues that program mobility does, but there are additional factors to consider if local/foreign partnerships are involved. Setting up a physical presence requires that attention is paid to national regulations regarding status of the entity, total or joint ownership with local bodies, tax laws, for-profit or non-profit status, repatriation of earned income, boards of directors, staffing, granting of qualifications, selection of academic programs and courses, and so on. In spite of these issues, the growth in the number of international branch campuses has been dramatic in the last decade. In 2002, there were 24 registered branch campuses around the world and by 2011, there were

200 (Observatory on Borderless Higher Education, 2012a). Table III illustrates the distribution and growth of these new initiatives by region and Table IV lists the top source or sending countries in the world.

Region	2009	2011	Planned
Middle East	55	55	1
Asia	44	69	31
Europe	32	48	3
Latin America	18	10	0
North America	8	10	1
Africa	5	18	1
Total	162	200	37

Table III. Distribution of international branch campus by region.
Source: OBHE (2012).

Source countries	2009	2011
USA	78	78
Australia	14	12
UK	13	25
France	11	27
India	11	17

Table IV. Top five source countries of branch campuses.
Source: OBHE (2012).

Third Generation: education hubs

Education hubs are the latest development and constitute the third wave of crossborder education initiatives. Education hubs build on and can include first- and second-generation crossborder activities, but they represent a wider and more strategic configuration of actors and activities. An education hub is a concerted and planned effort by a country (or zone, city) to build a critical mass of education/knowledge actors and strengthen its efforts to exert more influence in the new marketplace of education. The concept of a national education hub rests on the assumption that it is a country's plan to position itself within the region and beyond as a reputed centre for higher education and research. Therefore an education hub is not an individual branch campus, or a science and technology park, or a large number of international students. It is more than that. The proposed working definition is generic enough to apply to all levels of education hubs (city, zone, country): 'an education hub is a planned effort to build a critical mass of local and international actors strategically engaged in crossborder education, training, knowledge production and innovation initiatives' (Knight, 2011a, p. 227).

As of 2012, there are six countries around the world which are seriously trying to position themselves as an education hub. Two of them are located in the Gulf region – United Arab Emirates and Qatar, three are in Asia – Hong Kong, Malaysia, and Singapore, and one is in Africa – Botswana. There are other countries that may be using the term *hub* as a branding label or are in early stages of development. Bahrain, Mauritius, and Sri Lanka can be described as emerging hubs as there is no clarity on the plans or investment to date. There is no single model or one-size-fits-all approach for establishing an education hub. Each country has its own set of drivers, approaches, and expectations. It is worth noting that to date, all education hub countries are relatively small and share an interest in shifting from a natural resources or manufacturing economy to one that places more emphasis on knowledge and service industries (Knight, 2011a). These initiatives differ but all encourage closer relationships between higher education institutions and private industries to allow for fuller participation in the production of new knowledge and for ensuring that graduates are equipped with relevant skills and knowledge.

The diversity of rationales, actors, and activities characterizing education hubs is clear. Some countries see hubs as a means to build a critical mass of foreign students and providers to generate income as well as modernize and internationalize their domestic higher education institutions; others want to be a hub in order to train foreign and local students and employees as part of a skilled labour force; while other countries focus on attracting foreign students, institutions, and companies to build a vibrant research, knowledge, and innovation sector to lead them into the knowledge economy.

In order to capture these differences and allow for a more nuanced understanding and exploration of education hubs, a typology of three categories of hubs is suggested (Knight, 2011b). The three types of hubs include student hub, talent hub, and knowledge/innovation hub. The typology is based on the rationales and nature of the activities – not on the location, level, or scope of hubs.

The student hub is the most focused and prevalent type of education hub. The key activity is the education and training of local, expatriate, and international students. In addition to recruiting students, it also focuses on attracting foreign higher education institutions to offer franchised and twinning programs or establish branch campuses in order to increase access for all types of students. The primary objectives for student hubs are: 1. to provide increased access to higher education for students; 2. to modernize and internationalize domestic higher education institutions; 3. to generate revenue from international student fees; and 4. to build profile and increase competitiveness within the regional higher education sector and beyond.

The talent hub focuses on student education and training but differs from the student hub because the overarching goal is to develop a skilled workforce. Thus, foreign students are encouraged to remain in the host country for employment purposes. International higher education institutions as well as private training/education companies offer academic programs and professional development opportunities aimed at international and national students as well as local employees. The overall goal is human resource development. The driving key objectives are: 1. to educate and train students to be skilled labour workers for a knowledge- and service-led economy, and 2. to establish geopolitical status in the region and beyond. The education/training institutions and companies are often, but not necessarily, co-located in a zone in order to share facilities and promote collaboration amongst themselves and with industry. In order to develop a critical mass there can be more than one co-location site in a country.

The knowledge/innovation hub broadens its mandate beyond education and training to include the production and distribution of knowledge and innovation. Foreign actors including universities, research institutes, and companies with major research and development activities are attracted through favourable business incentives to establish a base in the country and to collaborate with local partners to develop applied research, knowledge, and innovation. The primary objectives are: 1. to help build a knowledge- and service-based economy; 2. to educate and train skilled labour for knowledge/innovation; 3. to attract foreign direct investment; and 4. to increase regional or global economic competitiveness and soft power. Collaboration among the key players – foreign and local education institutions, industries, research centres, and companies – is a key factor in building a knowledge and innovation hub.

Education hubs are full of lofty expectations and fraught with potential challenges. There are a myriad of issues that require further reflection and examination by researchers, policy-makers, and the hub sponsors. Issues vary by the type of hub but include regulatory and policy questions related to registration and quality assurance of education and training providers; recognition of qualifications for further study and employment in different countries; university–industry partnerships; intellectual property rights for new knowledge and innovation; employment and immigration policies; incentives to attract foreign education providers and companies; relevance of teaching/training methods in light of cultural diversity; and compliance with regional and international trade laws.

There are macro and more theoretical issues to be explored including higher education as an economic and soft power actor; the centrality of commercial competitiveness in education hubs; implications from the intercultural, interdisciplinary, and cross-sectoral nature of education hubs: the role of education hubs in region building; impact of brain gain through a hub; the relationship between local and foreign actors; and the sustainability of education hubs. These are but a few examples of the issues related to establishing an education hub to further a country's engagement and competitiveness in the knowledge economy (Knight, 2014).

Emerging Issues, Challenges and Unintended Consequences

Student Access

Does crossborder education help countries satisfy the growing demand for higher and continuing education? Many would answer yes and that increased access for students is a driving motivation for all forms of crossborder education (Wilkins & Huisman, 2010). But the critical issue of equity of access and whether it will be available only to those who can afford it or have the language skills (primarily English) prevails. No precise data exists on the rate of participation of students in crossborder programs at the national or international levels. Only a handful of countries around the world collect reliable data on enrolments in crossborder education programs, although this situation is improving. Thus, there is inconclusive evidence as to whether crossborder education in the form of program and provider mobility is a successful and sustainable way to increase access to higher education for the general cohort of students wanting higher education.

Quality Assurance of Crossborder Education

In the last decade, increased importance has been given to quality assurance at the institutional and national levels. More national quality assurance and accreditation agencies have been created. The primary task of national quality assurance agencies has been quality recognition and assurance of domestic higher education provision by public and/or private higher education institutions. However, the increase in crossborder education by foreign institutions has introduced a new challenge (and gap) in the field of quality assurance. Historically, national quality assurance agencies have generally not focused their efforts on assessing the quality of imported and exported programs. The question now facing the sector is how to deal with the increase in crossborder education by traditional higher education institutions and the new private commercial providers who are not normally part of nationally based quality assurance schemes (Knight, 2010).

Recognition of Qualifications

Increased academic mobility raises the issue of credential recognition to a more prominent place in international education policy. The credibility of higher education programs and qualifications is extremely important for students, their employers, the public at large, and the academic community itself. It is critical that the qualifications awarded by crossborder providers are legitimate and will be recognized for employment or further studies both at home and abroad. To establish a credential review and assessment agency is still a challenge facing many countries of the world, especially in developing countries.

Capacity-Building

It is clear that crossborder education can be considered a double-edged sword. On the one hand, it can increase access for local students and in many cases regional students. But, on the other hand, by importing foreign programs and providers, one can question the relevancy of the curriculum to local context and needs. More importantly, it often does not help to develop the human capacity of the domestic higher education institutions and faculty to design and offer these programs themselves. Critics of crossborder education believe that relying on foreign expertise to prepare and teach courses for local populations introduces issues of dependency, sometimes neo-colonization, and also sustainability.

Education Hubs – fad, brand, or innovation?

Education hubs are important new developments. They represent a new generation of crossborder education activities where critical mass, co-location, and connection between international/local universities, students, research institutes, and private industry are key. But are they just a fad? Are they more rhetoric than reality? A common perception is that being recognized as an education hub will increase a country's reputation, competitiveness, and geopolitical status within the region and beyond. Are education hubs nothing more than a branding exercise designed to increase status and a sense of soft power?

Brain Drain/Gain/Train

While 'brain drain and brain gain' are well-known concepts, research is showing that students are increasingly interested in taking a degree in country A, followed by a second degree or perhaps internship in country B, leading to employment in country C and probably D, finally returning to their home country after 8 to 12 years of international study and work experience. Hence, the emergence of the term *brain train* (Knight, 2008). From a policy perspective, higher education is becoming a more important actor and is now working in closer collaboration with immigration, industry, and the science and technology sectors to build an integrated strategy for attracting and retaining knowledge workers. Crossborder education and especially international student recruitment campaigns are seen as major contributors to the great brain race of the twenty-first century. Who would have believed that the generous scholarship schemes of the 1960s and 1970s for developing country students would morph into the big business of international student recruitment of 2012?

Double Degrees – double the benefit or double counting?

The interest in double degree programs is increasing around the world. But, so is concern about the necessary academic requirements and the validity of a double or multiple degree qualification. For many academics and policy-makers, double degree programs are welcomed as a natural extension of exchange and mobility programs. For others, they are perceived as a troublesome development leading to double counting of academic work and the thin edge of academic fraud. A broad range of reactions exist owing to the diversity of program models, the uncertainty related to quality assurance and qualifications recognition, and finally, the ethics involved in deciding what academic workload or new competencies are required for the granting of joint, double, or multiple degrees (Knight, 2011c).

Cultural Diversity or Homogenization – cultural tensions?

Debates on the impact of crossborder education on indigenous knowledge and cultural diversity often provoke strong positions and sentiments. Some take a positive view and believe that modern information and communication technologies and the movement of people, ideas, and cultures across national boundaries promote the fusion and hybridization of culture. Others contend that these same forces are eroding national cultural identities and leading to cultural homogenization, most often in the form of Westernization. And still others speculate that crossborder mobility of student, providers, and programs will only increase cultural tensions within host institutions and countries.

Concluding Remarks

Words like diversity, innovation, complexity, confusion, risks, benefits, opportunities, and challenges have been used repeatedly in this chapter to describe the development and evolution of crossborder education. The mobility of students, professors, knowledge, and values has been part of higher education for centuries but it has only been in the last two decades that there has been a significant growth in the mobility of programs and providers and the establishment of education hubs.

With innovation come new opportunities and threats, benefits and risks, promises, and perils. The potential for increased benefits are many and diverse and include:

- access to higher education;
- strategic alliances between countries and regions;
- production and exchange of new knowledge through academic/industry partnerships;
- greater mobility of graduates and professionals;
- human resource development and institutional capacity-building;

- income generation or attraction of foreign investment;
- improvement of academic quality;
- new intercultural skills and international understanding;
- increased mutual understanding.

While the list of potential benefits is long and varied, so is the list of potential risks:

- an increase in low-quality programs and providers;
- a potential decrease in public funding if foreign providers are providing increased access;
- courses being driven by short-term needs of the labour market;
- non-sustainable foreign provision of higher education if profit margins are low;
- double degrees which devalue the integrity of a qualification;
- foreign qualifications not recognized by domestic employers or education institutions;
- elitism in terms of those who can afford crossborder education;
- overuse of English as the language of instruction;
- little importance being given to collaborative research;
- national higher education policy objectives not being met.

In conclusion, much is at stake with the increase in crossborder education. The pros and cons differ in relation to whether a country is a sending or receiving country, or a developed or developed country, the maturity and stability of the higher education system, and the national priorities and policies driving the increase in crossborder education. The political, economic, cultural, and social contexts all influence whether the benefits outweigh the risks or vice versa. Usually the stakes are higher for a receiving country as the impact of foreign education programs and providers definitely affects the local higher education sector and access. One size does not fit all in determining the best combination of crossborder education strategies for a sending or receiving country. The short- and long-term impacts, as well as sustainability, are serious considerations. There is no 'silver bullet' formula in terms of crossborder education provision. The potential benefits, risks, and impacts need to be carefully calculated for each institution and country. It is important to acknowledge the huge potential of crossborder education but not at the expense of academic quality and integrity.

Note

[1] This article is adapted from Knight (2012).

References

Altbach, P.G. & Knight, J. (2007) The Internationalization of Higher Education: motivations and realities, *Journal of Studies in International Education*, 11(3-4), 290-305.

Boehm, A., Davis, D., Meares, D. & Pearce, D. (2002) *The Global Student Mobility 2025 Report: forecasts of the global demand for international education*. Canberra: IDP.

Chen, T. & Barnett, G. (2000) Research on International Student Flows From a Macro Perspective: a network analysis of 1985, 1989 and 1995, *Higher Education*, 39, 435-453.

Knight, J. (2007) Crossborder Tertiary Education: an introduction, in Organisation for Economic Cooperation and Development/World Bank, *Crossborder Tertiary Education: a way towards capacity development* (pp. 21-46). Paris: Organisation for Economic Cooperation and Development, World Bank and NUFFIC.

Knight, J. (2008) *Higher Education in Turmoil: the changing world of internationalization*. Rotterdam: Sense.

Knight, J. (2010) Quality Dilemmas with Regional Education Hubs and Cities, in S. Kaur, M. Sirat & W. Tierney (Eds) *Quality Assurance and University Rankings in Higher Education in the Asia Pacific: challenges for universities and nations*. Penang: Universiti Sains Malaysia Press.

Knight, J. (2011a) Education Hubs: a fad, a brand, or an innovation, *Journal for Studies in International Education*, 15(3), 221-240.

Knight, J. (2011b) *Three Types of Education Hubs – student, talent, knowledge. Are Indicators Useful or Feasible?* London: Observatory on Borderless Higher Education.

Knight, J. (2011c) Doubts and Dilemmas With Double Degree Programs, *Revista de Universidad y Sociedad del Conocimiento*, 8(2), 297-312. http://rusc.uoc.edu/ojs/index.php/rusc/article/view/v8n2-knight (accessed 20 November 2012).

Knight, J. (2012) *Internationalization: three generations of crossborder education*. Occasional Paper #38. New Delhi: India International Centre.

Knight, J. (2014) *International Education Hubs: student, talent, knowledge-innovation models*. Dordrecht: Springer.

Observatory on Borderless Higher Education (2012a) *International Branch Campuses: data and developments*. Authored by W. Lawton & A. Katsomitrous. London: OBHE.

Observatory on Borderless Higher Education (2012b) *MOOCs and Disruptive Innovation: the challenge of HE business models*. Authored by W. Lawton & A. Katsomitrous. London: OBHE.

Organization for Economic Cooperation and Development (OECD) (2010) *Education at a Glance 2010*. Paris: OECD.

Verbik, L. & Merkley, C. (2006) *The International Branch Campus – models and trends*. London: Observatory on Borderless Higher Education.

Wilkins, S. & Huisman, J. (2010) Student Recruitment at International Branch Campuses: can they compete in the global market? *Journal of Studies in International Education*, 15(3), 299-316.

CHAPTER 4

North–South Research Partnerships in Higher Education: perspectives from South and North

ANGELINE M. BARRETT, MICHAEL CROSSLEY & TITANJI PETER FON

ABSTRACT This chapter looks at the theme of internationalisation in higher education from the perspective of North–South cross-cultural collaboration and research capacity-building. It draws on the authors' experience of a collaboration which was directed towards strengthening teaching of research methods to postgraduate students. The project demonstrated how North–South research partnerships in higher education can create new possibilities for epistemology and pedagogy. In the Southern university, the dominance of an over-specified 'scientific' epistemology was challenged. In the Northern institution, pedagogic relations between academic staff and international research students were challenged. Dialogue over the nature of educational research and acceptable/legitimate forms of knowledge within North–South collaborations can be uncomfortable, as contestations and disagreements surfaced. The authors argue for mindfulness of influence of colonial heritage and of a global contemporary context where 'big science' approaches to research have a growing influence on modes of international collaboration.

Introduction

North–South research partnerships in higher education can be opportunities for dialogue that pushes back the horizons of epistemological and pedagogical possibilities within our universities. This chapter looks at the theme of internationalisation in higher education from the perspective of North–South cross-cultural collaboration and research capacity-building. It continues earlier work by the authors (Barrett et al, 2011; Crossley, 2011) and recent practical experience of a partnership between our two universities, the University of Buea in Cameroon and the University of Bristol in the United

Kingdom (UK). So far, the partnership has involved two projects. Four years apart, both were aimed at strengthening the teaching and learning of research methods within doctoral programmes. In the process, the project challenged the dominance of an over-specified 'scientific' epistemology within one university and pedagogic relations between academic staff and international research students in the other. This chapter brings together the perspectives of researchers involved in this collaboration in both the Southern and the Northern universities.

Internationalisation of Higher Education
Viewed from the North and South

Much literature on the internationalisation of higher education focuses on teaching and learning. Less is written about implications of internationalisation for research. One reason for this may well be, as Maringe et al (2013) point out, that universities are, almost by definition, international in character and this is especially true of their research activities. Internationalisation of teaching and learning, although not new, has intensified considerably over the last two to three decades, with very visible impact on student and civic populations, particularly in Western countries. The intensely international character of research has a longer history and one that is considered less remarkable except from the critical anti-Eurocentric perspective of postcolonial and indigenous theorists (Said, 1978; Tuhiwai Smith, 1999; Santos, 2012). Their analysis powerfully shows how internationalisation can look very different when viewed from the South and North:

> We live in a globalized world but not in a homogeneously
> globalized world. Not only are there different logics moving
> globalized flows but also different power relations behind the
> distribution of the costs and benefits of globalization. There is
> transnational greed as there is transnational solidarity. Which side
> will the university be on? (Santos, 2012, pp. 9-10)

The answer to Santos' question, according to Maringe et al's (2013) survey of 500 senior university administrators, depends on where in the world the university is located. Western Anglophone universities increasingly tend to adopt a 'commercial-value driven' perspective, largely concerned with 'developing a visible international presence and identity' through recruiting more international students and staff and the commercialisation of international collaborative research (Maringe et al, 2013, p. 32). Conversely, university administrators in sub-Saharan Africa see internationalisation as potentially damaging to their institutions, as talented individuals tend to be attracted away to universities in richer nations. In universities of the South, senior academics are more likely to express a purely academic rationale for internationalisation focused on stimulating research capacity and internationalising curricula. Similar divergent perspectives were evident in the first collaboration between Buea and Bristol in 2007-08. The project was aimed at strengthening the teaching of research methodologies on doctoral programmes within the education departments of the University of Buea and two other African universities. For the UK institution involved, benefits related to enriching the educational experience of their own international doctoral students, particularly those from Africa, and the research income associated with the project.

Scholars from both the North and South, including ourselves (Barrett et al, 2008, 2011), have written critically and self-critically on the unequal nature of North–South research collaborations (e.g. King, 1990; Pryor et al, 2009). Since the term *partnership* became popular within development discourses in the 1990s, North–South collaborations have been observed to serve the research agendas of North-based funders (King, 1990; Brown, 1992; Samoff, 2004; Olsson, 2008). Hence research partnerships funded by development organisations can contribute towards the perpetuation of what Fahey and Kenway (2010, p. 629) call 'empires of knowledge' centred on Europe and the USA and linked historically to European colonial empires. However, recently some researchers have questioned the extent to which such 'binary terms' (Desai, 2013, p. 266) capture the full dynamic of North-funded North–South collaborations, particularly within complex collaborations with more than one Southern partner (Holmarsdottir et al, 2013a). Through critical reflective dialogue and through 'sharing ideas, challenges and information' (Holmarsdottir et al, 2013b, p. 280), researchers create spaces within which dominant agendas emanating from the North can be contested by research partners from the South (Chege, 2008; Desai, 2013). Enabled by relations of trust and codes of mutual respect, these are not comfortable spaces of consensus but rather 'discursive and transgressive space[s]', within which 'disagreements and unevenness' are made apparent (Pryor et al, 2009, p. 781).

Many of these reflections by researchers acknowledge that, even when Southern partners gain some control over research agendas, complete equality between a Northern lead partner and Southern partners was not achieved. Exceptions do exist. These tend to be projects that are jointly funded by partners in the South and North (Crossley & Bennett, 1997), projects funded from East Asian countries which place a high value on cultural exchange (Chege, 2008) or projects initiated by academics seeking 'to pool the strengths each one had, to learn from each other, and to contribute to education in their different contexts' (Avalos, 2008, p. 102) rather than in response to a funding opportunity.

However, within the literature on North–South research collaboration, the forms of inequality that concern contemporary analysts extend well beyond funding flows to include the nature and influence of global epistemological hegemony, and the fact that this often goes unchecked by academic critique (Pryor et al, 2009; Holmarsdottir et al, 2013a). In an analysis of the form and nature of educational research capacity in the small Caribbean state of St Lucia, for example, Holmes and Crossley (2004) draw upon postcolonial theorising to reveal how much existing research carried out there is framed within traditional positivistic frameworks that prioritise quantitative surveys and detailed statistical analysis. In doing so, they argue that this is a limiting frame of reference, especially within social and cultural contexts where oral traditions and locally grounded understanding of educational needs and priorities have much to offer educational planners and policy-makers. They reflect upon extensive experience in the development of qualitative paradigms in a diversity of low-income countries (Crossley & Vulliamy, 1997) to argue that innovative qualitative developments in St Lucia could do more to stretch 'the boundaries of research to include more informal, but nevertheless intellectual, activities such as work by the storyteller and the calypsonian' (Holmes & Crossley, 2004, p. 207) to broaden the range of what might be understood as research data and research processes. This in turn has implications for what is considered as research capacity, what this means for research capacity-building, and how postcolonial analyses by authors such as Hoogvelt (1997), Tuhiwai Smith (1999), and Hayhoe and Pan (2001) could contribute to the genuine internationalisation of educational research capacity-building and cross-cultural research partnerships.

While such developments, and those reported by Pryor et al (2009), are encouraging, Crossley's (2010, 2012) more recent work is increasingly critical of the contemporary influence of 'big science' approaches to research on modes of international collaboration in the social sciences and the implications of this for the growing hegemony of expensive, large-scale, statistical modalities of educational research and research capacity-building. If such tendencies remain unchecked they will do much to reinforce the dominance of positivistic assumptions and values that already have a stronghold over social research throughout many universities in low-income countries, including the University of Buea in Cameroon, discussed below. As Vulliamy argues in his Presidential Address to the British Association for International and Comparative Education in 2003:

> A concern for sensitivity to cultural context has been a key part of
> the field of comparative and international education ... such
> concern for cultural context also pervades sociological traditions
> underpinning the development of qualitative research ... The
> challenge for future comparative and international researchers in
> education is to harness the symbiosis of these two traditions to
> resist the increasing hegemony of a positivist global discourse of
> educational research and policy-making. (Vulliamy, 2004, p. 277)

Today the challenges are much greater, in times when preoccupations with the potential of 'big data' are highly influential, and when the impact of large-scale data sets and cross-national surveys of student achievement is visible on educational policy-making worldwide. See, for example, work by Grek et al (2009) on the growing influence of the Programme for International Student Assessment (PISA) throughout European educational systems and Meyer and Benavot's (2013) edited book titled *PISA, Power and Policy*. This is not to deny the role and potential of such work, and the complex forms of statistical analysis that are emerging to pioneer new advancements, but it is important that, as Furlong (2004, p. 343) maintains, the research community does more to maintain 'a rich and diverse range of approaches to research'. We argue that this is especially important, as is research capacity-building from all paradigmatic and organisational perspectives, in international collaborative studies of education, where well-grounded understandings of local cultural differences, values and priorities are vitally important.

Botha and Breidlid (2013) discuss this further with reference to an international exchange programme that brought Masters students from a range of countries in the South to Norway. They found participating students talked about benefits in terms of technical and academic knowledge and skills but were silent on social and emotional learning, although the researchers were confident this had also occurred. Botha and Breidlid (2013, p. 274) relate this finding to the dominance, in both the global North and South, of a Western scientific epistemology that, through taking a segmented rather than holistic approach to knowledge, neglects 'learning as a social experience that affects the whole person'. Their analysis is influenced by the critique made by theorists adopting indigenous or feminist perspectives of the dominance of Western, segmented approaches to knowledge and also by the work of Boaventura de Sousa Santos, which associates the global dominance of Western, scientific epistemology with the emergence of global capitalism as a 'civilizational paradigm' (Santos et al, 2007, p. xix). Botha and Breidlid conclude with a challenge for international academic collaborations:

> Rather than echoing the message that education is about developing only one kind of knowledge and the elites and elitist practices that this epistemic dominance engenders in both the North and the South, we hope that North–South partners will take seriously Chomsky's (2010, as cited in Meyer 2010, 14) suggestion that the potential for challenging educational homogenisation is greater now than it has ever been. (Botha & Breidlid, 2013, p. 275)

In the remainder of this chapter we reflect on the extent to which the collaboration between the authors has opened up a space to challenge epistemic hegemony within the practice of educational research. We do so mindful of how our colonial heritage shapes and limits epistemological possibilities, whilst agreeing with Suárez-Krabbe (2012) that North–South dialogue is necessary for the decolonisation of universities in both Europe and Africa.

Education Research Capacity-Building in Practice: reflections on the Bristol–Buea partnership

The initial project partnering Bristol and Buea in 2007-08 was aimed at strengthening research methods training within the doctoral programmes of African education departments. Consistent with Harle's (2008, p. 86) advice that Africa–UK collaborations should be 'responsive to what African humanities and social science researchers define as their needs', the initial impetus for the project came from Buea. The Dean of the Faculty of Education at the time approached Bristol, requesting collaboration that would offer international exposure to Buea's doctoral students. Strengthening the research capacity of students and staff aligned with strategic objectives of the Government of Cameroon, the Ministry of Higher Education as well as the University of Buea (University of Buea, 2008; Republic of Cameroon, 2009). The project was funded through the British Council, funded by the UK Department for Education and Skills, as part of the England Africa Partnership capacity-building initiative. As UK leadership was a condition of the scheme, Bristol led the bidding process and consequently led on project administration, evaluation and reporting through the project's lifetime.

During the research design process, Bristol invited the Faculty of Education (as it was known at the time) at the University of Dar es Salaam and the Institute of Educational Planning and Administration at the University Cape Coast to join in the bid, having established they were also in the process of developing their doctoral programmes. This created a more complex partnership but one that contributed to developing intra-continental networks in Africa, also as recommended by Harle (2008). Since 2008, colleagues from the Universities of Buea, Dar es Salaam and Cape Coast have collaborated on further research bids and communicate regularly on academic and social issues. Buea and Bristol have maintained their partnership through a one-off contribution by Bristol staff to teaching on one of the Buea research programmes and ongoing communication with the former Dean.

By the end of the project, it was expected that the African partners would have developed a new teaching unit as part of their doctoral programmes and collaborated in bids for further funding. Bristol expected to enhance teaching for international postgraduates, most especially those from Africa, through the participant staff's experience of visiting an African university. Most African doctoral students at Bristol are teaching or administrative university staff and return to the institution where they formerly worked on completion of the degree. Project objectives and expected outcomes were expressed in the language of capacity-building mainly in the African universities. This included enhancing capacity for course design and programme development and support for leading research bids. Elements such as creating an opportunity for doctoral students to present to an international audience and enhancing supervision skills were generic to the British and African partners. However, the project design revolved around events that brought representatives from all four universities together in an African university or brought small teams of lecturers from each African university to Bristol to observe teaching units and discuss content with tutors. These events were also sites for contesting the research paradigms with their associated epistemological substance about the nature of scientific knowledge.

The largest event was a week-long 'Methods Conference' held at the University of Buea, in which sessions were led by academic staff and students from all four partner institutions. It was designed as a series of highly interactive teaching and learning events, with academics and doctoral students from each institution leading different sessions. Each session included group work that allowed for interaction across participating institutions and between staff and students of the same institution, on a more equal basis than was the norm in some partner institutions. Activities included critiquing journal articles, preparing brief research proposals, and designing and trialling data collection. The Methods Conference was followed by a doctoral conference, at which research students from all four universities presented on their own research. The two linked conferences were intended as the main opportunity for international exposure for Buea's research students that had been the initial motivation for Buea seeking a partnership with Bristol. As already indicated, the conferences were conducted within an institutional context where positivist research was (and still is) dominant, and viewed by proponents as the only 'scientific' way to do research. In response to this context, and reflecting the expertise and interests of participants from Bristol and Cape Coast, the conference included sessions comparing across diverse research approaches (positivist, interpretivist, critical and creative/narrative) and sessions focused on qualitative methods. Hence, the stage was set for debate and contestation over the nature of a 'PhD', the nature of educational research and acceptable/legitimate forms of knowledge within the academy. In the following sections we present a view of this debate from Buea and from Bristol.

The Buea Perspective

In her welcome address to participants at the Methods Conference, the Dean of the Buea Faculty of Education urged participants to conceptualise the Methods Conference 'as a learning journey ... a data collecting session that should be coded and stored for later use'. This partnership experience was indeed such a learning journey for staff and students from the University of Buea. The 'learning journey' provided graduate students enrolled in various academic programmes within the faculty to listen to and discuss with academics other than their own professors on research-related topics and issues. This was particularly helpful for doctoral students who were at the proposal stage of their degree programme as they discussed their research plans with staff and students from other universities and received valuable feedback from them.

One of the weaknesses of research in the Buea Faculty of Education and other departments in the humanities and social sciences is heavy reliance on positivist approaches. Little or no attention is paid to alternatives such as the post-positivist and interpretive paradigms. Doctoral programmes in the Faculty of Education were designed in response to acute shortages of teachers within the university and other higher education institutions in Cameroon. The quality of preparation of teachers for the higher education sector cannot be overemphasised. A good grounding in international developments in research methodologies is critical to staff, who presently control and perpetuate research cultures, and students, who are currently or likely to become staff members. Breaking the cycle, by which academic staff perpetuate their epistemological preferences by presenting research students with only one paradigmatic possibility, is critical in developing and sustaining a methodologically diverse research culture within the University of Buea in particular and the higher education system in Cameroon more generally. The project also helped in bringing out the importance of the contextual variable (Crossley, 2010) in shaping the research practices of students.

Since 2007, the University of Buea has been undergoing a far-reaching transition. With other higher education institutions within the Central African Economic and Monetary Community, Buea is in the process of implementing the Bachelor, Masters and doctorate system as an external dimension of the Bologna Process (Tchombe et al, 2009). At the same time, traditional, teacher-dominated, instructional practices are giving way to more student-centred approaches in a bid to 'train the whole person by giving the learners both professional and good citizenship skills' (Titanji, 2010). The Methods Conference brought staff and students together in group activities, based on the assumption that each can learn from the other. Group activities during the Methods Conference were both theoretical and practical. The hands-on components enabled participants to apply what they had learnt during the presentations by the various resource persons. Encouraging teachers and students to work together was not one of the objectives of the Methods Conference. However, inadvertently, it challenged colleagues from the University of Buea to work with students in groups as equals. This is not very typical of teaching and learning contexts within the university. By inadvertently challenging stereotypical instructional approaches, the project can be described as a success.

Though the project activities were very helpful, concerns were raised about their duration, and the content of some of them. It is very important to observe that all the activities associated with the project, especially the Methods Conference, were organised within a context of very tight timelines with the potential to constrain learning opportunities for all participants. The testimonials from postgraduate students and one member of staff suggest the need for more time to be devoted to future activities, rather than rushing them. However, concerns about the short duration of activities could be seen as indicative of their quality and the desire for more. Like Oliver Twist, adults will also ask for more of what is good. More time for programme design workshops, more time for auditing research methods courses in Bristol and more time for conversations during the Methods Conference would have definitely been welcome.

Some of the colleagues from Buea were of the opinion that a thorough needs assessment should have been conducted to inform the design and delivery of the activities, particularly the events held in Dar es Salaam and Bristol that only involved teaching staff. Involving staff from Buea in determining needs for their own professional development would have provided baseline data to inform the content and processes for professional development in line with principles of adult learning. Bristol had consulted lead researchers at all partner institutions in conceptualising and putting together the bid, however this communication had not extended to the wider team involved in project implementation and did not constitute a systematic needs analysis.

The Bristol Perspective

For Bristol staff involved in the project, the Methods Conference, more than any other event, challenged preconceptions and extended our understanding of teaching and supervision at the doctoral level. The first surprise was the number of Buea participants, almost twice as many as we had expected, owing to the participation of Masters students from Education and other faculties, and their enthusiasm. We had viewed the project as a small-scale intervention restricted to one academic department and had not imagined the readiness across postgraduate programmes and faculties to debate methodology. On the other hand, as is often the case, participation from students was more consistent than that of academic staff, particularly more senior academic staff, who were inevitably juggling competing demands on their time. We encountered different ways of conceptualising the doctorate, which placed greater emphasis on acquisition of expertise, handed from lecturer to student, and less on the individuality of each doctoral researcher's journey. The phrase 'terminal degree' that Buea staff used to describe a doctorate in philosophy seemed to capture its relationship to a hierarchical ordering of knowledge and status. The vehemence of opposition to qualitative research methods, reminiscent of the 'paradigm wars' of an earlier era in the UK, was not in itself a surprise given the orthodoxy that persists amongst policy-makers (Vulliamy, 2004). However, we had not anticipated the extent to which individuals' careers and professional identities were invested in maintaining the supremacy of their particular approach to quantitative research. The debate on methodologies became polarised as individuals presented epistemologies as paradigmatic, excluding the possibility of epistemological diversity. Accustomed to having a richly resourced library and electronic journals by the thousand at our fingertips, Bristol participants encountered for the first time the authority that can be invested in a single text when alternatives are hard to source. Research students at the University of Buea presenting in the conference adhered closely to the prescriptions of a single research methods textbook (Amin, 2005), which was written by one of their tutors, a well-respected professor. The book focused on quantitative methods and only admitted one 'scientific' epistemology.

Learning for researchers from the North was diffused to the level of the individual. Interacting with our doctoral students in the context of an African country, where the familiar roles of cultural insider/outsider were reversed, we found them to be more extroverted and confident. This raised questions concerning how the Bristol learning environment could disempower international students. This is an issue that we have continued to reflect upon particularly in relation to our supervision practices. We also learned from the facilitative skills of lecturers from the Universities of Cape Coast and Dar es Salaam, who created an assumption of equality and ensured that the voice of every group member, staff and student, host and visitor, was heard and given equal weight. We can now make use of the same techniques in our own teaching.

Conclusion

In this chapter we have focused on North–South research partnerships, as one manifestation of internationalisation in higher education. We have explored their potential to contribute towards diversifying epistemologies and the pedagogies with specific reference to a capacity-building collaboration for developing research methods teaching programmes for postgraduate researchers. Such small-scale research partnerships generate opportunities for critical dialogue between researchers and universities that expands our epistemological, methodological and pedagogical horizons. However, they are enacted within a global context where 'big science' approaches to research have a growing influence on modes of international collaboration in the social sciences. The emergence of new technologies, the rise of 'big data' and powerful statistical techniques add urgency to the imperative for researchers to create 'discursive and transgressive space[s]' (Pryor et al, 2009, p. 781), through engaging in critical reflection and dialogue. Few detailed studies of such research partnerships exist in the available literature, although Stephens' (2009) edited collection is a useful resource. One area, for example, in which more work is needed is the ethics of international research collaboration to inform the design and implementation of mutually beneficial research partnerships and to avoid new forms of intellectual imperialism (Bond & Tikly, 2013). This could include work such as that contained in a special issue of the journal *Comparative Education* on the theme of

'Educational Research in Confucian Heritage Cultures' (Evers et al, 2011), and further critical analyses of collaborative practice as presented here.

References

Amin, M.E. (2005) *Social Science Research: conception, methodology and analysis.* Kampala: Makerere University.

Avalos, B. (2008) Individual and Institutional Partnerships: some experiences, *NORRAG News*, 41, 101-102.

Barrett, A.M., Crossley, M. & Dachi, H.A. (2011) International Collaboration and Research Capacity Building: learning from the EdQual experience, *Comparative Education*, 47(1), 25-43.

Barrett, A.M., Rubagiza, J. & Uworwabayeho, A. (2008) Critical Reflections From a Partnership in Progress: the case of EdQual, *NORRAG News*, 41, 76-78.

Botha, L.R. & Breidlid, A. (2013) Challenging Hegemonic Knowledge Production Through North–South Collaboration, *Compare*, 43(2), 270-275.

Brown, L. (1992) Higher Education and the Reality of Interdependence, *International Journal of Educational Development*, 12(2), 87-94.

Chege, F. (2008) Experiences of Partnerships from Kenya: North-South and South-South, *NORRAG News*, 41, 103-105.

Crossley, M. (2010) Context Matters in Educational Research and International Development: learning from the small states experience, *PROSPECTS*, 40(4), 421-429.

Crossley, M. (2011) Strengthening Educational Research Capacity in Small States, in M. Martin & M. Bray (Eds) *Tertiary Education in Small States: planning in the context of globalisation*, pp. 101-108. Paris: UNESCO International Institute for Educational Planning.

Crossley, M. (2012) Comparative Education and Research Capacity Building: reflections on international transfer and the significance of context, *Journal of International and Comparative Education*, 1(1), 4-12.

Crossley, M. & Bennett, J.A. (1997) Planning for Case-Study Evaluation in Belize, Central America, in M. Crossley & G. Vulliamy (Eds) *Qualitative Educational Research in Developing Countries: current perspectives*, pp. 221-243. Oxford: Routledge.

Crossley, M. & Vulliamy, G. (Eds) (1997) *Qualitative Educational Research in Developing Countries: current perspectives.* New York: Garland.

Desai, Z. (2013) North–South–South Collaboration: internationalising higher education, capacitating the South or furthering donor agendas? *Compare*, 43(2), 266-270.

Evers, C.W., King, M. & Katyal, K.R. (Eds) (2011) Special Issue: Educational Research in Confucian Heritage Cultures, *Comparative Education*, 47(3).

Fahey, J. & Kenway, J. (2010) Thinking in a 'Worldly' Way: mobility, knowledge, power and geography, *Discourse*, 31(5), 627-640.

Furlong, J. (2004) BERA at 30. Have We Come of Age?, *British Educational Research Journal*, 30(3), 343-358.

Grek, S., Lawn, M., Lingard, B., Ozga, J., Rinne, R., Segerholm, C. & Simola, H. (2009) National Policy Brokering and the Construction of the European Education Space in England, Sweden, Finland and Scotland, *Comparative Education*, 45(1), 5-21.

Harle, J. (2008) Framing Research Between Africa and the UK, *NORRAG News*, 41, 84-87.

Hayhoe, R. & Pan, J. (Eds) (2001) *Knowledge Across Cultures: a contribution to dialogue among civilizations*. Hong Kong: Comparative Education Research Centre, University of Hong Kong.

Holmarsdottir, H.B., Desai, Z., Botha, L.R., Breidlid, A., Bastien, S., Mukoma, W., Ezekiel, M.J., Helleve, A., Farag, A.I. & Nomlomo, V. (2013a) COMPARE Forum: the idea of North–South and South–South collaboration, *Compare*, 43(2), 265-286.

Holmarsdottir, H.B., Farag, A.I. & Nomlomo, V. (2013b) North–South–South Collaboration: old ideas in new boxes? *Compare*, 43(2), 281-286.

Holmes, K. & Crossley, M. (2004) Whose Knowledge, Whose Values? The Contribution of Local Knowledge to Education Policy Processes: a case study of research development initiatives in the small state of Saint Lucia, *Compare*, 34(2), 197-214.

Hoogvelt, A. (1997) *Globalization and the Postcolonial World: the new political economy of development*. Baltimore: Johns Hopkins University Press.

King, K. (1990) The New Politics of International Collaboration in Educational Development: Northern and Southern research in education, *International Journal of Educational Development*, 10(1), 47-57.

Maringe, F., Foskett, N. & Woodfield, S. (2013) Emerging Internatoinalisation Models in an Uneven Global Terrain: findings from a global survey, *Compare*, 43(1), 9-36.

Meyer, H.-D. & Benavot, A. (Eds) (2013) *PISA, Power, and Policy: the emergence of global educational governance*. Oxford: Symposium Books.

Olsson, B. (2008) Symmetry and Asymmetry in Research Partnerships: lessons from 20 years experience, *NORRAG News*, 41, 78-80.

Pryor, J., Kuupole, A., Kutor, N., Dunne, M. & Adu-Yeboah, C. (2009) Exploring the Fault Lines of Cross-Cultural Collaborative Research, *Compare*, 39(6), 769-782.

Republic of Cameroon (2009) *Growth and Employment Strategy Paper: reference framework for government action over the period 2010-2020*. Yaounde: Republic of Cameroon.

Said, E.W. (1978) *Orientalism*. London: Routledge & Kegan Paul.

Samoff, J. (2004) The Promise of Partnership and Continuities of Dependence: external support to higher education in Africa, *African Studies Review*, 47(1), 67-199.

Santos, B.D.S. (2012) The University at a Crossroads, *Human Architecture*, 10(1), 7-16.

Santos, B.D.S., Nunes, J.A. & Meneses, M.P. (2007) Opening up the Canon of Knowledge and Recognition of Difference, in B.D.S. Santos (Ed.) *Another Knowledge is Possible: beyond Northern epistemologies*, pp. xix-lxii. London: Verso.

Stephens, D. (Ed.) (2009) *Higher Education and International Capacity Building: twenty-five years of higher education links*. Oxford: Symposium Books.

Suárez-Krabbe, J. (2012) 'Epistemic Coyotismo' and Transnational Collaboration: decolonizing the Danish university, *Human Architecture*, 10(1), 31-44.

Tchombe, T., Nnane, P. & Titanji, P.F. (2009) The Bologna Process in Cameroon's Higher Education System: challenges and prospects, paper presented at the European Conference on Educational Research, University of Vienna, 28-30 September.

Tikly, L. & Bond, T.N. (2013) Towards a Postcolonial Research Ethics in Comparative and International Education, *Compare*, 43(4), 422-442.

Titanji, V.P.K. (2010) Vice-Chancellor's Speech, The 15th Convocation Ceremony for the Award of Degrees, University of Buea, 17 December.

Tuhiwai Smith, L. (1999) *Decolonizing Methodologies: research and indigenous peoples*. London: Zed Books.

University of Buea (2008) *The University of Buea: strategic plan, 2007-2015*. Buea: University of Buea.

Vulliamy, G. (2004) The Impact of Globalisation on Qualitative Research in Comparative and International Education, *Compare*, 34(3), 261-284.

CHAPTER 5

Social Inclusiveness, Development and Student Mobility in International Higher Education: the case of the Ford Foundation International Fellowships Program

JOAN DASSIN, JÜRGEN ENDERS & ANDREA KOTTMANN

ABSTRACT This chapter argues that strong disparities in access and success continue to mark higher education systems at the national, regional and global levels, including persistent inequalities in access to global student mobility. The case of the Ford Foundation International Fellowships Program (IFP), assessed through a decade-long formative evaluation, illustrates how greater social inclusiveness in international education can be achieved by providing educational services and support systems for students from marginalized communities.

Introduction

It is widely accepted that internationalization is transforming the nature of higher education. Information and communications technology has irreversibly connected higher education institutions and systems throughout the world. Global student flows have increased more than fourfold over the past 30 years (Organisation for Economic Cooperation and Development [OECD], 2012). Cross-border networks, partnerships, projects and new types of institutional arrangements, such as branch campuses, are flourishing. Global studies courses, collaborative research, increased numbers of foreign students and scholars, as well as multiple other international contacts, now bring the outside world to even the most isolated domestic campus.

Scholars who study these trends recognize their benefits but also warn about their unanticipated consequences (Knight, 2012). Concerns revolve around maintaining academic quality in the face of unregulated expansion and privatization. Will encroaching commercialization and economic competition replace traditional values of academic cooperation? A faint nostalgia can be heard in the observation that global student mobility, still central to many internationalization policies, has changed from 'simple student exchange' within 'an incredibly small elite group' to a 'mass phenomenon' driven by 'the big business of recruitment' (Brandenburg & De Wit, 2011, p. 16).

The debate over quantitative growth versus academic quality overshadows another key point in international student mobility: that international higher education is still a long way from being a truly open and global system. Expansion and diversification are not inherently democratizing trends. On the contrary, strong disparities in access and success continue to mark higher education systems at the national, regional and global levels.

This chapter reviews some of these persistent inequalities in global student mobility. It presents the case of the Ford Foundation International Fellowships Program (IFP), a pioneering effort to develop an equity-based scholarship model. IFP was a natural laboratory for testing whether a program intended to increase the participation and academic success of students who lack systematic access to higher education in their own developing countries, could operate successfully in a wide variety of international settings and educational systems. IFP's experience also offers insights into the relationship between educational opportunity and broader social justice outcomes in developing countries. Finally, IFP's results suggest areas for further research and analysis that are central to contemporary studies in international and comparative education.

Persistent Inequalities in International Higher Education

Streitwieser (2012) stresses the importance of understanding the impact of worldwide student mobility on 'social and economic systems at a variety of levels, from the local and national to the regional and global' (p. 1). One could also argue the reverse, namely the importance of studying the impact of social and economic systems at various levels on global student mobility. This supplementary perspective helps to account for the limitations in the number of foreign students as well as the types of people who participate in international education.

In most developing countries, the number of places in higher education is still highly restricted, and is rather small compared with those in advanced industrial countries. For example, despite nearly increasing by more than two percentage points in the preceding 10 years, tertiary gross enrollment rates in sub-Saharan Africa stood at just 6.3% in 2009. In Latin America and the Caribbean – the highest performing developing regions – the rate in 2009 was

36%, compared with rates in excess of 70% in the United States, Northern Europe, Russia, Australia and Japan (World Bank, 2012). Participation in national higher education systems is also highly stratified. Access is usually limited to elites, who not only have financial resources but also benefit from privileged access to high-quality education at the primary and secondary levels. Rather than promoting social mobility, national education systems tend to reinforce existing social stratification, especially in countries with high levels of inequality.

Rapid growth of higher education does not necessarily lead to a more diverse participation. Among other factors, access to higher education is in particular stratified by gender, class, race, ethnicity and rural versus urban location. To overcome these disparities, many countries have implemented legal frameworks and targeted programs. Compensatory policies may help disadvantaged groups to participate in higher education but cannot completely offset structural inequalities in the short term. In Brazil, for example, nearly 45% of Brazilian higher education institutions have adopted affirmative-action measures since 2003. By 2009, participation of blacks and mixed-race people in higher education had increased by nearly 100% (Rosemberg, 2012), to 35.1% of the student population. Yet these groups, which constitute 51% of the Brazilian population, still lag far behind whites, who make up 63.9% of higher education students (Rosemberg, 2012).

Global student flows show rapid expansion but unequal participation as well. The number of foreign students enrolled in tertiary education increased from 0.8 million in 1975 to 4.1 million in 2010 (OECD, 2012). Yet student flows are still primarily from poorer to richer countries, with almost two-thirds of foreign students in the OECD areas coming from outside OECD countries. Moreover, overall participation in international study is still low at the global level. Despite the unprecedented expansion in student mobility, only 1-3% of the student population typically participate in international study. The rate is higher in some of the Erasmus participating countries – a notable but rare exception (Streitwieser, 2012).

Participation in international student mobility is affected by low and inequitable participation rates in higher education at the regional and national levels. Asian students comprise more than half of all international students. Students from Africa, in contrast, comprise only 12% of all international students enrolled in the OECD area. Only one African country, Nigeria, is among the top 25 sending countries to the United States (Institute of International Education, 2012).

Cost is a major deterrent to all but the most affluent students considering study abroad. International students pay higher tuition fees than domestic students in the major English-language study destinations such as Australia, Canada, the United Kingdom and the United States (Beerkens, 2012). And although tuition rates continue to rise at US universities, nearly two-thirds of international students must rely on personal and family funds to finance their studies (Institute of International Education, 2012).

Social factors are also important, even within Europe, where 'non-traditional' students (e.g. coming from a family with a low level of educational attainment, part-timers, those over 30 years of age) are less likely to aspire to foreign study (Orr, 2012). There is no systematic body of scholarship on patterns of participation in international higher education from developing countries, much less from a comparative perspective. It is, however, highly likely that, because of inhibiting socio-economic factors, mobile students from the developing world who study in more economically advanced countries are 'academically ambitious and/or come from relatively wealthy backgrounds' (Teichler, 2012, p. 44).

Educational mobility, therefore, is still only for a selected few, and global student flows continue to be marked by regional and socio-economic disparities. The challenge of the Ford Foundation International Fellowships Program was to enable more diverse socio-economic groups from the global South to participate successfully in international higher education. This required a series of institutional and educational innovations that will be discussed below.

The Case of the Ford Foundation International Fellowships Program

IFP deliberately set out to test some key assumptions related to the principle established by the International Association of Universities which declared that 'international mobility, exchanges and cross-border education activities must integrate the twin goals of increased access and equitable participation' (2008, p. 1). First, the program had to recruit and select Fellows from marginalized groups with limited access to higher education, whether at home or abroad. In particular, if the number of qualified candidates far exceeded the supply of fellowships, the program would have demonstrated that a significant demand for international study exists among these groups.

Second, the program had to create enabling conditions so that the Fellows, many of whom had significant gaps in their previous education, could gain access to and succeed academically in highly competitive academic programs at leading universities in different world regions. Further, the program had to demonstrate that donor support for higher education, particularly scholarships for international study, would directly enhance the Fellows' capacity to contribute to development and social justice in their home countries and communities.

Above all, the program's success depended on mitigating 'brain drain' pressures and ensuring that the IFP Fellows, who come from vulnerable and excluded groups in some of the world's poorest countries, would draw on their new knowledge and global networks to address issues of poverty and underdevelopment at home. For IFP, the social justice outcomes needed to go beyond increasing access and equitable participation in international higher education through targeted fellowships. The longer-term question was whether educational opportunity would also lead to more sustainable development impacts.

Processes and Outcomes

Between 2001 and 2010, IFP provided more than 4300 scholarships for Masters (82% of the Fellows) and doctoral degree study (18% of the Fellows). Recipients pursued studies in development-related fields in the arts and humanities, the social and behavioral sciences, and in environment, health and applied sciences. As indicated in Figure 1, Fellows were selected from Russia and 21 countries in Asia, Africa, the Middle East and Latin America. IFP Fellows enrolled in almost 650 universities in nearly 50 countries. Approximately two-thirds studied internationally, and one-third studied in their home countries and regions.[1] By early 2013, nearly 4000 Fellows had completed their fellowships. The remaining Fellows are expected to conclude their fellowships by the end of 2013.

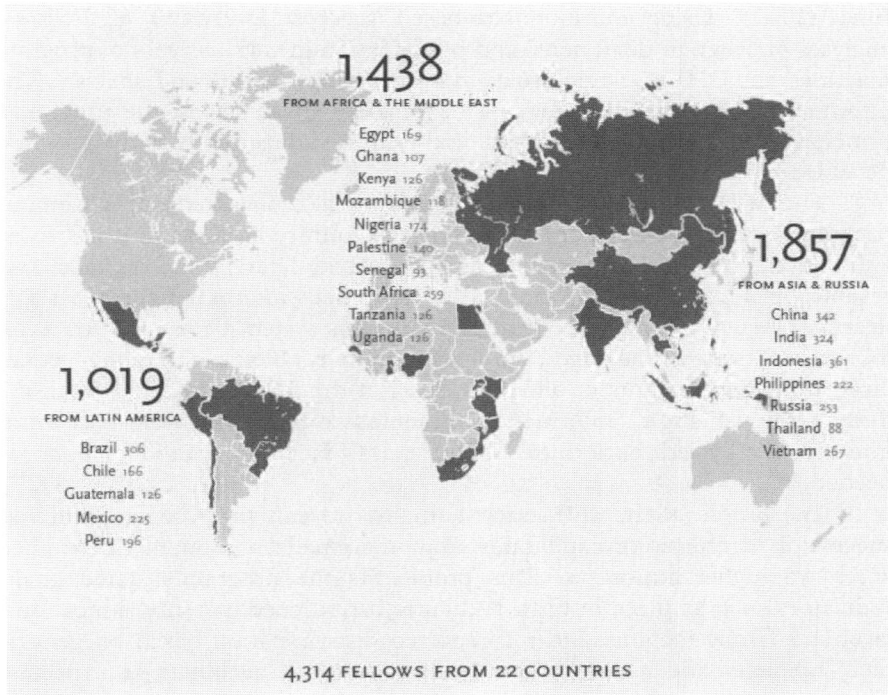

Figure 1. Selected IFP fellows by country.
Source: Dassin et al (2013, p. 5).

To operate effectively at the local, national, regional and global levels, IFP created a multi-actor, multi-level system. At the apex was the International

Fellowships Fund (IFF), created by the Ford Foundation to oversee the program. Based in New York, IFF hosted the IFP Secretariat, which developed the program's organizational structure and global policies. International Partner organizations (IPs) – technically sub-grantees based in the participating countries – adapted global policies to local conditions, devising strategies and implementing recruitment, selection, pre-academic training and monitoring of Fellows, as well as Alumni activities. International education organizations provided placement and monitoring services to Fellows based on their international study region.

Decentralized service provision within a unitary global framework was the IFP hallmark. It was especially important – and novel for international fellowship programs – that Fellows were selected by local committees comprised of independent professionals, and not in New York by the IFP Secretariat.

Formative evaluation was central to the program design. In 2002, the program contacted the Center for Higher Education Policy Studies (CHEPS) to develop and undertake a formative evaluation (Enders & de Boer, 2003). Using questionnaire-based surveys, interviews of Fellows, analyses of program documents and participation in various types of program meetings, the CHEPS study provided a steady flow of data and analysis. The information allowed IFP to assess its progress in achieving the program's principal goals on an ongoing basis, and to make adjustments as the program developed.

The IFP Secretariat and the IPs were also involved in continuous program assessment. Through grant reports, country-level studies, site visits, and national, regional and global meetings, the individuals and organizations responsible for the program built a locally based, internationally accessible 'learning system'. Collectively, the actors in this system developed strategies to address design challenges, implementation problems and policy issues faced by different actors at different stages of the fellowship cycle. With the formative evaluation, information obtained on an ongoing basis was immediately cycled back into the program, facilitating modifications as needed.

The profile of the IFP-selected finalists reveals that the program was successful in recruiting candidates from marginalized groups with limited access to higher education. This profile fits the program's stated goals. Indicators such as place of birth and current residence, parents' educational level and family income, and self-reported discrimination based on gender, race, ethnicity and rural location were taken into account. As expected, results varied by individual country and region, owing to different patterns of urbanization, levels of educational attainment and types of discrimination affecting marginalized groups.

Nonetheless, the data show significant convergence at the global level. As indicated in Figure 2, about two-thirds of all selected finalists were born in small towns or rural areas. About 79% of the selected finalists were first-generation students, and 45% of the finalists' fathers and 57% of their mothers did not even progress beyond primary school. Over 70% reported their family income at below average, and more than half indicated that they had experienced social injustice to a high extent because of poverty. Gender, age and family responsibilities can also pose obstacles to further study. Fifty percent of the IFP Fellows were women. Among all Fellows, 37% were older than 35 years of age at the time of selection, and nearly half were married, in a domestic partnership and/or had dependent children.

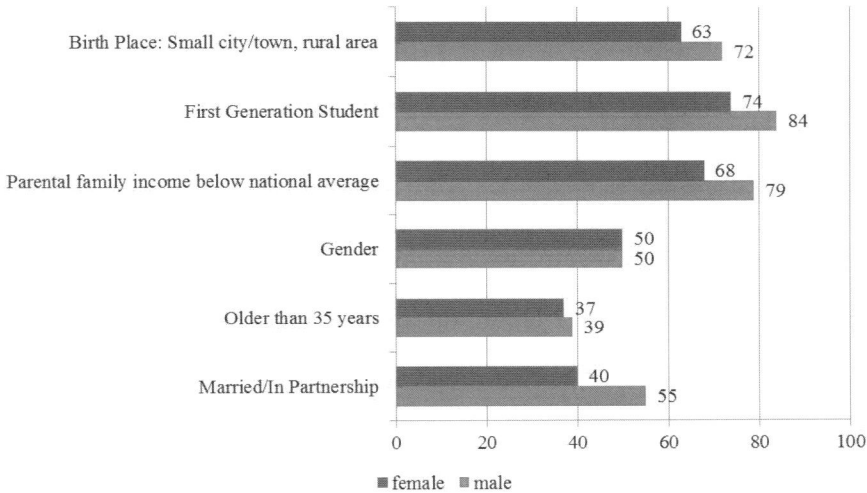

Figure 2. Socio-demographic and socio-biographic background of IFP selected finalists. (Finalists 2003-10, in %.)
Source: Enders & Kottmann (2011).

The program developed innovative academic support services for Fellows prior to and during their study period. One of the most effective services was pre-academic training: short- to medium-term courses designed to remedy gaps in the Fellows' preparation for graduate-level study. Low levels of English proficiency were an especially serious obstacle for those who sought international placements, and nearly all Fellows required short-term training to develop the necessary computer skills. Local universities and private providers based in the Fellows' home countries administered courses in English and other languages, academic writing, research methodology, computer skills and other relevant subject areas. Fellows studied in small groups; instruction was often online. In some countries, entire cohorts of Fellows gathered for more extended periods for residential courses held in a central location.

Over time, IFP established special relationships with approximately two dozen universities that hosted significant numbers of IFP Fellows. In many cases, these universities introduced more flexible admissions procedures, including conditional admissions, for Fellows who did not have the required language scores or whose transcripts showed inadequate undergraduate preparation in their chosen fields. About one-third of IFP Fellows attended bridging programs at their host universities that gave them extra time to improve their skills and adapt to the new environment. Designed for IFP Fellows, these new approaches allowed the universities to provide improved services for international students in general, and became standard practice in various universities. Examples include the University of Texas at Austin, where the International Student Services Office now takes a more proactive role in international student placement, and the Autonomous University of Barcelona, which expanded its support services for international students – both as a result of their experience with IFP Fellows (Bigalke & Zurbuchen, 2014).

Proactive monitoring was another element of IFP's academic support system. In addition to academic advisors and host university personnel, the Fellows' home-based IP kept abreast of their academic progress. IFP policy required that each Fellow received prior approval from his or her IP in order to renew multi-year fellowships. In practice, this administrative requirement fostered a close personal relationship between Fellows and their home country partners. The Fellows' ongoing interaction with the IFP scholarship managers at home reinforced their sense of personal responsibility and mitigated 'brain drain' pressures.

The program's comprehensive approach to academic readiness and student support was highly successful. Working through the Institute of International Education, the British Council and the Netherlands Organisation for International Cooperation in Higher Education as well as its own international partners, IFP successfully placed 97% of its Fellows in leading international universities in all major world regions, including the Fellows' home countries and regions. Ninety-eight percent of all Fellows placed in academic programs completed their fellowships, and the overall degree attainment rate of more than 3300 IFP Alumni surveyed in early 2012 was nearly 91%.

IFP's longer-term goal was to enhance the Fellows' capacity to contribute to social justice and development in their home countries and communities. For this reason, Fellows were selected on the basis of social commitment and leadership capacity, as well as academic achievement and potential. To assess progress toward IFP's social justice goals, the evaluation tracked key indicators through multiple Alumni surveys.

Some of these data are depicted in Figure 3. The first challenge in achieving IFP's longer-term goal was to avoid 'brain drain'. Just as international student mobility flows largely from poorer to richer countries, skilled labor also follows that pattern. Yet the vast majority of IFP Fellows return home. In the 2012 survey, 82% of Alumni reported that they were living in their home community or country. This included 77% of Fellows who studied internationally, 89% who studied in their home region and 97% who studied in their home country.

The same survey showed that over 90% of IFP Alumni were employed or continuing academic study. Nearly two-thirds held senior management or leadership positions. Nearly 90% reported that their current position is related to their social commitment; 84% agreed or agreed strongly (answer categories 4 and 5 on a 5-point Likert scale) that they are applying their knowledge in their professional activities; and 83% were confident that they are having a strong or very strong impact (answer categories 4 and 5 on a 5-point Likert scale) on their home countries and communities. Earlier alumni surveys, material from over 60 interviews, and hundreds of individual case studies collected in India, South Africa, Kenya, Palestine, and Mexico, among other countries, show similar outcomes.

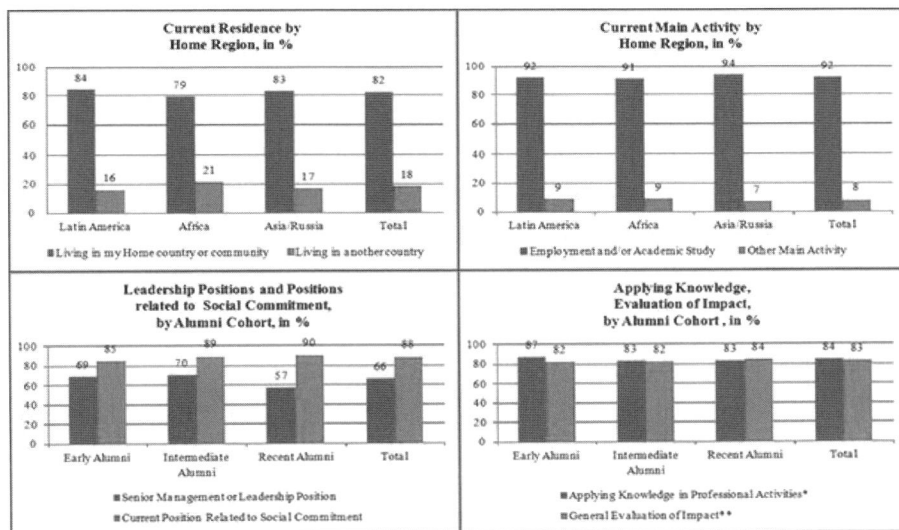

*Answer categories 4 and 5 on a scale from 1 'strongly disagree/not at all' to 5 'strongly agree/to a very high extent'.
**Answer categories 4 and 5 on a scale from 1 'not at all strong' to 5 'very strong'.

Figure 3. Current residence of IFP alumni, current main activity, leadership positions, and impact on social justice (Alumni-Survey 2012).
Source: Enders & Kottmann (2012).

Just a few examples make clear how IFP Alumni are bringing new research, policy analysis and professional skills to bear on persistent development challenges (http://www.fordifp.org, 2012). In Kenya, Alumni are designing and implementing urban and rural development projects, creating economic enterprises for youth and training farmers in new agricultural techniques. In India, former Fellows are providing revitalized leadership to local government and NGOs in remote regions by overcoming longstanding social divisions based on class, caste and gender. In Mexico, Alumni from indigenous groups are bringing innovations in communications such as Internet browsers and popular radio programming to their home communities, thus connecting them to contemporary society while preserving traditional languages and cultures. Complementing these individual achievements, IFP Alumni networks and associations – some now formally registered as independent NGOs – are also engaged in similar projects.

The IFP Experience: implications for research and policy in international education

We stated at the outset that IFP was a natural laboratory for challenging persistent inequalities in higher education at the regional and national level, and for exploring ways of supporting the inclusion of excluded groups in global student mobility. Program experiences and results suggest several issues for further research and analysis. This research, we argue, could have significant implications for policy-makers at donor agencies, national governments and universities working at the intersection of social inclusiveness in higher education, global student mobility and development. Various issues emerge that are relevant to scholarship in the two distinct yet overlapping epistemic domains of international and comparative education (Streitwieser et al, 2012).

The first issue is to gain better understanding of access and equity in global student mobility in international higher education in general and for developing countries in particular. IFP has proven that a targeted program can mobilize students from marginalized communities in developing countries for participation in high-quality international higher education (Dassin, 2012). Without such intervention, deep structural inequalities at home might, however, limit access to international higher education in ways that simply reproduce persistent inequalities in educational opportunities or might even create new inequalities for participation in a globalizing world. There is thus a need for further systematic, national and cross-national, comparative research into socio-economic backgrounds and characteristics of international students.

The second and related issue focuses on the demand and potential for international study among groups from developing countries that lack systematic access to higher education in their own country. IFP received nearly 80,000 applications over 10 years. The large candidate pool allowed IFP to be highly selective; only 5% of the total applicants were awarded fellowships. Thousands more would have been qualified for support, even for highly competitive graduate-level programs. Better information on potential students from marginalized groups would help policy-makers to extend opportunities for international education in ways that address deep structural inequalities at home.

The third issue for further research focuses on educational services and institutional changes that can support international (or domestic) students from marginalized groups. IFP demonstrated that with needs-based academic preparation and close monitoring, its Fellows could overcome substantial educational deficits and succeed in a wide variety of higher education institutions. This result counters the concern that social inclusion 'lowers academic standards' in highly competitive graduate-level programs. Universities can do their part by instituting flexible admissions policies, including conditional admissions, bridging programs and academic counseling.

Beyond academic support, universities also need to offer readily available services for students to resolve practical, cultural and health issues, which can be especially challenging for students lacking international experience and financial resources. These services may require new organizational structures and personnel, possibly at an additional cost. The relevant question, then, is what incentives exist for universities and other educational organizations to create more 'socially inclusive' policies and services. Further research is thus needed on the costs and benefits for institutions that not only increase but also diversify their international student populations.

Finally, recent years have seen more emphasis on 'value for money' in development assistance. Many donor countries, especially in Northern Europe, as well as Australia, Canada, Japan and the United States, provide individual scholarships to students from developing countries as part of their foreign assistance programs. Emerging countries such as China and Brazil are also starting to offer scholarships to foreign students, although their emphasis remains on sending domestic students abroad. Yet it is difficult to show that funding individual scholarships leads directly to broader foreign assistance outcomes like improving health and livelihoods in poor countries. While building human capacity in critical fields clearly supports development, it is difficult to attribute complex social change processes to improvements in individual knowledge and skills.

The IFP experience has shown that incorporating a formative evaluation into program design from the outset may help to address this problem. In the case of IFP, the formative evaluation has proven to be very useful in gathering robust, large-scale, global data on program effects on the recipients and in providing ongoing feedback into the policy learning of the program. Data collected over nearly 10 years show that IFP largely achieved its short-term goals: the program identified and recruited thousands of qualified candidates from designated target groups; nearly all the Fellows have had successful academic results in hundreds of universities in dozens of countries; and the vast majority of Alumni are advancing into influential positions where they exercise recognized leadership on social justice issues. Many Alumni are involved in policy-making at the local, national and even international levels, while others are engaged in research and advocacy.

An emerging literature on impact analysis suggests further improvements of such a formative evaluation approach, such as gaining insights into program effects on recipients by tracing trajectories of a control group of non-recipients (see, for example, Creed et al, 2012) and related micro-methods in evaluating policy interventions in development aid (Garcia, 2011).

For the long term, however, it will be very important to test the validity of IFP's ideas about higher education and social change in a variety of settings. Many questions could be asked. To what extent does educational opportunity, especially for international study at the graduate level, have a lasting effect in reversing discrimination and stigmatization? How does the personal empowerment that comes with advanced education translate into gains for the broader community in the long run? Is it possible to identify situations where economic, social and political constraints severely limit the kinds of transformational leadership that individuals or their communities can exercise, as opposed to more fluid contexts where change is truly possible? Clearly, these questions go beyond conventional research on study abroad, student mobility and international student exchange. Instead, they highlight the complex relationships between education and society in a globalizing world, one of the major purposes for contemporary studies in comparative education (Whalen, 2012).

Note

[1] The Ford Foundation considered IFP an international fellowships program because it offered international study opportunities to all Fellows, including periods abroad for those who studied in their home country or region.

References

Beerkens, Eric (2012) The Social Dimensions of Internationalization: social risks and responsibilities, in Bernd Wachter, Queenie K.H. Lam & Irina Ferencz (Eds) *Tying it All Together. Excellence, Mobility, Funding and the Social Dimension in Higher Education*, pp. 89-109. Bonn: Lemmens (ACA Papers on International Cooperation).

Bigalke, Terry & Zurbuchen, Mary (2014) *Leadership for Social Justice in Higher Education*. New York: Palgrave Macmillan, forthcoming.

Brandenburg, Uwe & De Wit, Hans (2011) The End of Internationalization, *International Higher Education*, 62, Winter, 15-16.

Creed, Charlotte, Perraton, Hilary & Waage, Jeff (2012) Examining Development Evaluation in Higher Education Interventions: a preliminary study. Unpublished paper, London International Development Centre.

Dassin, Joan (2012) Social Inclusion and Excellence in International Higher Education: necessary, achievable and compatible goals, in Bernd Wächter,

Queenie K.H. Lam & Irina Ferencz (Eds) *Tying it All Together. Excellence, Mobility, Funding and the Social Dimension in Higher Education*, pp. 128-148. Bonn: Lemmens (ACA Papers on International Cooperation).

Dassin, Joan, Clift, Rachel & Zurbuchen, Mary (2013) *The Ford Foundation International Fellowships Program: linking higher education and social change*. New York: Ford Foundation International Fellowships Program.

Enders, Jürgen & de Boer, Harry (2003) The IFP Evaluation Framework, Approaches and Instruments for Data and Information Gathering. Unpublished report, Center for Higher Education Policy Studies, University of Twente, the Netherlands.

Enders, Jürgen & Kottmann, Andrea (2011) The Profile of IFP Finalists 2010. Unpublished report, Center for Higher Education Policy Studies, University of Twente, the Netherlands.

Enders, Jürgen & Kottmann, Andrea (2012) First Results. Unpublished data from 2012 IFP Alumni Survey, Center for Higher Education Policy Studies, University of Twente, the Netherlands.

Garcia, M. (2011) *Micro-Methods in Evaluating Governance Interventions*. Evaluation Working Papers. Bonn: Bundesministerium für wirtschaftliche Zusammenarbeit und Entwicklung.

Institute of International Education (2012) *Opendoors 20/12 'Fast Facts'*. New York: IIE. http://www.iie.org/opendoors

International Association of Universities (2008) Equitable Access, Success and Quality in Higher Education: a policy statement by the International Association of Universities. Adopted by IAU 13th General Conference, Utrecht, July.

Knight, Jane (2012) Student Mobility and Internationalization: trends and tribulations, *Research in Comparative and International Education*, 7(1), 20-33.

Organisation for Economic Cooperation and Development (2012) 'Who Studies Abroad and Where' (2012). Indicator C4, in *Education at a Glance*, pp. 360-381. Paris: OECD.

Orr, Dominic (2012) Mobility is Not for All: an international comparison of students' mobility aspirations and perceptions of barriers to temporary enrolment abroad, in Bernd Wächter, Queenie K.H. Lam & Irina Ferencz (Eds) *Tying it All Together. Excellence, Mobility, Funding and the Social Dimension in Higher Education*, pp. 57-76. Bonn: Lemmens (ACA Papers on International Cooperation).

Rosemberg, Fúlvia (2012) Final Report Brazil, July 2012. Unpublished report for the Ford Foundation International Fellowships Program.

Streitwieser, Bernhard T. (2012) Editorial, *Research in Comparative and International Education*, 7(1), 1-4.

Streitwieser, Bernhard T., Le, Emily & Rust, Val (2012) Research on Study Abroad, Mobility, and Student Exchange in Comparative Education Scholarship, *Research in Comparative and International Education*, 7(1), 5-19.

Teichler, Ulrich (2012) International Student Mobility and the Bologna Process, *Research in Comparative and International Education*, 7(1), 34-49.

Whalen, Brian (2012) *Frontiers Journal* and the Forum on Education Abroad: building a research tradition on education abroad for the comparative education scholarship, *Research in Comparative and International Education*, 7(1), 61-69.

World Bank (2012) *Equity of Access and Success in Tertiary Education – conceptual approach*. http://web.worldbank.org

CHAPTER 6

Recent Trends in Student Mobility in Europe

BERND WÄCHTER

ABSTRACT This chapter, exploring developments in student mobility inside, into and out of 32 European countries, is based on the recent study *Mapping Mobility in European Higher Education* of the Academic Cooperation Association. It deals with methodological issues of international data collection and data definition, and it presents the current picture and development of both credit and degree mobility in Europe as a whole, as well as in individual European countries. Its main empirical finding is that Europe as a whole is a very 'mobility-active' world region, but that there are dramatic differences between individual countries.

This chapter explores recent trends in student mobility in Europe. Its findings are based on a recent study carried out by a consortium of organisations and individuals led by the Academic Cooperation Association (ACA), entitled *Mapping Mobility in European Higher Education* (Teichler et al, 2011). In the study and the chapter, 'Europe' refers to the 27 member states of the European Union, the four countries making up the European Free Trade Association, and Turkey. In this chapter, I refer to this set of countries as *the Europe 32 region*, *the Europe 32 zone* or simply *the region*.

Mapping Mobility (Teichler et al, 2011) covers a wide range of issues related to the international mobility of students and staff, among them methodological questions and issues of data definition, national mobility policies and mobility obstacles, amongst others. In this chapter, I concentrate exclusively on trends in student mobility in the most recently available comparable joint international database collections of UNESCO, the Organisation for Economic Cooperation and Development (OECD) and EUROSTAT (collectively UOE), the statistical office of the European Union. As in the *Mapping Mobility* study, I am looking at student mobility into, out of and between the above-specified 32 countries. The reference year is 2006-07, the last year for which UOE had comparable and quality-assured data available. At first glance these may appear to be old data but, by the standards of internationally comparable statistics, they are not. The speed of the compilation of these statistics is determined by the country which reports last, and the data need to go through a system of solid validity checks before they are published, thus the lag in reporting.

ACA has campaigned for a long time for the creation of international statistics based on *genuine mobility*, rather than on *foreign nationality*. The latter, which were until recently the only thing the international data collectors captured, are a very poor proxy for international mobility, as many students of foreign nationality have in fact been born, raised and educated in their country of study and thus did not become mobile across country borders when they engaged in their tertiary studies. But in *Mapping Mobility* (Teichler et al, 2011), as in this chapter, my co-authors and I had to rely on nationality data since not all countries collect genuine mobility data yet and the existing data sets are far from clean.

1. For Clarification: 'mobilities'

Student mobility is a hotly researched and discussed topic, but the debate suffers from a lack of differentiation. This is to quite an extent due to a slovenly use of terminology. In fact there is no such thing as mobility, there are different 'mobilities'. In the predecessor study of *Mapping Mobility* (Teichler et al, 2011), *EURODATA* (Kelo et al, 2006), ACA and the International Centre for Higher Education Research at the University of Kassel had developed a new terminology which was to be the basis of a more differentiated and enlightened discussion of student mobility. Below I explain the key concepts.

First, I differentiate between *degree (or diploma) mobility*, on the one hand, and *credit mobility (or temporary mobility)*, on the other. In the case of degree mobility, a student studies outside of his or her country of nationality for an entire degree (or another qualification). Credit mobility or temporary mobility consists of a period of one or two semesters (i.e. up to an academic year) which a student spends at a foreign university, after which he or she returns to finish his or her degree at the home institution. This differentiation is not made for the sake of methodology, but because the two kinds of mobility have in fact very different drivers.

Degree mobility mostly originates from countries and universities with quantitatively and/or qualitatively insufficient supply of higher education. The major driver of this mobility is a 'push effect'. Students leave their country for another with a better higher education provision. They do this out of need, not generally out of an interest in exploring another country or culture. An example is Cyprus, an EU country. For every 100 Cypriots enrolled in their own country, 138 enrol abroad. The reason is simple: there is not enough higher education capacity in Cyprus to educate all or even the majority of its young generation. As this example shows, most degree mobility is *vertical mobility*. It moves from countries with too little or too poor higher education to those where the qualitative and quantitative provision is better. Temporary or credit mobility is, in contrast, *horizontal mobility* – in Europe at any rate. The assumption is that, by and large, all universities in the EU are of at least decent quality, and exchanges therefore take place between relative equals. The expectation is not so much to move to a better university, but to a different one – in linguistic and cultural terms, in terms of teaching styles and so forth. The flow patterns of vertical and horizontal mobility differ sharply. For example, Spain has for years been the first country of destination in the Erasmus Programme (which organises credit mobility). But Spain is quite rarely the destination of degree-seeking students. In vertical mobility, students are seeking (perceived) academic quality. In horizontal mobility, students seek 'difference' and 'contrast'.

I have already referred to *genuine international mobility of students* as distinct from the *study of persons with a foreign nationality in the country of study*. In a not so small number of cases, the foreign citizens never migrated in order to enrol in their university. They were born in the country of study, or they went to school there. In a country like Germany, with a large percentage of Turkish citizens, this applies to about a third of all foreign-nationality students. On the other hand, there are also cases, though in no country over 10%, with a sizeable number of own-nationality students who in fact did enter the country for purposes of study. These had earlier lived and obtained their secondary-school-leaving examination abroad.

2. Inbound Degree Mobility

Europe has remained immensely attractive to international students. Slightly over 1.5 million of all foreign students worldwide were enrolled in the Europe 32 region in 2006-07. This translates into a European share of all foreign students worldwide of 50.9%. Compared with the year 1998-99, when Europe's share was 50.3%, this represents even a small rise – an astonishing fact in the light of new competitors and generally heightened competition for foreign students.

A Diverse Landscape

At the same time, looking at data or averages for the whole Europe 32 region hides very important differences between the single countries in this geographical area. In fact, the single most marked commonality between countries is difference. Almost one-third of the 1.5 million-plus students were enrolled in the United Kingdom (UK), with another one-third in Germany and France combined. Since mobility levels in these large countries are very high, this also means that mobility levels in many other countries of the region are quite low. Notwithstanding the atypical cases of Liechtenstein and Cyprus, the UK has the highest share of foreign students among the total student population, at 19.5%. Switzerland and Austria follow at 19.3% and at 16.7%, respectively. Germany, France and Sweden range above 10%. The Europe 32 average is 6.9% but most countries are below this level. At the bottom are countries like Lithuania, with just 1%, Slovakia with 0.9% and Turkey with a mere 0.8%.

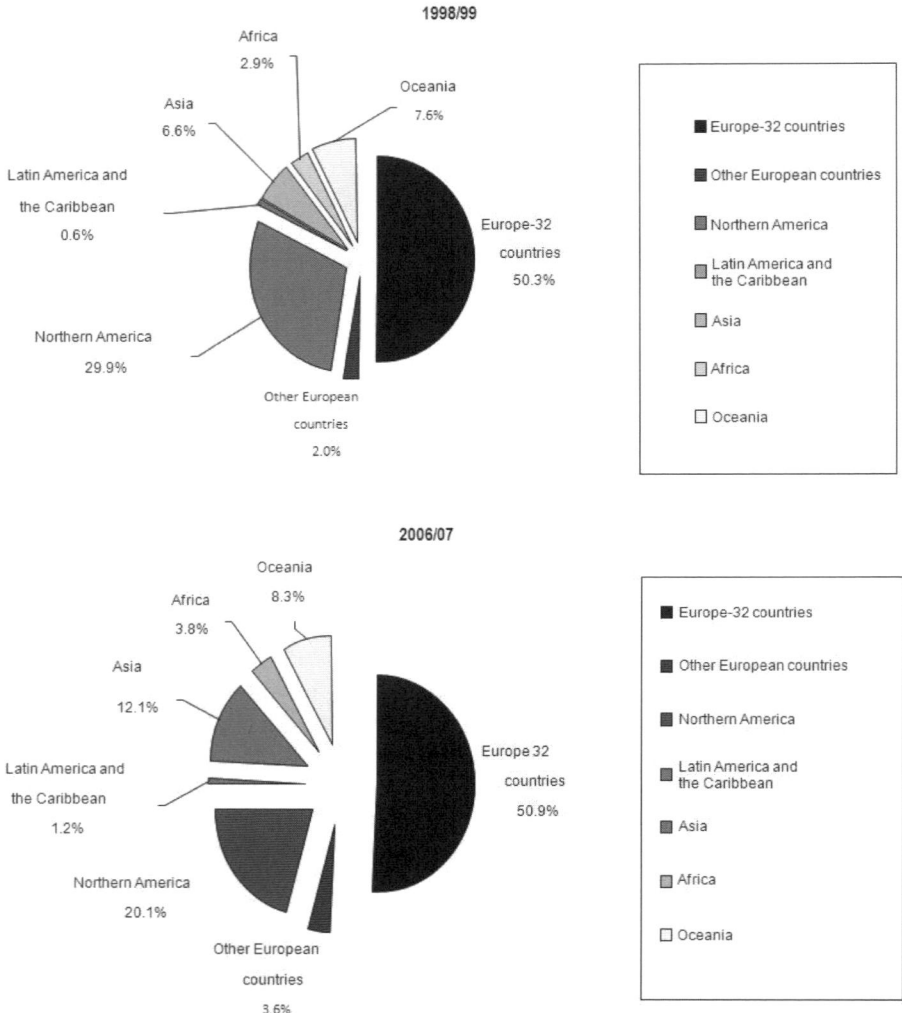

Figure 1. Distribution of students studying outside their country of nationality (foreign students) across world regions in 1998/99 and 2006/07.
Source: UOE data collection; ISCED 5/6.

Growth – above all from outside of Europe

The number of foreign students in the Europe 32 region grew very fast in the eight-year period between 1998-99 and 2006-07. Taking into consideration only those countries for which data were available for both years, growth was around 50%. Taking all countries into consideration, growth amounted to over 82%. There are reasons to believe that the real increase was nearer to the higher than the lower value. Total enrolment (home-nationality plus foreign-nationality students) also rose, but at about 28%, a much more modest pace. As a result, the share of foreign students of total enrolment grew from 4.5% in 1998-99 to 6.9% in 2006-07. The European development is mirrored at the national level, in the sense that almost everywhere enrolment numbers were up, although at very different levels. At the top end, numbers grew by 434% in the Czech Republic (but mainly due to an influx from one country: Slovakia) and by 302% in Lithuania. At the bottom end, Romania and Latvia saw slight decreases.

The main contributors to the strong growth in foreign enrolment were students from outside the Europe 32 region. Their share of all foreign students was 58% in 2006-07, or 870,000 in absolute numbers. In the earlier *EURODATA* study (Kelo et al, 2006), which used data from the reference year 2002-03, the share of non-Europe 32 citizens of all foreign students was 54%. As a result, the share of students with a Europe 32 nationality dropped to 38% [1] even though absolute numbers in this group also rose by about 104,000 to an overall 575,000.

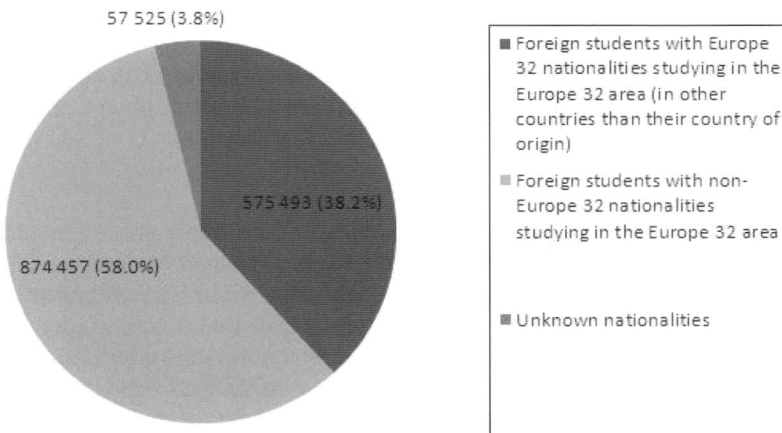

Figure 2. Foreign students in the Europe 32 area by region of origin ($n = 1,507,475$). *Source*: UOE data collection; ISCED 5/6.

Nationalities

The single largest nationality group among foreign students was Chinese, with about 123,000 students enrolled in 2006-07, 104,000 of whom studied in the UK, France and Germany. This translates into a share of the total of foreign students in the Europe 32 region of 8.2%. The second largest group is German, with a total of 75,000, followed by French (53,000), Italian (41,000), Polish (39,000), Turkish (38,000) and Greek (36,000).

In absolute terms, the Chinese saw the biggest growth between 2002-03 and 2006-07 of 42,000 students. But in relative terms, the rising star was India, with a growth rate of over 131% (though three out of four Indians studied in the UK). The largest community of foreign students in any single state in the Europe 32 zone was the Chinese in the UK (about 58,000). There were also sizeable communities of Indian and Irish students in the UK (about 30,000 and 27,000 respectively) and Chinese (27,000) and Turkish (25,000) students in Germany. Of the latter, however, few have probably been genuinely mobile, since Germany has a large Turkish community.

Graduation

It is one thing to enrol in a study programme, but quite another to graduate. In total, some 291,000 foreign students graduated in the Europe 32 region in 2006-7. This corresponds to 6.4% of all graduates in the respective year. This share is slightly lower than the share of foreign students in the same year (6.9%). However, at the time when the 2006-07 graduates entered higher education, the foreign student share was lower (4.5% in 2002-03). Taking this and further factors into consideration, I feel a good case can be made to argue that a larger share of foreign than of domestic students in the Europe 32 region manage to complete their studies successfully through graduation.

Genuine Mobility

As noted earlier, data on genuinely inwardly mobile students are not available from a number of countries in the Europe 32 region, and the quality of the data when they exist is not always satisfactory. But when extrapolating from the Europe 32 region as a whole onto those countries that produce such data, I would have to revise the number of 1.5 million foreign students down by about 25% or 375,000. This difference explains in unambiguous numerical terms why I insist that the criterion of foreign nationality is not a good proxy for real mobility. I am gratified that EUROSTAT and other data collectors are now pressing their member countries to start collecting data on genuine mobility (using the criteria of country of prior residence or country of prior education), in addition to collecting nationality data as well.

3. Outbound Degree Mobility

The total number of students of all Europe 32 countries studying outside their country of nationality was 673,000 in the year 2006-07. In comparison, the number of foreign students in the Europe 32 region the same year was slightly more than 1.5 million. In other words, the number of foreign students in the Europe 32 zone is more than twice as high as that of Europe 32 students studying abroad. The Europe 32 zone is a 'net importer' of students or a 'net exporter' of higher education, to use trade terminology. But this comes as no surprise. By global standards, Europe has high-quality systems of higher education, and it therefore, with few exceptions, lacks strong push factors that would make large numbers of students want to pursue degrees elsewhere. The comparatively low numbers of study abroad notwithstanding, degree study abroad has also grown between 1998-99 and 2006-07, but only by a relatively modest 37%.

Once Again, Difference Reigns Supreme

Across the Europe 32 region, the ratio of study abroad students to domestic students stood at 0.033 in 2006-07. To put this differently, for every 1000 home-nationality students enrolled 'at home', 33 studied abroad. Once again, however, this Europe 32 average hides significantly large differences between countries. The extremes are Cyprus at the high end and the UK at the low end. As mentioned earlier, more Cypriots study abroad than in their own country (for 1000 at home, there are 1380 enrolled abroad). The UK has the lowest study abroad rate of any country in the Europe 32 region, where for every 1000 British students enrolled at UK universities and colleges, only 12 are enrolled elsewhere in the world. In the European mobility landscape, British degree students abroad are indeed a very rare species. Almost as rare is study abroad of Spanish, Hungarian and Turkish students, with 17, 21 and 23 for every 1000 respectively.

Although there was moderate growth (37%) across the Europe 32 region in the eight-year period between 1998-99 and 2006-07, there were also countries that witnessed a decline. One of these is Greece, where numbers fell by around 42%. This must not be misinterpreted as a declining appetite of young Greeks for an international experience. Rather, it is a healthy sign. At the end of the 1990s, Greece was in much of the same situation in which Cyprus found itself in 2006-07. It did not yet have enough higher education capacity to educate its young generation in Greece. This had markedly changed by 2006-07, and the drop in Greeks studying abroad is a direct consequence of this.[2] The drop in UK study abroad numbers, from an already earlier low level, is an altogether different matter. Study abroad is neither a priority of UK higher education institutions, nor does it figure prominently in government policy. The UK puts all emphasis on attracting foreign (fee-paying) degree students into the country.

Still, and as earlier stated, study abroad rose in most countries of the Europe 32 zone. In absolute terms, the biggest increase was observed in Germany, where the numbers rose by 26,000 to almost 88,000. Every eighth student with a Europe 32 nationality is a German. In relative terms, study abroad of the nationals of some Baltic and southeast European states grew most, with Slovakia, which recorded a five-fold increase, in the lead.

Destinations

Where do Europe 32 students go when pursuing degree study abroad? The answer is simple: predominantly to another country in the same zone: 85.5% study elsewhere in the Europe 32 region. The rate of those staying in the region was already high in 1998-99, when it stood at 82.2%, but it has risen further since. Technically speaking, this trend is a result of two developments: an increase in study abroad to Europe 32 destinations and a decrease in non-European destinations, such as the USA and Australia. With 72,000 students from the Europe 32 region, the USA still attracts many nationals from this region, but the UK and Germany receive much higher numbers – about 160,000 and 112,000, respectively.

I am unsure how to evaluate the very strong preference for Europe 32 destinations. On the one hand, it is a clear vote of confidence in the quality of European higher education. If there were a large exodus, higher education in the region would need to seriously worry. On the other hand, the very small numbers of students from the region who study outside of the region (97,000 overall) and particularly in important emerging economies like China and India, to name only two, also appear as a cause for concern. One would think that Europe needs a critical mass of young, highly educated future leaders with first-hand experience in these economic and political powerhouses of tomorrow.

4. Credit Mobility

Most discussions about 'mobility' in Europe focus on credit or temporary mobility. In the Bologna context, the underlying concept of the (in)famous 20% goal was for a long time that of credit mobility only. It was only later that the emerging 'Bologna mobility strategy' started to integrate degree mobility as well. Politicians also tend to concentrate on this form of exchange. No doubt this has something to do with the immense success and popularity of the Erasmus Programme: almost every European by now has a family member or a friend who 'did Erasmus'. But this focus of the debate is at the same time quite irrational, to say the least. Even though our empirical knowledge of credit mobility is so much weaker than it is of degree mobility, all indications are that credit mobility in most countries is only a fraction of degree mobility. In other words: the focus of the main discourse is on the quantitatively less important form of mobility.

Weak Statistical Base

For credit mobility, we lack the information we have about degree mobility: a worldwide database like that of UOE. We also lack a clear definition, for example, on minimum duration. What we have detailed information on is credit mobility within the European Union's Erasmus Programme. But what share of all credit mobility Erasmus represents is far less clear. In some countries, such as Germany, there is a rich additional provision of nationally funded mobility programmes; in others, there is practically nothing. Some standard student finance instruments (state grants and loans) are 'portable' and fund temporary study abroad. Our best guess would be that Erasmus forms 70 to 80% of all programme-based credit mobility inside the Europe 32 region. But what about credit mobility to and from countries outside of the region? And what about credit mobility that occurs altogether outside of programmes, that is, such that it is self-organised and self-financed? There are no answers to these questions.

In light of the situation described, one can only present an analysis of volumes and directions of mobility inside Erasmus and try to assess how quantitatively important Erasmus is in comparison with degree mobility. The latter comparison must obviously focus on mobility inside the Europe 32 zone, as Erasmus funds only mobility inside this region.

Varied Picture

Erasmus, which celebrated its 25th anniversary in 2012, reached an annual turnover of 200,000 study abroad stays in the year 2008-09.[3] This is more than double the number in 1998-99, and thus constitutes impressive growth. However, only about 1% of all students in Europe become mobile with Erasmus every year. Assuming that a student is, on average, enrolled for four years, this translates into a share of 4% of the student population.

Credit mobility numbers can be expected to be considerably lower than degree mobility numbers, as explained earlier, but that does not mean that they are negligible. In the year 2006-07, incoming Erasmus students were about one-tenth of all foreign degree students in the Europe 32 region – including foreign degree students from outside of this region. Moreover, and what is more revealing, Erasmus students represented one-quarter of all types of inbound degree students including those from inside the Europe 32 zone.

Again, the relative importance of Erasmus mobility varies strongly between countries. In six countries – Spain, Finland, Malta, Poland, Portugal and Slovakia – incoming Erasmus students outnumbered foreign degree students. In most countries, the foreign-nationality degree students heavily outnumber incoming Erasmus students. In the UK, Bulgaria, Cyprus and Romania, the Erasmus Programme plays, in comparison with the degree study of foreign nationals, only a very marginal role.

5. Conclusion

The Europe 32 region as a whole has a very strong record of attracting foreign-nationality degree students. The 1.5 million students enrolled in the region represented 50.9% of all foreign-nationality degree students worldwide in the year 2006-07. This share was even higher than in 1998-99 (50.3%), when there were fewer active competitors on the foreign student market. The average share of foreign degree students in total enrolment in the region was 6.9%. But European averages say little when it comes to single countries. Three countries alone – the UK, Germany and France – together accounted for two-thirds of all foreign degree students in the region. This also means that a majority of the 32 countries have rather modest and, in some cases, downright insignificant numbers of foreign students.

Growth in the numbers of foreign students between 1998-99 and 2006-07 was considerable – 82%. A good deal of this growth is due to nationals from outside of the Europe 32 zone. In 2006-07, degree students with a non-Europe-32 nationality made up almost three-fifths of all foreign students, a sign of Europe's attractiveness – or that of its main players.

There are signs that present statistics which use nationality as a proxy of mobility overstate genuine mobility by around 25%. The over-count concerns mainly students with a foreign nationality who grew up and/or went to school in the country of tertiary study. I hope that the international data collectors will, in the future, be able to persuade all national governments to provide data not only on nationality but also on genuine mobility.

Our empirical base on temporary or credit mobility is so much weaker than that on the degree study of foreign nationals. In light of this, it is impossible to correctly assess the true volumes of temporary mobility. What I have attempted to do in this chapter therefore is to present data for Erasmus, the world's largest mobility programme.

Study abroad in a country other than that of the student's nationality is impressive, but it has not risen at the same rate as the inbound degree mobility of foreign students. Importantly, more than four-fifths of all outbound degree mobility students study in another country of the Europe 32 region. The trend towards concentrating degree study abroad on the region is a vote of confidence for European higher education. The opposite, a large outflow, would be a sign of a lack of trust. But the fact that so few of our future leaders will have gained first-hand knowledge of tomorrow's economic and political powerhouses could also one day become a problem.

ACA will continue to monitor the quantitative trends in international student mobility in the years to come. The big question is whether mobility volumes will continue to rise steeply, as they have done in the last four decades, or whether a saturation point is near. What would speak for the latter are important developments in the wider area of the internationalisation of higher education, such as the drive towards curricular internationalisation and 'internationalisation at home', as well as the growing importance of online study.

Notes

[1] The careful reader will have noticed that 58% and 38% do not add up to 100%. The missing 4% are students of unknown nationality.

[2] Few know that Norway was in a very similar situation in the post-Second World War years until the 1970s. Only when oil and gas drilling began to create sizeable revenues was Norway able to expand its higher education sector. Iceland has long been in the same situation, and study abroad out of Iceland is still more frequent today than in most other European countries.

[3] For Erasmus, I used the last year for which statistics were available. This was, at the time of publication of the *Mapping Mobility* study, 2008-09, and not 2006-07.

References

Kelo, M., Teichler, U. & Wächter, B. (Eds) (2006) *EURODATA. Student Mobility in European Higher Education.* Bonn: Lemmens.

Teichler, U., Ferencz, I. & Wächter, B. (Eds) (2011) *Mapping Mobility in European Higher Education. Volume I: overview and trends.* Bonn: German Academic Exchange Service.

CHAPTER 7

Liberal Education in the Erasmus Programme

THOMAS NØRGAARD

ABSTRACT In this essay the author explores the ideals and realities of the Erasmus Programme. His starting point is the educational vision of Sofia Corradi, an Italian educator who was instrumental in getting the Erasmus project off the ground in the 1980s. If we hold on to her thoughts about liberal education, culture, peace and social justice, the programme design immediately makes good sense. From this perspective, however, we may come to see Bologna as a process that undermines the Erasmus Programme. We may also come to wonder if Erasmus of Rotterdam really is a good patron of the programme. The author suggests that the cultural philosophy of J.G. Herder may provide a better philosophical grounding for Corradi's educational thought. Finally, he argues that Corradi's vision for Erasmus has one significant flaw: it is too optimistic about our ability to learn from travelling. For that reason, the current institutional means do not quite suffice to achieve her admirable educational ends. There is more work to be done.

1. Mama Erasmus

In 1958, a young Italian lawyer returned to Rome after a year in New York. Financed by Fulbright, she had completed a Master's degree at Columbia University. Back home, diploma in hand, she approached the administration at the University of Rome to have her Columbia exams recognised as a part of her *Laurea*. Her application was rejected, however, and one of the administrators she talked to felt the need to add insult to injury: 'Students shouldn't go and study abroad,' he said. 'If Italian students go abroad to study, they will pollute the culture we live in' (Corradi, 2012).

This unnamed administrator may deserve some sort of ignoble credit for what Europeans today know as the Erasmus Programme. Inspired by indignation, and by a keen sense of the educational value of studying abroad,

Sofia Corradi spent more than two decades as an activist pushing for change, within the university system and in public opinion generally. Her aim was to promote a 'culture of student mobility' (Corradi, 2006). She played a significant role in extensive conversations between German and Italian educators which prepared the ground for the EuRopean Community Action Scheme for the Mobility of University Students, commonly referred to as Erasmus, launched in 1987 (Corradi, 2006). As I write this, in 2013, about three million students have studied abroad under this scheme. Though many academics, administrators and politicians have contributed to this grand institution-building project, Sofia Corradi may be credited as an important inspiring force, sometimes fondly referred to as Mama Erasmus.

My aim in this essay is to understand and assess an institutionalised practice that has become prominent and widely celebrated in Europe. Corradi's vision for the Erasmus Programme provides me with a starting point that I will hold on to throughout the essay.[1] It should be evident that I admire her work, but towards the end I suggest that her vision has one significant flaw: it is too optimistic. The current institutional means do not suffice to achieve her admirable ends, so there is more work to be done.

2. Corradi's Vision

Sofia Corradi began publishing on the significance of studying abroad back in 1963. Since then her message has been quite clear: a well-arranged year abroad may be significant as a form of liberal education.[2] The point is not professional development, even if that may often be what motivates the student. Nor is it to learn from books. The educational end of the Erasmus Programme is for the student to learn from experience and so mature as a person (Corradi, 2006, pp. 55, 58). Maturation is a generic term under which we may include many kinds of personal development, but Corradi is particularly interested in the effect of the student's encounter with a foreign culture. In that encounter, the student has an 'opportunity to review those values (not necessarily all positive) which since his childhood he has considered to be self-evident and universal and to place them in a dimension of relativity' (Corradi, 2006, p. 55).

In conversation she gives me some examples:

> An Italian going abroad may come to learn that there are cultures in which civil servants actually understand that they are supposed to work. The same Italian may also come to appreciate aspects of Italian culture she had hitherto taken for granted. That Italians generally have a deep respect for children and those who take care of them, for example, is something to cherish.

If everything goes well, the review should result in a more mature understanding of one's own cultural roots and an ability to appreciate, or at least tolerate, the cultural commitments of foreigners. Corradi understands cultural maturation of this sort to be morally transformative (Corradi, 2006, p. 58) and of great political significance. Ultimately, she thinks of Erasmus as the first, systematic attempt in history to develop an intercultural education for peace (Corradi, 2006, p. 59).

Given this mission, we can begin to make sense of the Erasmus Programme design. It is important for Corradi that Erasmus students are neither tourists nor immigrants. The first are typically too briefly and superficially engaged to come to appreciate another culture, the latter often have to struggle too much to do so. Erasmus students stay in another country much longer than tourists, and unlike immigrants they have a ready-made institutional affiliation set up for them. Their stint abroad is limited in time, moreover, and has a concrete purpose. As a result, Erasmus students are more firmly anchored than both tourists and immigrants, and their anchor is reasonably familiar to them. They are affiliated with a foreign university, but it is still a university. They pursue their degree differently, but it is still the same degree. Anchored in this manner, students are challenged, but not over-challenged. They must learn to sail for themselves, but are unlikely to drift (Corradi, 2006, pp. 56-57).

The Erasmus Programme targets a fairly specific group of young adults. University students are young enough for fundamental character formation to be quite likely, old enough for most of the complications of adult life to be in play, sophisticated enough to appreciate the intricacies of a foreign culture. It is important, furthermore, that Erasmus students are volunteers and not conscripts. Self-selected, they are likely to possess curiosity, or some other drive, that will propel them towards others. Members of this group are likely to learn a lot from the great and complex laboratory of life they enter abroad (Corradi, 2006, pp. 56-57).

These features of the Erasmus Programme are meant to facilitate a successful liberal education for the individual, but the design does more than that. It is essential that students who return to their home university should experience no delay in their education. One might think that this shows a strong interest in certification, but that would be a misunderstanding. Given the obsession with certification in our day and age, it is worth stressing that two other points are much more important to Corradi.

First, the stress on recognition really comes from a concern about social justice. If the price for study abroad is an extra year of educational expenses, it will mainly be an experience for wealthy people's children. Corradi wants the Erasmus experience to be accessible to everyone. Her concern with educational justice runs like a red thread through her career. First educated as a lawyer, she worked on constitutional law and the right to education. She did not like fighting with people in a courtroom, however, and soon seized an opportunity to move into the field of educational theory. She brought her concern for social justice along with her.

Secondly, the stress on recognition is inspired by an ideal of inter-institutional trust. To appreciate this point fully, we need a distinction used by Corradi during her activist days: It is one thing for two universities to establish *equivalence* between their courses or degrees, another for them to *recognise* each other's courses or degrees. Equivalence is established through detailed empirical work, that is, by counting hours and studying course descriptions. Recognition may be based on established equivalence, but it may also be based on a trustful appreciation that needs no detailed comparisons. The practical significance of this distinction is hard to exaggerate and it has been crucial to Corradi's work. Seeing the diversity of educational systems as 'a precious resource' (Corradi, 2006, p. 36), she argues that:

> the desire for general or abstract evaluations of equivalence should be avoided ... ample flexibility is essential. The starting point must be the principle of reciprocal esteem and trust between the institutions of higher education of the European Union. (Corradi, 2006, p. 63)[3]

From an institutional point of view, the core of the Erasmus Programme is one university's recognition of another university, or one department's recognition of another department.

3. Ideals and Realities

An activist's vision is one thing but institutional realities are another. To what extent does the actual Erasmus Programme correspond to Corradi's educational vision? It took 18 months of 'bitter negotiations' (Pepin, 2006, p. 117) for the EU to agree on Erasmus and during this period it was far from clear that the political will of Europe was ready to create an institution of the sort Corradi hoped for. In June 1986, the Council of Education Ministers held a meeting but did not come to an agreement. In July, the United Kingdom, with Margaret Thatcher at the helm, took on the rotating EU Council Presidency and, in November, presented a new proposal. The idea was to reduce the budget dramatically by dropping the stipends that would support the students while abroad. In response, however, Manuel Marin, the Spanish Vice-President of the Commission, 'simply' decided to withdraw the entire proposal. To go ahead, he said, 'would be like buying a cookbook to assuage one's hunger' (Pepin, 2006, p. 117). His gamble paid off. The original proposal was eventually resubmitted and accepted the following year. Had he failed, however, his judgement would still have been correct, at least if we are looking at the matter from Corradi's point of view. Like John Rawls, she thinks that justice is 'the first virtue of social institutions' (Rawls, 1971, p. 3) and without the stipends, this would not have been a just institution. Sometimes nothing is better than something.[4]

Most of the time, however, something has to be better than nothing. The launch of Erasmus was far from easy, but today it may be difficult to imagine Europe without it. The programme is frequently put forth as an emblematic example of the successful work of the European Union (see e.g. Truszczynski, 2012) and widely celebrated by those who are invested in the European project (see e.g. Rifkin, 2005; Riotta, 2012). Now that Erasmus has been so happily adopted by the EU, it may seem obvious that it should be a European institution. For Corradi, however, it is little more than a historical contingency. She is no Eurocentric, and certainly not EU-centric. She does not seem to have a strong commitment to Europe as a cultural unity. Her horizon is better described as 'cosmopolitan' and originally she was hoping that the project might be picked up by UNESCO. She is nonetheless quite happy with what has been achieved, and proud to have contributed something to a culture of student mobility.

Something important has been achieved, it seems, but what does it amount to? One might think that Erasmus helps to spread some sort of 'feeling of Europeanness'. This is not entirely obvious, however. A statistical study by Emmanuel Sigalas suggests that, although Erasmus students do improve their language skills while abroad, and get to know something about another country's culture, they do not necessarily come to 'feel more European', which Sigalas defines in terms of pride, attachment and a sense of commonality. In fact, going to England seems to have the opposite effect, which may be unfortunate given the fact that this is one of the most popular destinations for Erasmus students (Sigalas, 2009, p. 20).

This study may be somewhat disappointing to European federalists, but not necessarily to confederalists. Those of us who are not seeking to build a United States of Europe, nor a Fortress Europe, do not have to insist on a strong and clear nationality-like feeling of Europeanness. Not only may we be content with less, we may actually be more excited about promoting an appreciation of European diversity. This could still be an education for peace as Corradi originally imagined. If Erasmus encourages young Europeans to understand and perhaps appreciate other European cultures, then we may have an antidote to excessive nationalism of the sort that prevents cooperation and leads to war.

This sounds good, to me at least, but it may not be a realistic description of the Erasmus Programme. Once again, a statistician, this time Kristine Mitchell, warns us not to misunderstand what the Erasmus experience amounts to. Those of us who imagine it to be an immersion experience through which a student comes to appreciate the local language and culture of another European country are wrong. Erasmus students do not typically engage in a sustained manner with the local citizens, culture and language of the host country. According to Mitchell's survey, larger and more multinational than previous studies, 'only 7 per cent of Erasmus students reported both socialising primarily with host country nationals *and* speaking primarily the host country language' (Mitchell, 2012, my italics).

Should we be worried about these results? Corradi does not think so. In her mind, the point of Erasmus is to develop a general capacity for engaging meaningfully with foreigners. An Italian going to Germany to study may befriend a Japanese person, learn something about Japan and develop a general ability to deal meaningfully with otherness. It is not crucial for Corradi that students engage with local culture or local language. Once again, it is clear that Corradi's horizon is more cosmopolitan than European. It is also clear that her vision for intercultural education is focused on an ideal of friendship. In her mind, the trust that develops in a friendship has intrinsic value, but it also helps preserve peace when crisis threatens. Holding this thought about friendship together with her sense of healthy institutional relations, we come to see that of the various values that inspire her vision for Erasmus, the most central one may well be trust.

4. From Erasmus to Bologna

We understand and assess institutions not only on their own merits, but as a part of a larger institutional landscape. When the Erasmus Programme was launched in 1987, educational cooperation in Europe was still in its infancy. In fact, educational cooperation was something like a taboo in the Commission, a form of integration that came all too close to challenging national sovereignty (Pepin, 2006, pp. 54, 56). Until the Maastricht Treaty was signed in 1992 there was no legal mandate for educational cooperation in the EU. In this situation, the birth of Erasmus must have seemed like a breath of fresh air (Henckel & Wright, 2008, p. 15).

Since then, educational cooperation in Europe has developed dramatically. In June 1999, the so-called Bologna Declaration was signed by ministers of education from 29 European countries. In the name of European peace, democratic development and competitiveness, they agreed to promote a 'Europe of Knowledge', characterised by student and citizen mobility.[5] In order to achieve this, they committed themselves to 'greater compatibility and comparability of the systems of higher education' through 'easily readable and comparable degrees'. The pursuit of peace through student mobility connects Erasmus and Bologna very closely. The same end and the same means.

Or so it may seem from a distance. When we take a closer look, however, it becomes clear that there are some fundamental differences between Erasmus and Bologna. In the latter project, the end of mobility is no longer just peace; in fact, it is focused primarily on European competitiveness and employability (Henckel & Wright, 2008, p. 4), something Corradi never mentions. More obviously, perhaps, the means are now decisively different. Whereas the Erasmus design facilitates educational cooperation bottom-up, Bologna is a forceful top-down process. Whereas Erasmus is based on educational pluralism and pursues cooperation through mutual trust, the Bologna process seeks cooperation through harmonisation. The Erasmus Programme is based on *recognition*, the Bologna process is focused on *equivalence* established with the help of the European Credit Transfer System. Corradi insists that educational diversity is a precious resource. The Bologna

Declaration claims to proceed with 'full respect of the diversity of cultures, languages, national education systems and of University autonomy'. But, given the goal of harmonisation, and given the time-frame – it is stressed in the Declaration that the changes have to be achieved 'in the short term' and certainly within a decade – one can only wonder how such respect could possibly be maintained.

In fact, it seems quite clear that the Bologna process has been implemented without much respect for national education systems. Germany is a prominent example (see Lemcke, 2010; Münch, 2010). Richard Münch, a sociologist from Universität Bamberg, has argued convincingly that when German students protested against Bologna in 2009, they were right to do so. Attempts to underplay the havoc caused by the Bologna process as superficial implementation difficulties were misleading. In fact, in Germany, 'the Bologna Process signifies a cultural revolution' (Münch, 2010). Traditionally, education and employment have been closely connected in Germany, Münch explains. The link is organised through professional organisations – *Fachgesellschaften* and *Berufsverbände* – that secure a close connection between degree descriptions and job descriptions. The new BA, however, is too short to secure the relevant depth and specialisation required by this system. Students who complete a BA have acquired general competence, but not really what Germans would call a *Fach* (Münch, 2010).

The architects of Bologna seem to have thought that, since they aim to regulate form only, not content, there must be ample space for substantial local variety, yet Münch's analysis shows this to be a misunderstanding. Curricular form matters. An analogous analysis shows that the other major structural imposition, the so-called modular form that all curricula have to take according to Bologna, also functions as a constraint on substantial educational variety. The forced organisation of a curriculum into modules, that is, elements that are 'capable of being replaced without requiring substantial change to the overall system' (Lemcke, 2010, p. 3), essentially undermines the work of educators who attempt to design strongly integrated curricula. Students and educators are forced to think of learning as something deliverable in 'bite-sized chunks' (Lemcke, 2010, p. 4). Sometimes it is both possible and desirable to look at learning in that way, but to impose this as a general perspective through forced curricular form is to take a step too far towards the industrialisation of education (Liessmann, 2006, pp. 7-11).

Why should we respect local educational institutions in Europe? One might argue, for example, that the conservative, hierarchical and quite bureaucratic German system is in need of a bit of modernisation. Perhaps so, but the point is, first, that this should not be done from above, and certainly not without *consulting* those who work in the system (Lemcke, 2010, p. 2). Secondly, it should not be done lightly (p. 1). As Nietzsche once pointed out, educational institutions 'do not hang around us like a garment'; they are 'living monuments of cultural movements' (Nietzsche, 2004, p. 14).

Münch's concrete analysis confirms this general Nietzschean point, but in order to appreciate it fully we need to look beyond the topic of professional training and remind ourselves of the extra-economic function of education. In the memorable words of Louis Menand:

> Knowledge is our most important business. The success of almost all our other business depends on it, but its value is not only economic. The pursuit, production, dissemination, application, and preservation of knowledge are the central activities of a civilization. Knowledge is social memory, a connection to the past; and it is social hope, an investment in the future. The ability to create knowledge and put it to use is the adaptive characteristic of humans. It is how we reproduce ourselves as social beings and how we change – how we keep our feet on the ground and our heads in the clouds. (Menand, 2010, p. 13)

In other words, education is of profound cultural significance, even if looked upon quite pragmatically. And if cultural diversity is a deep and valuable characteristic of Europe – something stressed over and over by thoughtful observers (Morin, 1988; Davies, 1996; Rifkin, 2005; Borgolte, 2008) – then we have a compelling reason to hold on firmly to the principle of subsidiarity in the field of education.[6] So, we should agree with Corradi when she insists that educational diversity is a precious resource for Europe. Unsurprisingly, she is sceptical about Bologna. From the point of view of the original Erasmus vision, Bologna is a bureaucratic take-over of a project that in principle should have only a very light administrative footprint.[7]

The road from Erasmus to Bologna was short, but the trip has been of great consequence, philosophically and politically. Erasmus and Bologna are not different means to the same end. They cannot be. They are institutional tools that point in different directions, essentially so. One may say that they both aim at integration in Europe, but then we have to distinguish between an Erasmic integration and a Bolognian integration. The Erasmic integration is facilitated from above, but developing freely from the ground up. The Bolognian integration is dictated from above, a straitjacket for those who work on the ground. Erasmic integration celebrates diversity. Bolognian integration superficially tolerates diversity, at best, but really undermines it. Both forms of integration promote peace in Europe, one may say, but they are two different forms of peace. Whereas the Erasmic peace is quite trustful and pluralistic, the Bolognian peace is more bureaucratic and monotonous.

Which sort of peace is the worthy ideal of Europe? Some might argue that the Erasmic peace is too fragile and anarchic, but I don't believe that many Europeans today would really think so. That is not the problem. The truth is that Bologna is not really about peace or social cohesion, but about money and Europe's ability to compete in global markets. Once we look carefully at the means, it becomes quite clear how different the ends of Erasmus and Bologna are. Erasmus is first of all inspired by an ideal of liberal education; Bologna is primarily concerned with education as an instrument for making a living. The only legitimate way to defend the road from Erasmus to Bologna is to argue that it is necessary for the sake of Europe's material future. But is it really? Or is that the claim of bureaucrats who have forgotten that there may be recognition without detailed equivalence, reductivists who worry about the price of education but do not really understand its full cultural value (Lemcke, 2010, p. 4)?

This is not an argument against uniformity per se. I am in favour of common regulations for air traffic, for example, and against genetically modified crops. It is quite clear, however, that the EU on occasion goes too far in this direction. As Hans Magnus Enzensberger has observed, economic integration has – ever since the birth of the European Coal and Steel Community – been pursued without much consideration for cultural and political diversity in Europe; bureaucratic institutions like the EU tend to expand beyond reason simply because that makes them more powerful; and finally, the EU tends to be run by a rootless, cosmopolitan elite for whom it is an ideal to elevate themselves above the European life-world (Enzensberger, 2011, pp. 43, 18, 35). Even if Enzensberger exaggerates somewhat, which may be the case, Bologna fits all too well into this picture.

While it would be a mistake to see Bologna as a solidification of Erasmus, it is probably an ironic fact nonetheless that Erasmus helped pave the way for Bologna (Henckel & Wright, 2008, pp. 15, 17-18; De Wit, 2012). In this situation, Erasmus may no longer seem like a fresh breeze, but more like part of a storm that is causing havoc in Europe. This would not be a fair assessment, however. Once we appreciate Corradi's educational vision, we may come to see the original Erasmus ideal of trust as an emblematic antidote to the Bologna bureaucracy. In fact, if cultural critics are right to point out that we increasingly live in an 'audit culture' and a 'culture of suspicion' (Power, 1997; O'Neill, 2002), Corradi's ideal of a peace built bottom-up through individual instances of trust becomes a precious reminder that things could be different. We might even come to hope that if there was a road from Erasmus to Bologna, perhaps there could be a road the other way too.

5. From Erasmus to Herder

It is commonly taken for granted that the Erasmus Programme was named fittingly after Erasmus of Rotterdam (Desiderius Erasmus Roterodamus). This is how the programme is advertised by the EU and the logo of the programme bears his profile. Sofia Corradi, however, insists that the substantial link between the programme name and the famous humanist has been forged *ex post facto* (Corradi, 2006, p. 51). Not that she minds. It is a trivial issue, she thinks, we just shouldn't make too much of it. But I am not so sure. It may be worthwhile investigating if Erasmus is a fitting patron for the programme. Not just because EU materials link the programme to

Erasmus's life and thought, but because a thorough understanding of an institution typically demands that we consider the philosophical and political assumptions that underpin it.

In official EU materials, Erasmus has been described as someone who 'lived and worked in several parts of Europe, in quest of the knowledge, experience and insights which only such contacts with other countries could bring' (Pepin, 2006, p. 116). His name is commonly associated with ideals of pacifism, cultural tolerance and impartiality. In many ways, it seems to make good sense to link the name of Erasmus with Corradi's educational vision.

If we look more closely, however, the link is weakened. It is true that Erasmus was a pacifist. A wise ruler, he argued, should seek 'peace with all nations but particularly with his neighbours'. He also believed that the ruler's interest in peace should motivate him to learn about 'the character and temperament of all races'. This knowledge, Erasmus pointed out, could be acquired 'partly from books and partly from the accounts of wise and well-travelled men' (Erasmus, 1997, pp. 94-95). Here we seem to get very close to the central thought behind Corradi's educational vision, but appearances deceive. For Erasmus, the point of acquiring cultural understanding was not really to *review* one's values, at least not in Corradi's sense. Erasmus knew about cultural diversity, but had no deep educational interest in it. He was convinced that 'social and political problems' could be resolved 'in one true religion, one classical culture, and one exquisite language' (Kimball, 1995, p. 88). Local cultures were not something to learn *from*, but to learn *about*, in order to deal with them prudently.

Erasmus began adult life as an Augustinian monk, but left monasticism behind for a life as a *peregrinatio academica*, a 'travelling scholar'. Corradi (2006) explicitly links the Erasmus Programme with this tradition, so Erasmus may again seem like a possible source of inspiration for her educational vision. Yet it is important to see the limits of this line of thought. Though Erasmus became one of the most well-travelled men of his time, he did not really travel to learn from experience, at least not in Corradi's sense. He first travelled to get away from his early life as a monk, later on often to avoid the plague or religious strife, but most of the time to find a good place to work.[8] He was a bookish person, a bibliophile actually, and mostly absorbed in quiet study (Huizinga, 1952, p. 63). He did not seek a liberal education through experience of things foreign, but in trusted books: the ancient classics and (primarily) the Bible. As he travelled, he took no deep interest in local culture or language (Zweig, 1935, p. 378). He generally refused to learn any vernaculars and one might say that he really 'passed by' the countries in which he travelled (p. 48). For Erasmus, local culture was little but an obstacle to a cosmopolitan Christian order and Latin the perfect living language in which to seek universal order and peace.

If this description of Erasmus is correct, he is not a particularly good patron for the Erasmus Programme. His educational focus on books is too far from Corradi's interest in experience, and he moves at a different level.

108

Stefan Zweig, who studied Erasmus closely and with deep sympathy, thought of him as someone whose admirable educational mission *had to fail* because he had elevated himself too high above the ground (Zweig, 1935, pp. 114, 116). The ground ignored by Erasmus seems to be exactly that upon which Corradi wants her educational institution to be built. For this reason, Erasmus is not of great help to her.

If we are looking for a companion with whom we can explore philosophically the essence of Corradi's educational vision, I would suggest that we turn from Erasmus to Johann Gottfried von Herder (1744-1803). In his writings we find a great deal of rich soil in which something like Corradi's educational vision could grow.

The meeting of cultures was a central theme in Herder's thought: 'Surely it matters,' he argued, 'according to which basic principles, peoples influence one another' (Herder, 1991, p. 706, my translation). He was struck by the negative impact that one people often have on another. Migrants, missionaries and crusaders have often been major disturbers of peace and local culture. So have colonisers, ancient and modern. He wrote before Germany became a colonial power, but the desirability of acquiring colonies was a topic in the German press of his time and the colonising activities of Spain, Portugal, England and Holland were well known through travel descriptions (Herder, 2002, p. 381). Today, Herder is recognised as one of the most unambiguous and vehement critics of colonialism in his time. He saw the colonial business as a cultural disaster, a 'crime of abusing humanity', something that should make the European collective spirit – if something like this actually existed – ashamed (pp. 380-381).

Herder also took a keen interest in cultural affairs within Europe. We may get a sense of his outlook by considering his attitude towards Joseph II, who ruled the Habsburg Empire from 1780-90. Joseph was what we today might call an 'enlightened despot' (Beales, 2005, pp. 263, 294). Inspired by French *philosophes*, at least to some extent, he introduced a series of reforms that were quite progressive: reduction in censorship, limitations on the use of capital punishment and torture, fighting against superstition and extension of the freedom of religion. Herder initially admired Joseph but grew more and more critical of his rule. Joseph was an impatient and autocratic reformer who alienated his subjects and his advisors by hasty and harsh decisions. He also pursued cultural uniformity top-down in ways that Herder found misguided. The decision to impose German on the entire empire, for example, was in Herder's view a clear instance of Joseph's unfortunate unwillingness to build his empire from the ground up (Herder, 1991, pp. 64-66). Herder probably never lost his sympathy for Joseph entirely; he writes with deep ambivalence and seems to think of Joseph as a tragic figure who, while well intentioned, did not appreciate the human significance of diversity and the fact that 'the best culture is slow' (p. 66).

These political attitudes, and Herder's cultural philosophy generally, were rooted in a pluralist understanding of value:

> Is not the good on the earth strewn about? Because one form of
> humanity and one region of the earth could not grasp it, it got
> distributed into a thousand forms, it roams forth – an eternal
> Proteus! – through all parts of the world and all centuries.
> (Herder, 2002, p. 298)

We are confronted not so much with anything we can refer to simply as 'the good', that is, some unified or uniform entity, but with many values and valuables, different not only in number but in kind, and constantly developing. Herder explains this protean behaviour of the good with reference to what we may call 'narrowness'. The human mind, no matter how cultured, is in some manner too narrow to contain or grasp everything good. The same goes for every part of the human abode, no matter how cultivated (Herder, 2002, pp. 288, 297). So, Herder's value pluralism goes hand in hand with cultural pluralism. There are many legitimate and precious forms of culture that deserve our respect and appreciation. Herder articulated his pluralism against the enlightenment Zeitgeist in which he grew up. He saw in the Enlightenment a tendency to cultural self-congratulation that he found maddeningly myopic (pp. 332-334).

A pluralist of Herder's kind has a straightforward reason to learn from other cultures, both in the past and in the present. The point is to enlarge and improve one's appreciation of 'the good'. 'A noble expansion takes place in the soul when it dares to venture outside the circle that climate and education have drawn around it' (Herder, 1989, p. 304, translation borrowed from Sikka, 2011, p. 21). This may happen through reading or travelling. As an empiricist, Herder stressed the significance of the latter approach. The combination of pluralism and empiricism provides a powerful incentive to travel. Book learning is important, but nothing can replace first-hand knowledge.

My suggestion here is that only a pluralist world-view makes proper sense of Corradi's educational vision and of the Erasmus Programme. A thinker like Erasmus, who was not inclined towards cultural pluralism, could not make the same straightforward sense of Corradi's central ideas about cultural education. Erasmus may well deserve more attention than he receives today, but he is no great help if we are trying to find a philosophical ground on which Corradi can rest her educational views.

An attentive reader may have noticed that Corradi makes use of the term 'relativity' in a crucial passage quoted above. A philosophically minded reader may point out that this could be a problem for my claim that Corradi ought to be something like a Herderian pluralist. This is a serious point that deserves an answer. In philosophical debates about the metaphysical and epistemological status of values, it is common to distinguish between relativism and pluralism (see e.g. Wolf, 1992; Berlin, 1998; Spencer, 2012). Outside philosophy these two technical terms are sometimes used more or less interchangeably, but for the purposes of this essay it is important not to conflate them. The relativist thinks that there are no objective values. The pluralist thinks that there are objective values, but that there are many of them, and that their mutual relation is one of deep or essential tension. Relativists and pluralists agree to reject what is commonly called 'monism': the view that there is only one (kind of) value or that the world of value is harmoniously ordered, or at least free of deep and disturbing conflict. If we use this technical vocabulary, Erasmus may be described as a monist, Herder as a pluralist.[9]

If Corradi makes significant use of the concept of relativity, why not read her as a relativist? For two reasons. During our conversations, I learned that the philosophical distinction between relativism and pluralism was unknown to Corradi at the time of writing. Her use of the word 'relativity' could therefore not have signalled a preference for one position over the other. But there is a more important reason. Whereas the pluralist world-view reveals the deep educational value of the Erasmus Programme, the relativist world-view would trivialise it. There is no particular reason for a relativist to be culturally tolerant or humble. Think of Nietzsche. There is no particular reason for a relativist to be a pacifist either. Mussolini was a relativist who thought that cultural clashes must be settled through war.[10] The pluralist, however, is humble because he has a sense of his own narrowness. He is tolerant because he knows that other cultures may teach him something about the good. And he seeks peace, not just because war involves horrible suffering, but because peace allows for fruitful complementary relations between different cultures. It does not follow that any culture is beyond criticism, nor that all cultures deserve to survive. But the pluralist will not be jumping to conclusions without a careful attempt to appreciate what seems foreign.

Whither Now?

As a former Erasmus student for whom that experience has been life-shaping, I am grateful to Sofia Corradi for her work. Nonetheless, we should not let gratitude and feelings of friendship deter us from a sober discussion of the programme. Is the institution successful? Does it need reform in any way? Recently, in an interview, Umberto Eco offered some interesting reformative proposals which provide us with a good starting point for discussing these questions. Eco, who thinks that Erasmus has been underappreciated so far, sees the programme as facilitating nothing less than a sexual revolution by encouraging international match-making. He would like the Erasmus Programme to be compulsory, however, and to apply more broadly. He suggests that taxi drivers, plumbers and workers of all kinds should be able to spend time abroad, just like university students (Riotta, 2012).

Making the programme compulsory would be a mistake, it seems to me. Corradi is right to stress the significance of self-selection. Forcing foreign culture down the throats of reluctant students is probably just wrong, but it is also unlikely to have the desired effect. Let's facilitate, nudge even, but not force anyone. This is a good prima facie principle for all educational thinking, at least for adults.[11]

Broadening the target group is a good idea, however. Not only would this move be a step towards educational justice, it might also be of genuine cultural significance in Europe. The current Erasmus design has a touch of that cultural elitism that was so characteristic of Erasmus, the humanist. In that sense, ironically, the programme is named appropriately. If we agree with Zweig's reluctant critique of Erasmus, and with Herder's ambivalent worries about Joseph II, then we have reason to appreciate Eco's proposal. What Zweig and Herder were saying was that a community cannot be built top-down. Solid building begins on the ground, or under, and is not built higher or heavier than the soil allows. Evidently this thought is still relevant in Europe. Many critics worry that the EU is primarily an elite project and some of the evidence for that view is very compelling (Haller, 2010). The sheer lack of interest in elections for the European Parliament speaks volumes. No wonder that the cry for a more solid foundation of the EU project is getting louder. As Ulrich Beck and Daniel Cohn-Bendit have argued in a recent manifesto, signed by an impressive list of famous Europeans, we need to 're-build Europe from the bottom up' (Beck & Cohn-Bendit et al, 2012). This thought ought to unite EU-builders, no matter how much 'Europe' they want.

Securing a broad basis for the EU project is not an easy task, but at least we have a fairly clear sense of what is required: inclusion and participation. Unfortunately, we are also confronted with another problem, one that looks much more intractable. Umberto Eco, helpful again, puts his finger on the sore spot. By now the sense of European identity is quite widespread, he observes (somewhat optimistically), but still shallow. The problem with this is easily illustrated if we hold on to the building metaphor. A solid building needs a sufficiently broad basis, but typically also foundations sufficiently deep. Part of the problem here is that, even if this thought commands some agreement, it will be difficult to find and agree on a solution. There is no simple recipe for acquiring depth, and there will be dramatically different conceptions of the depth needed.

Here we arrive at my main doubt about the current Erasmus design. While Corradi seems convinced that the Erasmus scheme tends to ensure a fruitful engagement with another culture, I am not convinced. Her thought seems to be that when a sufficiently curious student lives abroad for a year, a significant cultural maturation tends to follow, more or less automatically. It is not unreasonable to *hope* so, I agree, or feel that it *should* be so, but I don't think it is something we can expect in general.

As we learn from Mitchell, Erasmus students do not typically undergo some sort of immersion experience while abroad. While Corradi was left more or less unperturbed by these statistical results, I found them quite troubling. This can be explained partly by the fact that Corradi is less concerned with European identity than I am, which is fair enough, but the deeper reason concerns a disagreement about the process of cultural maturation. Corradi is relatively unconcerned with immersion because she believes in individual friendships as the vehicle of cultural maturation. While I value individual friendships highly, I don't think they typically inspire deep cultural understanding. Friendship, even when international, primarily concerns individual character, but collective culture only contingently, intermittently or superficially. Only those who think that character is always determined quite heavily by local culture can think otherwise. Those of us who don't subscribe to this reductive view have to admit that Erasmus students are not *systematically* invited to engage in a sustained manner with another culture.

And it does not, generally speaking, happen automatically. Most of us are rather helpless, it seems to me, when we really have to confront cultural differences; we mostly rely on clichés and stereotypes. It is not so easy to rise above, or dig below, the level of the tourist. This could just be a fact of human nature, but the problem may also be particularly acute in an era that does not particularly value or reward deep understanding (Liesmann, 2006). If this is true, the Erasmus student seeking cultural understanding is not only not helped by the institutional design, but is fighting the Zeitgeist also. In this situation we should not expect the average Erasmus student to learn much more about culture than the typical tourist.

Perhaps I am being unfair to the tourist. That is not my intention and in most moods I'm not inclined to throw stones at this ubiquitous creature.[12] Sometimes, I join the ranks myself. At the same time, the word 'tourism' has derogatory connotations for a reason. As tourists we tend to become somewhat pitiful creatures unable to engage with the culturally significant objects we pursue. As Eva Brann once observed:

> tourists pay dearly to be delivered to the sight catalogued as
> worthy to be seen. And what do you do before such a sight? Well,
> you have your picture taken with your back to it (that is your
> tourist's identity card; it shows that you are you and that it is it
> and the two were within one view-finder). And then you gawk and
> the sight goes blank with embarrassment. And then, greedy for a
> new experience, since the last one denied itself ... you traipse on
> until you finally come to a cafe, where your soul longed to be.
> (Brann, 2004, pp. 90-91)

I have been in that cafe many times, I have to admit, also while I was an Erasmus student. The coffee there is bitter and I always promise myself not to go back. But somehow we – I assume that some of you have been there too – keep taking it for granted that we can come to look at things with understanding simply by opening our eyes. Unfortunately that is rarely true. The result of simply opening our eyes does not typically deserve to be called understanding.[13] This is probably true in general, but almost certainly true when we travel. Herder felt the sting of this difficulty quite acutely. In 1769, for example, he hesitated before going to France because he worried that he might not be able to learn enough from the trip. He felt that the cultural riches of Paris were hidden behind a façade of French luxury that he might not be able to penetrate. He did not just blame French culture for the difficulty, however, but his own lack of preparation: he was in his mid-20s and thought of himself as someone who had not yet learned to travel (Herder, 1997, p. 100).

The *desire* to travel and learn was not lacking. Herder gave up his first job in order to travel and sold his belongings to afford it (Herder, 1997, pp. 862-863). He did not assume that sheer desire guarantees anything, however, and we should agree with him. For two reasons. First, because our desires to learn through travelling differ in quality. To see how much, consider two words used to refer to that desire. In English we often use the word 'curiosity', in German the typical term is *Neugier*, which means 'news greed'.[14] Though these terms are commonly used to translate one another, their etymological connotations point in different directions. Whereas 'curiosity' in principle suggests careful attention, that is, focus and depth, *Neugier* suggests the ongoing pursuit of novelty and so dispersion. These motivational states are not only not equivalent, but potentially conflicting. The person greedy for novelty will often not pause long enough at any one object to understand it. The desire that propels the self-selected Erasmus student to study does not have to be curiosity, it could be mere *Neugier*, or something related even more superficially to serious learning.[15]

Secondly, because desire, even the best, simply isn't enough. Herder knew this and discussed the problem with respect to Joseph II. Not only did Joseph travel, Herder suggests that he may have travelled *too much*. He probably saw more than he could digest and spread himself too thinly (Herder, 1991, p. 56). While he 'knew' many of the peoples of his empire very well, he did not really understand them (p. 66). Herder suggests that he lacked not so much the desire but the preparation to do so. His upbringing did not prepare him and he did not sufficiently prepare himself either. Not only was Joseph not bookish, he had no interest in book-learning at all (p. 60). He lacked the taste for *Wissenschaft*, systematic learning, without which – Herder suggests – our action will never be truly insightful. Even if we think there is an exaggeration here, the basic point is clear enough: while experience is necessary, it is not sufficient. Travelling to learn is no trivial matter.

Lack of depth does not just mean that something important is missing, it may also lead to the presence of something quite pernicious. My primary worry about the Erasmus Programme, as it currently stands, is that it may encourage 'facile cosmopolitanism', the quickly produced but quite unfounded feeling of being a world citizen. Confidence is a desirable part of maturity, but let it be of the healthy humble kind and not the bloated proud one. This is morally desirable, but of immense political significance also. Of all internal tensions in Europe, the potential conflict between a self-appointed 'elite' and despised 'mass' may be one of the most dangerous.[16] The nations of Europe may end up superficially united through a rootless cosmopolitan elite, but deeply divided by distinctions of class and culture. If this is a realistic worry, we have reason to support Eco's suggestion to broaden the target group of the Erasmus Programme. Moreover, we have reason to improve the institutional design in order to encourage the humble pursuit of cultural depth. How exactly to do this is a matter for discussion and educational experiment. One might begin by encouraging local language study. This is already done, but the effort could be intensified. Or we could make it possible and attractive for Erasmus students to live with local families. These are just the most obvious options, however. What we need first of all is to revive a concept that seems to have gone out of use. From the sixteenth to the eighteenth centuries, the concept went under the name *ars apodemica*, literally 'the art of going away from one's people'. If we are trying to benefit from Herder's company, however, we could revive a helpful neologism he coined: *hodopaedia*, literally 'road-learning' (Herder, 2002, p. 397). In any case, it is time to realise that 'a culture of student mobility' is not enough. If we really want to learn from travelling, we have to learn how to travel.

Acknowledgements

I am grateful to Zsofia Barna, Peter Hajnal, David Hayes, Sofiya Skachko, Bernhard Streitwieser and students at Humboldt University for discussing the material of this essay with me. I am particularly grateful to Sofia Corradi for being so generous with her time during my visit to Rome in March 2012.

Notes

[1] The following interpretation of Corradi's educational vision is based on a text (Corradi, 2006), a TV interview (Corradi, 2012) and about 10-12 hours of conversation with her in Rome in March 2013. She has retired from her position as Professor of Lifelong Learning at Roma Tre University, but is still actively promoting Erasmus in lectures and interviews. She can be reached by email at s.corradi@lifelong.it.

[2] In this essay 'liberal education' refers to any education that is more than a preparation for a job or profession narrowly conceived. The word 'narrow' is meant to allow space for professional education with a liberal element or aspect. I also want to leave open a more detailed discussion about the nature of liberal education.

[3] See also Pepin (2006, p. 74).

[4] Corradi still thinks the stipends are insufficient for Erasmus to be entirely just, however.

[5] All quotes in this paragraph are taken from the Bologna Declaration of 19 June 1999 (European Ministers of Education, 1999).

[6] This principle is explicitly established in the Maastricht Treaty, but apparently is not playing a very forceful role. Cf. Henckel and Wright (2008, p. 17).

[7] Of course some worry that the Erasmus Programme itself is becoming too bureaucratic. See De Wit (2012).

[8] This is the impression we get from Huizinga (1952) and Zweig (1935).

[9] This understanding of Herder is common enough, but not universally agreed on. For helpful discussion, see Linker (2000), Sikka (2011) and Spencer (2012).

[10] I have taken these examples from Graham (1996).

[11] For the idea of a prima facie principle, see Ross (1930).

[12] Here I follow Santayana (1968, p. 15).

[13] Or even 'seeing' (Murdoch, 1997, pp. 330, 368).

[14] Here I am developing a point from Brann (2004).

[15] CV building, for example.

[16] For a disturbing report from Germany, see Friedrichs (2009).

References

Beales, Derek (2005) *Enlightenment and Reform in Eighteenth-Century Europe*. International Library of Historical Studies (Book 29). London: I.B. Tauris & Co.

Beck, Ulrich & Cohn-Bendit, Daniel et al (2012) Let's Create a Bottom-up Europe, *The Guardian*, 3 May.

Berlin, Isaiah (1998) The First and the Last, *New York Review of Books*, XLV(8).

Borgolte, Michael (2008) How Europe Became Diverse: on the medieval roots of the plurality of values, in H. Joas & K. Wiegandt (Eds) The Cultural Values of Europe, pp. 77-114. Liverpool: Liverpool University Press.

Brann, Eva (2004) *Open Secrets/Inward Prospects: reflections on world and soul*. Philadelphia: Paul Dry Books.

Corradi, Sofia (2006) *Erasmus Programme: the origin, preparatory years (1963-1986) and foundation of the European Union initiative for the exchange of university students, reported and documented by the scholar who first conceived of it*. Rome: Laboratories of Lifelong Learning and of Comparative Education of the University 'Roma Tre'.

Corradi, Sofia (2012) Will Erasmus Live Forever? Interview, Europarltv, 121205, 30 November. http://europarltv.europa.eu/en/player.aspx?pid=594cc29c-b025-4a54-bfcb-a11c00ff68f1

Davies, Norman (1996) *Europe: a history*. Oxford: Oxford University Press.

De Wit, Hans (2012) Erasmus at 25: what is the future for international student mobility? *The Guardian*, 21 May.

Enzensberger, Hans Magnus (2011) *Sanftes Monster Brüssel oder die Entmündigung Europas*. Berlin: Suhrkamp Verlag.

Erasmus, Desiderius (1997) *The Education of a Christian Prince with the Panegyric for Archduke Philip of Austria*, ed. Lisa Jardine. Cambridge Texts in the History of Political Thought. Cambridge: Cambridge University Press.

European Ministers of Education (1999) *The Bologna Declaration.* http://www.bologna-berlin2003.de/pdf/bologna_declaration.pdf

Friedrichs, Julia (2009) *Gestatten: Elite: Auf den Spuren der Mächtigen von morgen.* Munich: Heyne Verlag.

Graham, Gordon (1996) Tolerance, Pluralism, and Relativism, in David Heyd (Ed.) *Toleration: an elusive virtue*, pp. 44-59. Princeton: Princeton University Press.

Haller, Max (2010) *European Integration as an Elite Process: the failure of a dream?* New York: Routledge.

Henckel, Ole & Wright, Susan (2008) The Bologna Process: a voluntary process of coordination and marketisation? *Learning and Teaching*, 1(2), 1-24.

Herder, Johann Gottfried (1989) *Werke 6: Ideen zur Philosophie der Geschichte der Menschheit.* Herausgegeben von Martin Bollacher. Frankfurt am Main: Deutscher Klassiker Verlag.

Herder, Johann Gottfried (1991) *Werke 7: Briefe zu Beförderung der Humanität.* Herausgegeben von Hans Dietrich Irmscher. Frankfurt am Main: Deutscher Klassiker Verlag.

Herder, Johann Gottfried (1997) *Werke 9/2: Journal meiner Reise im Jahr 1769/Pädagogische Schriften.* Herausgegeben von Rainer Wisbert unter Mitarbeit von Klaus Pradel. Frankfurt am Main: Deutscher Klassiker Verlag.

Herder, Johann Gottfried (2002) *Philosophical Writings*, ed. Michael N. Forster. Cambridge: Cambridge University Press.

Huizinga, J. (1952) *Erasmus of Rotterdam*, trans. F. Hopman. London: Phaidon Press.

Kimball, Bruce (1995) *Orators and Philosophers: a history of the ideal of liberal education.* New York: Teachers College Press.

Lemcke, Dietrich (2010) Mourning Bologna, *e-flux*, #14. http://www.e-flux.com/journal/mourning-bologna/

Liessmann, Konrad Paul (2006) *Theorie der Unbildung: Die Irrtümer der Wissensgesellschaft.* Vienna: Paul Zsolnay Verlag.

Linker, Damon (2000) The Reluctant Pluralism of J.G. Herder, *The Review of Politics*, 62(2), 267-293.

Menand, Louis (2010) *The Marketplace of Ideas: reform and resistance in the American university.* New York: W.W. Norton & Company.

Mitchell, Kristine (2012) Student Mobility and European Identity – Erasmus study as a civic experience, *Journal of Contemporary European Research*, 8(4), 490-518.

Morin, Edgar (1988) *Europa denken*, trans. Linda Gränz. Frankfurt: Campus Verlag.

Münch, Richard (2010) Bologna, or the Capitalization of Education, *eurozine.* http://www.eurozine.com/articles/2010-07-01-munch-en.html

Murdoch, Iris (1997) *Existentialists and Mystics: writings on philosophy and literature*, ed. Peter Conradi. New York: Penguin.

Nietzsche, Friedrich (2004) *On the Future of Our Educational Institutions*, translated and introduced by Michael W. Grenke. South Bend: St Augustine's Press.

117

O'Neill, Onora (2002) *A Question of Trust*. The BBC Reith Lectures 2002. Cambridge: Cambridge University Press.

Pepin, Luce (2006) *The History of European Cooperation in Education and Training*. Luxembourg: Office for Official Publications of the European Communities.

Power, Michael (1997) *The Audit Society: rituals of verification*. Oxford: Oxford University Press.

Rawls, John (1971) *A Theory of Justice*. Cambridge, MA: Harvard University Press.

Rifkin, Jeremy (2005) *The European Dream: how Europe's vision of the future is quietly eclipsing the American dream*. Cambridge: Polity Press.

Riotta, Gianni (2012) Umberto Eco: it's culture, not war that cements European identity, *The Guardian*, 26 January.

Ross, W.D. (1930) *The Right and the Good*. Oxford: Oxford University Press.

Santayana, George (1968) *The Birth of Reason and Other Essays*, ed. Daniel Cory. New York: Columbia University Press.

Sigalas, Emmanuel (2009) *Does ERASMUS Student Mobility Promote a European Identity?* *Con*WEB. Webpapers on Constitutionalism and Governance beyond the State, No. 2. https://www.wiso.uni-hamburg.de/fileadmin/sowi/politik/governance/ConWeb_Papers/conweb2-2009.pdf

Sikka, Sonia (2011) *Herder on Humanity and Cultural Difference: enlightened relativism*. Cambridge: Cambridge University Press.

Spencer, Vicky A. (2012) *Herder's Political Thought: a study on language, culture and community*. Toronto: University of Toronto Press.

Truszczynski, Jan (2012) Is Erasmus Europe's Success Story? *OpenDemocracy*, 17 December. http://www.opendemocracy.net/can-europe-make-it/jan-truszczy%C5%84ski/is-erasmus-europes-success-story

Wolf, Susan (1992) Two Levels of Pluralism, *Ethics*, 102(4), 785-798.

Zweig, Stefan (1935) *Triumph und Tragik des Erasmus von Rotterdam*. Vienna: Herbert Reichner Verlag.

CHAPTER 8

International National Universities: migration and mobility in Luxembourg and Qatar

JUSTIN J.W. POWELL

ABSTRACT Located in small states with extraordinary migration flows, the University of Luxembourg and Qatar University reflect global norms relating to research universities. Each has opened its doors widely in recent decades to scholars and students from around the world. Higher education in both countries relies to a considerable extent on global mobility; indeed, the international dimension of higher education is a precondition for their development. Elaborated internationalisation strategies characterise the universities in Luxembourg and Qatar, embedded in hyper-diverse and very wealthy nation-states as well as in significant regional and global networks. In these two cases, the 'national' flagship universities are thoroughly 'international'. These recently founded universities rely on global scientific collaboration, without which higher education and science could not flourish. Likewise, these young international national universities facilitate the accelerating global reach of higher education and science as they systematically foster the worldwide recruitment, cross-border mobility and multicultural networks of faculty, staff and students.

Introduction

Higher education and science, producing intellectual dialogue, conferences and publications in the lingua franca of the day, are thoroughly worldwide activities. Research universities offer spaces for multicultural and multilingual learning and for scientific discovery. Increasingly, national ideals of 'progress' rely on successfully institutionalising universities that promise to generate the 'knowledge society' as well as economic development (Ramirez & Meyer, 2013). Today, all countries invest in higher education, the smaller ones often doing so through a national university, despite the considerable state

119

expenditures this requires. Creating new institutions from the ground up may involve high costs and myriad challenges – especially for small states – due to limited highly qualified human resources and lack of economies of scale (Bacchus, 2008; Crossley et al, 2011; Martin & Bray, 2011). The costs of tertiary education have risen by 15% across the developed world since 2000 (Organisation for Economic Cooperation and Development, 2011), yet scientific productivity varies considerably. Numerous successful universities have provided considerable returns to national investments in education and science as they reach beyond their home contexts to attract the best and brightest internationally, while others struggle to develop their reputations (Salmi, 2009).

Two nascent national universities with ambitious agendas – the University of Luxembourg and Qatar University – are embedded in very small but exceptionally wealthy states in which each university emulates global goals simultaneously with serving national and local needs. These examples show how small states compensate being on the perceived periphery of a scientific world characterised by stark and increasingly global rivalry. While geographically central in their respective regions, both countries lack hundreds of years of (higher) education institutionalisation that have conferred a massive head-start to many competitors in Europe and North America. The comparison of Luxembourg and Qatar emphasises similarities and differences in national 'internationalisation strategies' (see, e.g., Graf, 2009) and education and science policies. In distinct contrast to many federal countries like Canada, Germany, Switzerland or the USA, in which regional differences prevail and a plethora of universities exist (see, e.g., Braband, 2011), these highly centralised nation-states provide their few research universities with generous funding but limited autonomy.

From the beginning, universities have been standard-bearers of the nation-states in which they are located, often serving to train elites – from civil servants and business leaders to clergy and intellectuals. Yet they have also reached beyond such boundaries, be they political, linguistic or disciplinary, oriented as they are to universal goals such as truth-seeking and cross-cultural understanding. Higher education, more than ever owing to massive educational expansion in societies worldwide (Schofer & Meyer, 2005), is often viewed as the most assured pathway to elevated social status for individuals and to economic growth for societies, as those with tertiary education qualifications often enjoy higher salaries and lower unemployment rates than other groups. Higher education, while exhibiting durable national differences, has become even more international in orientation over recent decades, for example, due to successful European programmes like Erasmus that foster spatial mobility (Powell & Finger, 2013) and supranational coordination processes such as Bologna and Copenhagen (Powell et al, 2012).

To analyse the contemporary internationalisation of higher education, this contribution compares two relatively recently founded national universities striving for international reputation: the University of Luxembourg in Europe and Qatar University in the Middle East. These universities exemplify major trends in tertiary education globally. Delving into the two case studies, this chapter compares these universities in their respective contexts, investigating how each national university relies on cross-border migration and global mobility to establish itself.

Transnational Higher Education and Science

The on-going transnationalisation of higher education and science challenges traditional nation-based analyses of institutional change in education. In response, neo-institutional analyses have explored the diffusion of worldwide ideas and norms (Drori et al, 2003; Schofer & Meyer, 2005). Such work has uncovered the ideologies, values and assumptions that guide educators and policymakers as they continuously attempt to optimise their institutions and organisations based on comparisons with other countries. Trends in internationalisation, such as increased student and faculty mobility, are incontrovertible (see, e.g., the 'Open Doors' survey, Institute of International Education, 2012; Streitwieser, 2012). Continued growth in the numbers of youth and adults attending all types of higher education institutions is a key element behind both growing scientific capacity and the role of the university in knowledge production. For example, about half a million students, or just 1% of the youth age-cohort, were enrolled in higher education worldwide in 1900; a century later approximately 100 million youth were enrolled, representing 20% of the college-aged cohort (Schofer & Meyer, 2005). This phenomenal growth forms a critical base for the recruiting and training of the world's future scientists and scholars (Altbach, 2005). The rationale and vision shared by many governments of how to build capacity for science is not difficult to understand: infrastructure for research lies at the heart of the knowledge triangle – 'the beneficial combination of research activity, specialised education/training and innovation that advances our knowledge' (European Commission, 2010, p. 3). Internationally oriented universities aim to prepare students for employment as well as for global citizenship, especially in states that rely to a large extent on foreign workers and the worldwide export of goods and services. In terms of research, governments hope universities will strengthen institutional capacity and broaden networks, to contribute to knowledge production on key issues, to enhance prestige and visibility and to generate revenue (Salmi, 2009). In both Luxembourg and Qatar, key challenges are to develop research infrastructure and to recruit the necessary expertise (on Luxembourg, see Meyer, 2008; on Qatar, see Qatar Foundation, 2013).

Justin J. W. Powell

(Inter-)national Research Universities between the Global and the Local

National universities have developed and attempt to realise their ambitions on different levels: within transnational, national and local contexts. The Universities of Luxembourg and Qatar are based in different world regions, grow within contrasting institutional environments and utilise very different resource-bases. Yet they are similar in aiming to become part of global dialogue and to compare favourably in world rankings with hundreds of other research universities, to be regional leaders and to address local needs. To reach these goals, they have chosen particular emphases and selected different internationalisation strategies; however, both states rely heavily on cross-border migration and international mobility to achieve their visions.

Evident in the cases of Luxembourg and Qatar, even very small states may exert influence via elite networks, supranational coordination and business acumen far beyond their population size or land area. For example, these countries host powerful media companies, Radio-Television-Luxembourg [1] and Al Jazeera [2] in Qatar, that wield considerable regional influence by shaping political consciousness. Import/export flows and labour migrations are vital because these countries are not self-reliant or self-sustaining; this is also true in academic markets. Owing to the reliance on other countries' universities to train their citizens, both their labour forces and their education systems reflect a high degree of internationalisation, especially at tertiary level. Both have chosen to invest in founding and expanding their own (inter-)national university to respond to changing global norms and economic conditions. Most importantly, Luxembourg and Qatar now attempt to convert their current economic success into long-term affluence via education and science.

As a correlate of heavy in-migration and cultural diversity, multiculturalism and multilingualism are further hallmarks of life in these states, although languages are also often highly stratified in their usage and prestige – and even politicised. Internally, less functional differentiation and tight social ties can ease decision-making and bundle resources across boundaries that in other contexts would be challenging. Cosmopolitan life and elite communication in both countries is centred in a single dominant city: Luxembourg and Doha, respectively. Other strategies to compensate for their lack of military force are advanced diplomacy (as seen in regional integration attempts, such as the Benelux or the Gulf Cooperation Council) or political neutrality, which led Luxembourg to host several European Union institutions such as the European Court of Justice. Perhaps decisively, these small states have amassed vast wealth from their strategic dominance in key industrial sectors. They have done so whether through discovery and extraction of national resource holdings, like Qatar's traditional pearl trade or its current natural gas reserves, or in highly profitable global industries, such as Luxembourg's traditional steel foundries, increasingly replaced by banking. Thus, while small in terms of population and geographic area, these states are large in resources and influence.

Both countries have fashioned high-tech campuses for their universities as well as attempting to extend their networks far afield. The University of Luxembourg participates in the Université de la Grande Région,[3] a cooperative venture between universities in Belgium, France, Germany and Luxembourg. Education City, in the capital of Doha, Qatar, hosts a number of prominent foreign universities' branch campuses; Qatar University's own campus is also modern – but segregated by sex. The University of Luxembourg, while still housed in several regal structures, will soon move into a completely refurbished former steel factory site in Esch-sur-Alzette along the border with France. Campus Belval, initially budgeted at €600 million and comprising two dozen new buildings, has begun to accommodate research institutes, banks and retail stores, and R&D companies. Both states have invested heavily in top-quality foundations for education and science – and rely on migration and mobility to a significant extent. Elites are devoted to international education experience even as they have marshalled support for these universities. They recognise the importance of education and science for the future development of their countries. More than ever, these countries are embedded in transnational economic, political and cultural networks.

Migration and Mobility as Foundations of the Global Research University

How are migration and mobility driving the development of the young universities in Luxembourg and Qatar, putting them on the path to becoming global research universities? Alongside excellence in research (top-quality faculty), academic freedom, and adequate facilities and funding, crucial factors in establishing the global research university include the internationalisation of students, staff and faculty and the resulting diversity (Levin et al, 2006). Inexorably, universities compete in a growing number of university rankings (e.g. *Times Higher Education*, Shanghai Jiao Tong), even if their worth and methodologies have been criticised (Steiner-Khamsi, 2010; Münch, 2011; Hazelkorn, 2013). Newer rankings, like U-Multirank, include all types of tertiary education, from all parts of Europe and the world. What is methodologically challenging is that most universities in Qatar are international branch campuses, with their home institutions ranked without the contributions directly attributable to developments in Qatar (on the myriad contemporary types of international university engagement in the Middle East, see Miller-Idriss & Hanauer, 2011). Unmistakably, direct comparison and competition as well as regional coordination, as in the Bologna Process in Europe, are key factors that have intensified institutional change.

Justin J. W. Powell

Both the universities in Luxembourg and Qatar are oriented toward global standards, at least according to their mission statements and annual reports, and seek to become 'elite' universities by recruiting talent globally. Yet the target is shifting as 'super research universities' (SRUs) have undergone striking recent developments (Mohrman et al, 2008). This model emphasises certain qualities a handful of universities have pioneered – extraordinary research capacity, science and technology parks, and preeminent faculty clusters. The principles upon which the SRUs have developed emphasise particular qualities of universities in producing scientific knowledge: their missions are explicitly global; they are research intensive; they contribute to the expanding 'scientification' of all types of societal challenges (Drori et al, 2003); they focus on knowledge and economic integration and form public–private partnerships in the firm belief that university-based knowledge production enhances both social and economic progress. On the cutting edge, SRUs proclaim that they are at the forefront and should define global norms, whether related to graduate/professional training or research production and patent development. Growing budgets dedicated to these twin tasks and their prominence intensify the university's role as a major leader in scientific knowledge production (Baker, in press). Even if only very few of the thousands of universities actually achieve membership in this 'world-class' group, the model they provide is significant for all stakeholders; the principle of knowledge generation builds upon the conception of the SRU as vital both to worldwide economic competitiveness and national social development (Geiger & Sá, 2008).

The emphasis differs by university, with some world-class universities remaining very much an 'ivory tower' and others embracing strong roles in improving living conditions in their countries (Ramirez, 2006). Depending on region and especially languages spoken and scientific traditions practised therein, universities appeal to scientists, who more often than not publish their cutting-edge research in English and train their most ambitious students in multiple languages to facilitate career advancement. To analyse the extent to which these ascendant national universities reflect these broader global trends in higher education, each country and its national university will be placed in its cultural context.

University of Luxembourg in Context

The Grand Duchy of Luxembourg, nestled between Belgium, France and Germany, is home to half a million people, of whom three-fifths are natives. The country is trilingual, with Luxembourgish, German and French the official languages. Daily, many tens of thousands of workers commute from surrounding countries, bringing their native language and cultural sensibilities with them. More than half the workforce consists of cross-border workers; with its strong financial industry, demographic growth and the EU

124

institutions, Luxembourg has the second highest per capita GDP worldwide (International Monetary Fund, 2011), encouraging such tremendous migration flows.

As its three founding principles, the leaders of the University of Luxembourg chose multilingualism, interdisciplinarity and internationalisation. These foci accentuate the strategy developed to capitalise on Luxembourg's history as a trading crossroads and its contemporary situation of cultural and linguistic diversity, as well as to compensate for being a new university in a very small state through strategic investments in promising research areas.

The University of Luxembourg, building upon the legacies of several postsecondary training institutes, was founded in 2003 as a private, government-dependent institution (*établissement public*) directed by a seven-member council, the Conseil de gouvernance. Most funding is provided by the state, although external sources have risen rapidly over the past several years (University of Luxembourg, 2013). From the very beginning, Luxembourg has relied heavily on student mobility and tertiary education provided in neighbouring countries to supply qualified personnel, especially teachers, judges and physicians; this has generated cultural hybridity (Rohstock, 2010, p. 44; Rohstock & Schreiber, 2013). The university's antecedents can be traced back to the early 1800s when the national school system was first established, yet not until 1974 was the Centre universitaire du Luxembourg, hosting several humanities and social science departments, opened alongside teacher training institutes and an Institut supérieur de technologie, which offered technological courses of study (Meyer, 2008).

The mission statement emphasises that as 'a small-sized institution with an international reach, [it] aims at excellence in research and education. ... to be among the world's top universities. UL intends to be innovative, centred on research, ... and attentive to the needs of the society around it'.[4] With nearly 100 nationalities represented among the 6288 students (2012-13), and around half non-native, the university is extraordinarily diverse (University of Luxembourg, 2013). If the country has three official languages, the university replaces the local language with the current international scientific lingua franca, English. Regardless of nationality, each student pays tuition of just €200 per semester. Thus, state investment ensures that Luxembourg's national university can attract students from around the world.

In a hyper-diverse society marked by migration and mobility, internationalisation has been present from the start. A key challenge is to attract a talented undergraduate student body since the tradition in Luxembourg has long been to study abroad; elites continue to send their children abroad in large numbers. As Rohstock and Schreiber (2013) note, more students from Luxembourg study abroad than stay home, with Germany, Belgium, France, Austria and Switzerland the preferred destinations. Funded by the EU, the network of universities of the 'Greater Region' connects universities in the countries that share borders with

Luxembourg. At the same time, the small classes, low tuition fees and high quality of the faculty and campus also attract students from everywhere to Luxembourg. Today, all Bachelor-level students are expected to spend a semester abroad as a required part of their course of study, thus expanding European and global networks and ensuring the spatial mobility of University of Luxembourg students – and migration-driven transnationalisation.

Aiming to develop strengths based on both international trends and local/regional needs, the university has three faculties, all decidedly multidisciplinary: (1) Science, Technology & Communication; (2) Law, Economics & Finance; and (3) Humanities, Arts & Education. Further, two major interdisciplinary research centres aim to advance the cutting-edge goals internationally, namely the Interdisciplinary Centre for Security, Reliability and Trust, focusing on information systems, and the Luxembourg Centre for Systems Biomedicine. The university's total budget for 2012 from all sources was over €150 million (University of Luxembourg, 2013). By identifying in advance the most promising research areas that also reflect Luxembourg's economic and geographic contexts, the university concentrates its resources.

The university aims to achieve excellence in research by recruiting top faculty members worldwide. Although the funds provided by the national government are considerable (top-ranked in financial autonomy in Europe), organisational autonomy is limited.[5] In sum, Luxembourg has invested both considerable capital and strategic planning in the establishment of its national university, aiming to compete on a global scale by concentrating its resources, both intellectual and financial, and by building on the country's strengths and priorities. Alliances with other universities in the region and internationally underscore its international outlook. Hallmarks include its hyper-diverse faculty, staff and student body.

Qatar University in Context

The State of Qatar gained its independence in 1971 and is a member of the Gulf Cooperation Council and the League of Arab States. Although this small Gulf state has a massively growing overall population (currently around 1.7 million; 15 times what it was in 1970), only about 15% (roughly 250,000) are ethnic Qataris (Qatar, 2012). Its native Arabic society and the bulk of its population and labour force, migrants mainly from Asia (especially India and Nepal), are highly stratified with the latter facing exploitation (Human Rights Watch, 2012). In the face of the undeniable, nearly complete reliance on the work of migrants, a government priority is 'Qatarisation' of the private sector and professional jobs currently held mainly by expatriates (Rubin, 2012). Considerable social and economic investments are needed to implement Qatar's ambitious national development programme – the *Qatar National Vision 2030* (Qatar, n.d.), especially because of the lack of an 'indigenous knowledge economy' and only several decades of educational expansion (Donn & Al Manthri, 2010, 2013). Explicitly or implicitly, Qatar and the other Gulf states borrow foreign (especially American) models without sufficiently reflecting their costs and benefits or necessary adaptation to a contrasting cultural context (Phan, 2010; Hanauer & Phan, 2011; Kane, 2013).

Higher education in Qatar is bifurcated, with Qatar University, first established in 1973 as a college of education, joined recently by the 2500-acre campus Education City, funded by Qatar Foundation, which has attracted Western universities to establish international branch campuses (IBCs) (Lane & Kinser, 2011; Miller-Idriss & Hanauer, 2011). As of 2012, the following universities operate there, bringing expertise in targeted fields: Carnegie-Mellon (computer science), Georgetown (foreign affairs), HEC Paris (business), Northwestern (journalism), Texas A&M (engineering), University College London (museum studies), Virginia Commonwealth (design) and Weill-Cornell (medicine). These institutions seek to draw the elite of Qatari students who aspire to the 'gold standard' in tertiary education (Lewin, 2008). To do so, these IBCs must compete with the tradition of elite families sending their offspring to foreign, mainly anglophone, countries for university studies. If successful, this strategy may reduce the education-motivated study abroad of Qatari youth. Especially compared with the tremendous investments in capacity in Qatar, the programmes for Qataris to study elsewhere are limited.

In part to enhance Qatar University's competitiveness given the exclusive offerings of the new, mostly North American, IBCs, since 2003 the university has enjoyed considerable government funding as part of the country's major development programme. This significant reform has transformed and expanded the university, which aims to achieve the vision that it 'be a model national university that offers high quality, learning-centred education to its students' (Moini et al, 2009, p. 75). President Professor Sheikha Al-Misnad, herself an alumna (1977), is responsible for the curricular and organisational transformation of Qatar University into a leading university in the Arab world. The IBCs of Education City, as well as further institutions not housed there, bring their own principles, personnel and 'student cultures' (Wood, 2011), even as they contribute their home-grown reputations to Qatar. By contrast, Qatar University clearly reflects indigenous priorities and is set to facilitate their attainment.

Thus, higher education in Qatar is characterised by duality: Even as foreign research universities are invited to become pillars of the higher education system (now under the umbrella of the HBKU, or Hamad bin Khalifa University), the country has invested in the construction and expansion of a significant local university that reflects the country's particular heritage and is oriented toward local traditions and labour markets (Crist, 2013). This institutionalisation process emphasises the entire country becoming a world territory that operates as an ascendant node in multinational higher education and science – a hub situated between the West and the East.

If the vision is to serve national needs, the mission statement emphasises that Qatar University is 'the national institution of higher education in Qatar. It provides high quality undergraduate and graduate programs that prepare competent graduates, destined to shape the future of Qatar. The university community ... contribute[s] actively to the needs and aspirations of society' (Moini et al, 2009, p. 75). Furthermore, Qatar University seeks to 'promote the cultural and scientific development of the Qatari society while preserving its Arabic characteristics and maintaining its Islamic cultural heritage ... The University shall provide the country with specialists, technicians, and experts in various fields, and equip citizens with knowledge and advanced research methodologies' (p. 75). While crucial to remember that education in Qatar has only been formalised beginning in the 1950s, with the state replacing within-family instruction, this development is being cemented with tremendous investments – US$4 billion was spent on education and science in 2008 alone (Fromherz, 2012, p. 152). 'Qatar has set the bar high with its goal of becoming a knowledge-producing economy at record speed. But the country holds some strong cards: a clear vision, highly committed leadership, and abundant resources to devote to the cause' (Rubin, 2012, p. 4). While Qatar University has long been considered among the better universities in the Middle East, the recent reforms have counteracted what many viewed as lack of academic standards and deteriorating performance (Moini et al, 2009).

The university, emphasising undergraduate teaching in particular, had 8706 students in 2009-10, with 38% being Qatari nationals and three-quarters women. Students of Qatari origin study tuition-free. Students are taught by a large group of 653 faculty (all ranks), with non-Qataris (70%) on one-year contracts and tenure held by Qatari faculty members (30%) (Qatar University, 2010); thus the teaching staff is highly stratified by origin. Addressing the needs of its community has been the hallmark of an institution located in a society experiencing massive demographic and economic change.

In terms of resources, Qatar has chosen to use its wealth to rapidly develop a high-quality education system – and to fund scientific research with 2.8% of GDP. In 2009-10, the research funding for Qatar University amounted to US$60 million (Qatar University, 2010). The university sets out to improve its teaching and research by recruiting researchers globally. Generous funding from the national government (and through Qatar Foundation, especially for Education City) provides excellent facilities. Yet, both academic freedom and self-governance remain partial; the university is not led democratically. Recognising the discordance with global academic norms, reform initiatives aim to strengthen these dimensions to which most world-class universities conform.

As in Luxembourg, the internationalisation of all status groups is the rule due to the extraordinarily diverse population of the country, although there are inequalities; for example, only Qataris can study at Qatar University free of charge. Attracting a talented undergraduate student body is difficult because traditionally the brightest students have gone abroad for their studies, similarly to Luxembourg. The large majority of female students at Qatar University results from their higher probability of seeking tertiary educational opportunities closer to home. In both country and university, Arabic and English are the two key languages, although this duality is contentious. Debates about the language of instruction emphasise the continuous challenge of serving different groups and aiming to place graduates in labour markets at home and abroad. Qatar University has chosen to focus on preparing qualified graduates for Qatar's dramatically expanding labour market, as have the Western universities' branch campuses. As in Luxembourg, it remains to be seen when these considerable investments in education and science will provide the university with a reputation to compete with the best universities worldwide.

In sum, Qatar has chosen a two-pronged strategy: to entice Western universities to provide their know-how and reputations and to establish and grow its own national higher education institution. In the past few decades, Qatari education, economy and society have experienced transformative growth. The fit between the diverse international branch campuses of Education City and the local initiatives to strengthen Qatar University and the goals of the family-led state will require further adjustment and strenghtened cooperation. Similarly to the Luxembourg case, significant economic prosperity provides visionary leaders with myriad opportunities to construct some of the newest and most impressive university campuses anywhere. Yet international scientific collaboration and reputations must be established over the long term – and these require sustained international mobility and migration.

Conclusions

Unlike many other small states, Luxembourg and Qatar are international, ethnically diverse and unusually prosperous. Almost completely dependent on international trading relationships and global markets for capital and labour, both countries have experienced extraordinary recent growth made possible mainly through immigration of the most highly qualified and less educated workers. Over the past decade, Luxembourg *and* Qatar have further intensified their investments in education and science, attracting scientists and students from around the globe. The institutional actors in Luxembourg and Qatar have compensated perceived vulnerabilities of small population, small size or peripheral geopolitical position with economic prowess and media influence – and by taking the lead in regional governance, whether the European Union or the Gulf Cooperation Council.

The two ascendant national universities reflect their ethnically and linguistically diverse host countries, yet their ambitions are not limited to their national contexts. Indeed, the governments of Luxembourg and Qatar seem to have found promising mechanisms to compete globally, such as significant investment in selected, high-potential and often multidisciplinary research fields; the building of cutting-edge campus facilities; and the establishment of a range of undergraduate and graduate programmes to train local elites and attract individuals from around the world to help develop these dynamic organisations. Yet recruitment of international scholars and students to these lesser-known universities takes considerable effort, as do international and regional partnerships of differing depth and significance. Where the University of Luxembourg is weakly linked to other universities in the Greater Region, Qatar invests heavily in IBCs located at Education City; yet these too could work more collaboratively. Youth in both countries continue to be highly mobile in studying abroad. The time required to convert material resources into human capital or scientific advancement and reputation is much longer than the government-directed investment plans suggest. Arguably, competition in tertiary education and scientific activity will continue to increase worldwide, especially due to the massive expansion of education and science systems in East Asia and elsewhere.

Both Luxembourg and Qatar have shown their dedication to funding ambitious experiments in capacity-building via university institutionalisation. Whatever the future holds, these young universities are now the official national standard-bearers; simultaneously, they are thoroughly internationally oriented. Despite their historical, social and political differences and the similarity of being extraordinarily economically successful in recent times, both Luxembourg and Qatar have leaders who accept the principle that the future belongs to education and science, though they have not granted their universities full autonomy. Elites in these countries believe that to be successful, their countries must have a research university that adequately meets national needs, attracts their country's best students and competes worldwide. Without sustaining considerable cross-border migration and relying on the global mobility of faculty, staff and students, these international national universities would have to close their doors.

Acknowledgements

My thanks to Bernhard Streitwieser for valuable feedback on an earlier draft of this chapter, portions of which have appeared in Powell (2012). For helpful comments, I also thank the participants in the project on 'Science Productivity, Higher Education Research Development and the Knowledge Society' (SPHERE), especially John Crist of Georgetown University School of Foreign Service in Qatar. This publication was made possible by NPRP Grant 5-1021-5-159 from the Qatar National Research Fund, a member of Qatar Foundation. The views expressed herein are solely those of the author.

Notes

[1] http://www.rtl.com

[2] http://www.aljazeera.com

[3] http://www.uni-gr.eu

[4] http://www.uni.lu (2012).

[5] see http://www.university-autonomy.eu

References

Altbach, P.G. (2005) Globalization and the University: myths and realities in an unequal world, in *The NEA 2005 Almanac of Higher Education*, pp. 63-74. Washington, DC: National Education Association.

Bacchus, M.K. (2008) The Education Challenges Facing Small Nation States in the Increasingly Competitive Global Economy of the Twenty-First Century, *Comparative Education*, 44(2), 127-145.

Baker, D.P. (in press) *The Schooled Society: the educational transformation of global culture*. Redwood City, CA: Stanford University Press.

Braband, G. (2011) Eine gesamtstaatliche Aufgabe? Hochschulpolitik in Kanada und Deutschland, *Die Hochschule. Journal für Wissenschaft und Bildung*, 20(1), 95-109.

Crist, J.T. (2013) International Perspectives: the growing presence of social science in Qatar, *ASA Footnotes*, 41(2), 9-10.

Crossley, M., Bray, M. & Packer, S. (2011) *Education in Small States: policies and priorities*. London: Commonwealth Secretariat.

Donn, G. & Al Manthri, Y. (2010) *Globalisation and Higher Education in the Arab Gulf States*. Oxford: Symposium Books.

Donn, G. & Al Manthri, Y. (Eds) (2013) *Education in the Broader Middle East: borrowing a baroque arsenal*. Oxford: Symposium Books.

Drori, G.S., Meyer, J.W., Ramirez, F.O. & Schofer, E. (2003) *Science in the Modern World Polity*. Stanford: Stanford University Press.

European Commission (2010) *A Vision for Strengthening World-Class Research Infrastructures in the European Research Area*. Luxembourg: European Commission.

Fromherz, A.J. (2012) *Qatar: a modern history*. Washington, DC: Georgetown University Press.

Geiger, R. & Sá, C. (2008) *Tapping the Riches of Science: American universities and the promise of economic growth*. Cambridge, MA: Harvard University Press.

Graf, L. (2009) Applying the Varieties of Capitalism Approach to Higher Education: comparing the internationalization of German and British universities, *European Journal of Education*, 44(4), 569-585.

Hanauer, E. & Phan, A. (2011) Middle East: global higher education's boldest step, *University World News Global Edition*, no. 185, 21 August. http://www.universityworldnews.com/article.php?story=20110819173149188&query=hanauer

Hazelkorn, E. (2013) Reflections on a Decade of Global Rankings, *Beiträge zur Hochschulforschung*, 35(2), 8-33.

Human Rights Watch (2012) Qatar: migrant construction workers face abuse. http://www.hrw.org/news/2012/06/12/

Institute of International Education (2012) *Open Doors: report on international educational exchange.* New York: IIE.

International Monetary Fund (2011) World Economic Outlook Database. http://www.imf.org/external/ns/cs.aspx?id=28

Kane, T. (2013) Higher Education in Qatar: does a US medical school break the baroque arsenal? In G. Donn & Y. Al Manthri (Eds) *Education in the Broader Middle East: borrowing a baroque arsenal*, pp. 85-105. Oxford: Symposium Books.

Lane, J. & Kinser, K. (Eds) (2011) Multinational Colleges and Universities: leading, governing, and managing international branch campuses. *New Directions for Higher Education*, no. 155. San Francisco: Jossey-Bass.

Levin, H.M., Jeong, D.W. & Ou, D. (2006) What is a World Class University? Teachers College Working Paper C12. http://www.tc.columbia.edu/centers/coce/pdf_files/ c12.pdf

Lewin, T. (2008) In Oil-Rich Mideast, Shades of the Ivy League, *The New York Times*, 11 February. http://www.nytimes.com/2008/02/11/education/11global.html

Martin, M. & Bray, M. (Eds) (2011) *Tertiary Education in Small States: planning in the context of globalization.* Paris: International Institute for Educational Planning/UNESCO.

Meyer, M.B. (2008) The Dynamics of Science in a Small Country: the case of Luxembourg, *Science and Public Policy*, 35(5), 361-371.

Miller-Idriss, C. & Hanauer, E. (2011) Transnational Higher Education: offshore campuses in the Middle East, *Comparative Education*, 47(2), 181-207.

Mohrman, K., Ma, W. & Baker, D.P. (2008) The Research University in Transition: the emerging global model, *Higher Education Policy*, 21(1), 5-27.

Moini, J.S., Bikson, T.K., Neu, C.R., DeSisto, L., Al Hamadi, M. & Al Thani, J. (2009) *The Reform of Qatar University.* Doha: Rand-Qatar Policy Institute.

Münch, R. (2011) *Akademischer Kapitalismus.* Frankfurt am Main: Suhrkamp.

Organisation for Economic Cooperation and Development (2011) *Education at a Glance 2011: OECD indicators.* Paris: OECD.

Phan, A. (2010) A New Paradigm of Educational Borrowing in the Gulf States: the Qatari example. Middle East Institute, 14 December. http://www.mei.edu/content/new-paradigm-educational-borrowing-gulf-states-qatari-example

Powell, J.J.W. (2012) Small State, Large World, Global University? Comparing Ascendant National Universities in Luxembourg and Qatar, *Current Issues in Comparative Education*, 15(1), 100-113.

Powell, J.J.W., Bernhard, N. & Graf, L. (2012) The Emergent European Model in Skill Formation: comparing higher education and vocational training in the Bologna and Copenhagen processes, *Sociology of Education*, 85(3), 240-258.

Powell, J.J.W. & Finger, C. (2013) The Bologna Process's Model of Mobility in Europe: the relationship of its spatial and social dimensions, *European Educational Research Journal*, 12(2), 270-285.

Qatar (n.d.) *Qatar National Vision 2030*. Doha: General Secretariat for Development Planning.

Qatar (2012) *Qatar in Figures 2012*. Doha: Qatar Statistics Authority.

Qatar Foundation (2013) *Qatar National Research Strategy 2012*. Doha: Qatar Foundation. http://www.qf.org.qa/news/347

Qatar University (2010) *Qatar University 2009-2010*. Doha: QU.

Ramirez, F.O. (2006) Growing Commonalities and Persistent Differences in Higher Education, in H.-D. Meyer & B. Rowan (Eds) *The New Institutionalism in Education*, pp. 123-142. Albany: SUNY Press.

Ramirez, F.O. & Meyer, J.W. (2013) Universalizing the University in a World Society, in J.C. Shin & B.M. Kehm (Eds) *Institutionalization of World Class Universities in Global Competition*, pp. 257-273. Heidelberg: Springer.

Rohstock, A. (2010) Wider die Gleichmacherei! Luxemburgs langer Weg zur Universität 1848-2003, *Forum für Politik, Gesellschaft und Kultur in Luxemburg*, no. 301, 43-46.

Rohstock, A. & Schreiber, C. (2012) The Grand Duchy on the Grand Tour: a historical study of student migration in Luxembourg, *Paedagogica Historica*, 49(2), 174-193.

Rubin, A. (2012) Higher Education Reform in the Arab World: the model of Qatar. Middle East Institute, 31 July. http://www.mei.edu/content/higher-education-reform-arab-world-model-qatar

Salmi, J. (2009) *The Challenge of Establishing World-Class Universities*. Washington, DC: World Bank.

Schofer, E. & Meyer, J.W. (2005) The Worldwide Expansion of Higher Education in the Twentieth Century, *American Sociological Review*, 70(6), 898-920.

Steiner-Khamsi, G. (2010) The Politics and Economics of Comparison, *Comparative Education Review*, 54(3), 323-342.

Streitwieser, B. (2012) Editorial, *Research in Comparative and International Education*, 7(1), 1-4. Special issue on 'Research on Study Abroad, Mobility, and Student Exchange in Comparative Education Scholarship'.

University of Luxembourg (2013) *Facts and Figures 2013*. Luxembourg: University of Luxembourg.

Wood, C.H. (2011) Institutional Ethos: replicating the student experience, *New Directions for Higher Education*, no. 155, 29-39.

CHAPTER 9

Seek Knowledge Throughout the World? Mobility in Islamic Higher Education

ANTHONY WELCH

ABSTRACT While Southeast Asia as a region is generally poorly represented in scholarship on higher education, this is even more the case when considering Islamic higher education in the region. While patterns of mobility within the Islamic world are ancient, with medieval scholarly centres such as Baghdad, Cairo and Alexandria attracting scholars and students from many parts, scholarly mobility in Southeast Asia also has its own history. The earlier part of the chapter concentrates on the flowering of Islamic scholarly centres, with a particular focus on mobility. Subsequently, contemporary Islamic higher education in Southeast Asia, particularly in countries such as Malaysia and Indonesia, is analysed, focusing particularly on international mobility patterns, particularly of students. This includes both regionalism (students from within Southeast Asia travelling to other countries within the region to pursue Islamic higher education) and efforts by countries such as Malaysia to recruit significant numbers of students from the Gulf states and Arab world, thereby reversing traditional paths of mobility.

... the Qur'an and Hadith ... made it obligatory for [Muslims] to pursue truth freely from all possible sources, but also contained certain guiding principles that could provide a secure foundation for the development of religious and secular sciences. ... several traditions ... indicate that a scholar's sleep is more valuable than an ignorant believer's journey for pilgrimage (hajj) and participation in holy war, and that the drops of a scholar's ink are more sacred than the blood of a martyr. (Akhtar, n.d.)

Another very telling feature of contemporary Islamic societies is the near absence of world-class universities. The standard of publicly funded universities is dismal by international standards. (Hassan, 2008, p. 293)

He who travels in search of knowledge travels along Allah's path to Paradise. (Mohammed [Hadith 1631])

According to many scholars of Islam, the evidence for the prophet Mohammed's injunction 'Seek knowledge throughout the World, even if you have to go to China' in the Hadith is unreliable.[1] Whatever its status, there can be no doubt as to the longstanding, rich tradition of scholarly mobility within Islamic higher learning. Both the history of academic mobility within Islam and current patterns of mobility reveal the important role of knowledge mobility, as well as that of scholars and teachers.

The Beginnings

The history of education is still markedly biased towards the West and the evolution of Graeco-Roman intellectual traditions. This is no less true when referring to the history of scholarly mobility (Welch, 2008). This intellectual bias ignores the enormous contributions of often-peripatetic scholars from non-Western traditions, such as Confucianism and Islam, to the development of knowledge, including in both the natural and social sciences (Welch, 2005; Connell, 2007).

For Islam, this included more than the few who appear in (some) Western histories, such as the widely travelled Persian Ibn Sina (980-1037), the Cordoban Ibn Rushd (1126-98), who died in Marrakech, and the peripatetic Tunisian Ibn Khaldun (1332-1406). Other notables among this crop of great Islamic scholars included al-Jabir, al-Biruni, al-Uqlidisi, al-Khwarizmi, al-Kindi, Ibn al-Haytham, al-Tūsi and al-Birūni. Several were peripatetic scholars, frequenting some of the major intellectual hubs of the Islamic world.

Of several centres of Muslim higher learning from the ancient world, the Great Library of Alexandria, founded by Ptolemy I (323-283 BCE), was probably the earliest. Before its destruction, responsibility for which has been variously ascribed to, *inter alia*, Julius Caesar, Aurelian, Theophilus or the Caliph Omar (Phillips, 2010), Alexandria was perhaps the first library to systematically set out to collect works from throughout the known world: the obsession of the early Ptolemys extended to, 'if possible, all the books in the world' (El-Abbadi, 1990, p. 159). Situated at a strategic point that made it an international trade hub, a royal mandate assigned scholars to travel from Alexandria to centres such as Rhodes and Athens, to purchase works from their book fairs. At the same time, vessels that visited Alexandria were combed for books, which were then removed and copied (with the originals being held and only copies subsequently returned to their owners) (Phillips, 2010). Works in different languages that were plundered in this way were translated into Greek, providing standardised (re)constructions of major Greek works (Blum, 1991; Casson, 2001). As a leading producer of papyrus, Alexandria also became a scholarly centre for scribes to transcribe copies of books that were then sent abroad; the income from such activities helped sustain the Library's activities. The library's holdings were estimated to total between 400,000 and 700,000 papyrus scrolls.

Great libraries comprise more than books, however; they also demand scholars. A handsome endowment by Ptolemy ensured that the Library was able to offer scholars from abroad 'free board, lodgings, servants, tax exemptions, and handsome salaries – for life' (Phillips, 2010). Scholars attracted by such generous benefits included Strabo (the geographer), Zenodotus (literary critic and scholar of Homer), Aristophanes, Eratosthenes (Libyan-born scholar and librarian), Herophilus (scholar of medicine), Euclid and Archimedes, while Aristotle's own library, complemented by that of his follower Theophrastus, was an early acquisition.

But Alexandria was by no means the only early example. As early as the ninth century CE, numerous scholars were drawn to the intellectual hub of Baghdad, where Greek science and philosophy were being translated and transmitted to the Arabic-speaking world, a project that enabled not only the flowering of medieval Islamic civilisation but also paved the way for the Western twelfth-century renaissance.

Inspired by a dream in which he was visited by Aristotle, the then Caliph of Baghdad Abū Ja'far al-Ma'mūn, acclaimed by some as perhaps the greatest patron of science among Islamic rulers, founded both an observatory and his Bayt al-Hikma (House of Wisdom) in the ninth century. At a time that has often been characterised as the Dark Ages in the West (albeit with some exaggeration), Arabic was one of the key languages of science, and al-Ma'mūn is credited as initiating what was (at least until the Mongol invasion that destroyed Baghdad in 1258) perhaps the most substantial era of scholarship since ancient Greece. A keen student of the Koran, as well as mathematics, philosophy and theology (especially *Kalam*, a form of dialectical debate), al-Ma'mūn invited scholars weekly to the palace, where they were wined, dined and engaged in scholarly debate.

Scholars from throughout the Islamic empire were drawn to Baghdad and the House of Wisdom, while al-Ma'mūn's passion for knowledge saw emissaries sent great distances to obtain treasured texts: Salman, for example, was sent to Constantinople to secure Greek texts from the emperor Leo V (Leo the Armenian), while defeated enemies were at times able to pay their tribute in the form of treasured texts, rather than in gold. Perhaps the greatest translator of the time, Hunayn ibn Ishāq, for whom we have to thank the translations of Galen's work, travelled widely in search of valuable texts. Works were collected from India, Persia and Greece, then painstakingly translated into Arabic. Scholars from many regions were attracted to the intellectual hub of Baghdad. They included the polymath al-Kindi (Alkindus) (801-73), who was born in Basra but is known for introducing the work of Aristotle to the Arab world, as well as making diverse contributions in areas such as mathematics, cryptanalysis and theory of music. The great mathematician Muhammad ibn Mūsa al-Khwārizmi (c.780-c.850) was another. Hailing from Khorezm (then part of greater Persia/Iran, but in current Uzbekistan), he came to settle in Baghdad and is credited (with al-Kindi) for having introduced the Hindi decimal numerals to the Arab world as well as algebra, through his book *al-Kitab al-mukhtasar fi hisab al-jabr wa'l-muqabala* or The Book of Calculation by Completion and Balancing, in which he produced solutions to linear and quadratic equations.

Although, sadly, no trace remains of the Bayt al-Hikma, it was at the time an institution of learning comparable in stature with the great Library of Alexandria (also destroyed, but reincarnated at much the same site in 2002).

Hence it can fairly be said that knowledge, students and scholars were mobile, at a time of flowering of knowledge within the key intellectual centres of the Islamic world. Filled with texts from India, Persia and Greece, many of which were translated, by the mid-ninth century Baghdad became the intellectual centre of the civilised world, comparable to the major centres of Chinese learning of the Tang dynasty, from which they had learned how to produce paper (as opposed to papyrus or parchment), a technical advance that was subsequently used as the basis for key texts.

Of the scholars who were drawn to Baghdad from places such as Basra, Khorezm (in Uzbekistan) or the largely Christian Hira (in current Iraq), some were responsible for original advances in fields such as maths, astronomy, physics, medicine and engineering, in the great flowering of Islamic science between the eighth and fifteenth centuries, when scholarly centres of the Islamic world popularised Arabic as the language of science (Nakosteen, 1964; Makdisi, 1981), attracted scholars from far and wide, and produced teachers whose fame spread via their peripatetic profession and who, according to Makdisi, were responsible for introducing the lecture and disputation, two centuries before their inception in the West (Makdisi, 1981, 1990; Welch, 2005, pp. 73-74). The scholarly centre of Baghdad was described by Al-Khalili (2010) as 'the seed from which sprouted all the subsequent achievements of this golden age of science, from Uzbekistan in the east to Spain in the west' (*The Observer*, 2010, see also Nakosteen, 1964; Al-Khalili, 2010).

A third scholarly centre was based in Egypt's Cairo. Al-Azhar, founded by Shīites in Cairo in 970, and whose name supposedly derives from Fatima, the daughter of Mohamed, who was called Al-Zahra ('the luminous/brilliant'), was revived under the Sunni Mamluks in the mid-thirteenth century and became another magnet for scholars and students from throughout the Islamic world, especially after the defeat of the Mongols led many scholars from the East to migrate to Cairo. Based on a core curriculum of Islamic theology, law and Arab language, the programme expanded to included history, rhetoric and literature, together with Islamic philosophy, astronomy, medicine and logic.

Its fame as a centre of learning attracted, *inter alia*, Persian poet Naser-i-Khusru and the founder of the Hashashin order in Persia, Hassan-i-Sabbah. Prominent early scholars such as al-Hufi (a grammarian), Abu Abd-Allah al-Quda'i (scholar of the Hadith), and ibn-Babshad and ibn-Barakat (both grammarians) were supplemented by Abd-el-Latif, who lectured on medicine, and the great Jewish philosopher Moses Maimonides, who lectured on medicine and astronomy during the time of Saladin (c.1138-93).

That this occurred at much the same time that the army of Castille were progressively destroying Islamic centres of learning (between 1236 and 1261) in Qurtuba (Cordoba), Ishbilyya (Seville) and Balansiya (Valencia) led many scholars from Spain to migrate to Al-Azhar. The increasing expulsion of Islamic scholars from notable centres of learning on the Iberian peninsula (alluded to above), such as Seville, Granada, Valencia and Cordoba, from at least the middle of the thirteenth century, provoked widespread lamentation:

> The tap of the white ablution fount weeps in despair,
> like a passionate lover weeping at the departure of the beloved,
> over dwellings emptied of Islam, whose inhabitants now live in
> unbelief, where the mosques have become churches in which only
> bells and crosses are found. (ar-Rundi, in Monroe, 1974, p. 333)

but helped seed centres such as Al-Azhar. The swift abandonment of the Treaty of Granada, developed by Ferdinand and Isabella after conquering the city, that had vouchsafed Muslims the right to retain their language, laws and customs, led by 1499 to the mass burnings of books: 'Muslim religious leaders were persuaded to hand over more than 5000 priceless books with ornamental bindings, which were then consigned to the flames; only some books on medicine were spared' (Boase, 1990; see also Boase 2008). During the reign of Phillip III, perhaps 300,000 Muslims, of whom nominally converted individuals were known as Moriscos, were expelled between the years 1609 and 1614.

Al-Azhar also became a magnet for Western scholars, in part due to its library that is now thought to be second in importance only to the Egyptian National Library.

Islamic Mobility in Southeast Asia

The great era of Islamic higher learning did not endure, however, and, somewhat like China, was largely overtaken by the rise of Western science from the seventeenth century, and the later developments in social sciences. As has oft been lamented by Muslim scholars, and reports, universities in the Islamic world are now conspicuously absent from the world's leading research institutions (Selvaratnam, 1985; Malaysian Ministry of Higher Education, 2006; Hassan, 2008). Indeed, among the much-cited Shanghai

Jiao Tong Academic Ranking of World Universities index of the world's leading 500 universities, only one, the University of Istanbul, is included (and it languishes in the lower reaches).

On the other hand, Islamic centres of learning have spread throughout the world, including to the diverse region of Southeast Asia (Day & Bin Muhammad, 2011), containing the most populous Muslim-majority nation, Indonesia, with a total population of approximately 240 million, 90% of whom are Muslims, and Malaysia (total population 25 million, of whom around 60% are Muslims).

Significant patterns of mobility among students, scholars and knowledge persist in these two notable regional examples (Welch, 2012; Welch & Syafi'i, 2013). And this is not new: Islamic higher learning in the region now known as Malaysia and Indonesia is centuries old, as are connections to other centres of Islamic scholarship, for example the venerable Al-Azhar (Welch & Syafi'i, 2013). Smaller centres of Islamic higher education also exist in the Southern Philippines, Thailand and Brunei. While Myanmar has a significant Islamic population, of whom the Rohingya are the largest group, there are no designated Islamic universities in the country (Welch & Hayden, 2013). Indeed, there are significant regional dimensions to Islamic higher education in Southeast Asia, as well as important trans-regional currents (Welch, 2011b, 2012; Welch & Syafi'i, 2013).

Scholarly Mobility in Indonesia and Malaysia

The remaining sections of the chapter treat the mobility surrounding Islamic higher education in these two nation-states, each of which faces different mobility scenarios, it is argued, as a result of different levels of development. An example is per capita GDP, which was US$9120 for Malaysia compared with US$3230 for Indonesia (United Nations Development Programme [UNDP], 2005, p. 20), while Human Development Index rankings also differ appreciably: from 59 (Malaysia) to 111 (Indonesia) (UNDP, 2005). Even the term *Islamic higher education* embraces a spectrum of institutions; yet, although each of the two presents a strikingly different picture, Islam figures significantly in each, as do patterns of mobility. It is argued, however, that the patterns of mobility evident in each reflect not merely differential states of development, but also alternative cultural and linguistic profiles (Crystal, 1997; Malaysia, 2011; Welch, 2011b, pp. 1-20). There is clearly a significant regional dimension to Islamic higher education in Southeast Asia, as well as some important trans-regional dimensions (Welch, 2012; Welch & Syafi'i, 2013).

Of the two ministries responsible for education in Indonesia, one is specific to Islamic institutions of education, funding both *Madrassahs* at the secondary level and Islamic higher education institutions (HEIs), of various kinds. Although Islam lacks the formal status within the Indonesian constitution accorded by its neighbour (although an attempt was made in

1959 to enshrine its status within the constitution), some 90% of the populace are adherents. Islamic HEIs are administered by the Ministry of Religious Affairs, a fact that, rather like the same organisational distinction at the secondary level (the *Madrassah*), condemns Islamic HEIs to very modest funding (Amirrachman et al, 2008). In effect, then, Islamic HEIs in Indonesia are a periphery within a periphery (see Altbach, 1994, 1998, 2002; Welch, 2011b; Welch & Syafi'i, 2013).

Malaysia

The particular constitutional position of Islam in Malaysia, by contrast, is one in which *Bumiputras* (ethnic Malays) are constitutionally defined as Muslims. In turn, this is part of a wider picture whereby funding for public HEIs comes from the state, and where longstanding ethnic quotas have restricted enrolments in public HEIs by non-*Bumiputras* (the Chinese and Indian minorities, some of whom, notably among the latter, are Muslims), forcing many into the private sector or overseas.

Some ethnic Chinese or Indian graduates do not return, leading to a persisting problem with brain drain. Most recently, however, as lamented in a recent parliamentary report, brain drain has extended to significant numbers of high-skilled *Bumiputras*, enticed either by targeted migration schemes in countries such as Canada or Australia (the latter of which has moved to establish several branch campuses in Malaysia [Welch, 2011a]) or the significantly enhanced incomes available in neighbouring Singapore (whose economy recently outgrew that of Malaysia, despite a population less than 20% its size). In the report, push factors were also cited as being important:

> 140,000 left the country, probably for good, in 2007. Between March 2008 and August 2009, that figure more than doubled to 305,000, as talented people pulled up stakes, apparently disillusioned by rising crime, a tainted judiciary, human rights abuses, an outmoded education system and other concerns. (Asia Sentinel, 2010)

Against this, however, Malaysia has attracted substantial numbers of students to its universities, from within and without the region. Many are Muslims. Malaysia's determined efforts to develop itself into an Eduhub, attracting students from the region and beyond to its HEIs, have in part traded on its status as an Islamic culture, in order to attract international students who wish to study in an Islamic environment, using the international languages of Arabic or English. While by no means all international students enrolled in Malaysian higher education stemmed from Islamic countries, by 2007 Indonesia had replaced China as the largest regional source by 2007, while Bangladesh was the third largest source. Extra-regional sources contributed much less overall, although again the three largest sending countries were Islamic, at least in part: Iran, followed by Nigeria and Yemen. Table I shows that, of the almost 87,000 international students enrolled in Malaysian HEIs in 2010, with by far the largest proportion in the more entrepreneurial private sector, a large number of the top 10 source countries are those with a substantial Muslim proportion.

Country	Public sector total	Private sector total	Total
China	2168	8046	10,214
Iran	4814	7009	11,823
Indonesia	6119	3769	9888
Nigeria	737	5080	5817
Yemen	1809	3522	5331
Libya	1125	2805	3930
Sudan	596	2241	2837
Botswana	–	1909	1909
Saudi Arabia	668	1584	2252
Bangladesh	538	1503	2041
Total	18,574	37,468	56,042

Table I. Top ten source countries, Malaysian higher education, public and private, 2010.
Source: Ministry of Higher Education (2010a, b).

Evident from Table I is that the public sector has been far less dynamic in promoting itself to prospective international students relative to the private sector, which by 2008 was attracting 50,000 students alone, with some HEIs also establishing branch campuses in Islamic countries such as Pakistan and Indonesia. Overall, the private sector attracts around two-thirds of total international enrolments, although data about the extent to which such enrolments are from Islamic countries or contexts are less clear. This is because some of the source countries for Malaysia's international enrolments, such as China, Nigeria and India, which in 2007 accounted for 6468, 2884 and 1350 students respectively, are only partly Muslim. Overall, however, the proportion is substantial. Part of the attractiveness of private sector HEIs is their freedom to offer programmes in English (Crystal, 1997), something long denied to their public sector peers although, as Table II shows, international enrolments have grown faster in the public sector for the years 2003-10, off a much lower base.

A clear intention to attract Muslim students was enunciated in recent ministerial pronouncements and followed up by visits by the then Minister, Mohamed Khaled Nordi, to countries such as Dubai. The stated rationale was as follows:

> We're providing access to our higher education, places in our universities, because we believe that this is one way of contributing towards the development of our fellow Muslim countries. (Bernama, 2009a)

	2003	2004	2005	2006	2007	2010
Public HEIs	5239	5735	6622	7941	14,324	24,214
Private HEIs	25,158	25,939	33,903	36,449	33,604	62,715
Total	30,397	31,674	40,525	44,390	47,928	86,929

Table II. International enrolments, Malaysian
higher education, public and private, 2003-10.
Source: Ministry of Higher Education (2010a, b), Welch (2011b, p. 70).

At the same time, more pragmatic considerations were also apparent, with Minister Khaled citing the fact that in the Middle East and North Africa (MENA) region, some 43 million young people were eligible for higher education. As part of its effort to raise its educational and strategic profile internationally, the Islamic world was being systematically targeted:

> You will see that there will be a consistent and constant effort by Malaysia, especially my Ministry, to come over to this region to establish closer ties with governments and officials responsible for higher education so that they will always consider Malaysia whenever they decide to send their students for further studies. (Bernama, 2009a)

While, as indicated above, it is not possible to be entirely precise about the proportion that Muslim students occupy of total international enrolments, it is clearly significant. According to the Minister, statistics indicated that Malaysia was then home to a total of 60,000 foreign students (including not merely those in higher education). Of these, he claimed about 18,000 (30%) were from the MENA region. Source countries included Yemen, Sudan, Iran, Iraq, Saudi Arabia, Somalia, Libya, Jordan, Oman, Palestine, Syria, Egypt, Turkey, Algeria, Bahrain, Lebanon, Qatar and the United Arab Emirates. While it is not possible to extrapolate from these overall figures to higher education, examination of the data on international enrolments in public and private HEIs indicates that the proportion is at least 50%. Ministry figures for 2010 register 10,024 students from Middle Eastern countries enrolled in public HEIs (Ministry of Higher Education, 2010a). As was seen in Table I, Iran alone had 11,800 students studying for degrees in Malaysia. And, as was seen above, the traffic is in both directions – it is still the case that some young Malaysians take the opportunity to further their studies in an Islamic context by enrolling in institutions such as Egypt's famed Al-Azhar.

This was by no means new: Islam had been a significant dimension of mobility within Malaysian higher education for some time. The distinctive role played by the International Islamic University of Malaysia (IIUM), in part funded by eight other Islamic states and which has representation from the Organisation of the Islamic Conference, has for some time been an important component of overall mobility in public sector HEIs. Founded in

1983, it offered courses in the international languages of Arabic and English, and was shortly followed by Universiti Utara Malaysia (the University of North Malaysia) in 1984. IIUM was founded on a different premise to the other HEIs, however, in that its teaching and ideology were to be based specifically on Islamic beliefs:

> The purpose of this university is to strengthen cooperation and friendship among Islamic intellectuals, provide facilities for Islamic studies, and train skilled manpower for development – on the basis of Islamic Principles. (Selvaratnam, 1985, p. 192)

Its role in internationalising Islamic higher education in Malaysia is particularly significant. The fact that teaching was conducted in Arabic and English provided a solid platform for attracting international students, particularly from the Islamic world. International enrolments at the institution rose from 1800 (or 13.7% of total enrolments) in 1997-98, to 2629 in 2000, although the latter figure represented a declining proportion (8.6%), since overall numbers had risen sharply. By 2003-04, IIUM attracted 31.2% of all international enrolments in public sector universities and 38.4% of all international staff (Kaur et al, 2008, p. 15).

Indonesia

Despite a population almost 10 times that of Malaysia, Indonesia is far less able than its much smaller neighbour to project its presence as a centre of Islamic learning that might attract tertiary students from within and beyond the region to its HEIs. This is due both to its lower level of development and to its much lower capacity to deliver programmes in international languages, notably English (Welch, 2012). As was seen above, it is far more likely that its own students travel to study in nearby Malaysia, where, despite intermittent bilateral difficulties, the languages are similar and the cultures are similar, including Islam.

The earliest forms of Indonesian higher learning were Islamic, with some of its brightest pupils going on to postgraduate studies at universities in the Middle East, such as Al-Azhar in Cairo. After independence in 1945, Islamic HEIs such as the Indonesian Islamic University in Yogyakarta were established. Muhammadijah University in Jakarta and Nahdatul Ulama University in Bandung were associated with their respective Islamic political parties (Buchori & Malik, 2004; Welch, 2007, 2011b, pp. 21-52).

Demand for Islamic higher education was substantial, especially in the provinces, although the structure, content and duration of degrees broadly paralleled that of public HEIs. Graduates of accredited institutions currently have equivalent status to public HEI graduates.

Both the State Islamic University and the nine other Islamic Institutes receive funding from overseas, including from Arab states such as Saudi Arabia. Universitas Al-Azhar, Indonesia, was established by a foundation

(Yayasan Pesantren Islam Al-Azhar) with six faculties, including Economics, Science and Technology, Psychology and Education, Languages (comprising Japanese, English, Arabic and Chinese), Law and Agama Islam. While it takes its name from the ancient Islamic university in Cairo, it is difficult to determine the precise flows of students and staff to and from other parts of the Islamic world.

Malaysia and Indonesia Compared

In this context, including some tensions between an overall mainstream, syncretic Islam and more conservative and fundamentalist elements (Hefner & Zaman, 2007; Dhume, 2008), an overall model of Islamic higher education is untenable, yet it is clear that while the cultural imaginary differs, Islam occupies an important place within the higher education system of each. Clearly however, Malaysia's greater wealth and better developed universities, and ability to offer programmes in English and Arabic, position it far better than Indonesia to offer programmes to Muslims who wish to study abroad in an Islamic context. In 2010, it chose one of its major public universities, the Universiti Sains Malaysia, to become an 'Apex' university, with clear expectations of a swift rise in international rankings (Bernama, 2009b).

It has already moved to position itself as an Eduhub within the region, and currently attracts over 80,000 international students to its universities and colleges, with plans to reach 100,000 within the next few years. As indicated above, significant numbers of these international students will be Muslims. While both Indonesia and Malaysia could still be argued to be peripheral within the global knowledge system (Altbach, 1994, 1998, 2002), Malaysia's situation is far stronger than its neighbour's, with an ambitious agenda to extend its influence, both regionally and trans-regionally. Its capacity to attract Islamic students and staff is much enhanced relative to Indonesia, as is its capacity to contribute meaningfully to pan-Islamic initiatives in higher education, such as the Federation of the Universities of the Islamic World, the Islamic Body for Quality and Accreditation, the Draft Strategy on the Promotion of University Education in the Islamic World, and Islamic Conference of Ministers of Higher Education and Scientific Research (*University World News*, 2010). More broadly, this includes contributions to the development of an Islamic Higher Education Area, which takes its inspiration from the European initiative of the same name, and which has, as one of its key aims, to 'foster stronger cooperation among its member states and their universities and higher education learning institutions' (ScienceDev, n.d., p. 16).

Conclusion

Mobility in Islamic higher learning has a long and illustrious history, having contributed notably to the development of knowledge worldwide. While over the last several centuries its scientific lead was lost, largely to the West, this did not inhibit Islamic higher learning from spreading throughout many parts of the world. Southeast Asia, including the most populous Muslim-majority nation of Indonesia, represents a dynamic and diverse arena of Islamic higher education, including smaller pockets in states such as Thailand and the Philippines.[2]

Current pan-Islamic efforts include key aims to foster more mobility, such as 'furthering cooperation in such a way as to enhance the exchange of experiences, studies, programmes and visits in the fields of education, science, culture and technology' (ScienceDev, n.d., p. 22), and 'encouraging a significant increase in the number of joint programmes and the creation of flexible curricula, as well as urging their institutions to take greater responsibility for staff and student mobility, more equitably balanced between countries across the IHEA [Islamic Higher Education Area]' (ScienceDev, n.d., p. 27). This may take some doing, given that, of Malaysia's major scientific collaborators, for example, none of the top eight were Islamic nations (Day & Bin Muhammad, 2011, p. 91), but if successful, and with greater progress in rebuilding leading centres of Islamic learning (Lysaght, 2008; BBC, 2011), it may be possible that such centres could once again become magnets for scholars and students, and contribute significantly to the advancement of knowledge worldwide.

Notes

[1] Although cited by some, other scholars argue that this injunction does not appear in any reliable Hadith collection, but only in some less authoritative works. According to such scholars, the evidence for this saying is based on a weak and unreliable chain of narrators; see Al-Mawrid (2011).

[2] Narathiwat University, in southern Thailand, for example, has an agreement with Egypt's Al-Azhar University that brings a teacher from the latter to teach Islamic Studies to students at Narathiwat, while also offering 80 places to such students to study at Al-Azhar. Scholarships for the Thai students are provided by the Egyptian government.

References

Akhtar, S. (n.d.) The Islamic Context of Knowledge, *Al Tawhid*, 12(3), p. 3.

Al-Khalili, J. (2010) *Pathfinders. The Golden Age of Arabic Science*. London: Allen Lane.

Al-Mawrid (2011) Question and Answer. http://www.al-mawrid.org/pages/questions_english_detail.php?qid=1084&cid=511

Altbach, P. (1994) International Knowledge Networks, in T. Husen & T.N. Postlethwaite (Eds) *The International Encyclopaedia of Education*. Oxford: Pergamon.

Altbach, P. (1998) Gigantic Peripheries: India and China in the world knowledge system, in *Comparative Higher Education: knowledge, the university and development*. Greenwich: Ablex.

Altbach, P. (2002) Centres and Peripheries in the Academic Profession: the special challenges of developing countries, in *The Decline of the Guru. The Decline of the Profession in Middle and Lower Income Countries*. New York: Palgrave.

Amirrachman, A., Syafi'i, S. & Welch, A. (2008) Decentralising Indonesian Education. The Promise and the Price, *World Studies in Education*, 9(1), 31-54.

Asia Sentinel (2010) Malaysia's Brain Drain. http://www.asiasentinel.com/index.php?option=com_content&task=view&id=230 8&Itemid=199

BBC (2011) Turning Knowledge into the New Oil. http://www.bbc.co.uk/news/business-12680358

Bernama (2009a) Malaysia to Boost Muslim Progress Through Education. http://www.bernama.com/bernama/v3/news_lite.php?id=381479

Bernama (2009b) USM is Malaysia's APEX University. http://www.bernama.com/bernama/v3/news_lite.php?id=356958

Blum, R. (1991) *The Alexandrian Library and the Origins of Bibliography*. Madison: University of Wisconsin Press.

Boase, R. (1990) The Morisco Expulsion and Diaspora: an example of racial and religious intolerance, in D. Hook & B. Taylor (Eds) *Cultures in Contact in Medieval Spain: historical and literary essays presented to L.P. Harvey*. London: Kings College, Medieval Studies.

Boase, R. (2008) The Muslim Expulsion from Spain: an early example of religious and ethnic cleansing. theamericanmuslim.org/tam/php.features/articles/the_muslim_expulsion_from_sp ain_an_early_example_of_religious_and_ethnic_cl/

Buchori, M. & Malik, A. (2004) Higher Education in Indonesia, in P. Altbach & T. Umakoshi (Eds) *Asian Universities. Historical Perspectives and Contemporary Challenges*, pp. 249-278. Baltimore: Johns Hopkins University Press.

Casson, L. (2001) *Libraries in the Ancient World*. New Haven: Yale University Press.

Connell, R. (2007) *Southern Theory. The Global Dynamics of Knowledge in Social Science*. Sydney: Allen & Unwin.

Crystal, D. (1997) *English as a Global Language*. Cambridge: Cambridge University Press.

Day, N. & Bin Muhammad, Amran (2011) *Malaysia. The Atlas of Islamic-World Science and Innovation. Country Case Study No. 1.* The Royal Society. http://royalsociety.org/uploadedFiles/Royal_Society_Content/policy/publications/ 2011/4294976146.pdf

Dhume, S. (2008) *My Friend the Fanatic. Travels With an Indonesian Islamist*. Melbourne: Text Publishing Company.

El-Abbadi, M. (1990) *The Life and Fate of the Ancient Library of Alexandria*. Paris: UNESCO.

Hassan, R. (2008) *Inside Muslim Minds*. Melbourne: Melbourne University Press.

Hefner, R. & Zaman, M. (Eds) (2007) *Schooling Islam. The Culture and Politics of Modern Muslim Education*. Princeton: Princeton University Press.

Kaur, S., Sirat, M. & Azman, N. (2008) *Globalisation and Internationalisation of Higher Education in Malaysia*. Penang: Universiti Sains Malaysia Press.

Lysaght, G. (2008) The Need for Higher Education in the Developmental State: Indonesia and Malaysia, in M. Shuib, S. Kaur & R. Jamaludin (Eds) *Governance and Leadership in Higher Education*. Penang: Universiti Sains Malaysia Press.

Makdisi, G. (1990) *Religion, Law and Learning in Classical Islam*. Aldershot: Variorum.

Makdisi, G. (1981) *The Rise of Colleges. Institutions of Learning in Islam and the West*. Edinburgh: Edinburgh University Press.

Ministry of Higher Education (2006) *Report by the Committee to Study, Review and Make Recommendations Concerning the Development and Direction of Higher Education in Malaysia*. Kuala Lumpur: MOHE.

Ministry of Higher Education (2010a) *Institusi Pengajian Tinggi Awam (IPTA)* [Public higher education institution (Public HEI)]. Kuala Lumpur: MOHE.

Ministry of Higher Education (2010b) *Institusi Pengajian Tinggi Swasta (IPTS)* [Private higher education institution (Private HEI)]. Kuala Lumpur: MOHE.

Monroe, J. (Ed.) (1974) *Hispano-Arabic Poetry: a student anthology*. Berkeley: University of California Press.

Nakosteen, M. (1964) *History of Islamic Origins of Western Education. AD 800-1350*. Boulder: University of Colorado Press.

The Observer (2010) When Baghdad Was Centre of the Scientific World, 26 September.

Phillips, H. (2010) The Great Library of Alexandria? http://unllib.unl.edu/LPP/phillips.htm

ScienceDev (n.d.) Towards the Islamic Higher Education Area. sciencedev.net/Docs/ISESCO_document_2.doc

Selvaratnam, V. (1985) The Higher Education System in Malaysia: metropolitan, cross-national, peripheral or national? *Higher Education*, 14(5), 477-496.

United Nations Development Programme (2005) Southeast Asia Human Development Report (SEAHDR). In *Regional Economic Integration and Regional Cooperation in Southeast Asia: deepening and broadening the benefits for human development*. New York: UNDP.

University World News (2010) Islamic States. Boosting Scientific Cooperation, 31 October. http://top-colleges.onlineschoolnet.com/2010/10/31/ISLAMIC-STATES-Boosting-higher-education-cooperation-University-World-News/

Welch, A. (2005) From Peregrinatio Academica to the Global Academic: the internationalisation of the profession, in A. Welch (Ed.) *The Professoriate. Profile of a Profession*. Dordrecht: Springer.

Welch, A. (2007) Blurred Vision. Public and Private Higher Education in Indonesia, *Higher Education*, 54(5), 665-687.

Welch, A. (2008) Myths and Modes of Mobility: the changing face of academic mobility in the global era, in M. Byram & F. Dervin (Eds) *Students, Staff and Mobility in Higher Education*. Newcastle: Cambridge Scholars Publishing.

Welch, A. (2011a) The Dragon, the Tiger Cubs and Higher Education. University Relations Between China and SE Asia in the GATS Era, in D. Jarvis & A. Welch (Eds) *ASEAN Industries and the Challenge From China*. London: Palgrave Macmillan.

Welch, A. (2011b) *Higher Education in SE Asia. Blurring Borders, Changing Balance*. London: Routledge.

Welch, A. (2012) Locating Indonesia Within the Emergent Regionalism of Southeast Asian Higher Education, in J. Hawkins, K.-H. Mok & D. Neubauer (Eds) *Higher Education Regionalization in Asia Pacific. Implications for Governance, Citizenship and University Transformation*, pp. 91-116. London: Palgrave Macmillan.

Welch, A. & Hayden, M. (2013) Higher Education Subsector. Myanmar Comprehensive Education Sector Review (CESR). Phase 1: Rapid Assessment. http://www.adb.org/projects/46369-001/documents

Welch, A. & Syafi'i, S. (2013) Indonesia: Islamic higher education – periphery within periphery?, in L. Symaco (Ed.) *Education in South-East Asia*, pp. 95-114. London: Bloomsbury.

CHAPTER 10

Gateways and Guest Homes: how US area studies centers serve as arbiters of scholar mobility

JONATHAN Z. FRIEDMAN
& CYNTHIA MILLER-IDRISS

ABSTRACT International mobility is central to the study of the world's cultures; yet, the quotidian ways in which it is fostered among scholars and university students are little understood. Focusing on the case of area studies centers – centers at American universities for the study of world regions – this chapter examines how these academic units serve as arbiters of global mobility, by serving both as gateways and as guest homes. In these dual and reciprocal roles, they facilitate fieldwork abroad for the students and faculty from their campuses, and host scholars from their regions of study in the USA. Drawing on a large cache of interviews with directors and administrators at 25 area studies centers from eight American universities, this chapter offers insight into the institutional factors that promote and constrict the flow of scholars across national borders. This chapter offers a unique contribution to existing scholarship, as rather than present mobility as an individual decision, this study explores the institutional dynamics that constrain the ways in which mobility is organized and facilitated. These processes are necessary to comprehend if internationalization as a broad project is to be advanced.

In recent years, much discussion of the globalization of higher education has centered on the increasing cross-national mobility of students and faculty as a key indicator of change. Whether called 'brain exchange' (Bhandari & Blumenthal, 2011), the 'brain train' (Knight, 2009), or 'free trade in minds' (Wildavsky, 2010), scholars argue that the unprecedented scale of individuals moving about the globe bespeaks a significant shift in students' college experience, as well as in the academic production of knowledge. Much research in this area has focused on tracking the global movements of individuals – as exemplified in the Institute of International Education's *Open Doors* report and *Project Atlas*. Yet while this work has contributed much to our understanding of trends in student and scholar mobility, it has told us little about the actors and processes that facilitate or constrain this movement. Largely unexamined are the institutional apparatuses that shape academic mobility beyond an individual's decision to go abroad.

In this chapter we begin to attend to this gap, drawing on interview data from a long-term, mixed-methods study of area studies centers at eight American universities, conducted by a team of researchers at the US Social Science Research Council. Centers for the study and promotion of different world regions, area studies centers have long been involved in the formal exchange of students and scholars across borders, helping their constituents travel abroad to conduct research and bringing in people from their regions of study for speaking engagements or as visiting faculty. Though not an original aim of the large-scale research project, analysis of the data revealed that area studies centers are reliant on the flow of individuals between the USA and their respective regions of study to fulfill their main mission: namely, the production, promotion, and dissemination of knowledge. Offering the perspective of academic units deeply engaged in facilitating international exchange, these centers form an insightful example to explore the mechanics of how mobility is organized, facilitated, and accomplished. What emerges, as will be detailed below, is the central role of these academic units as arbiters of the circulation of scholars, as they serve both as gateways to different world regions for their own campus community, and as guest homes for the visitors they host.

Existing Research on Academic Mobility

There can be little doubt that the flow of students and scholars around the world is increasing (Bhandari & Blumenthal, 2011; Brooks & Waters, 2011; De Wit et al, 2013). Individual scholars are more likely than ever to leave their native countries to take positions abroad, and there has been an increase in academic collaborations across national borders (Wildavsky, 2010). While the international exchange of ideas has long been central to the production of knowledge, the dominant view among scholars of higher education is that this increasing mobility is indicative of broader changes in how the university works and how knowledge is produced (Byram & Dervin, 2008; Gürüz, 2008).

To date, the main approach to studying academic mobility has been to examine the origins and destinations of students, and changes in this movement over time (e.g. Gürüz, 2008; Bhandari & Blumenthal, 2011; Brooks & Waters, 2011; Institute of International Education, 2012). This has been complemented by analyses of individuals' motivations for moving, and the barriers they face. Kondakci (2011), for example, looked at the 'push' and 'pull' factors that motivate international students to study in Turkey.

Caudery et al (2008) examined the motives of European students coming to study in Sweden and Denmark. Among Canadian graduate students in the social sciences and humanities, Knight and Madden (2010) found that funding was selected most often as the greatest barrier to mobility. Various studies of faculty, meanwhile, have shown that personal costs, health and safety, having a family, and the insignificance of international experience to promotion and tenure are all factors that can impede scholars' motivation to go abroad (Goodwin & Nacht, 1991; Van de Bunt-Kokhuis, 1996; Miller-Idriss & Shami, 2012).

These contributions have added much to our understanding of academic flows in the global context, but macro-level analyses of trends in student and scholar mobility tend to obscure the variety in types of movement – in terms of duration, single versus repeated trips, and reasons for travel (for discussions of this variety see Goodwin & Nacht, 1991; Altbach et al, 2010). Moreover, they tell us where people are going and where they are coming from, but not how mobility pathways are established, maintained, and promoted. For example, Knight and Madden (2010) note the existence of formal institutional linkages as a factor mediating student mobility, but they do not examine how these linkages come about. Existing scholarship has thus tended to prioritize mobility as an individual undertaking, largely presuming the institutional arrangements and supporting actors that organize and facilitate movement to be incidental. In the sections that follow, we attend to this gap in existing literature, drawing on the case of area studies centers as one such institutional arbiter of academic mobility. As we will argue, mobility ought also to be understood as a collective endeavor, where the movement of one individual takes the work of multiple people, and can serve multiple purposes as well as multiple actors' interests.

Data and Methodology

Data for this study are drawn from semi-structured interviews conducted from 2005 to 2008 with the staff of 25 area studies centers at eight American universities, as part of a long-term research project.[1] Campuses were chosen to capture variation between degree-granting and non-degree-granting centers as well as public and private institutions, and include centers drawn from across the USA geographically (including the Northeast, the South, the West Coast, and the Midwest). In total, we analyzed interviews with 57 people, which included 31 center directors, 20 assistant directors, and 6 center staff, all involved in running centers for the study of four world regions: the Middle East, Russia-Eurasia, South Asia, and Latin America. In-depth interviews allowed for rich insight into the many facets of these centers' operation, as interviewees discussed their missions, how they interface with their regions of study, and issues of internationalization on their campus.[2] Transcribed interview data were analyzed using a set of inductive codes in a computer-assisted, qualitative data analysis software program (Atlas.ti). An illustrative sample from the data codebook is presented in the Appendix.

It is difficult to generalize among area studies centers (Biddle, 2002, p. 76), much less from area studies centers to university mobility initiatives more broadly. The work of area studies centers is only one part of any given campus's efforts to internationalize; individual colleges, schools, departments, and thematic centers, to name just a few, also have funding opportunities, study abroad programs, and other initiatives to promote or facilitate student and faculty mobility. But area studies centers are also an intriguing case because they were founded in the 1950s and 1960s, and thus have a relatively long history in the context of American universities' internationalization efforts. They offer much rich experience and detail about institutional processes for facilitating mobility.

In the section that follows, we analyze area studies centers' roles in supporting the mobility of students and faculty, both outgoing from the centers to various world regions, and incoming from the regions into the center. These dual roles emerged through analysis of interviewees' explanations of how their centers support student and faculty research abroad, how they form and maintain institutional linkages to their regions of study, and how they host visiting scholars, both from the region and from across the USA. Each of these aspects of center operation proved to be multifaceted. Although there was some variation among centers, these differences did not follow any clear pattern among center demographics, such as public versus private institutions, and they were minor when compared with the overwhelming similarities in how centers facilitate mobility. The centers are thus discussed below as a homogenous group, as we summarize the range of mechanisms they use and the various challenges they face in maintaining the international exchange central to their mission.

Institutional Mechanisms for Facilitating Mobility

Area studies centers emerged during the Cold War at various American universities to promote the production and dissemination of knowledge on world regions. They were initially funded by a coalition of private foundation and federal government support. In 1958, federal support was enshrined under Title VI of the National Defense Education Act, in response to a wider recognition that producing and promoting knowledge about the world beyond America's borders was instrumental to national security (McCaughty, 1984; Biddle, 2002; Engerman, 2009). Reauthorized under the Higher Education Act of 1965, Title VI funding remains the core source of funding for many area studies centers today. Centers compete for funding in three- or four-year grant cycles administered by the US Department of Education, with those receiving funding designated as 'National Resource Centers' (NRCs). In exchange for financial support for their core operation, NRCs dispense fellowships for students to study languages around the world, and run outreach activities to educate the wider American public about their world regions, in particular through teacher education programs.

A chief method for centers to fulfill the multiple aspects of their mission is to aid in the global circulation of scholars, supporting both outgoing mobility of their own students and faculty, and incoming mobility of visiting scholars. Although these two routes may be conceived as quite different, our analysis found tremendous similarity in the mechanisms by which area studies centers support each of them. We treat them here as two sides of the same coin, seeing both avenues as integral to the overall account of academic mobility. While past accounts have examined the rationales that motivate individuals to go abroad, we ask here: by what mechanisms do area studies centers facilitate the international mobility of students and scholars? Our findings illustrate five such mechanisms through which centers aid in the mobility process. Many of these mechanisms overlap in practice, but we separate them here into discrete activities so that each can be articulated.

Housing and Administering Mobility Opportunities

First, it is common for centers to offer a variety of funding programs for their faculty and students to travel abroad as well as for visiting scholars to come in from the region. There is variation in scale and scope across the cases we studied, but most centers both provide support with their own internally competitive funding, and also serve as administrators for a variety of scholarships and programs supported by outside donors such as the US government's Foreign Language and Area Studies (FLAS) fellowships. Visitors from the region and experts on the region from elsewhere in the USA are brought in on short- and long-term programs, whether funded internally or externally, through, for example, Fulbright. Often centers co-sponsor long-term visitors with other departments on campus; many center staff gave examples of finding funding to support a visitor by approaching other departments or their supervising deans or vice-provosts for co-sponsorship. By housing and administering a variety of funding opportunities, area studies centers facilitate pathways to the region for their constituents, as well as avenues to their campus for scholars in their field. In this way, they act as arbiters of academic mobility.

Maintaining Formal Linkages

Second, centers maintain formal linkages with institutions in their regions. This mechanism for facilitating mobility includes formal exchange programs for faculty and students as well as paying membership dues to the American Overseas Research Centers, independent research centers throughout the Middle East, North Africa, and South Asia, which enable their students to study abroad more easily. As one Middle East center director explained, the center uses these memberships to 'facilitate students going there. The students get – like in Turkey – they get discounted housing, they get, they get help with visas, and with access to archives, you know, so these are very, very helpful.' Membership in these research centers, as well as in other foreign associations, aids in the mobility of students and scholars by providing an institutional home for them when abroad. Meanwhile, multiple centers gave examples of how formal exchange programs act as conduits of student and faculty exchange, facilitating traffic between foreign universities and their own campuses. While in some cases center directors felt that such formal channels were underused, in other cases they spoke of their great success. Many highlighted the work necessary to ensure spaces for their students in appropriate courses at foreign universities, and easy transfer of credits afterward. In these ways, area studies center staff form and manage the connections necessary for students and scholars to travel to their regions of study and for experts from their regions to come to the USA.

Clearinghouses

Third, most area studies serve as clearinghouses for information about their regions. Center staff discussed providing 'sensitivity training' for faculty and students from other schools across their campuses, where they summarize the 'dos and don'ts' of travelling to their regions. Centers also pass on information and publicize opportunities about funding or study abroad, as one assistant director explained, 'when they come across our radar screen.. Many centers host brown bag lunches where students returning from the region present on what they were doing abroad. One assistant director explained how she was more proactive, asking students to send her 'a very informal email' with what they liked about their programs or internships in the region, which she would then compile in a manner for other students to reference in the future. Similarly, center staff explained how they serve as information sources for visiting scholars they host, providing information about their own university and its environs, an aspect which will be discussed in more detail below. Serving as a formal channel for information exchange and a clearinghouse for travel opportunities, area studies centers thus promote and facilitate both the outgoing and incoming mobility of students and scholars.

Connecting Hubs

Fourth, area studies centers and their academic staff serve as hubs for connecting students, faculty, and visiting scholars with each other and with mobility opportunities. In addition to simply informing students about opportunities, for example, center staff can put them directly in touch with others who can help, using their personal networks. One center administrator discussed putting current students interested in internships in the region in touch with students recently returned from them. The director of a Latin

America center explained that this role turns them into 'facilitators more than active organizers', as they connect students with faculty or graduate students who know the region and its resources. A Middle East center director similarly explained: 'I usually know who to go to. So let's say the student really wants to go to Jordan to work on healthcare ... I might know someone who works in Jordan and might know someone in healthcare. And I've been able to place people that way.' Such examples were common as various interviewees discussed the informal ways in which students are linked to regional scholars through the personal networks of faculty and center staff.

Center staff also spoke of their responsibility as hosts for connecting visiting scholars to their own communities, including both the students and faculty on campus and the wider public communities they serve. In selecting and attracting visiting scholars, centers rely on their faculty's connections to the region, and in many cases use these mobility opportunities to foster stronger international collaborations. A key mechanism by which area studies centers facilitate international mobility, then, is by developing informal connections among academic communities.

Handling Logistics and Welcoming Visitors

Finally, centers support mobility simply by assisting their students and faculty with the logistics of their travel, and similarly so for visiting scholars. Some centers complete much of the paperwork for faculty to go abroad, even organizing their itineraries. Others run fellowship-writing workshops, formal exchange and study abroad programs, and help students enroll in foreign universities, including arranging home stays with local families. Interviewees also described in depth the logistical work that goes into hosting visitors. Beyond the visa process, with which other campus offices usually provide significant assistance, centers often provide office space, a mailbox, and computer access, organize and pay library fees, and advise on temporary housing, local schools, and neighborhoods. All of this logistical work takes significant time and effort, and is an important mechanism by which centers help facilitate the inflow of international scholars and the outflow of their own students and faculty.

Summary

From the discussion of these five mechanisms it is clear that there is much that area studies centers do to facilitate the mobility of students and scholars: they house and administer opportunities; maintain formal linkages and exchange programs; act as clearinghouses for information; serve as hubs connecting academic communities; and directly aid in the logistics of sending and receiving individuals. These various mechanisms can be further simplified into two essential functions that area studies centers serve, namely, as *gateways* and *guest homes*. We use the term *gateway* to encompass the multiple ways area studies centers serve as liaisons between their constituents and the foreign region. They are the institutional mediator through which students and scholars pass en route to the region, either by being awarded a travel scholarship, using information, advice or the personal connections of center staff, or even by having their trips arranged by the center on their behalf. The term *gateway* similarly encompasses the ways centers serve as a liaison for visiting scholars who utilize the center to find out information about the US campus and its environs, and to become connected to the campus community. In this way, area studies centers' *gateway* function is two-sided, helping in both incoming and outgoing mobility. Meanwhile, we use the term *guest home* to encompass the hosting function that area studies centers provide for incoming visitors. In essence, centers' role as guest home refers to their role facilitating visitors' abroad *experience*.

Exploring an institutional perspective on mobility as undertaken here reveals the importance of these two functions to the accomplishment of international movement. Though drawn from the case of area studies centers, the notion that institutional gateways and guest homes underpin international mobility is likely applicable to the mobility carried out by various programs, departments, centers, and schools in the university at large. Hence, in the following section we turn to the implications of these two dimensions for understanding how these infrastructures condition academic mobility.

Impediments to Gateways and Guest Homes

As discussed, hindrances to academic mobility are often conceived in individualistic terms, focused on personal motivations and factors that constrain international mobility (e.g. Goodwin & Nacht, 1991; van de Bunt-Kokhuis, 1996; Knight & Madden, 2010; Souto-Otero et al, 2013). While there has been some attention to institutional factors such as the availability of funding, none have explored an institutional perspective on the promotion of mobility or endeavored to understand the range of institutional factors that can constrain and shape individual trajectories. Utilizing the framework put forward above, we explore five factors that condition the operation of institutional gateways and guest homes, continuing to draw on our empirical data. As above, these factors often overlap, but they are treated discretely here to explore each individually.

Funding

While financial considerations have been found in the existing literature to have a significant impact on whether individuals go abroad (Knight & Madden, 2010; Souto-Otero et al, 2013), we find it also affects how institutions promote mobility. For example, while many center staff talked about the limitations of their resources for offering a robust array of travel opportunities to students and faculty, they also focused on the problem of existing limitations on the funding they do have being used in the ways they want. Some centers are constrained in their ability to support faculty research, for example, since Title VI funding must support core center activities directly. Various center staff also expressed frustration with the prohibition of certain countries as destinations for students to go to for language training with federal FLAS funding, such as Iran. 'It's really a problem,' stated one South Asia center director with regard to such restrictions, 'especially if we actually want to have, you know, really good quality scholarship on those countries. It's very difficult to do if you can't actually go there.'

In this sense, while centers do face funding challenges, most being extremely reliant on Title VI funding, it is not only lack of funding that poses a challenge to mobility, but also other factors that influence the ways in which center funding can be spent. On one campus, for example, an assistant director of a South Asia center was adamant that travel restrictions against going to Pakistan were resulting in students choosing other areas in which to specialize. The center's ability to serve as a gateway to that area was thus hampered by funding rules.

Personnel

As outlined above, serving as an adequate gateway and guest home takes work. Most centers are staffed by a director and an assistant director, one or two administrative assistants in charge of programming or outreach activities, and casual student employees. The overwhelming consensus from interviewees was that this was inadequate. With regard to the visa process, for example, one assistant director discussed how she had to do this herself, since it was too technical to leave to a student employee. Indeed, many commented about the challenge of high turnover rates among their student employees for maintaining their programming quality and oversight. Center staff also discussed time-consuming activities needed to properly host visitors. One assistant director explained:

> We want to make sure that they are comfortable and they know what they are doing. But we are pretty much at our limit with the amount of time that we are able to spend on it because it is very time-consuming … . to miss, you know, a few hours a day to go out and take them around and get them their card and get them their library fees paid and all this stuff. You know, it's a lot of time away from the center.

When asked, various center directors said they would use additional funding to hire another administrator in the center, to work in part either on organizing more opportunities in the region, or on the visa paperwork and logistics of hosting visitors. For many centers, the prospect of having another worker seemed to make a significant difference in what they imagined they could handle in terms of their support of outgoing and incoming students and scholars. In this sense, administrative personnel are a condition on mobility as they affect how it is organized and supported.

Space

An additional factor affecting mobility raised consistently by center staff was that of their campus space. This impacted their function as guest homes, as many listed office space as something they give to visitors. 'If they're going to be here as your guest and colleague,' stated one Russia-Eurasia center director, 'you should be seeing them on a regular basis.' The common sentiment among multiple centers was that without an office to give visiting faculty, it was impossible to host them properly. A South Asia center director stated likewise: 'We don't want someone to come in, then we have nowhere to put them and we can't do very much for them.'

On some campuses, center staff were dismayed with the amount of office space they had been delegated, and the topic of visiting faculty seemed to provide a venue for them to discuss these frustrations, usually directed at senior university administrators who, as one center director explained, do not always find a lot of visitors 'entirely welcome'. Staff at another center, which had recently acquired new space, saw it as contributing to their visibility 'exponentially', aiding their ability to bring in visitors through co-sponsorship with other departments. In these ways, office space forms an important institutional factor conditioning the incoming mobility of scholars to universities in the USA.

Relationships

In addition to funding, personnel, and office space, the relationships of the center staff proved a significant factor in conditioning the flow of scholars internationally. In their role as a gateway, center staff spoke about using their connections to faculty and personal networks in different ways: to connect students to internships in the region; to link students to people and institutions in the region that can help them when doing fieldwork; to attract visiting scholars to come to their campus; and to connect visiting faculty to scholars on campus with whom they may want to work. As one Russia-Eurasia center director explained, formal linkages are built from faculty relationships: 'It's usually a single or a couple of faculty members who set up the first contact. It always starts that way in a kind of one-to-one, face-to-face ... then when it, the decision is made to formalize, we go to the international office.'

Centers also rely on faculty relationships in the region to help structure and lead study abroad programs. One assistant director for a South Asia center explained how they use their financial resources to develop such relationships:

> We pay for a number of faculty to travel to the region; it is a regular activity, what we do. We are often able to fund them to a substantial extent of what they need, and we try to make them remember that they owe us one (laughs). You know this is, it is about relationships, and it is about various forms of exchange that makes a center like this function. So you know we have a few things that we can offer, and then we, then we'll turn to them and say give us something back, by doing something for us. I mean I'm not saying it's you know, it's not a market relationship, it's a barter relationship.

These examples suggest that the way centers serve as gateways to the region is reliant on their ability to foster relationships, with both partners in the region and with faculty from their own campus. The importance of such relationships was commonly recognized among interviewees. Meanwhile, when speaking of the possibility of expanding what they do, various centers emphasized their interest in expanding their *relationships* with non-governmental organizations or developing other internship opportunities for students in the region, with some even suggesting this is how they would make use of additional administrative personnel.

There was thus a common understanding among center leaders that, as one assistant director stated, 'You really have to cooperate with so many people to be an effective center, to get your faculty to help. You can't do it all yourself, you have to develop these relationships.' In various cases center staff also spoke about positive relationships with their deans or vice-provosts as helping them to find more funding when they need it to bring in visitors. In various ways, then, international mobility is conditioned not just by cross-border relationships among institutions and scholars, but also by relationships among personnel on a single campus.

The Interconnected Nature of Mobility

A final factor that emerges from our interview data as salient to the successful circulation of students and scholars is the interconnected nature of the mechanisms that support it. Just as centers rely on reciprocal relationships with faculty to adequately serve as gateways to the region, so too is their ability to serve as a gateway impacted by their ability to serve as a guest home. Serving as good hosts for visitors, in this sense, results in good hosting for their own faculty and students when they go abroad. This was accentuated by multiple references among interviewees to the 'back and forth' movement of students and scholars from the region. One Middle East center's assistant director explained the dynamics of this ongoing exchange well:

161

> We'll bring faculty here, and we've done that several times. And
> we'll either, you know, it will sometimes begin just by bringing
> someone here to give a lecture then they'll meet students here.
> Students will want to go study with that person for a semester.
> Then the faculty member will come back here for a year or
> something.

The development of these international relationships relies not just on
hosting visitors once, but on their *continual* hosting over multiple return
visits. Consider the following comments from a Russia-Eurasia center
director:

> We get more visitors from the region through Fulbright and
> government-to-government programs of that kind and they're
> typically very good and they tend to be older... And, sometimes
> they'll even come under wearing one hat one time, and wearing
> another hat the next time, which is fine. You get to know them for
> that.

This idea was echoed across many centers, as they understood their
exchanges with the region to be ongoing, deep, and long-term, rather than
singular, temporary, or brief. For example, one center that was hosting two
visiting scholars had already hosted each of them twice before. The functions
of gateway and guest home thus affect one another, as two sides of the same
coin. Their interconnected nature reveals that each is simultaneously a
mechanism for supporting mobility and a condition affecting the operation of
the other.

Conclusion: implications for existing theory

The institutional perspective explored herein reveals a new set of factors that
condition mobility, beyond the decisions of individuals to go abroad. As
discussed above, mobility has primarily been studied as a phenomenon of
individual choice, rather than by examining the institutions and actors that
facilitate and organize these experiences. In the discussion below, we
articulate three implications of these findings for our understanding of
academic mobility.

First, our data reveal that academic mobility relies on collective action
and serves multiple people's interests. Whereas the act of crossing borders
alone is inarguably individualistic, in the case of knowledge production on
world regions it is reliant upon a large infrastructure of administrative
personnel, hosts, and relationships. Area studies centers send faculty abroad
for various reasons, and their mobility often fulfills multiple interests, not just
those of the individual moving: from the donor who choses to fund a
fellowship, to the center that uses the trips of their faculty to establish formal
linkages; from the scholar who will get to conduct research abroad, to the
foreign scholar who hosts them with the expectation of being reciprocally

welcomed in the USA in the future. In this sense, the time horizon for our understanding of the phenomenon of mobility must be widened. Mobility does not just happen; it requires openings. Visiting scholars need an opening in the curriculum at the American university that they can fill. Outgoing faculty need an opening in their schedule and an existing opportunity that will send them abroad. It takes time to form, plan, and arrange these openings, to advertise them once they exist, to prepare for people to go and to arrive, and to facilitate travelers' experiences. Since mobility pathways require multiple contingencies to coalesce, they are often dependent on various personal and institutional relationships, which also require time to form and develop. Current research on mobility has not attended adequately to the multiple actors involved in accomplishing academic mobility, nor the significant time horizon for its facilitation.

Second, the case of how area studies centers facilitate academic mobility reveals the importance of institutional arbiters in actually exchanging people across borders. An analysis of the ways in which these centers send and receive visitors reveals the multiple mechanisms they use in the process: housing and administering programs, maintaining institutional linkages, serving as clearinghouses of information, hosting brown bag lunches, connecting students and scholars to opportunities, and organizing trip logistics. The gateway role performed by these centers is thus multifaceted, as they can even be understood to simply attract students to go abroad by virtue of their physical presence as an academic unit on campus. Similarly, their role of guest home is critical to the flow of scholars as their hosting of visitors helps them maintain relationships, and hence, their ability to serve as a gateway in the future. As illustrated, these dual functions are interconnected, and each is an important factor that can condition the mobility of students and scholars. Centers offer a catalogue of potential avenues to their regions of study and make visitors feel welcome, two services that are critical to the outflows and inflows of scholars and students. In this way, institutional gateways and guest homes can be understood to underpin all official academic mobility. Attending to this concept requires new approaches to investigate the administrative underpinnings of the internationalization of higher education more generally.

Finally, the case of area studies centers leads us to concur with other scholars who have argued that there are multiple kinds of academic mobility (e.g. Altbach et al, 2010; Brooks & Waters, 2011). In connoting single one-way trips by a variety of students and scholars, much existing discussion of 'mobility' does not adequately portray the varied international exchanges characteristic of area studies fields, where faculty, students, and visiting scholars often travel back and forth between the USA and other countries repeatedly, and for different durations. Bhandari and Blumenthal (2011), among others, use the term 'brain circulation' as a means of emphasizing the multiplicity of ways in which academic exchange now happens globally, contrasted with the 'brain drain' of the past. Our case suggests, however, that academic mobility is not just a travelogue of numerous destinations in a broad, indeterminate way, but can include concentrated mobility among a narrow range of places.

What emerged in our interview data then was the centrality of *circulation* of scholars to area studies centers' missions, as they rely on students and faculty not just going to the region, but also *returning from it*. In most cases, center staff discussed mobility in terms of multiple trips back and forth, for example, sending a PhD student to the region once for language training and another time for dissertation fieldwork, or inviting a visiting scholar who, after returning to their home university, will help supervise students coming from the USA doing research 'in the field'. Our data points to the intertwined nature of such circulation, as in the case of area studies, both student and scholar mobility is furthered over time by the development and sustainment of cross-national relationships.

Ultimately, this suggests that scholars pay more attention to the different *circuits* of mobility that exist, rather than continuing to talk of academic mobility as though it were all a single undertaking. It is significant that the work of area studies centers, and thereby the production of knowledge on world regions, requires not just academic mobility but a specific type of ongoing reciprocal flow of scholars in and out of the USA. This is quite different from discussions of student and scholar movement through multiple sites around the globe (e.g. Knight, 2009). To date though, there has been no exploration of how mobility matters to those students who aspire to be regional experts, or the scholars who have attained that mantle. Further, there is little sense of how the kind of academic mobility particular to American area studies compares with other mobilities in the higher education landscape. How this institutional apparatus for international mobility designed during the Cold War compares with more contemporary infrastructures for academic mobility remains little explored.

As discussed above, the ability to serve effectively as gateways and guest homes is critical to area studies centers, because they rely on mobility for their study of world regions. These are functions, however, that also underlie much student and faculty mobility in the 'American university' writ large. Thus, while centers vary in whether they prioritize travel funding for faculty research, invest in formal exchanges with foreign institutions, or even run study abroad programs for K–12 teachers, they collectively serve as gateways between the 'American university' and its publics, whether at home or abroad. In employing the variety of mechanisms detailed above, these centers serve as institutional arbiters of academic mobility. Our argument, as outlined here, suggests that more attention be paid to understanding the institutional factors such as space, funding, and personnel that condition their ability to do such arbitration effectively. Study of academic mobility must thus be widened beyond the individual choice perspective and current method of mapping individual movement, if we are to truly understand the range of factors that shape and condition its occurrence.

Note

[1] This chapter is part of a long-term study at the US Social Science Research Council (SSRC), 'Producing Knowledge on World Regions', which was funded from 2004 to 2010 by the US Department of Education's International Research and Studies Program (grants PO17A040075 and P017A060034). We are indebted to co-PI Seteney Shami and senior consultant Mitchell Stevens for years of generative discussions related to this research and its findings, to Elizabeth A. Worden, Nick Gozik and Anthony Koliha for conducting field research, and to Holly Danzeisen, Christian Bracho and Jesse Foster for research assistance. See Miller-Idriss & Worden, 2010; Miller-Idriss & Shami, 2012; Miller-Idriss et al, forthcoming. See also: http://www.ssrc.org/programs/producing-knowledge-on-world-regions/

[2] For the purposes of protecting the identities of the interview subjects, the universities in this study are confidential. In some instances the quotations in this chapter have been edited slightly for brevity or to maintain the confidentiality of participants, but in no case have such alterations changed the meaning of the original statements.

References

Altbach, P.G., Reisberg, L. & Rumbley, L.E. (2010) *Trends in Global Higher Education: tracking an academic revolution*. Rotterdam: UNESCO.

Bhandari, R. & Blumenthal, P. (Eds) (2011) *International Students and Global Mobility in Higher Education: national trends and new directions*. New York: Palgrave Macmillan.

Biddle, S. (2002) *Internationalization: rhetoric or reality?* ACLS Occasional Paper, #56. New York: American Council of Learned Societies.

Brooks, R. & Waters, J. (2011) *Student Mobilities, Migration and the Internationalization of Higher Education*. New York: Palgrave Macmillan.

Byram, M. & Dervin, F. (Eds) (2008) *Students, Staff and Academic Mobility in Higher Education*. Cambridge: Cambridge Scholars Publishing.

Caudery, T., Petersen, M. & Shaw, P. (2008) The Motivations of Exchange Students at Scandinavian Universities, in M. Byram & F. Dervin (Eds) *Students, Staff and Academic Mobility in Higher Education*, pp. 114-130. Cambridge: Cambridge Scholars Publishing.

De Wit, H., Ferencz, I. & Rumbley, L.E. (2013) International Student Mobility: European and US perspectives, *Perspectives*, 17(1), 17-23.

Engerman, D.C. (2009) *Know Your Enemy: the rise and fall of America's Soviet experts*. Oxford: Oxford University Press.

Goodwin, C.D. & Nacht, M. (1991) *Missing the Boat: the failure to internationalize American higher education*. Cambridge: Cambridge University Press.

Gürüz, K. (2008) *Higher Education and International Student Mobility in the Global Knowledge Economy*. Albany: State University of New York Press.

Institute of International Education (2012) *Open Doors 2012: report on international educational exchange*. New York: IIE.

Knight, J. (2009) New Developments and Unintended Consequences: whither though goest, internationalization? In R. Bhandari & S. Laughlin (Eds) *Higher Education on the Move: new developments in global mobility*. New York: Institute of International Education.

Knight, J. & Madden, M. (2010) International Mobility of Canadian Social Sciences and Humanities Doctoral Students, *Canadian Journal of Higher Education*, 40(2), 18-34.

Kondakci, Y. (2011) Student Mobility Reviewed: attraction and satisfaction of international students in Turkey, *Higher Education*, 62(5), 573-592.

McCaughey, R.A. (1984) *International Studies and Academic Enterprise: a chapter in the enclosure of American learning*. New York: Columbia University Press.

Miller-Idriss, C. & Shami, S. (2012) Graduate Student Training and the Reluctant Internationalism of Social Science in the USA, *Research in Comparative and International Education*, 7(1), 50-60.

Miller-Idriss, C., Stevens, M.L. & Shami, S. (forthcoming) *Teaching the World: how American universities organize knowledge about the rest of the world*. Princeton: Princeton University Press.

Miller-Idriss, C. & Worden, E.A. (2010) Internationalization in US Higher Education: studying the Middle East in the American university, *Globalisation, Societies and Education*, 8(3), 393-409.

Souto-Otero, M., Huisman, J., Beerkens, M., De Wit, H. & Vujić, S. (2013). Barriers to International Student Mobility: evidence from the Erasmus program, *Educational Researcher*, 42(2), 70-77.

Van de Bunt-Kokhuis, S.G.M. (1996) *Academic Pilgrims: determinants of international faculty mobility*. Tilburg: Tilburg University Press.

Wildavsky, B. (2010) *The Great Brain Race: how global universities are reshaping the world*. Princeton: Princeton University Press.

APPENDIX. Sample Inductive Codes

CENTERROLE_CAMPUS	Roles of a center on campus
CENTERROLE_COMMUNITY	Roles of a center beyond campus, in the wider public community
CENTERROLE_GOVT	Roles of the center serving the US government
HOST_DIGNITARIES	Center's role hosting dignitaries
HOST_MISC	Center's role hosting miscellaneous other visitors (e.g. musicians, artists)
HOST_POSTDOCS	Centers' role hosting postdocs from the US

HOST_VISITORSREGION — How centers bring in scholars from the region to the center, both short and long term

HOST_VISITORSUS — How centers bring in scholars from the US to the center, both short and long term

OPERATION_FUNDING — Explanations of how centers are funded, and what they would do with more funding, how they attract more funding

OPERATION_PERSONNEL — Descriptions of who works there and what they do, and what would they do with more personnel

OPERATION_SPACE — How space is part of the center's operation

RELATIONS_DIASPORA — Links of the center to the diaspora community from their region in the US

RELATIONS_FACULTY — How centers rely on relationships with faculty

RELATIONS_LIBARTS — How centers have relationships with smaller liberal arts colleges

RELATIONS_REGIONCENTER — Institutional links of the center to the region of study, formal exchanges, memberships

RELATIONS_REGIONPERSONAL — Mentions of personal links of faculty or center staff to the region

RELATIONS_SNRADMIN — How centers rely on relationships with senior administrators (deans, vice-provosts, presidents)

RELATIONS_USUNIVS — How centers rely on relationships with other universities in the US, or other area studies centers on different campuses

SEND_FACULTY — How centers send faculty abroad, including grant competitions, solicitation of external funds

SEND_STUDENTS — How centers send students abroad; support study abroad programs; host travel fellowships; facilitate internships

167

CHAPTER 11

When the Diaspora Returns: analysis of Ethiopian returnees and the need for highly skilled labour in Ethiopia

ROSE C. AMAZAN

ABSTRACT The changing nature of international skilled migration may allow developing countries that have been victimised by brain drain to regain some control over the way it impacts them. The two giants of India and China, for example, have benefited in different ways from the shift from brain drain to brain gain. Despite the successes of some countries in mobilising their diaspora and the rapid growth of technology, many countries still struggle to counteract the flight of skilled personnel; Ethiopia is one such country. Ranking first in Africa in terms of the rate of loss of human capital, it has yet to find an effective strategy to manage the comings and goings of its skilled professionals. However, Ethiopia's desire to join the global knowledge economy has pushed the government to massively expand higher education. Such ambitious targets, however, have placed further strain on the meagre-skilled personnel resources. These facts suggest that mobilising the skilled diaspora to contribute to national development would benefit Ethiopia both socially and economically. However, the findings suggest lack of policies to strengthen the government's relationship with Ethiopian professionals in the diaspora is a barrier to engagement. This chapter discusses Ethiopian diaspora mobility and the barriers they encounter in contributing, including after having returned. It focuses attention on the potential impact that the Ethiopian skilled diaspora can have on educational development.

Introduction

Over the centuries, human resources have become one of the most prized and valuable commodities in the quest for economic growth and development. They have become a vital component in the developmental

169

processes of countries and in keeping ahead of global competition. Since the value of knowledge and skilled individuals has been recognised, countries have been investing millions of dollars to ensure the future of their country in the global market. This human capital approach holds that when a government invests in an individual's educational qualifications, abilities, skills and competencies, it is entitled to expect a future return on its investment (Brown, 2000). This investment, which was once regarded as 'safe' due to its profit margin and return, is now being challenged by the mass migration of skilled professionals.

This professional skilled migration, often referred to as brain drain, has attracted significant interest in the international community. This is mainly due to reports that have associated this phenomenon with developmental constraints (Sako, 2002). Brain drain is not a new phenomenon; it has been around since the 1950s and was used to describe British intellectuals and scientists migrating to the Unites States (Gaillard & Gaillard, 1997). Today, brain drain is mostly used to refer to the exodus of highly skilled professionals from developing countries to developed countries. It has crippled the developmental prospects of many countries, particularly in Africa where the numbers of highly skilled Africans leaving their countries of origin have reached disturbing proportions.

In Africa alone it is estimated that one-third of the most highly qualified are residing outside their country of origin, mainly in Western Europe and North America (World Bank, 2000). According to the International Organization for Migration (2005) there are currently 300,000 highly qualified Africans in the diaspora, 30,000 of whom have PhDs. Similarly, the World Bank (2002) estimates that some 70,000 highly qualified African professionals, experts, scholars and managers with internationally marketable skills leave Africa each year. Woldetensae (2007) reports that this continuous outflow of skilled professionals from Africa has widened the gap in scientific and technological development.

The skilled migration has negatively impacted some countries more than others. In Africa, Ethiopia ranks first in terms of the rate of loss of human capital, followed by Nigeria and Ghana (Integrated Regional Information Networks, 2004). The International Organization for Migration estimated that between 1980 and 1991, Ethiopia lost about 74.6% of its human intellectual capital from various institutions. Ethiopia spends over US$5.3 million every year in hiring expatriate staff to compensate for the shortage of qualified staff in the country (Kefela & Rena, 2008).

With an estimated population of 84 million in 2011, Ethiopia remains a poor country, ranking 173 among the 186 countries of the Human Development Index (United Nations Development Programme, 2013). Faced with this grim picture, many dream of migrating and turn to international migration as a way to improve the livelihood of their family. International migration of qualified professionals has become a coping mechanism, thus leaving many sectors in Ethiopia, especially the health sector, depleted of personnel and further impeding the progress of the country.

The government has yet to manage the inflow and outflow of the migration of Ethiopians. The International Centre for Migration Policy Development (ICMPD) in 2008 identified lack of financial and human resources; poor transport and communication infrastructure causing discrepancy between central and regional levels; and limited regional and bilateral cooperation as impediments to Ethiopia's migration management. The consequences of these impediments include a lack of data, lack of structure and inefficient migration management (ICMPD, 2008).

As part of the knowledge economy and global processes, diaspora mobility has made it imperative to challenge the traditional nation-state unit of analysis in comparative education (see Welch, 2010). Diaspora mobility of the skilled and the highly skilled has in a way fractured the mould of comparative education discourse and presents us with a platform/opportunity to reconstruct comparative education. More recently, the acknowledgement of the skilled and the highly skilled in the diaspora as a major resource that needs to be harnessed and utilised for the economic growth of developing countries has spearheaded new developmental hope, not only in terms of remittances but also in generating new knowledge and ideas for economic growth. Higher education in Ethiopia as it stands today remains in a state of reform and expansion. Although not solely responsible, the exodus of trained professionals has weakened the quality of higher education in Africa. This study does view diaspora mobility as a realistic choice for developing countries to spearhead development, especially in the area of higher education. As such this article will analyse the Ethiopian skilled and highly skilled returnees against the context of Ethiopia's need for skilled labour.

The data presented in this chapter is from a larger study on mobilising the Ethiopian highly skilled, knowledge diaspora. A mixed-method exploratory design was employed in order to provide a holistic picture of the complexity of mobilising the Ethiopian knowledge diaspora. All data were collected from North America (United States and Canada) and Ethiopia. Participants were drawn from highly skilled Ethiopians in the diaspora, as well as returnees who are currently residing in Ethiopia. The data set consisted of 165 questionnaires and 13 interviews in North America and 19 questionnaires and 31 interviews in Ethiopia.

Higher Education: the Ethiopian context

The historical background of Ethiopian higher education is unlike that of any other African higher education context. Modern higher education in Ethiopia was established in 1950 under the imperial regime of Haile Selassie, with the United Kingdom (UK), the United States and Germany being the dominant external influences. With the establishment of modern higher education in Ethiopia came expectations of economic growth, poverty reduction and development. Unfortunately, the establishment of modern higher education in Ethiopia fell short of its promise. According to Yizengaw (2003), 'higher education institutions in Ethiopia have deprived our country of the opportunity of getting out of poverty and underdevelopment' (p. 1).

Nevertheless, the Federal Democratic Republic of Ethiopia government's belief that education is the way to reduce poverty has underpinned the massively expanded higher education system in Ethiopia; in addition, it has instigated several reforms such as cost-sharing. As of 2012 there were 34 government higher education institutions (HEIs) in Ethiopia, of which 75% had opened in the previous few years. The term massification was used by Scott (1995) to describe the phenomenon of rapid growth in student enrolment, whereby larger proportions of the age cohort were engaged in higher education. In Africa, this progressive massification of HEIs has often been at the expense of quality, however.

This is particularly the case in Ethiopia. Mohamedbhai (2008) points out that 'most African countries have a very low higher education enrolment ratio but experience a very rapid increase in actual numbers of students enrolled in higher education' (p. 4), and that, in itself, should be considered as one form of massification. A consequence of this is a decline in the quality of education being offered. Indeed, the key difference between massification in Ethiopia and in the Western system is expressed by Ashcroft (2004) in her article about the UK's higher education system versus that of Ethiopia, where she stated that 'the expansion of higher education experienced by the UK was very large, but occurred over a longer time period than in Ethiopia' (p. 26), allowing the government to implement systems to maintain the quality of education (Ashcroft, 2004).

Higher education in Ethiopia has expanded beyond the government's capacity to provide quality education and appropriate knowledge that is relevant to the context of the country. In fairness, this has always been an issue, not only in Ethiopia but also in many developing countries. The rapid expansion and fast changes within the tertiary education system in Ethiopia bring both positive and negative consequences; arguably, however, the downside dominates this rapid transformation. Rising enrolments and the growing number of new universities have led to a high demand for PhD and Master's degree-holders in all disciplines, especially in the fields of business, marketing, accounting, computer science and technology (Tessema, 2009). As a solution to this shortage, the government implemented a new capacity-building policy known as the 70:30 plan as a way to increase natural science, engineering and technology enrolment to 70% and bring down enrolment for social sciences and humanities to 30%.

There were numerous obstacles to implementing this initiative, however; not only were the resources (students, staff, materials etc.) not available, but also the infrastructure simply was not there to accommodate such an ambitious plan. In response to the shortfall of qualified academic staff, the Ministry of Education has taken some actions that are questionable, including the hire of young, inexperienced and under-qualified local educators (Tessema, 2009) and increasing the usage of expatriates, mostly from India, the Philippines and Nigeria. Hiring less qualified staff is understandable because of the high demand and the insufficient numbers of teaching staff with PhD degrees. However, most universities do not have the resources or the funding to supervise or mentor these young and inexperienced lecturers effectively. Fewer than 20% of the current instructors hold Master's degrees and fewer than 4% hold PhDs (Reisberg & Rumbley, 2010). The government currently has an initiative to increase the number of qualified teaching staff in the country. The Ministry of Education has pledged to produce 10,000 Master's degrees and 2000 PhD degree graduates in five years' time (Addis Ababa University–Business Process Reengineering, 2008). Achieving this target is likely to prove difficult, however, considering there are not enough senior academics in Ethiopia to supervise these students. Furthermore, in the last 50 years Ethiopia has produced fewer than 100 PhD-holders (Nordling, 2008), of whom all graduated via so-called 'sandwich' programmes in collaboration with foreign HEIs. Reaching these ambitious targets using domestic higher education capacity, then, is very much against the odds.

Hence, despite the government's efforts, the substantial expansion has not strengthened the quality of higher education; in fact, it has had the opposite effect. Expansion has neither solved its own unemployment issues, nor has it remedied the acute shortage of locally qualified Ethiopians. Instead it is weakening quality and creating more disparities in the system. Tessema (2009) outlines a range of trends relating to the expansion including the deterioration of teacher–student ratios and growing class sizes and workloads. Quality improvement is effectively paralysed because of attrition, lack of adequate educational materials and shortage of qualified education staff (Dufera, 2005). Judging by the evidence presented above, the expansion of higher education in Ethiopia is clearly failing to meet the objective of quality enhancement. The Ethiopian government is still struggling to retain qualified teaching staff at the university level. The brain drain of academics has become a major problem to a point where it is seriously affecting the quality of education and weakening the capacity of HEIs. This in turn exacerbates the shortage of qualified academic staff.

Government Initiatives in Engaging the Ethiopian Diaspora

The Ethiopian government has long been aware of the social and economic ramifications of brain drain and has been promising to mitigate brain drain with a national policy that has not, however, materialised. Irrespective of this, the Ethiopian government has acknowledged the value of mobilising the Ethiopian diaspora for development. Both the Sustainable Development and Poverty Reduction Programme of 2002-05 and the Plan for Accelerated and Sustained Development to End Poverty of 2006-10 explicitly reference the 'positive impact of the diaspora and their roles in providing a cross-fertilisation of ideas, skills, and injections of capital and remittances that can help accelerate development' (Ministry of Finance and Economic Development, 2006, p. 216). The government has also acknowledged that in order to fully engage the Ethiopian diaspora community and all its resources, there must be institutional structures in place both at national and regional levels to encourage and facilitate diaspora involvement.

Examples include the establishment of two departments (i.e. the Ethiopian Expatriate Affairs General Directorate and the Diaspora Coordinating Office) in relevant federal ministries to promote diaspora involvement. Their priority is to facilitate diaspora activities in Ethiopia. The Ministry of Capacity Building was also part of the government's initiative to accelerate economic growth and enhance national institutional capacity. The government has also set up at the federal level a committee under the Expatriate Affairs General Directorate composed of the Ministry of Foreign Affairs, the Ministry of Trade and Industry, the Ministry of Culture and Tourism, the Ministry of Labour and Social Affairs, the Ministry of Revenue, the Department of Immigration and the National Bank of Ethiopia to ensure interagency coordination and share information on diaspora engagement activities (Association for Higher Education and Development [AHEAD], 2007; ICMPD, 2008). The involvement of Ethiopia's regions in diaspora engagement replicates and complements federal initiatives (AHEAD, 2007) and in particular helps with dissemination of information because the regional division of Ethiopia correlates with ethnic groups. A similar cooperation committee between the federal and the regional governments was set up to ensure an environment conducive to investment (ICMPD, 2008).

The Ethiopian government has also taken some legislative measures to facilitate the mobility of resources and investment from the Ethiopian diaspora community. In 2002, the Ethiopian government established Proclamation No. 270/2002: 'A Proclamation to Provide Foreign Nationals of Ethiopian Origin with Certain Rights to Be Exercised in their Country of Origin' (Federal Democratic Republic of Ethiopia [FDRE], 2002, p. 1710). Directive FX 25/2004, issued in 2006, allow non-resident Ethiopians to open fixed accounts, varying maturity terms or accounts where they can make withdrawals in US dollars, pound sterling or euros. Originally, non-resident Ethiopians were not allowed to deposit more than US$5000 in these accounts, however in August 2006 the National Bank of Ethiopia raised the limit to US$50,000 (National Bank of Ethiopia, 2004, 2006a, b).

The Ethiopian government has done more in the area of facilitating diaspora investment than any other area in the diaspora mobility sector. Under the domestic investors' scheme, Ethiopians in the diaspora are treated like domestic investors, which allows them to invest much less than the minimum of US$100,000 that foreign investors must have in order to be allowed to invest in Ethiopia. There are several different agencies, such as the

Ethiopian Investment Authority, the Ethiopian Investment Commission, the Addis Ababa City Administration Investment Authority and Regional Investment Offices, all of which work as a 'one stop shop' to provide services to potential investors. The different initiatives set in place by the Ethiopian government to attract investment have been successful in increasing foreign investment by Ethiopians in the diaspora. There are about 800 non-resident Ethiopians, including foreign citizens of Ethiopian background, who invested in Ethiopia, bringing the foreign investment total to 7.5 billion birr (US$863 million) and a total of US$1.3 billion in the period since July 1992 (Xinhua, 2006; AHEAD, 2007). This, according to Xinhua (2006), is due to the government's liberal economic policies which were implemented in the early 2000s, paving the way for enhanced flows of foreign investment. There is no evidence to suggest that some of these investments are being made by highly skilled Ethiopians or that the money is going toward the greater good of the country.

The Ethiopian government has used various methods, mentioned above, to channel its diaspora's knowledge, skills and financial resources for development. Many have praised the various initiatives and directives by the Ethiopian government to improve communication with, and involvement of, the diaspora. However, the government still faces many challenges in mobilising the Ethiopian diaspora, especially its intellectual capital. According to AHEAD (2007), the lack of financial and human resources, as well as political divisions and polarisation, limit the government's ability to fully and effectively reach out to the Ethiopian diaspora community.

Some argue that part of the government's difficulties in attracting the diaspora is due to its financially focused strategies where the government appears to be more interested in investment and what money the diaspora have to offer, rather than the diaspora's direct involvement in knowledge transfer and capacity-building. According to Yacob (2005), the government's initiatives and directives, such as land lease privileges for Ethiopians living abroad, investment and importation of goods, and incentives to maintain foreign currency accounts in Ethiopia, are all targeted to attract financial capital instead of the intellectual resources of the diaspora community. Both Shinn (2002) and AHEAD (2007) concur with Yacob's (2005) statement; AHEAD (2007) points out that 'despite the political will expressed to involve the diaspora formally and the many incentives provided, measures taken appear to be *ad hoc* and confused, with more emphasis seemingly on encouraging remittances and investments, to the neglect of attracting diaspora intellectual capital' (p. 53). The few policies that are set in place to attract Ethiopian professionals for knowledge transfer have not been effective in tempting highly qualified Ethiopians in the diaspora to return. Yacob (2005) went further in saying, 'the Ethiopian Embassies and the General Directorate for Diaspora Affairs in the Ministry of Foreign Affairs have been dismal failures in effectively executing mandates' (p. 7).

Key Findings

Repatriation Experiences

Many returnees have similar stories of how their efforts and hard work were not considered and where they wasted much time in producing something that was ultimately not implemented. Experiences like the following echo throughout, damaging both self-esteem and national development:

> this past year they said okay ... we'll get together and revise the curriculum. And we say do you want a three year curriculum or a four year curriculum? No don't mention the years, just revise the curriculum. So, we spent the whole year revising the curriculum. And most of the programs came up with a four year programs ... Some schools five years, like pharmacy and so forth, medicine, a little longer than that. And then ... all the university staff got together from all over the country and from all the other universities discussed it ... then they moved it to the Ministry of Education and this one guy said 'nah make it three years'. ... that's the kind of system we live in okay. This one guy with a stroke of a pen said it's not going to work. ... So this is the kind of thing you have to fight ... even after you've done all that work ... you are not looking for thank you, at least putting in practice will say, 'you know what I work on this and now we are using it', but it was trashed. (AZ)

Sadly, all returnees in the study experienced at least one such disappointment, which made them question both their contribution and ongoing involvement in Ethiopia.

Nonetheless, there are some exceptions. Although many give up, some returnees keep trying and will not let the system beat them, no matter how much they have to put up with, or how often their ideas are turned down. Some returnees manage to maintain a positive mindset, propose solutions, are innovative, visionary and still committed to making a difference, regardless of who is in charge because their approach is at the grassroots level. As one participant put it, 'if I do my part right, if I teach my students the right way of management and the real, the universal truth about management ... and make them think critically, that might be my contribution. That's why I am staying' (GH).

The returnees have reason to be worried as academic promotions (tied to salary increases) are difficult, even with returnees' skills and experience. Even those who have been promoted have difficulty sustaining a standard of living which reflects their skilled status and provides for their family. As confirmed by Assefa (2008) in his study, many participants find it very difficult to support their family with just their full-time academic salary, which then forces them to take on additional work (teaching, researching etc.) in order to supplement their income and cope with the ever-increasing cost of living. This phenomenon (called moonlighting) is common among academics in developing countries (see Teferra & Altbach, 2003; Welch, 2011). These supplementary jobs, combined with other academic obligations, make it difficult for academic staff to find time to do research and thus get promoted. All the returnees found it impossible to do their own research, not only because of time but also, as one participant explained:

> there is a lot of work here, you can teach more than your load ...
> you are also expected to participate in ... committee work and in
> addition to that you are also expected to work ... at the university
> at administrative positions. And in addition to that if you want to
> do some research work ... there is no incentive for that. It's just for
> your mental satisfaction, otherwise it will contribute to nothing ...
> oh well, not nothing except ... for the rank of Assistant Professor
> ... Associate Professor. If you fulfil that, that's all, you don't need
> it anymore. There is no additional thing that you can get from
> your research ... no additional incentive at all. Then this will not
> attract you ... to put additional effort on your research direction.
> (SMK)

Attracting and Retaining the Diaspora/Returnees

Attracting the diaspora community to contribute to Ethiopian development is as important and as relevant as retaining skilled professionals at home. The Ethiopian government has failed to recognise that the two are interconnected and should be treated as such. The idea is substantiated in their 70:30 plans and their plans to generate 2000 PhDs in the next five years (2008-13) to fill the shortage of staff in the 21 universities that have been opened, as well as in their ultimate plan to mitigate brain drain. There were good reasons for the development of these initiatives, as many students who leave for overseas to obtain higher degrees tend to stay there; thus these programmes, conferences and training sessions often serve as opportunities for migration (Welch, 1997, 2002; Welch & Zhang, 2007).

An issue raised by all returnees was that retaining and attracting involves recognition, and they felt that they were not being acknowledged or recognised for their efforts. They did not need praise for their sacrifices, but would have liked to have been recognised, thought of as competent and to have been included in the country's development process:

> I used to work in the Ministry of Housing in a master plan project,
> I was developing a Master plan for Addis Ababa and the World
> Bank gave the consultancy work to an Irish company, those people
> come in the economists ... we had thousands of economists that
> could have done the job. Why hire expatriates and pay them
> thousands of dollars ... that money could have been used in such a

wise way in terms of maximising the output or the benefit of that project. (FC)

Even when the diaspora seek to help, they encounter difficulties. Many participants from the diaspora relate stories of initiating contact without success. For instance, the highly skilled and educated GH, with six degrees, finally gave up after many attempts with Ethiopian Airlines, and decided to apply to Addis Ababa University. His application was rejected on the basis of having too many degrees. 'When they rejected my application and Ethiopian Airlines did not return my call ... I thought there is something going on here, they don't want this country to grow up or people to come to ... you know it makes you to wonder' (GH).

There were many who tried and failed, due to the lack of follow-up. Stories like GH's are not unknown in other countries and dominated the Ethiopian diaspora's experiences of trying to contribute. These difficulties discourage the highly skilled diaspora, reinforcing the message that their knowledge, skills and experiences are unwanted, despite rhetorical calls by the government to engage the diaspora.

A major inhibitor for Ethiopia is the lack of systems to support inquiries by the diaspora who are trying to initiate contact and contribute; the entire process is left to the individual. The contribution of the diaspora and returnees, especially from developing countries, is about making sacrifices for the homeland, whether for family reasons or a sense of belonging. The findings repeatedly show that strong connections to home and a sense of belonging drive many of the diaspora to return to Ethiopia. The love of country, family, relatives and friends is what drives many to contribute. It is these basic desires to return home that are

> usually tied to factors that include wanting to play a constructive role in the development of the country, the desire for a simpler and in some ways more fulfilling lifestyle or a never-ending hunger for the cultural aspects of living in Ethiopia that can never be duplicated elsewhere no matter how many Ethiopian restaurants, injera bets, markets and churches are built there. The perception of opportunity can certainly play a significant part as well but it is usually not at the very core of someone's contemplation to return home. (Sahlu, 2009, p. 1)

This drive needs to be harnessed and cultivated in order to mobilise the diaspora community. Connection and a sense of belonging may be underestimated by the government; they are far more powerful than is acknowledged (Amazan, 2012).

Factors Inhibiting Further
Involvement by the Ethiopian Diaspora

The lack of active involvement by the Ethiopian consulates in engaging the diaspora, or the failure to disseminate appropriate information, were common themes among both the North American respondents and the returnees: 68.4% of returnees received no assistance from the Ethiopian consulate in their host country when ready to return. Furthermore, before returning, 72.2% of intending returnees were not aware of any government policies or programmes established to attract the highly skilled diaspora. It is important to note here that the government set in place certain directives (mainly for those who are interested in doing business in Ethiopia) to attract the diaspora to contribute. Unfortunately, some of them were abandoned and others modified, but the diaspora were not made aware of such changes until it was too late.

It may be true that the consulates are not active in informing the diaspora of government policies and initiatives, or even that they are poor at disseminating the right information. However, the nature of the relationship between the diaspora and the government is that of mutual mistrust. Thus, although not excusable, it is not at all surprising that the majority of both the returnees and the diaspora were not aware of government initiatives. Many, if not the majority, simply want peace and are apolitical; however, some hold extreme views and, unfortunately, create an image of the diaspora that is used by the government to judge all diasporas.

This deep-rooted suspicion and mistrust inhibits the recruitment of the diaspora. Thus, one of the reasons why the consulates are not more involved in disseminating information to the diaspora could be due to the fact that:

> anything Ethiopian that's promoted through the embassy
> especially ... areas like DC [Washington, DC], if you are even
> seen with the ambassador, you're like labelled for life and they'll
> close down your restaurant. People are just like rabid about their
> anti-government stance ... it's almost infantile sometimes. It's like
> they cut off your nose to spite your face sort of thing ... . (MT)

At times, those who associate with the embassy or the government are disparaged as government sympathisers. Consequently, the diaspora must rely on the Ethiopian community, and often hearsay, to get information. As one participant put it, if you need information:

> you would call somebody who knows somebody who's done it
> ahead of you or whatever, but the government as a source of
> information and the government as a source of support for ... its
> citizens; that sense does not exist. I think the generalised view of
> the government is somebody who ... as an institution that's there
> to make your life difficult, not to make your life easy, that's the
> general sense. (AT)

This mutual mistrust, together with the government's response by putting all the diaspora into one group, is very harmful to Ethiopia's development. Too often, 'all this desire to go back and do something suffers or gets lost in personal bickering and personal vendettas' (DD).

Even when an individual from the diaspora decides to return, they suffer a backlash from both sides. Some returnees currently residing in Ethiopia felt that they were being judged by their family and friends overseas for returning to Ethiopia, while at the same time being mistrusted by the government, who thinks they are on the side of the diaspora. One returnee pointedly highlighted his frustration with this phenomenon:

> this summer I was in the United States, ... everybody was thinking that I am a sell out there, in the United States. ... they think I am here [Ethiopia] for a position [government job]. They think I am here exploiting the people ... those people most of them did not even want to talk to me just because they thought that ... I am one of the sell outs. And then you come here and this government considers you also as one of them [the diaspora]. (GH)

Concluding Observations

Transnational mobility research is influencing the discussion and contributing to the next phase of comparative education by embracing both the national and the global spheres (see Little, 2000). As such this study is quite relevant as it is part of the economic, social/cultural and political manifestations of the push and pull of globalisation. It shifts away from the pure nation-state as a main unit of analysis (Welch, 2010) and rather promotes educational dialogue across the North and South. The phenomenal growth of knowledge and skills exchange, educational goods and services within and between the North and South reinforces the importance of the need for comparative education to be grounded not only in the local but also in the global context (see Little, 2000). The understanding of the role of knowledge exchange (Kuznetsov, 2006; Wescott, 2006) and brain circulation (Saxenian, 2006) as part of the global processes of education should be strongly considered as part of the development of comparative education.

The discussion above shows that the obligation that individuals feel toward their homeland is a strong motivator to participate in the developmental process, driving many to return and seek opportunities to give something back. The obligation that people from the diaspora feel toward the country they love, the country that has provided them an education and a pathway for a better life, is the driving force for many. They are willing to make sacrifices to contribute to the homeland because they understand the sacrifices that Ethiopia and the Ethiopian people have made for them. This sentiment too needs to be nurtured so as to benefit the country and bring about change.

The findings also reveal that the majority of the returnees returned for the love of their country and because they thought they could contribute to national development. Within both the North American and the Ethiopian groups, family ties and the need to belong were identified as critically important. These two concepts drive many of the returnees to return and sacrifice their personal comfort to help in any way they can. The need to belong, coupled with the sense of obligation, motivated many in the diaspora to return or strongly consider returning. Family ties affect the drive to return, the level of difficulty encountered upon returning, as well as life satisfaction after returning. The findings show that the stronger the family attachments in Ethiopia, the easier it is for the returnees to adjust after returning home. This sense of obligation to their country is closely tied to the educational status of the participants when they migrated overseas – the higher the level of education before migrating overseas, the greater the sense of obligation to their country. Most of the returnees and the diaspora in this study left Ethiopia with at least a university degree, which would then explain the strong need to give back expressed by the participants.

The main reason cited for migrating varied between the North American diaspora and the returnees. The primary reason for migration among the North American group was the impossibility of personal development and improvement in Ethiopia, followed by the political situation (for men and for women). The leading reason for the returnee group's migration was education and research opportunities, followed by the political situation (for men and for women). Once again the political status of the country played a part in the migration of many highly skilled individuals.

Another sore point is salary differences between expatriates (i.e. Indians, British, Nigerians etc.), returnees and local university staff. The issue is not so much about the money but rather about the message it sends to Ethiopians. The findings reveal that expatriate staff were paid on average at least four times that of returnees (who are paid local salaries). This sends a message to Ethiopian university staff that their expertise is not valued. This struck a particularly negative chord with returnees who often have qualifications that are similar to or better than those of expatriates. In effect, their hard work and sacrifices are not being acknowledged. Both returnees and local staff have difficulty providing for their families and, as a result, have to find other jobs to supplement their income, thereby weakening the quality of their input to Ethiopian universities and national R&D. Diaspora returnees may conclude that employers prefer expatriates to themselves.

The government justifies this disparity in salary by stating that there is no need to pay returnees the same wages as expatriates because the latter did not receive the benefits of the Ethiopian education system. The government also claims that maintaining equal pay between locals and returnees is designed to maintain the morale of the locals so that they do not feel undervalued or feel that they have to leave Ethiopia for better pay. The government's stance is understandable but in reality creates difficulties with engaging the diaspora as it claims to want to do. This dedication to mobilising the diaspora for tertiary contribution needs to find a better solution than that which is currently in place. While it is understandably difficult to find a workable solution that suits all stakeholders, the government must provide more effective solutions, not just content itself with the default situation. The returnees and the highly skilled diaspora who want to contribute are frustrated that the government's approach to finding a solution is to maintain the status quo, rather than better decision-making. The government's attitude toward some of these issues inhibits effective diaspora engagement and reveals its unwillingness to mobilise the Ethiopian knowledge diaspora.

It cannot be said that the Ethiopian government is doing nothing to attract its people in the diaspora. The government has several strategies and directives in place and has formed two offices to deal with diaspora issues and concerns. But the primary focus of the government remains financial. Government efforts do not go beyond encouraging remittances and investment from the diaspora (Shinn, 2002; Yacob, 2005; AHEAD, 2007). Ineffective policies to strengthen the government's relationship with Ethiopian professionals in the diaspora remain a barrier to engagement. A diaspora policy framework and a holistic national approach are needed to form a systematic and much-needed linkage between national development needs and diaspora capacities (International Organization for Migration, 2005; AHEAD, 2007). This failure is partially due to inadequate attention to using the skills of such individuals effectively, and to there simply being not enough places for them, as well as ongoing political concerns (the suspicion of ideological pollution). Despite ineffective government initiatives, individuals and professional networks overseas are doing what they can to attract skilled Ethiopians to return, re-engage and contribute.

References

Addis Ababa University–Business Process Reengineering (2008) Teaching and Learning in Graduates Programs at AAU.
http://www.aau.edu.et/index.php/component/content/article/172-bprcat/609-teaching-and-learning-in-graduates-programs-at-aau

Amazan, R.C. (2012) Gender, Diaspora and Development: the Ethiopian highly-skilled diaspora's notion of home and belonging, in N. Bagnall (Ed.) *Education and Belonging*, pp. 139-152. New York: Nova Science.

Ashcroft, K. (2004) The Massification of Higher Education: a comparison of the UK experience and the emerging Ethiopian response, *Ethiopian Journal of Higher Education*, 1(1), 20-42.

Assefa, T. (2008) Academic Freedom: conceptualization and determinants., in T. Assefa (Ed.) Academic Freedom in Ethiopia: perspectives of teaching personnel, pp. 1-18. Addis Ababa: Forum for Social Studies (FSS).

Association for Higher Education and Development (2007) *Enabling Diaspora Engagement in Africa: resources, mechanisms and gaps: case study: Ethiopia*. Ottawa: AHEAD.

Brown, M. (2000) Using the Intellectual Diaspora to Reverse the Brain Drain: some useful examples. Paper presented at the Economic Commission for Africa, University of Cape Town, South Africa, 22-24 February.

Dufera, D. (2005) Prospects, Challenges and Policy Options of Ethiopian Educational System Towards the Achievement of EFA Goals. http://home.hiroshima-u.ac.jp/cice/paper67.pdf

Federal Democratic Republic of Ethiopia (FDRE) (2002) Providing Foreign Nationals of Ethiopian Origin with Certain Rights to be Exercised in their Country of Origin. Proclamation No. 270/2002.

Gaillard, J. & Gaillard, A.M. (1997) Introduction: The International Mobility of Brains: exodus or circulation? *Science, Technology and Society*, 2(2), 195-228.

Integrated Regional Information Networks (2004) Ethiopia: IOM and government wooing skills and funds from diaspora. http://www.irinnews.org/report.aspx?reportid=49412

International Centre for Migration Policy Development (2008) *East Africa Migration Route Initiative Gaps & Needs Analysis Project Country Reports: Ethiopia, Kenya, Libya*. Vienna: ICMPD.

International Organization for Migration (2005) *World Migration 2005: costs and benefits of international migration*. Geneva: IOM.

Kefela, G. & Rena, R. (2008) Human Capital Investment is a Continuous Proposition: a study of North East African states, *Indus Journal of Management & Social Sciences*, 2(1), 54-70.

Kuznetsov, Y. (Ed.) (2006) *Diaspora Networks and the International Migration of Skills: how countries can draw on their talent abroad*. Washington, DC: International Bank for Reconstruction and Development/World Bank.

Little, A. (2000) Development Studies and Comparative Education: context, content, comparison and contributors, *Comparative Education*, 36(3), 279-296.

Ministry of Finance and Economic Development (2006) *Ethiopia: building on progress. A Plan for Accelerated and Sustained Development to End Poverty (PASDEP) – 2005/06-2009/10*. Addis Ababa: MoFED.

Mohamedbhai, G. (2008) *The Effects of Massification on Higher Education in Africa*. Accra-North: Association of African Universities, Working Group on Higher Education and Association for the Development of Education in Africa.

National Bank of Ethiopia (2004) Directive No. FXD/25/2004: amendment to directive no. FXD/24/2004 – issued for the establishment and operation of foreign currency account for non-resident Ethiopians and non-resident Ethiopian origin.

National Bank of Ethiopia (2006a) Directive No. FXD/31/2006: amendment to directive no. FXD/25/2004 – establishment and operation of foreign currency account for non-resident Ethiopians and non-resident Ethiopian origin. http://www.nbe.gov.et/gallery/Directives/Etablishement%20and%20operation%20directives.html

National Bank of Ethiopia (2006b) Directive No. FXD/30/2006: provisions for international remittance services. http://www.nbe.gov.et/gallery/Directives/international%20remittance%20directiv es.html

Nordling, L. (2008). Growing apace in Africa, *The Guardian*. http://www.guardian.co.uk/education/2008/may/13/highereducation.international educationnews

Reisberg, L. & Rumbley, L.E. (2010) Ethiopia: the dilemmas of higher education expansion. *University World News*, no. 45. http://www.universityworldnews.com

Sahlu, M. (2009) Welcome Mat Pulled from under Diaspora, *Capital Newspaper*.

Sako, S. (2002) Brain Drain and Africa's Development: a reflection, *African Issues*, 30(1), 25-30.

Saxenian, A. (2006) *The New Argonauts: regional advantage in a global economy*. Cambridge, MA: Harvard University Press.

Scott, P. (1995) *The Meanings of Mass Higher Education*. Buckingham: Society for Research into Higher Education and Open University Press.

Shinn, D.H. (2002) Reversing the Brain Drain in Ethiopia, paper presented at the Ethiopian North American Health Professionals Association, Alexandria, Virginia, 23 November.

Teferra, D. & Altbach, P.G. (Eds) (2003) *African Higher Education: an international reference handbook*. Bloomington: Indiana University Press.

Tessema, K.A. (2009) The Unfolding Trends and Consequences of Expanding Higher Education in Ethiopia: massive universities, massive challenges, *Higher Education Quarterly*, 63(1), 29-45.

United Nations Development Programme (2013) *Human Development Report: 'the rise of the south' or the disappearance of the south*. New York: UNDP.

Welch, A.R. (1997) The Peripatetic Professor: the internationalisation of the academic profession, *Higher Education Policy*, 34(3), 323-345, Special Issue on the Academic Profession.

Welch, A.R. (2002) Going Global? Internationalising Australian Universities in a Time of Global Crisis, *Comparative Education Review*, 46(4), 433-471.

Welch, A.R. (2010) Nation-State, Diaspora and Comparative Education: the place of place in comparative education, in D. Mattheou (Ed.) *Changing Educational Landscapes: educational policies, schooling systems and higher education – a comparative perspective*. New York: Springer.

Welch, A.R. (2011) *Higher Education in Southeast Asia. Blurring Borders, Changing Balance*. London: Routledge.

Welch, A.R. & Zhang, Z. (2007) The Chinese Knowledge Diaspora: communication networks among overseas Chinese intellectuals, in D. Epstein, R. Boden, R. Deem, F. Rizvi & S. Wright (Eds) *Geographies of Knowledge, Geometries of Power: framing the future of higher education*, pp. 338-354. New York: Routledge.

Wescott, C.G. (2006) Harnessing Knowledge Exchange Among Overseas Professionals, *International Public Management Review*, 7(1), 30-69.

Woldetensae, Y. (2007) Optimizing the African Brain Drain: strategies for mobilizing the intellectual diaspora towards brain-gain, paper presented at the Conference of

Rectors, Vice Chancellors and Presidents of African Universities, Tripoli, 21-25 October.

World Bank (2000) *Entering the 21st Century: world development report*. New York: Oxford University Press.

World Bank (2002) *Constructing Knowledge Societies: new challenges for tertiary education*. Washington, DC: World Bank.

Xinhua (2006) Overseas Ethiopians Increase Investment at Home, *People's Daily Online*, 30 May.
http://english.peopledaily.com.cn/200605/30/eng20060530_269582.html

Yacob, Y. (2005) Reversing Ethiopia's Brain Drain: a national imperative. Online monograph. http://www.ethiomedia.com/newpress/braindrain_033005.html

Yizengaw, T. (2003) Transformations in Higher Education: experiences with reform and expansion in Ethiopian higher education system, paper presented at the conference Improving Tertiary Education in Sub-Saharan Africa: Things That Work, Accra, Ghana, 23-25 September.

CHAPTER 12

Global Climate, Local Weather: perspectives of internationalisation in Chinese higher education

JÜRGEN HENZE

ABSTRACT Internationalisation of higher education in China has become a hot topic in international comparative research, in education as well as across disciplines. Despite vast numbers of publications on the topic already, this chapter introduces basic elements of the state-of-the-art discussion as it is taking place outside of China, as well as perspectives from the discourse occurring within China. The chapter takes Jane Knight's definition of internationalisation as a starting point for classification of certain elements of internationalisation, but then proposes an enlargement of the scope of her definition by introducing the term 'reflexive internationalisation' in reference to Beck's theory of reflexive modernity. Reflexive internationalisation represents the enlightened analysis of processes, structures and interrelatedness (dependencies) of intended action within the frame of global internationalisation and its critical reflexive analysis. This analysis also includes various kinds of reach-out 'influences' of internationalisation strategies in cross-national and cross-cultural perspectives. The chapter provides an overview of developments in Chinese state-controlled internationalisation in higher education and the regional and institutional variations in strategy and policy outcomes.

Introduction

Internationalisation in Chinese higher education appears as a process of state-controlled frame setting, regionally and institutionally translated in different forms of policy design and action, strongly related to international mainstream discourse of globalisation and internationalisation with well-informed academia, and well aware of the possibilities and constraints of market-driven designs of internationalisation. Internationalisation in China seems to be directed inwardly and outwardly at the same time. As such, China has become an interrelated space of a worldwide process, inwardly driven but at the same time outwardly shaping the internationalisation space in parts of the western world. Internationalisation in Chinese education, especially in higher education, has increasingly become an area of international concern. This seems to be mainly due to the rising number of Chinese international students and scholars who have become the world's largest floating intellectual population from/in Asia in the twenty-first century.

In a broader perspective, if internationalisation means confrontation with otherness and the challenges of coping with otherness, China has a long history of cultural and political encounters. At least since the middle of the nineteenth century, Chinese academia has been forced by internal and external pressures to cope with and react to different views of the world, education and science and the way knowledge is produced and shared in society. As part of this tradition, the articulation of some kind of Chinese cultural 'substance', which has to be protected against non-Chinese influence and infection, has always been on the agenda of discourse about modernisation, globalisation and internationalisation (Hayhoe, 1996). As a matter of fact, a certain sensitivity for protecting the cultural 'self' – however defined by different interest groups – has always been an important perspective of the Chinese brand of critical thinking (Wang, 2012).

It is in the light of these intellectual traditions that current international and internal Chinese discourse and practice of internationalisation has to be seen in a broader perspective, a perspective that moves beyond very recent semantic constructions of 'comprehensive internationalisation' or similar notions (Hudzik, 2011). The embeddedness of current internationalisation processes in deep-level cultural webs/meanings leads to a degree of complexity which can hardly be dealt with in this chapter. Instead, the following analysis is intended to serve as a first and introductory mapping of research on internationalisation in Chinese higher education, to sketch out core areas of research and possible options for further research. The chapter predominantly refers to research that has been undertaken by Chinese scholars abroad, a community which has been described elsewhere as Chinese 'knowledge diaspora' or 'academic-intellectual diaspora' (Welch & Zhang, 2007; Wang & Zweig, 2009; Welch, 2010; Welch & Cai, 2011; Henze et al, 2013). Mainly during the last decade this community has been very successful in the production of a new genre of research literature, very often in cooperation with foreign colleagues. The combination of Chinese language and culture origins, in combination with a first academic degree from a tertiary institution in China and a PhD at a western university, has created a new academic space (and identity formation) beyond disciplinary, cultural and national boundaries. The chapter will apply non-Chinese frames of classification and categorisation for the analysis of internationalisation as orientation, and will also try to review their value and appropriateness for meaningful interpretations of Chinese internationalisation in higher education.

Setting the Stage: China as a new player in the world market of international education

During the last decade China has increasingly caught the world's attention for its massification of higher education and the resulting expansion on all levels in higher education. Currently international sources project China's tertiary enrolment ratio (based on the 18-22 age group population) to rise to 38% in 2020 from 24% in 2009 (British Council, 2012). In combination with the mid- and long-term demographic development, this increased participation in higher education will lead to higher levels of international mobility among Chinese students (Han & Zweig, 2010). This development is further accelerated by a rising middle class, mainly in urban spaces (Kharas, 2010).

Recent publications by the Organisation for Economic Cooperation and Development (2013, p. 304ff.) and the British Council (2012, p. 39ff.) estimated the total number of tertiary students enrolled outside their country of citizenship as around 4.3 million; among them students from Asia accounted for 53% and the majority originated from China, India and South Korea. According to a new United Kingdom (UK) government study on international education (Department for Business, Innovation and Skills, 2013b, p. 18), 'by 2010, nearly a fifth of internationally mobile students were Chinese (548,500; 18.2%), with Indian (192,000; 6.4%) and German (93,700; 3.1%) students the next biggest group'.

	2000			2010	
	Number	% of global int'l mobile students		Number	% of global int'l mobile students
China	140,500	8.1	China	548,500	18.2
South	71,100	4.1	India	192,000	6.4
Greece	63,600	3.7	German	93,700	3.1
Japan	59,300	3.4	USA	55,000	1.8
India	55,900	3.2	Malaysi	53,900	1.8
German	54,500	3.1	France	53,300	1.8
France	50,200	2.9	Vietnam	47,200	1.6
Turkey	48,000	2.8	South	46,500	1.5
Italy	44,400	2.6	Canada	44,900	1.5
Morocco	42,500	2.4	Turkey	42,600	1.4

Table I. Top 10 countries of origin for internationally mobile students.
Source: Department for Business, Innovation and Skills, 2013b, p. 19 (based on World Bank Education statistics, excluding North Korea).

By 2020 India, China, the USA and Indonesia will account for over 50% of the world's 18-22 population and China and India will see half of the world's manpower entering the labour market with a higher education degree. Although China's current role as leading country for outbound students will be overtaken by India soon – due to demographic changes – its role as the most attractive participant in the education market will hardly be challenged due to the growing importance of the middle class and its preparedness to invest in education. Not surprisingly, this is of great interest for all national higher education systems that charge tuition to international students and rely on their overall spending on living costs as a major element of national budgeting. Among other countries, Australia, Canada, the USA, New Zealand and the UK have already started intensive marketing campaigns with far-reaching consequences for their national higher education systems (as an example see Australia International Education Advisory Council, 2013; Department for Business, Innovation and Skills, 2013a, b; for a more critical discussion see Fazackerley & Worthington, 2007; Chiang, 2012).

A second area of international concern is the gradual development of China as an attractive host country for inbound international student mobility. The number of international students in China has increased by four times in the past 10 years. In 2003, the number of international students was 77,715, while in 2012, the number reached 328,330.

Furthermore, the Chinese government makes strenuous efforts to attract international students to China by offering scholarship. In 2003, 7.92% of international students were sponsored by the Chinese government, while in 2012, 8.76% of international students received scholarship. Students from neighbouring Asian countries are still the largest international student group in China; in 2012, 63.22% of all international students came from Asia. However, compared with the data in 2003, when 81.93% of international students came from Asia, students from Europe (16.58%) and the USA (10.62%) became important sources of international students in China as well (statistics according to the Ministry of Education, Beijing, webpages, 2003-12).

The third area of international attraction has evolved around the complex of knowledge production, dissemination and international cooperative sharing by joint research and publication activities. This also includes China's continuous share in patent development (Wilsdon & Keeley, 2007; Royal Society, 2011; Department of Industry, Innovation, Science, Research and Tertiary Education, 2012).

Finally, the strong presence of Chinese students in a number of host countries (USA, Australia and UK) has forced their academic systems to respond to different teaching and learning expectations among Chinese students (Hou, 2011; Commonwealth of Australia, 2012). The research into culturally dependent learning styles, the awareness of different communicative behaviours in classroom interaction and a growing sensitivity among the teaching staff of an alternative architecture of scientific work, including reasoning and writing, have increasingly produced a new landscape of discourse and research (Henze & Zhu, 2012). As an overall result, there is a new openness to non-western theory-building in various scientific disciplines (see Chan & Rao, 2009; Kember, 2009; Jin & Cortazzi, 2011; Li, 2012; Jarvis 2013; Wright & Schartner, 2013).

Concepts of Internationalisation – do they fit the Chinese case?

This chapter accepts the interpretation of the international dimension in education by Jane Knight, who defined 'internationalization at the national/sector/institutional levels as the process of integrating an international, intercultural or global dimension into the purpose, functions or delivery of post-secondary education' (Knight, 2004, p. 11). Internationalisation is seen as a process at home or abroad, where specific outcomes are defined in detail or more general terms. According to de Wit (2011, p. 245):

> the literature ... identifies four broad categories of rationales for internationalisation: political, economic, social and cultural, and academic. These rationales are not mutually exclusive, they may vary in importance by country and region, and their dominance may change over time. At the present time, economic rationales are considered to be more dominant than the other three. In relation to these, academic rationales such as strategic alliances, status and profile are also becoming more dominant ... .
> Rationales vary over time and by country/region, they are not mutually exclusive, and they lead to different approaches and policies. Currently, changes are taking place at a rapid pace in many parts of the world, and rationales are becoming more and more interconnected.

As far as China is concerned, these categories of rationales may serve well to capture the variety of orientations, activities and landscapes of discourse in the policy domain of internationalisation, in China as well as abroad. It is against this finding that I selected the weather metaphor as a title for this chapter: 'Global climate' stands for the appropriateness of the rationales as an analytical tool to cope with the various perspectives of internalisation in Chinese higher education. 'Local weather' on the other hand denotes the overall effect of the varying importance of each category of rationales and their different degree of interrelatedness and direction as well as speed of development at different levels of the higher education system (and society in general). As a matter of fact, Knight's (2008, 25) listing of rationales and its differentiation into those of 'existing rationales' and of 'emerging importance' appears as a highly appropriate categorisation for the case of China (see Table II).

Rationales	Existing rationales	Of emerging importance
Social/cultural	National cultural identity	*National level*
	Intercultural understanding	Soft power
	Citizenship development	Human resources
	Social and community	development
	development	Strategic alliances
	Improving the quality of the	Income generation/
	nation	commercial trade
		Nation-building/
Political	Foreign policy (Confucius	institution-building
	Institutes)	Social/cultural development
	National security	and mutual understanding
	Technical assistance	
	Peace and mutual understanding	
	National identity	
	Regional identity	
Economic	Economic growth and	*Institutional Level*
	competitiveness	International branding and
	Labour market	profile
	Financial incentives	Quality enhancement/
		international standards
Academic	Extension of academic horizon	Income generation
	Institution-building	Student and staff
	Profile and status	development
	Enhancement of quality	Strategic alliances
	International academic	Knowledge production
	standards	Development of reward
	International dimension to	systems/ incentives
	research and teaching	Sharing the world's elite
	Knowledge production and	publication system (SCI,
	dissemination	SSCI ...)

Table II. Rationales driving internationalisation of higher education in China.
Source: Knight (2008, p. 25) and adjustments by the author.

Internationalisation in higher education in China is strongly related to a vision of modernisation conceptually rooted in the earlier state policy of the 'four modernisations' (*sige xiandaihua*) in the 1980s. As such, modernisation, internationalisation and globalisation have been strategic keywords used for policy implementation in different directions and with varying degrees of intensity at different levels of society. As a *terminus technicus* for anticipated change, internationalisation 'hints at a trend towards more' (Teichler 2010, 265) with higher quality for more people in society. In its core elements, internationalisation is predominantly seen as a necessary process for improving the 'quality of education', especially in higher and vocational education. While the term 'globalisation' is more often used in conjunction with economic developments (*jingji quanqiuhua*, economic globalisation), internationalisation has been used to describe the educational 'opening to the world'. While internationalisation seems to be more often used to denote intended processes of cross-cultural encounters framed by clear boundaries – like nation-states – and regulatory acts, globalisation is related to interconnected phenomena and processes with blurred or hybrid boundaries. Altbach et al (2009, p. 7) prosed a definition which comes close to related concepts in the Chinese context:

> We define globalization as the reality shaped by an increasingly integrated world economy, new information and communications technology, the emergence of an international knowledge network, the role of the English language, and other forces beyond the control of academic institutions ... . Internationalization is defined as the variety of policies and programs that universities and governments implement to respond to globalization.

This definition also mirrors the basic world view encoded in the most up-to-date document for educational development in the period 2010-20, released by the Chinese Ministry of Education in 2010.

Internationalisation as the Road to Modernisation: outline of China's National Plan for Medium and Long-Term Education Reform and Development (2010-2020)

Although only one in a series of related documents on China's modernisation, the *Outline of China's National Plan for Medium and Long-Term Education Reform and Development (2010-2020)* – hereafter referred to as the *Outline* – provides a key to understanding the overall perspectives of internationalisation in higher education. This blueprint for intended, state-controlled processes of change in all sectors of the education system seems to be the result of an intensive academic and political competition for mapping out different approaches of modernisation in Chinese education. A closer look at this central document may reveal a multifaceted approach which corresponds to the internationally prevailing interpretation of 'comprehensive internationalisation'.

In its preamble, the *Outline* refers to internationalisation as an ongoing process which has to be seen in the broader context of

> increasing pressure from its vast population, limited natural resources, the environment, and its transformation of economic growth pattern. All those have highlighted the pressing need to enhance citizens' quality and cultivate innovative personnel. The future development and great rejuvenation of the Chinese nation are predicated on talents or professionals, and on education. (Ministry of Education [MoE], 2010, p. 6)

As far as the higher education sector is concerned, institutions shall be urged to open their best faculties to the world, and to participate in or set up collaborative international academic organizations or global science plans; they shall also be encouraged to join top-notch education and research institutes abroad in establishing united research and development centers. The building of world-class and high-level universities shall pick up speed, so as to cultivate top-notch innovators and world-class disciplines, achieve original results at advanced level in the world. (MoE, 2010, p. 21)

Very much in contrast to earlier policy documents on educational development, the *Outline* not only provides a clear reference to 'opening up' (*kaifeng*) but also a more detailed prescription on form, content and orientation of internationalisation at various level of higher education.

It is essential to reform and develop education by opening it to the outside world, carrying out education exchanges and collaboration at multiple levels and in a broad scope, and raising education's internationalization level. Advanced concepts and experience in education in the world shall be assimilated to boost education reform and development at home, and to enhance the nation's global position, influence and competitiveness in the field of education. To meet the requirement of opening up the Chinese economy and society to the world, large numbers of talents shall be cultivated that are imbued with global vision, well-versed in international rules, and capable of participating in international affairs and competition. (MoE, 2010, p. 34)

In spite of this overall request for opening up to the world, internationalisation becomes a 'must' for educational institutions as well as for individual actors. A specific frame of reference is laid out for optional references and for the design of institutional and individual forms of implementation, but framed by state guidelines. Orientation towards 'world-class' standards, whatever that is in specific circumstances, serves as the new standard for highest quality:

It is necessary to seek the cooperation of renowned schools, education institutions, research institutes and companies outside this nation to establish education, teaching, training and research organizations or undertake such projects. Schools at all levels and of all varieties should be encouraged to engage in diverse forms of international exchanges and cooperation, and a good job should be done in running demonstrative joint schools or joint projects in cooperation with foreign partners. Multiple approaches to utilizing quality education resources from abroad shall be searched for. Efforts should be made to attract more world-class experts and scholars to teaching, research and managerial jobs in China, and invite high-level professionals and academic teams from overseas in a planned way. Quality textbooks shall be imported, and the percentage of foreign teachers in college faculty increased. More outstanding Chinese students shall be attracted to serve the nation after they have finished their studies in other countries and regions. (MoE, 2010, p. 34)

It should be of no surprise that this interpretation of internationalisation leads to similar forms of international cooperation as it has been observed in other parts of the world: open and contracted institutional exchange and cooperation in teaching and research; the development of well-known forms of transnational educational provision; an extension of the scope and dimensions of student and scholarly international inbound and outbound mobility and a gradual intensification of China´s participation in supra-national policy design (UNESCO):

China should facilitate the mutual recognition of academic credentials and degrees between its colleges and academic institutions from more countries and regions. More support shall be given to exchanges of students and teachers, mutual recognition of academic credits, and mutual or joint conferment of academic degrees between Chinese and foreign colleges. Collaboration between Chinese colleges and their counterparts abroad shall be stepped up, platforms for collaborative teaching and research projects set up, and collaborative high-level researches in basic or high technology promoted. Exchanges and cooperation between Chinese and foreign primary and middle schools and vocational schools shall be boosted. Education aimed at enhancing international understanding shall be stepped up to promote level of cross-cultural communication and to help students better understand different countries and cultures ... Cooperation with UNESCO and other international organizations shall be intensified. This nation will take a more active part in bilateral, multilateral, regional and global collaboration in education. (MoE, 2010, p. 34-35)

Of special importance for mid- and long-term development is the extension of existing, and the formation of new, transnational forms of education delivery, thereby in two directions, inbound and outbound:

Assistance shall be granted to set up a cluster of exemplary Sino-foreign cooperative education institutions, build joint laboratories and research centers in colleges by international cooperation, introduce a large number of high-level professionals from overseas countries and regions, and dispatch college presidents and faculty members, and primary and middle school principals and

backbone teachers for advanced studies or training in overseas
institutions. (MoE, 2010, p. 46)

Increasingly, the Chinese government will take measures to increase the
importance of Chinese as a foreign language in other parts of the world.
'Confucius Institutes', which may be viewed as a state project to increase
China's soft power in the world, implemented within the responsibilities of
the Ministry of Education, play a decisive role:

High-quality Chinese educational institutions shall be encouraged
to run branches overseas, undertake international exchanges,
cooperation and education service extensively. Efforts should be
made to support the teaching of Chinese as a foreign language in
other countries, and elevate the education quality of Confucius
Institutes. International aid to education shall be boosted, so as to
cultivate and train professionals for other developing countries. A
framework shall be established to make Chinese college graduates'
overseas volunteer service available in more fields and through
more channels. (MoE, 2010, p. 35)

Finally, China is going to promote itself as a new and important player in the
education world market more actively than ever:

More international students shall be admitted for studies in this
country. Chinese government scholarships shall be increased, with
financial assistance offered mainly to students from other
developing countries, and the composition of students coming to
this country for studies shall be optimized. Foundation courses
shall be given to international students before they start college
education in China; more disciplines shall be taught in foreign
languages in Chinese colleges; and education quality for those
studying in China shall be improved. (MoE, 2010, p. 35)

At this stage of the chapter, the informed reader might be reminded of de
Wit's more recent attempt to clarify various 'misconceptions' and 'challenges'
in the construction and interpretation of internationalisation in higher
education. De Wit refers to Jane Knight's five myths of internationalisation'
(de Wit, 2011, p. 245):

– Myth one: Foreign students as internationalization agents: 'more
foreign students on campus will produce more internationalized
institutional culture and curriculum'.
– Myth two: International reputation as a proxy for quality: 'the
more international a university is ... the better its reputation'.
– Myth three: International institutional agreements: 'the greater
number of international agreements or network memberships a
university has the more prestigious and attractive it is'.

– Myth four: International accreditation: 'the more international accreditation stars an institution has, the more internationalized it is and ergo the better it is'.
– Myth five: Global branding: 'an international marketing scheme is the equivalent of an internationalization plan'.

While de Wit himself agrees with Knight's myths one and three, he presents a collection of nine misconceptions altogether (2011, p. 246), which are:

1. Internationalisation is similar to teaching in English.
2. Internationalisation is similar to studying abroad.
3. Internationalisation is similar to teaching an international subject.
4. Internationalisation means having many international students (see Knight's myth one).
5. Internationalisation can be implemented successfully with only a few international students in the classroom.
6. Intercultural and international competencies do not necessarily have to be assessed as such.
7. The more agreements an institution has, the more international it is (see Knight's myth three).
8. Higher education is international by its very nature.
9. Internationalisation is an objective in itself.

The analysis of developments in Chinese higher education since the government's decision in favour of mass higher education in 1999 reveals that virtually all the misconceptions listed appear in academic discourse and institutional orientation and behaviour in China (Zha, 2003, 2009, 2011, 2012; Hayhoe et al, 2011). But, to be fair, it must be noted that these misconceptions – partly by referring to de Wit and Knight – are clearly recognised among a growing number of Chinese intellectuals. Still, from the organisational point of view, de Wit's listing of misconceptions is more or less exactly what forms the policy background for internationalisation in Chinese higher education, on the state level as well as on the regional and organisational levels. While the *Outline* served as an example for central state-controlled guidelines with some kind of visionary character, Tables IIIa and IIIb list a number of indicators that have been in use in one of the more affluent regions in China, in Zhejiang province (Gu, 2013, p. 10). These indicators, in conjunction with the general orientation of the *Outline*, serve as a road map for testifying the success and failure of internationalisation at the institutional level within the provincial space.

Indicators (college average)*	Status quo**		
	Doctoral/Master's degree-granting colleges	Other undergraduate colleges	Vocational & technical colleges
Percentage of foreign students		0.86	
	1.6	0.6	0.1
Percentage of outbound exchange students	0.9	0.6	0.1
Percentage of foreign experts for culture and education***	4.5	3.9	1.1
Percentage of full-time teachers as visiting scholar over 3 months****	20.0	11.2	4.1
Percentage of foreign language and bilingual instruction	4.3	1.6	2
Sino-foreign cooperative education programmes	2.8	0.7	0.7
International academic conferences (organiser or contractor)	15.4	1.6	0.4
International cooperated research platform (including international research base)	2.0	1.1	0.2
Overseas or international organisation-funded projects	14.4	1.4	0.2

Indicators (college average)*	2015		
	Doctoral/Master's degree-granting colleges	Other undergraduate colleges	Vocational & technical colleges
Percentage of foreign students		2	
	4.5	1.3	0.2
Percentage of outbound exchange students	4.0	1.0	0.3
Percentage of foreign experts for culture and education***	8.0	4.0	2.0
Percentage of full-time teachers as visiting scholar over 3 months****	30.0	18	6.0
Percentage of foreign language and bilingual instruction	6.0	4.0	3.0
Sino-foreign cooperative education programmes	4.0	2.0	2.6
International academic conferences (organiser or contractor)	22.0	3.0	0.5
International cooperated research platform (including international research base)	5.0	2.0	0.5
Overseas or international organisation-funded projects	30.0	1.5	0.4

Indicators (college average)*	2020		
	Doctoral/Master's degree-granting colleges	Other undergraduate colleges	Vocational & technical colleges
Percentage of foreign students		4.0	
	8.6	3.0	0.4
Percentage of outbound exchange students	8.0	2.0	0.5
Percentage of foreign experts for culture and education***	10.0	5.0	3.0
Percentage of full-time teachers as visiting scholar over 3 months****	40.0	25.0	8.0
Percentage of foreign language and bilingual instruction	12.0	8.0	6.0
Sino-foreign cooperative education programmes	6.0	3.0	3.0
International academic conferences (organiser or contractor)	25.0	5.0	1.0
International cooperated research platform (including international research base)	9.0	3.0	0.6
Overseas or international organisation-funded projects	40.0	2.0	0.5

*Planning indicator reflects the average level of similar colleges and universities across the province.
**Status data and the starting year are based on data from 2008.
***Foreign experts for culture and education: foreign experts for culture & education, project experts, foreign teachers, administrative staff, etc., engaged in teaching, research and management in colleges of the province.
****Status data is indeed the 'percentage of persons with experience abroad'.

Table IIIa Planning indicators – internationalisation of higher education, Zhejiang.

Indicators (total province)	Status quo **	2015	2020
Sino-foreign cooperative education institutions	1	≥ 7	≥ 10
Confucius Institutes	8	≥ 15	≥ 20
Educational institutions abroad	0	≥ 1	≥ 2

**Status data and the starting year are based on data from 2008.

Table IIIb. Planning indicators – internationalisation of higher education, Zhejiang.

While this type of indicator is in use all over China, there can be no doubt about the in-built mechanism of (re)producing regional and institutional inequality and disadvantages. Because the internationalisation processes are embedded in historically transmitted hierarchies of social orientation and practice, controlled and maintained by governmental action, the internationalisation is good and bad at the same time, just depending on the actor's position in society. Contradictions which derive from this situation have been clearly recognised among the academic community in China and elsewhere.

Current Research on Chinese Higher Education: findings and prospects

From an international perspective, research on Chinese higher education has produced an enormous amount of knowledge and critical awareness concerning those perspectives of internationalisation that have been discussed here so far. Not necessarily under the heading of 'internationalisation', but in the light of modernisation and globalisation, change in China's higher education system has been analysed extensively. A new community of scholars of Chinese origin, with a first university degree from China and further educational credentials (mostly PhD) from abroad, has become an important and influential resource for new insight into content, structure and interrelatedness of higher education in China. This community of scholars has been called a 'knowledge diaspora' or 'academic-intellectual diaspora'; the majority of them now hold university positions in Australia, the UK, the USA and Hong Kong and, if they have returned to China, at universities there as well. Often their international publications are based on research during a doctorate first, followed by individual effort or (increasingly international) collaboration in research and publication. Although the number of such influential scholars is still fairly small, it is on the rise.

What are the main areas of research, then? So far it is possible to identify a number of important research areas based on an initial literature overview. I think it is reasonable to map out the following:

1. A large number of publications try to provide a balanced picture of the results in higher education development since the end of the 1980s and treat the dimension of internationalisation as one among others of the dramatic move to mass higher education and China's open door policy (Hayhoe, 1996; Yang, 2000, 2002, 2003, 2010, 2011, 2012; Mok, 2005, 2009; Ross & Lou, 2005; Wan, 2006; Li et al, 2008; World Bank, 2009, 2012; Cai, 2010; Hayhoe et al, 2011; Morgan & Wu, 2011; Ryan, 2011; Schulte, 2012; Wang & Liu, 2011).
2. Of particular interest is the development of transnational education and China's growing involvement in the world education market. This leads to a variety of studies on cultural, organisational-structural and economic consequences for both, the internal situation in China and the world community of host countries for Chinese international students and scholars (Wang, 2006; Gu, 2008; Ding et al, 2009;

H. Li, 2010; Anderson, 2011, 2013; GHK Consulting, 2011; Griffith University, 2012; Ong & Chan, 2012, Quality Assurance Agency for Higher Education, 2013a, b).

3. A special genre of research has been created on how to cope with the 'Chinese' or 'Asian' learner (whatever that is!) in non-Chinese learning environments and how the host education systems can assure the most efficient teaching and learning for this target group (Chan & Rao, 2009; Kember, 2009; Jin & Cortazzi, 2011; Yan & Berliner, 2011).

4. Research on adaptation problems among Chinese students abroad has also been en vogue for a number of years (Zhu, 2012). Basically, there is a new direction of research and theory-building, moving away from the interpretation of Chinese students as 'deficit' learners (as a result of culturally determined learning style and orientation), to more open approaches and interpretations of context-dependent learning behaviour (Gu, 2009; FitzPatrick et al, 2012; Tan, 2012; Wang et al, 2012; Ruble & Zhang, 2013).

5. A more recent development has produced a line of research on re-entry problems among Chinese students and scholars, on their influence at the institution that offers employment and on the frame of reference for their decisions about which employer to select (and vice versa) (Cai, 2012, 2013; Cai et al, 2012; Hao & Welch, 2012; Zweig & Wang, 2013).

Perhaps the next phase of research on internationalisation in Chinese higher education will move in the direction of comparative theoretical research with a broader historical background and stronger affiliation to current discourse in modernisation and globalisation theory. There is a vast amount of research available that could be used in cooperative research activities with Chinese colleagues in China and with members of the intellectual diaspora in other parts of the word. What seems to be necessary is a research that takes the basic understanding of Beck's reflexive modernisation and cosmopolitan view as a starting point and puts internationalisation in a broader frame of reference beyond the current understanding of 'comprehensive internationalisation': for Beck, '"reflexive modernisation" means self-confrontation with the effects of risk society that can not be dealt with and assimilated in the system of industrial society' (Beck, 2004, p. 6; Beck & Grande, 2010). For the complex relation between internationalisation, modernisation and globalisation, the case of China might be a good fit to be looked at from a reflexive point of view. It seems that current change in higher education – as well as elsewhere in the education system – that has been induced by elements of internationalisation is embedded in a social and cultural matrix which is responsible for a constant production of conflict and contradictions beyond the control of social actors. Research is needed to find new paradigms of thinking about this complexity of development in modern societies.

References

Altbach, P.G., Reisberg, L. & Rumbley, L.E. (2009) *Trends in Global Higher Education: tracking an academic revolution.* A report prepared for the UNESCO 2009 World Conference on Higher Education. Paris: UNESCO.

Anderson, S. (2011) *The Impact of the Children of Immigrants on Scientific Achievement in America.* NFAP Policy Brief May 2011. Arlington: National Foundation for American Policy.

Anderson, S. (2013) *The Importance of International Students to America.* NFAP Policy Brief July 2013. Arlington: National Foundation for American Policy.

Australia International Education Advisory Council (2013*) Australia – educating globally. Advice From the International Education Advisory Council.* Canberra: Commonwealth of Australia.

Beck, U. (2004) The Reinvention of Politics: towards a theory of reflexive modernization, in U. Beck, A. Giddens & S. Lash, *Reflexive Modernization: politics, tradition and aesthetics in the modern social order,* pp. 1-55. Cambridge: Polity Press.

Beck, U. & Grande, E. (2010) Varieties of Second Modernity: the cosmopolitan turn in social and political theory and research, *The British Journal of Sociology,* 61(3), 409-443.

British Council (2012) *The Shape of Things to Come: higher education global trends and emerging opportunities to 2020 (Going Global 2020).* London: British Council.

Cai, Y. (2010) Global Isomorphism and Governance Reform in Chinese Higher Education, *Tertiary Education and Management,* 16(3), 229-241.

Cai, Y. (2012) International Graduates From Finland: do they satisfy the needs of Finnish employers abroad? *Journal of Research in International Education,* 11(1), 19-31.

Cai, Y. (2013) Graduate Employability: a conceptual framework for understanding employers' perceptions, *Higher Education,* 65(4), 457-469.

Cai, Y., Pekkola, E. & Shumilova, Y. (2012) *Employability of International Graduates Educated in Finnish Higher Education Institutions.* Helsinki: VALOA-project, Career Services, University of Helsinki.

Chan, C.K.K. & Rao, N. (Eds) (2009) *Revisiting the Chinese Learner.* Hong Kong: Comparative Education Research Centre, University of Hong Kong.

Chiang, L.-C. (2012) Trading on the West´s Strength: the dilemmas of transnational higher education in East Asia, *Higher Education Policy,* 25, 171-189.

Commonwealth of Australia (2012) Australia in the Asian Century. White Paper. Canberra. http://asiancentury.dpmc.gov.au/white-paper

De Wit, H. (2011) Globalisation and Internationalisation of Higher Education [Introduction to online monograph], *Revista de Universidad y Sociedad del Conocimiento (RUSC),* 8(2), 241-248. http://rusc.uoc.edu/ojs/index.php/rusc/article/view/v8n2-dewit/v8n2-dewit-eng

Department for Business, Innovation and Skills, UK Government (2013a) *International Education: global growth and prosperity.* London: BIS.

Department for Business, Innovation and Skills, UK Government (2013b) *International Education – global growth and prosperity: an accompanying analytical narrative*. London: BIS.

Department of Industry, Innovation, Science, Research and Tertiary Education, Australian Government (2012) *Science and Research Collaboration Between Australia and China*. Canberra: DIISTRE. http://www.innovation.gov.au/Science/InternationalCollaboration/ACSRF/Docu ments/DIISRTE-AustraliaChinaCollaboration.pdf

Ding, X., Yue, C. & Sun, Y. (2009) The Influence of China's Entry into the WTO on its Educational System, *European Journal of Education*, 44(1), 9-19.

Fazackerley, A. & Worthington, P. (2007) *British Universities in China: the reality beyond the rhetoric. An Agora Discussion Paper*. London: Agora: the Forum for Culture and Education.

FitzPatrick, M., Davey, J. & Dai, L. (2012) Chinese Students' Complaining Behavior: hearing the silence, *Asia Pacific Journal of Marketing and Logistics*, 24(5), 738-754.

GHK Consulting (2011) *EU–China Student and Academic Staff Mobility: present situation and future developments*. Joint study between the European Commission and the Ministry of Education in China, April. Brussels: GHK Consulting.

Griffith University (2012) The Australia–China Relationship at Forty: building a pathway for the future, an Outcomes Paper from the Second Track Dialogue, Peking University, Beijing, 25-26 September. http://goo.gl/8OTOJX

Gu, J. (2008) *Transnational Education Development: concept and strategy*. Shanghai: Xuelin Chubanshe.

Gu, J. (2013) *Development of Internationalisation in Higher Education in Zhejiang Province: Annual Report*. Hangzhou: Higher Education Research Institute, Hangzhou University. (In Chinese.)

Gu, Q. (2009) Maturity and Interculturality: Chinese students' experiences in UK higher education, *European Journal of Education*, 44(1), 37-52.

Han, D. & Zweig, D. (2010) Images of the World: studying abroad and Chinese attitudes towards international affairs, *The China Quarterly*, no. 202, 290-306.

Hao, J. & Welch, A.R. (2012) A Tale of Sea Turtles: job-seeking experiences of hai gui (high-skilled returnees) in China, *Higher Education Policy*, 25, 243-260.

Hayhoe, R. (1996) *China's Universities 1895-1995*. New York: Garland.

Hayhoe, R., Li, J., Lin, J. & Zha, Q. (2011) *Portraits of 21st Century Chinese Universities: in the move to mass higher education*. Hong Kong: Hong Kong University, Comparative Education Research Centre.

Henze, J. & Zhu, J. (2012) Current Research on Chinese Students Studying Abroad, *Research in Comparative and International Education*, 7(1), 90-104.

Henze, J., Zhu, J. & Xu, B. (2013) Perspektiven der Entwicklungsdynamik im chinesischen Hochschulwesen, in M.F. Buck & M. Kabaum (Eds) *Ideen und Realitäten von Universitäten*, pp. 53-81. Berlin: Peter Lang.

Hou, J. (2011) Learning on Two Campuses: students' transition experiences in a China–UK articulation programme. Dissertation. Newcastle: University of Newcastle.

Hudzik, J.K. (2011) *Comprehensive Internationalization: from concept to action.* Washington, DC: NAFSA: Association of International Educators.

Jarvis, P. (2013) Learning to a Person – East and West, *Comparative Education,* 49(1), 4-15.

Jin, L. & Cortazzi, M. (Eds) (2011) *Researching Chinese Learners. Skills, Perceptions and Intercultural Adaptations.* Basingstoke: Palgrave Macmillan.

Kember, D. (2009) International Students From Asia, in M. Tight, K.H. Mok, J. Huisman & C. Morphew (Eds) *The Routledge International Handbook of Higher Education,* pp. 47-60. New York: Routledge.

Kharas, H. (2010) *The Emerging Middle Class in Developing Countries.* Paris: Organisation for Economic Co-operation and Development. http://www.oecd.org/dev/44457738.pdf

Knight, J. (2004) Internationalization Remodeled: definition, approaches, and rationales, *Journal of Studies in International Education,* 8(1), 5-31.

Knight, J. (2008) *Higher Education in Turmoil: the changing world of internationalization.* Rotterdam: Sense.

Li, D. (2012) Easing Transition and Promoting a Positive Student Experience Within an International Partnership Scheme for British and Chinese Teachers, *Journal of Research in International Education,* 11(1), 32-49.

Li, H. (2010) Higher Education in China: complement or competition to US universities? In C.T. Clotfelter (Ed.) *American Universities in a Global Market,* pp. 269-304. Chicago: University of Chicago Press. http://www.nber.org/chapters/c11599

Li, Y., Whalley, J., Zhang, S. & Zhao, X. (2008) *The Higher Educational Transformation of China and Its Global Implications.* Cambridge, MA: National Bureau of Economic Research.

Ministry of Education (2010) *State Outline Program for Medium Long-Term Education Reform and Development (2010-2020).* Beijing: MoE. https://www.aei.gov.au/news/newsarchive/2010/documents/china_education_refor m_pdf.pdf

Mok, K.-H. (2005) Globalization and Educational Restructuring: university merging and changing governance in China, *Higher Education,* 50(1), 57-88.

Mok, K.H. (2009) Globalisation and Higher Education Restructuring in Hong Kong, Taiwan and Mainland China, in M. Tight, K.H. Mok, J. Huisman & C. Morphew (Eds) *The Routledge International Handbook of Higher Education,* pp. 285-295. New York: Routledge.

Morgan, J.W. & Wu, B. (Eds) (2011) *Higher Education Reform in China. Beyond the Expansion.* New York: Routledge.

Ong, K.C. & Chan, D.K.K. (2012) Transnational Higher Education and Challenges for University Governance in China, *Higher Education Policy,* 25, 151-170.

Organisation for Economic Cooperation and Development (2013) *Education at a Glance 2013.* Paris: OECD.

Quality Assurance Agency for Higher Education (2013a) *Review of UK Transnational Education in China 2012. Case Studies: setting and maintaining academic standards.* Gloucester: QAA.

http://www.qaa.ac.uk/Publications/InformationAndGuidance/Pages/TNE-China-2012-case-studies.aspx

Quality Assurance Agency for Higher Education (2013b) *Review of UK Transnational Education in China 2012: overview.* Gloucester: QAA. http://www.qaa.ac.uk/Publications/InformationAndGuidance/Pages/TNE-China-Overview.aspx

Ross, H. & Lou, J. (2005) 'Glocalizing' Chinese Higher Education: groping for stones to cross the river, *Indiana Journal of Global Legal Studies*, 12(1), 227-250.

Royal Society (2011) *Knowledge, Networks and Nations: global scientific collaboration in the 21st century.* London: The Royal Society. http://royalsociety.org/uploadedFiles/Royal_Society_Content/Influencing_Policy/Reports/2011-03-28-Knowledge-networks-nations.pdf

Ruble, R.A. & Zhang, Y.B. (2013) Stereotypes of Chinese International Students Held by Americans, *International Journal of Intercultural Relations*, 37, 201-211.

Ryan, J. (Ed.) (2011) *China's Higher Education Reform and Internationalisation.* New York: Routledge.

Schulte, B. (2012) World Culture With Chinese Characteristics: when global models go native, *Comparative Education*, 48(4), 473-486.

Tan, C. (2012) *Learning From Shanghai. Lessons on Achieving Educational Success.* Singapore: Springer.

Teichler, U. (2010) Internationalising Higher Education: debates and changes in Europe, in D. Mattheou (Ed.) *Changing Educational Landscapes, Educational Policies, Schooling Systems and Higher Education – a comparative perspective*, pp. 263-283. Dordrecht: Springer Science+Business Media.

Wan, Y. (2006) Expansion of Chinese Higher Education Since 1998: its causes and outcomes, *Asia Pacific Education Review*, 7(1), 19-31.

Wang, H. (2012) What Are the Implications of a Chinese University Model? In K. Mundy & Q. Zha (Eds) *Education and Global Cultural Dialogue: a tribute to Ruth Hayhoe*, pp. 139-163. Basingstoke: Palgrave Macmillan.

Wang, H. & Zweig, D. (2009) China's Diaspora and Returnees: impact on China's globalization process, paper presented at the annual meeting of the ISA's 50th Annual Convention, 'Exploring the Past, Anticipating the Future', New York, 15 February. http://citation.allacademic.com/meta/p313910_index.html

Wang, K.T., Heppner, P.P., Fu, C.C., Zhao, R., Li, F. & Chuang, C.C. (2012) Profiles of Acculturative Adjustment Patterns Among Chinese International Students, *Journal of Counseling Psychology*, 59(3), 424-436.

Wang, L.-W. (2006) *China's Higher Education Trade and the Impact of the WTO/GATS Liberalization.* Dissertation, Columbia University. http://goo.gl/I6npHR

Wang, X. & Liu, J. (2011) China's Higher Education Expansion and the Task of Economic Revitalization, *Higher Education*, 62(2), 213-229.

Welch, A.R. (2010) Nation-State, Diaspora and Comparative Education: the place of place in comparative education, in D. Mattheou (Ed.) *Changing Educational Landscapes Educational Policies, Schooling Systems and Higher Education – a comparative perspective*, pp. 285-308. Dordrecht: Springer Science+Business Media.

Welch, A.R. & Cai, H. (2011) Enter the Dragon: the internationalisation of China´s higher education system, in J. Ryan (Ed.) *China's Higher Education Reform and Internationalisation*, pp. 9-33. New York: Routledge.

Welch, A.R. & Zhang, Z. (2007) Communication Networks Among the Chinese Knowledge Diaspora: a new invisible college? In R. Boden, R. Deem, D. Epstein & F. Rizvi (Eds) *Geographies of Knowledge, Geometries of Power: framing the future of higher education* (World Yearbook of Education 2008), pp. 338-354. New York: Routledge.

Wilsdon, J. & Keeley, J. (2007) *China: the next science super power*? London: Demos. http://goo.gl/hdFKfur

World Bank (2009) *Economic Growth, Spatial Income Inequality, and the Role of Education and Training in China*. Washington, DC: The World Bank.

World Bank (2012) *China 2030. Building a Modern, Harmonious, and Creative High-Income* Society. Washington, DC: The World Bank.

Wright, C. & Schartner, A. (2013) 'I Can't ... I Won't?' International Students at the Threshold of Social Interaction, *Journal of Research in International Education*, 12(2), 113-128.

Yan, K. & Berliner, D.C. (2011) Chinese International Students in the United States: demographic trends, motivations, acculturation features and adjustment challenges, *Asia Pacific Education Review*, 12, 173-184.

Yang, R. (2000) Tensions Between the Global and the Local: a comparative illustration of the reorganization of China's higher education in the 1950s and 1990s, *Higher Education*, 39(3), 319-337.

Yang, R. (2002a) *Third Delight: the internationalization of higher education in China*. New York: Routledge.

Yang, R. (2002b) University Internationalization: its meanings, rationales and implications, *Intercultural Education*, 13(1), 81-95.

Yang, R. (2003) Globalisation and Higher Education Development: a critical analysis, *International Review of Education*, 49(3-4), 269-291.

Yang, R. (2010) International Organizations, Changing Governance and China's Policy Making in Higher Education: an analysis of the World Bank and the World Trade Organization, *Asia-Pacific Journal of Education*, 30(4), 419-431. http://www.tandfonline.com/doi/abs/10.1080/02188791.2010.519692

Yang, R. (2011) Chinese Ways of Thinking in the Transformation of China's Higher Education System, in J. Ryan (Ed.) *China's Higher Education Reform and Internationalisation*, pp. 34-47. New York: Routledge.

Yang, R. (2012) Education and Global Cultural Dialogue: analyses of the Chinese knowledge diaspora at a major Canadian university, in K. Mundy & Q. Zha (Eds) *Education and Global Cultural Dialogue: a tribute to Ruth Hayhoe*, pp. 125-137. Basingstoke: Palgrave Macmillan.

Zha, Q. (2003) Internationalization of Higher Education: towards a conceptual framework, *Policy Futures in Education*, 1(2), 248-270.

Zha, Q. (2009) Diversification or Homogenization: how governments and markets have combined to (re)shape Chinese higher education in its recent massification process, *Higher Education*, 58(1), 41-58.

Zha, Q. (2011) China's Move to Mass Higher Education in a Comparative Perspective, *Compare*, 41(6), 1-18.

Zha, Q. (2012) Transnational Higher Education in China: toward a critical culturalist research agenda, in K. Mundy & Q. Zha (Eds) *Education and Global Cultural Dialogue: a tribute to Ruth Hayhoe*, pp. 107-123. Basingstoke: Palgrave Macmillan.

Zhu, J. (2012) Academic Adjustment of Chinese Students at German Universities. Dissertation, Humboldt-Universität zu Berlin. http://edoc.hu-berlin.de/dissertationen/zhu-jiani-2012-11-21/PDF/zhu.pdf

Zweig, D. & Wang, H. (2013) Can China Bring Back the Best? The Communist Party Organizes China's Search for Talent, *The China Quarterly*, no. 215, 590-615.

CHAPTER 13

Higher Education and International Student Mobility: the extraordinary case of Cuba

ANNE HICKLING-HUDSON & ROBERT F. ARNOVE

ABSTRACT This chapter considers the extraordinary case of Cuba in promoting international student and scholarly mobility. It outlines the Latin American context, and examines Cuba's role as a regional and international 'hub' for university and polytechnic education that attracts thousands of international students to apply for places and Cuban-provided scholarships each year. The chapter considers whether the Cuban approach illustrates an alternative to the traditional forms of international student mobility. It discusses the character and features of the type of higher education that internationally mobile students receive in Cuba, and the nature of programs in which Cuba shares the work of its highly-trained professionals in collaborative projects with other countries. It examines this model of internationalism in higher education in the context of a global system of international student flows to other countries that can be considered educational 'hubs', and raises the question of the extent to which the Cuban model has the potential of countering the incentives offered by countries of the Global North towards the emigration and 'brain drain' of international students and professionals from the Global South.

I dream of the day when these, the African mathematicians and computer specialists in Washington and New York, the African physicists, engineers, doctors, business managers and economists, will return from London and Manchester and Paris and Brussels to add to the African pool of brain power, to enquire into and find solutions to Africa's problems and challenges, to open the African door to the world of knowledge, to elevate Africa's place within the universe of research, the information of new knowledge, education and information. (Thabo Mbeki, 1998)

Higher education is now widely recognized as an important driver of socioeconomic growth and human development. UNESCO researchers report that since the 1970s, there has been a great expansion in higher education enrollment across the world. In 2009, over 165 million students participated in higher education, which is a five-fold increase since 1970 and a three-fold increase since 1980. Cross-national higher education is a significant aspect of this increase, involving movement across national borders of some 3 million people (students, scholars, researchers, and consultants), programs (courses and degrees), and providers (institutions, consortia, and companies) (Chien & Kot, 2012). Countries of the global North, including the USA, Canada, the United Kingdom (UK), Germany, France, and, more recently, Australia, with their highly developed education systems, have constituted the most sought-after destinations for internationally mobile students, but some countries of the developing world such as Malaysia, Singapore, South Korea, and Cuba, are also important destinations.

In this chapter, we consider the extraordinary case of Cuba in promoting and hosting international student mobility. We outline the Latin American context, and examine Cuba's role as a regional and international 'hub' for higher education. We consider the character and features of the type of higher education that internationally mobile students receive in Cuba, discussing implications of this type of education for development issues.

Cuba, with a small population (11.3 million in 2010) and the relatively low per capita income, $10,000 annually in 2010 (see Central Intelligence Agency, 2013), has achieved the remarkable role of becoming a significant provider of education not only for large numbers of students from neighboring Latin American and Caribbean countries, but also for many thousands of international students from Africa, as well as some from the Middle East and Asia. Jaramillo and de Wit (2009) offer the definition of a regional 'hub' as a country where students from neighboring countries go to study, giving examples of Singapore and Malaysia in Asia, and South Africa in Africa. Their view is that such hubs do not exist in Latin America, but that currently Cuba is the 'only regional receiver' – that is, of Latin American students.

We feel that Cuba's role in educating international mobile higher education students from African, Latin America, the Caribbean, and other regions justifies its being thought of as an educational hub, a provider of university and polytechnic education which attracts thousands of international students to apply for scholarships each year. This role is more 'a result of its special political position than its economic status' (Jaramillo & de Wit, 2009). In this chapter we set out some of the political and social considerations that have enabled Cuba to become an educational hub. We discuss the significance of the model of education in which Cuban-trained international students are immersed for their five-year degrees, and the implications of this for development in their home countries.

International Student Mobility: context

International student mobility and scholarly exchange are important dimensions of a country's educational profile. It has been argued that such educational mobility is an aspect of cultural programs, which constitute the fourth dimension of foreign policy (Coombs, 1964), added to the diplomatic, military, and commercial dimensions of a country's image and influence abroad. Individual institutions, especially at the higher education level, have sent and received students and academic staff as a way of attracting talent, enriching their curricula, and expanding intellectual horizons. Study abroad may form part of a country's strategic plans, as in Brazil, to 'make a quantum leap in the formation of scientific and technological elites' (Downie, 2011). During the last decade, international student enrollment in higher education has become a significant source of higher education financing for some countries. Between 2002 and 2009, Australia and the UK promoted and expanded the policy of attracting full fee-paying international students and marketing degree programs, to the extent that international student enrollment grew by 81% and 47% respectively, compared with 18% in the USA, where visa requirements had been tightened after '9/11', the attack on the World Trade Center (Choudaha, 2011). In countries with inadequate higher education infrastructure, the most mobile students and scholars seeking placements overseas have tended to come from the most prosperous families or the most prestigious universities. This may contribute to exacerbating the already inequitable outcomes of stratified education systems. The tendency towards elitism in international student mobility is countered to some extent by the role that Cuba has played in enabling many thousands of international students from impoverished or modest backgrounds to study on full scholarships in Cuban higher education institutions.

International mobility of students and scholars is also driven by war, conflict, and oppressive political regimes. In Latin America, for example, in the 1970s and 1980s, many academics and intellectuals were forced into exile by brutal military regimes in Argentina, Brazil, Chile, and Uruguay. Countries such as Venezuela and Mexico (as well as the United States) provided a refuge for them. Interestingly enough, Venezuela's social democratic administrations during that period used the country's enormous oil wealth to send thousands of university students to North America and Europe to develop its human resources but also to win normally radical university students over to more centrist political orientations supportive of Acción Democrática (see, for example, Arnove, 1977).

A common problem faced by many of countries of the global South is the 'brain drain', or loss of skilled intellectual and technical workers who decide to stay as migrants in the more favorable geographic, economic, or professional environments of the developed countries in which they studied. Some argue that 'brain circulation' might be a more appropriate term than brain drain, since some of the migrants contribute the skills and knowledge they have gained when they return either temporarily or permanently to their countries of origin. The tertiary education that they have gained overseas is particularly valuable if their country of origin has insufficient tertiary places or no comparable tuition. Additionally, the flow of remittances from diasporas to home countries can often make an important contribution to national economies (for further discussion, see the chapter by Amazan in this volume). However, it is more usually a large cost to home countries, since they lose not only the highly educated and skilled workers necessary to drive socioeconomic development, but also the investment in having provided them with years of the country's best education, either at the tertiary level, or to qualify them for college entry overseas. This situation is particularly serious for many African and Caribbean countries. A 2000 study quoted by Mpinganjira and Rugimbana (2009) found that almost half of those who leave Africa do so to study abroad, and that fewer than 7% leave for political reasons. Chien and Kot (2011) point out that brain drain not only leads to very substantial outflows of African graduates and scholars, but it also comes at a considerable financial cost. It has been estimated, for instance, that each year $4 billion is spent on salaries for approximately 100,000 Western expatriates who 'help make up the loss of professionals in Sub-Saharan Africa' (Teichler & Yağcı, 2009, quoted by Chien & Kot, 2011, p. 3). A majority of Caribbean countries have lost to North-bound emigration more than 50% of their tertiary-educated and more than 30% of their secondary-educated populations. These countries are among the top 20 in the world with the highest tertiary education migration rates. As Mishra (2006, p. 5) points out, '[T]he tertiary educated labor force (with more than 12 years of schooling) in Jamaica and Guyana has been reduced by 85 percent and 89 percent, respectively, due to emigration to OECD member countries'. More than 60% of Caribbean tertiary-educated migrants go to the USA. The losses due to high-skill migration outweigh the financial gains in official remittances to the region (Mishra, 2006). South and Central American countries, too, have suffered a significant loss of tertiary-educated graduates, though proportionally not as much as the Caribbean.

Most internationally mobile students from Africa, Latin America, and the Caribbean go to study in the USA, the UK, Canada, and Australia. These countries have in place deliberate policies aimed at attracting postgraduate students to become residents, on the grounds that this form of skilled migration can strengthen competitiveness in key industries (see Mpinganjira & Rugimbana, 2009; Lehr, 2012). Therefore, from the point of view of developing countries that suffer from these policies, an alternative form of student mobility is critically important in strengthening their higher education systems and helping to build the human capacity that will contribute to sustainable development in the South. In Africa, an alternative form of mobility has been taking place in the form of increasing numbers of mobile African students choosing to travel and study at South African universities. However, the majority of outbound students still choose to study in North America or Europe where they have linguistic and/or colonial links (Chien & Kot, 2012). The emergence of economic blocs such as MERCOSUR (Southern Cone countries of Latin America with Venezuela) and CARICOM (Caribbean Community countries) includes initiatives to regulate academic degree equivalencies to facilitate the efficient flow of tertiary-educated workers among member states, a policy that, it is hoped, will encourage highly educated people to stay and work in their region.

Does Cuba as an education hub for internationally mobile students represent an alternative form of mobility? As is pointed out by Lehr, it is important to consider whether the Cuban scholarship program and the Cuban educational model have the potential of encouraging decisions of Cuban-trained graduates 'to return and stay in their home country, thus outweighing the demand incentives offered by countries of the Global North towards emigration' (Lehr, 2012, p. 88).

Latin American students account for only 5%, or some 140,155, of the worldwide number of 2.7 million students who travel to a different country to study. While this is a small proportion, the percentage has increased by 20.8% in the last five years, representing a growth of almost 2% in the last 10 years compared with other continents (Chiche-Portiche, 2013, also see Casallas, 2010). The USA has historically represented by far the largest destination for internationally mobile Latin American students, attracting some 40%, or 53,000 students. As Chiche-Portiche (2013) puts it, 'Cuba – and to a lesser extent Venezuela since 1998 – now offers a strong alternative to the mobility that the United States has captured up until now.' Between 2007 and 2012, Cuba doubled the number of Latin American students in its higher education system to 22,769, an increase of 142%. Spain occupies third place in Latin American student mobility, with 19,392 students, also representing a doubling of numbers of these students since 2007 (they comprise some 50% of the international students who study in Spain). France takes fourth place as a destination for Latin American students, with 12,488 enrollments. Although data are not readily available on the numbers of Latin American and Caribbean students who decide to stay in the countries where they receive a higher education, some insights are provided by Özden's (2006, p. 9) US case study. This found that there were large migration flows to the USA of college-educated people from small and poorer countries (mostly in the Caribbean and Central America) which are 'losing a large portion of their highly educated citizens'. The proportion of migration was less from larger countries (Argentina, Brazil, Chile, and Venezuela), and the proportion of loss of educated people was also less, but it was still significant for these countries. In addition to a 'brain drain' there has been considerable 'brain waste' due to the fact that at least 40% who arrived in the United States with a college degree failed to find a job commensurate with their skills.

While Özden's study is limited to the United States, it does imply that, as the quality of higher education improves in Latin America and the

Caribbean, there is a greater incentive for students to pursue an undergraduate education at home or in the region. Moreover, because of the possible mismatch between education received and adequate job opportunities found abroad, there are strong reasons for countries to support policies favoring studying in higher education programs of quality in the region, especially those that prepare individuals with the knowledge, skills, and values that contribute to national development. The case of Cuba represents a country that provides such an education.

Cuba as an International Education Hub

On 8 August 2012, National Public Radio in the United States aired a program on Café Havana in Juba, the capital of South Sudan. There each week, a dozen or more South Sudanese congregate to speak Spanish, partake of Cuban rum drinks, listen to Cuban music, and reminisce about the years they spent as students, refugees from a war that raged between the northern and southern regions of the country. Nostalgia is heavy as those gathering in Café Havana consider the Cuban experience to be the most formative and pleasant of their lives.

Between 1983, the outbreak of the Sudanese civil war, and the late 1990s, nearly 700 South Sudanese studied and lived in Cuba. As the program noted, 'Cuba has a long tradition of giving free college educations to young people from leftist movements and friendly countries' (Burnett, 2012).

Cuba represents perhaps the most extraordinary example of a low-income country providing exemplary opportunities for the South–South exchange of students and scholars. At the same time, it sends tens of thousands of teachers, doctors, and health workers to countries of the global South. The goals, workings, and outcomes of Cuban internationalism in education have been documented by Hickling-Hudson, Corona Gonzalez and Preston (2012). Their book, *The Capacity to Share. A Study of Cuba's International Cooperation in Educational Development*, provides a detailed study of the arrangements that Cuba, since its revolution, has put in place to receive and educate scores of thousands of students from primary through graduate school from Africa, the Middle East, Asia, and other Latin American countries – and even a few from the United States (notably with regard to medical education). The book shows that Cuba's educational internationalism not only provides full scholarships for studying in Cuba, it also lends teachers to needy education systems overseas including those in conflict locations, implements adult literacy programs, assists with university administration, research, and curriculum development, and organizes systematic and regular conferences and short professional development courses for international education professionals (see Hickling-Hudson et al, 2012). This internationalism constitutes a significant way in which the Cuban people express their solidarity with other developing countries. Agreements based on the philosophy of solidarity involve mutual support and assistance based on need and capability, rather than on market principles, as is discussed below.

In considering important factors in the education of internationally mobile students in Cuba, we start with documenting the figures involved in this mobility by showing, in Table I, the numbers of Cuban-trained graduates by geographical region up to 2009. Next, we discuss political and educational factors that throw light on the significance of international student mobility in Cuba.

Geographical regions	Total	%
Latin America and the Caribbean	17,359	55.1
Sub-Saharan Africa	11,012	34.9
North Africa and Middle East	1799	5.7
Asia	1143	3.6
North America	162	0.5
Europe	53	0.2
Total	31,528	100.0

Table I. Overseas graduates from Cuban universities, by region of origin, 1961-2009. Source: *Prontuario* (Higher Education Compendium 2010), p. 12, cited by Martinez Perez (2012, p. 75).

A useful overview of the Cuban higher education scholarship program is provided by Francisco Martinez Perez (2012), who was for some years in charge of the program in Cuba's Ministry of Higher Education. More than 55,000 foreign scholarship holders from 148 different countries graduated in Cuba between 1961 and 2008. Of these, over 30,000 are university graduates and over 24,000 are graduates of vocational and technical post-secondary, diploma-level programs. During the 1990s, a decade of severe problems that followed the collapse of economic partnership with the former Soviet bloc, the numbers of university scholarships offered to overseas students for studying in Cuba decreased by half (from an average of 6000 to about 3000). However, by the turn of the twenty-first century, the Cuban government had put in place strategies for economic recovery and in the 1999-2000 academic year, 8220 university scholarships were awarded to overseas students, the highest number in the history of the program. By 2008, the number of international students in Cuban higher education went up to 31,000, of which about half are in universities. Cuba's Latin American School of Medicine takes in about 1500 students every year and has overall 10,000 students mainly from Latin America and the Caribbean enrolled at any given time. Another institution that provides opportunities for international students is the International School of Physical and Sports Education, which by 2010 had enrolled students from 78 countries.

Cuba's 1959 revolution was the culmination of many decades of resistance and struggle against a system in which a majority of impoverished workers and peasants were controlled by a wealthy minority of landowners and industrial corporations. The new revolutionary government, led by Fidel Castro, made radical changes across Cuba, with social reform, assistance to the very poor, and nationalization of much private enterprise including US-owned agribusinesses. Following the Bay of Pigs invasion, the missile crisis, and the US commercial embargo in 1961, Cuba became more closely aligned with the Soviet Union, which provided it with economic assistance, trade, and military support.

Cuba developed its education system with the help of the Soviet bloc, and utilized many socialist education policies and structures. Between the 1960s and 1980s, thousands of Cubans went to the Soviet Union and East Germany to study on scholarship, and returned as professionals and skilled technicians who applied their knowledge to the island's socioeconomic development. Cubans make no secret that this important help from Eastern European countries became the foundation of the ability of revolutionary Cuba to extend its own help to other impoverished developing countries. The collapse of the Soviet bloc in 1989 was an economic disaster for Cuba, as it had accounted for over 80% of the island's trade. But in spite of intense material hardship over the next 10 years, the Cuban government and people worked out new ways of structuring their economy and society with new strategies (more free market enterprise within the ongoing socialist structure), new alliances, and a greater variety of partners. During the hardships of restructuring, great efforts were made to maintain the essentials of the education system and by the twenty-first century, when the economy started to recover and grow as a result of the new policies, changes were launched in an effort to improve every sector of education (Martin Sabina et al, 2012).

In the 1960s, many countries were involved in liberation struggles from European colonialism, emerging from their colonial histories. Sharing postcolonial goals, Cuba interacted with the new nations through the Non-Aligned Movement, in which it continues today to play a key role. Cuban scholarships from the 1960s to the 1980s went mainly to countries in Africa and the Middle East. At that time, only a minority went to Latin American and Caribbean countries, constrained in their interaction with Cuba because of political fears surrounding challenges to the US embargo. The Cuban scholarships supported young people, predominantly from Africa, to study in middle secondary schools (grades 7 to 9) and in polytechnic institutions that trained them to become skilled workers in areas such as agriculture, construction, electricity, and accounting. Most of these students returned to their home countries with polytechnic training, and a minority went on to higher education at Cuban universities. In the academic year 1986-87, there were 6000 overseas scholarship students in Cuban universities and 12,000 in secondary and polytechnic schools (Martinez Perez, 2012, p. 74).

By the beginning of the new century, Latin American and Caribbean countries were more confident about making alliances with Cuba, in spite of the continuing US embargo. The pattern of overseas scholarships changed. Fewer scholarships supported secondary education, while the number of university scholarships increased. By far the majority of university scholarships now went to Latin American countries. In 2005-06, Cuba was providing about 15,000 university places, which went to 11,368 students from Latin America, especially Bolivia and Venezuela, to just over 2000 students from the Caribbean (mainly Haiti, the Dominica Republic, Jamaica, and Guyana), and to just over 1000 students from Africa (Martinez Perez, 2012, p. 76).

With the formation of ALBA (the Bolivarian Alliance for the Peoples of Our America), the number of students studying in Cuba from the region is likely to increase even further in the coming years. Initiated in 2003 by Venezuela, with the support of Cuba, and subsequently incorporating Bolivia, Ecuador, Nicaragua, and the Caribbean island countries of Antigua, Barbuda, Saint Vincent and the Grenadines, and Dominica, ALBA views itself as a counter-hegemonic bloc to US influence in the area. The Alliance advocates an expanded role for the state in redirecting resources to the poorest areas and populations within a country while advancing regional integration and cooperative relations among countries. Cooperation in education, for example, has involved Cuba sending teachers to Venezuela and Nicaragua to advise on literacy campaigns as well as sending doctors to staff health clinics in poor urban neighborhoods (Arnove et al, 2013). In turn, statistics show that Cuba now receives the largest number of its international students from partner ALBA countries. Cases in point include Bolivia ($n = 5801$), Ecuador ($n = 1711$), Nicaragua ($n = 951$) – where Cuba is the leading destination for students going abroad – and Venezuela ($n = 3144$), second only to those going to the United States ($n = 4914$) – those going to the United States coming overwhelmingly from those families opposed to the socialist agenda of the Venezuelan government. Venezuela, at the same time, is an important destination for students from partner ALBA countries: Bolivia ($n = 796$), Nicaragua ($n = 173$), and Ecuador ($n = 171$).

Most of the places for overseas students in Cuban higher education are funded by full scholarships from the Cuban government. It was only during the 'Special Period' of restructuring in the 1990s that fee-playing places were introduced, mainly in medical education. Students who had not been awarded scholarships were allowed to pay fees to study at Cuban universities; this amounts to about 10% of the overseas undergraduate students. Since the Cuban government still heavily subsidizes these university places, the fees are much lower than for comparable places in developed countries.

Politically, it is unique that a small, low-income country such as Cuba has been able to offer higher education scholarships on such a large scale to other low-income countries. Initially, the indirect foundation for this help was the fact that Cuba was receiving significant assistance from the Soviet bloc and was able to develop its people educationally to the extent where they, in turn, could offer help to others. But by the time the Soviet bloc collapsed, Cuba had become developed enough to continue educational assistance on its own, and, in spite of a decade of hardship in the 1990s, to increase this assistance once it had restructured its economy.

The ability of the Cuban government to carry out its internationalist policies in education rests on the revolution's expansion of the system of education. Cuba became one of the few developing countries to achieve, in the second half of the twentieth century, universal primary and secondary schooling of a high quality, universal adult literacy, a network of universities and polytechnic schools throughout the country, and a deep cultural and practical link between university and society (see Martin Sabina et al, 2012). By the 1990s, there were 48 universities, and some half a million Cubans held degrees. At that time, Cuba ranked closely with much wealthier countries such as Australia and the UK in the number of tertiary students (between two and three thousand) per 100,000 inhabitants (UNESCO, 1993, pp. 144-147). Currently, Cuba has embarked on a policy of reducing university places and increasing diploma-level polytechnic education to match the needs of the economy more closely (see Martin Sabina et al, 2012). An estimated 24% of Cuba's 18-24 age cohort is enrolled in its higher education institutions, a drop in its position compared with many countries of the Global North, where tertiary enrollment ranges between 50 and 72% (*Education Statistics*, 2013). However, Cuba's higher education network is well developed and maintains its ability to absorb increasing numbers of internationally mobile students.

Discussing the quality assurance context in which Cuban higher education operates, Martinez Perez (2012, pp. 80-81) points out that most governments accepting higher education student scholarships from Cuba acknowledge the value of degrees earned in Cuba as being equivalent to degrees granted by their own countries' accredited higher education institutions. Thousands of collaboration agreements have been negotiated between Cuban and overseas higher education institutions. The Cuban Ministry of Higher Education has established a self-evaluation and accreditation system for each university discipline, Cuban scholars are frequently invited to do collaborative work overseas, some obtain postgraduate degrees overseas, and Cuban universities have achieved several UNESCO chairs and other kinds of international recognition.

Solidarity: 'offering the kind of help we are able to give'

Why does Cuba invest so much of its material and human resources into providing generous educational assistance to other countries? A country does not provide help to others simply because it can. Decisions about the level of expenditure on international scholarships are possible because of the centralized planning of Cuba's socialist economy. But it is the philosophy of solidarity, a hallmark of the Cuban revolution, together with the material strength of the education system, that explains and provides a foundation for Cuban internationalism. Operating in a very different way from the traditional North–South model of official development assistance, Cuban solidarity principles specify that countries must negotiate agreements with the utmost respect for each other's sovereignty, that there must be no conditionalities, and that account must be taken of the different levels of economic development so that countries can help each other in ways that do not necessarily follow the rules of the market. As is pointed out by Corona-Gonzalez et al (2012, p. 43), in education, this means that a cost-sharing principle that includes paying local salaries to Cuban educators overseas is worked out with countries that can afford it, while the poorest countries, such as Haiti, are given Cuban assistance for little or no payment.

It can be argued that Cuba's practice of socialist internationalism is based on a strong critique of exploitation, inequality and social injustice, which is not necessarily the case with liberal internationalism (see Harris, 2009). Cubans believe that their provision of overseas scholarships makes an important contribution to economic growth and development in the poorer countries. They see themselves as sharing some of the benefits of their high achievements in education because of their desire to build solidarity in the global South. The scholarships were a way in which Cuba could assist partner countries 'by offering the kind of help we are able to give', in the words of a professor interviewed in Havana in the 1990s (Hickling-Hudson, 2012, p. 122). As well as idealistic goals, educating thousands of young people from across the globe in a socialist university system must have benefits for Cuba in creating an international reservoir of goodwill. This must be important for a country as pressured as Cuba has been by the hostility of the US government.

Most Cuban scholarships are given to students who are from modest or impoverished backgrounds in their own countries. Because of the shortage of university places in these countries, most would be unable to go to university without this scholarship. The majority of scholarships are in medicine and the health sciences, engineering, and agriculture, fields of critical necessity to the development process. Students in Cuba are trained for tackling development problems, and many commit to offer their services mainly in the most remote and socioeconomically deprived regions of their home countries once they return. The intention of the Cuban government is to use education as a means of managing socioeconomic inequalities to support the development process (see Lehr, 2008). When partner countries utilize this principle by negotiating with Cuba for scholarships for their young people, the capacity-building effect can be remarkable. For example, from 1980 to the early 1990s, nearly a thousand teachers from Zimbabwe were trained in mathematics and science on Cuba's Isle of Youth, studying in a pedagogical institute affiliated with the University of Havana. In the mid-1990s, this institute was still providing scholarships not only to Zimbabweans, but also to Angolans and Namibians.

In the case of the English-speaking Commonwealth Caribbean, there are contradictions surrounding the role of the Cuban scholarships in expanding access to tertiary education. Since the 1970s, Cuba has provided Commonwealth Caribbean students with almost a thousand scholarships, an unprecedented gesture of South–South solidarity. Yet, because fears and hostilities of the 'Cold War' have persisted to this day, the region has not taken up as many scholarships as Cuba has offered. This is remarkable, given the great need of this region for tertiary-educated graduates particularly in scientific fields. Some nationals are worried that Cuban degrees will be associated with a Marxist perspective. Thousands of Caribbean students have flocked to North America to study, most of them without scholarships, and many remain there as residents. Some of the Cuban-trained graduates interviewed in Hickling-Hudson's **2012?** research in the English-speaking Caribbean said that they occasionally encountered employers who, knowing little of the nature and standards of the Cuban degree, were initially cautious about offering long-term employment. Some graduates had succeeded in obtaining postgraduate qualifications in the Caribbean or in North America after their Cuban degrees, which put them in a stronger position in the workplace. Since the advent of fee-paying degree places in Cuba, several English-speaking Caribbean students have opted to pay to study there, and currently Cuba hosts over 600 Caribbean students, most of them on scholarships negotiated by their governments or through CARICOM.

The Nature of the Cuban Degree

The Cuban university degree provides students with a type of education that appears to be different in ethos and organization to the degrees provided by universities that have not been influenced by revolutionary and socialist ideas. Cuba's universities were developed to counter what revolutionary ideology analyzed as the problems of colonial capitalist education, particularly its elitism, its imitative Eurocentrism, and its insufficiently practical orientation. Besides contributing to the expansion of access to tertiary education, an important impact of the Cuban scholarships is that they have demonstrated a model of university education different from what previously colonized countries inherited from Western Europe.

The foundations of higher education in Cuba are the three pillars of *Académico, Laboral e Investigación* – academic study, labor, and research. Most degree courses are five years in length, ending with a research component (medicine takes longer). In the first and second years, students concentrate mainly on the academic aspects of the program. In the third and fourth years, they integrate theoretical studies with 'labor' (practical work in an industry or profession), and in the fourth and fifth years they write a research thesis that combines all three aspects. Labor of a different sort, that is, non-academic manual work, is also expected of students for two weeks each year. Overseas students are told that, for them, this is on a voluntary basis. This usually takes the form of assisting with food production, sometimes for student meals, in the fields or in the university kitchens, and sometimes in the general agricultural harvest.

Between 1996 and 2011, Hickling-Hudson interviewed a number of Cuban-educated graduates working in four Caribbean countries – Jamaica, Grenada, St Lucia, and Guyana. This gave an insight into the kind of study and research they had completed for their degrees in Cuba, and how this prepared them for working as Caribbean professionals in engineering, medicine, agronomy, veterinary science, teaching, physical education, media studies, and community work. These broad themes – the work–study degree, and the graduates' understanding of how this education influenced their work as professionals – are illustrated by a few examples from these interviews (Hickling-Hudson, 2012).

During the first year, the Spanish language was studied intensively, and foundation studies in the student's chosen discipline were introduced in the language. Nearly all of the graduates interviewed expressed appreciation for having had to acquire Spanish as a highly developed second language. This opened their horizons to Cuba and Latin America, and gave them a lingua franca with which to relate to other international students from many countries of the world.

All of the graduates explained how their university carried out the goal of integrating theory and study with practical, reflective work in their particular discipline. The subjects studied in the degree were both broad-ranging and specialist. Subjects were combined with annual work placements that introduced students to every aspect of the job, including the manual work that in many other countries is likely to be regarded as unsuitable for university students. This was particularly noticeable in the information received from engineers. In the first year of studies, the students were placed in work projects for a month. Each year this time increased, until in the fourth year the work project lasted for three months. These placements, supervised by professionals approved by the university, provided experience in the practical side of production at factories, farms, and enterprises. Students learned how to relate academic subjects to their practical work. For example, an agronomy graduate related how puzzled he was at first, that in agronomy, which is 'the study of crops and things related to them, like soils, climate, plant diseases and pest control' (see Hickling-Hudson, 2012, p. 111), students were given a thorough grounding in the pure sciences – mathematics; physics; organic, general, and inorganic chemistry; biostatistics; and calculus. His understanding of the usefulness of this academic training developed through his practical work, where he learned to apply it to soil chemistry, fertilizers, pest control, and his research project.

Most international students in Cuba are studying the sciences and medicine, fields in which university places are particularly limited in their own countries. Hickling-Hudson interviewed graduates in other fields, one studying modern languages, another, education. The language graduate related how she became fluently trilingual by adding French and Spanish to her native English. Her work placements were in libraries, at Radio Havana's news desk, and in conferences that required instantaneous translation. The education graduate did his practical work in schools during each year of his five-year degree, specializing in methods of teaching Spanish both to foreigners and to Spanish speakers, while academically he specialized in the literatures of Spain and Latin America. The young woman who had done a diploma program in film studies at the International Film and Television 'School of the Three Worlds' described how film students were required to complete a 'polyvalent' process, taking part in several aspects of the film production process while specializing in one skill, such as sound engineering, production, or cinematography (Hickling-Hudson & Springer, 2012).

Reflecting on how the Cuban degree had influenced their work as professionals, the graduates felt that their Cuban education had deliberately trained them to be a certain kind of professional, one who is oriented toward researching the needs of people or of industries in a particular field, and gearing his or her career toward meeting these needs. Especially striking was the Jamaican doctor who made it his business to penetrate deep rural areas, sometimes in peasant mode on the back of a donkey or on foot, to talk with people about public health. The closeness of study with work placements geared the graduates toward thinking about what their own countries could do to increase the production of food, non-traditional crops, or goods and services. The two Cuban-trained linguists were striking for the variety of linguistic fields to which they applied their skills, spanning teaching, interpreting, training students to interpret, helping with teacher training, and a community-oriented business consultancy. The film graduate is the director of her own Barbados-based media production company that provides multimedia products and services in the Caribbean.

The Cuban Scholarships and the Potential for Regional Development

The globalization of the international economy has presented developing countries, including the English-speaking Caribbean, with a crisis of development. The structure of global production has changed along lines made possible by developments in microelectronics and information technology, fields in which most of these countries are barely at the margins. The previous raw material mainstays of their economies are becoming less relevant and less in demand. Multinational corporations are becoming stronger rather than weaker in their ability to exploit the cheap labor of these countries. At the same time, the conditions of globalization, the huge foreign debt, the reduction in foreign aid, and the reduction in the opportunity for migration are combining to worsen the poverty and social plight of the majority. Latin American and Caribbean governments have made such inadequate commitment to the development of science and technology that the education system, inherited from the colonial era, even if expanded and improved, is unlikely in the short term to produce populations that are highly educated and skilled enough to respond effectively to these global changes. At the same time, as observed earlier, many countries lose significant proportions of their highly educated nationals to migration, particularly to North America.

There is no large-scale research on the career destinations or locations of Cuban-trained graduates. Some of the students interviewed in the studies by Hickling-Hudson (2012) and Lehr (2012) suggested that the nature of the Cuban degree oriented them to want to work on development problems in their own countries. However, as Lehr found in her study of Cuban-trained graduates from Ghana, the relevance of higher education is not enough to encourage all to work at home. It is necessary for the home country to have in place infrastructure that absorbs graduate skills (Lehr, 2012, pp. 100-101). The enormous gaps in higher education in the Latin American/Caribbean region are unlikely to be filled without significant external help. These countries need to put in place an education system that enables them to develop their human resources in a culturally suitable way and in appropriate fields. Among the Caribbean scholars who have explored such scenarios for development and education are Bacchus (1980), Hall and Benn (2000), Hickling-Hudson (2000, 2004) and Howe (2000). The effectiveness of this strategy would depend on a system of national and regional development and planning that could guarantee appropriate utilization of skilled people and some reduction of skilled migration. Cuba has excess university capacity that could help immensely in the rapid development of regional science and technology skills – arguably to a greater extent than any other country would be willing to do. In the development process, Cuba lacks the entrepreneurial experience, expertise, and connections needed to seize the opportunities of producing for constantly changing 'niche markets' in a globalized economy. Latin America and some Caribbean countries, such as Guyana and Trinidad, have considerable natural resources and pockets of expertise in market-oriented business, tourism, and commerce that could be expanded. If it were possible to put in place a Latin American and Caribbean regional project that combined the research capacity of Cuba with the physical and entrepreneurial resources of the rest of the region, immense changes would become feasible.

Concluding Reflections

The latest UNESCO data on international student mobility by region indicate that the top three destinations for students from Latin America and the Caribbean are the United States (33%), Spain (15%), and Cuba (11%) (UNESCO, 2012). In 2011, Cuba hosted over 30,000 mobile students from abroad. In light of the preceding discussion of Cuba's internationalism in education, this may not seem so surprising. But, taken within the context of the size of the country (approximately 11.3 million in 2011) with an average per capita income of approximately US $10,000 – substantially less than wealthier countries in the region – the number of students studying in Cuba is very impressive. Politically, the significance of Cuba's education of such large numbers of international students is, as Lehr (2012, p. 89) expresses it, that: 'The Cuban model is notably different in that it rejects colonial intellectualism and attempts to invalidate the hegemonic conception of development and underdevelopment ... [T]he Cuban curriculum is responsive to the needs of other countries with similar socioeconomic structures.'

From the point of view of further understanding Cuba's international education assistance and linkages, it would be interesting to compare the international education policies of an emerging power, China. In recent years, China has made strong efforts through its diplomacy to establish a number of alliances with leftist countries in Latin America. As a formerly semi-colonized country, China is interested in developing South–South/East–West relations with postcolonial countries in Africa and Latin America. It should be noted that China ranked third among countries sending higher education students to Cuba ($n = 1783$). Developing students with Spanish-language mastery and knowledge of Latin America is one aspect of its internationalizing strategy. The top destinations for Chinese students remain the United States, Europe, and Japan.

While China sends students abroad, it also provides capacity-building programs for its partners and many thousands of scholarships to Chinese universities: 88,000 between 1950 and 2000, and currently over 4000 a year to African students (see King, 2007, 2010; Brautigam, 2010; Dong, 2011; Li Wei, 2011). China also promotes Chinese language and culture instruction through its Confucian Institutes in over 280 centers in 88 countries as of 2010 (*Hanban News*, 2010). In considering the position of China with regard to international students, an important question is the extent to which China experiences the problem of 'brain drain'. Between 1978 and the end of 2011, the total number of students from China (counting all types of students) who had studied abroad was over 2,245,100, and the total number of returned overseas students was 818,400 (Australian Education International, 2012, quoting Chinese Ministry of Education sources). In 2006, the number of Chinese students worldwide was 134,000, and 42,000, or 25.09% of this number, returned home. The USA benefits significantly from the international mobility of Chinese students and scholars. Between 2001 and 2007, the number of Chinese students in the USA ranged from 63,200 thousand to 67,700 thousand, the second largest number of international students from one source in the USA (11.6% in 2006-07). From 2000, the number of Chinese scholars remaining in the USA rose from 14,772 or 18% of the total, to 2006-07, when there were 20,149 Chinese scholars or 20.5% of the total (see sciencenet.cn). Researching similarities and differences between the international education policies and experiences of China and of Cuba is likely to be of interest to comparative education scholars, especially given the context that both countries see themselves as pursuing South–South strategies for solidarity and mutual benefit.

Another interesting comparison could be made between international education policies in Cuba and those in Brazil. As an emerging regional center for students in Latin America and the Caribbean, Brazil in 2011 hosted over 27,000 students from abroad. Given its outreach to Portuguese-speaking populations of Africa, it is worth noting that the top two countries sending students to Brazil are Angola ($n = 1831$) and Cape Verde ($n = 892$), with Guinea-Bissau and Portugal tied for third place ($n = 830$). Between 2000 and 2010, the Brazilian government awarded 6311 undergraduate scholarships to students from 44 countries in Africa, Latin America, and the Caribbean, and in the same period awarded over 1500 scholarships at the postgraduate level to 38 countries as well as several hundred short-term visiting research programs (Barros, 2011).

In an increasingly multipolar world that involves emerging superpowers such as China and regional giants such as Brazil and South Africa (a continental hub for sub-Saharan students), the destinations for internationally mobile students are expanding beyond North America and Europe. An important question for further discussion is the appropriateness for these students of overseas higher education programs – whether in the newer centers of the East and South or the more traditional ones of the North, or indeed, in the online courses that are being increasingly offered by countries such as the United States and Australia, seeking new higher education 'markets'.

In this chapter, we have discussed the special role that Cuba plays in educational internationalism, within a context of global trends in the international mobility of students from developing countries. The fact that so many students from numerous countries of the global South have found the education they received in Cuba to be relevant to their societies' existential struggles is a remarkable achievement. What lessons may be derived from the Cuba case, as documented by Hickling-Hudson and colleagues, merits further study, as does the overall flow of students between Latin America and the rest of the world.

References

Arnove, Robert F. (1977) Students in Politics, in John D. Martz & David D. Myers (Eds) *Venezuela: the democratic experience*, pp. 195-214. New York: Praeger.

Arnove, Robert F., Franz, Stephen & Alberto Torres, Carlos (2013) Education in Latin America: from dependency and neoliberalism to alternative paths to development, in Robert F. Arnove, Carlos Alberto Torres & Stephen Franz (Eds) *Comparative Education: the dialectic of the global and the local*, pp. 215-340. Lanham, MD: Rowman & Littlefield.

Australian Education International (2012) Chinese Students Abroad: 2011 figures released. Australian Government, 9 March. https://aei.gov.au/News/Latest-News/Pages/Article-Chinesestudentsabroad-2011figuresreleased.aspx

Bacchus, M.K. (1980) *Education for Development or Underdevelopment? Guyana's Education Systems and its Implications for the Third World (Development Perspectives)*. Waterloo, Ontario: Wilfrid Laurier University Press.

Barros, Helio (2011) Scholarships for Foreigners in Brazil, *NORRAG News*, Special Issue, 'The Geopolitics of Overseas Scholarships and Awards: Old and New Providers, East & West, North & South', no. 45, April, 81-88.

Brautigam, Deborah (2010) China in Africa: think again, *The European Financial Review*, 16 August.

Burnett, John (2012) Summer Nights: Cuban 'Jubans' in South Sudan. http://www.npr.org/2012/08/08/158448841/summer-nights-cuban-jubans-in-south-sudan

Casallas, Liliana (2010) Where Do Latin American Students Choose to Study? QS Intelligence Unit, 31 March. http://www.iu.qs.com/2010/03/31/latin-american-students-where-do-they-choose-to-study/

Central Intelligence Agency (2013) *World Book*. https://www.cia.gov/library/publications/the-world-factbook/geos/cu.html

Chiche-Portiche, Olivier (2013) Panorama of Student Mobility in Latin America. http://www.iesalc.unesco.org.ve/index.php?option=com_content&view=article&id=2729:panorama-de-la-movilidad-estudiantil-en-america latina&catid=194&Itemid=746&lang=en

Chien, Chiao-Ling & Kot, Felly Chiteng (2011) New Patterns in Student Mobility in the Southern Africa Development Community, in *Building Regional Higher Education Capacity through Academic Mobility,* edited and published by the Southern African Regional Universities Association. Reprinted in *Bulletin No. 7*, UNESCO Institute for Statistics, February 2012.

Choudaha, Rahul (2011) GLOBAL: the future of international student mobility, *University World News*, no. 191, 2 October.

Coombs, Philip (1964) *Fourth Dimension of Foreign Policy: educational and cultural affairs*. New York: Harper & Row.

Corona-Gonzalez, Jorge, Hickling-Hudson, Anne & Lehr, Sabine (2012) Challenging Educational Underdevelopment: the Cuban approach as a mode of South–South Cooperation, in A. Hickling-Hudson, J. Corona Gonzalez & R. Preston (Eds) *The Capacity to Share. A Study of Cuba's International Cooperation in Educational Development*, pp. 35-51. New York: Palgrave Macmillan.

Dong, Lili (2011) China's Educational Assistance, *NORRAG News*, Special Issue, 'The Geopolitics of Overseas Scholarships and Awards: Old and New Providers, East & West, North & South', no. 45, April, 84.

Downie, Andrew (2011) Quote Attributed to Alozio Mercadante, Brazil's Minister of Science and Technology in the Government of President Dilma Rousseff. See Downie, Andrew (2011) How Brazil is Sending 75,000 Students to the World's Best Colleges, *Time*, 21 September. http://www.time.com/time/world/article/0,8599,2094119,00.html

Education Statistics: tertiary enrollment by country,
     http://www.nationmaster.com/graph/edu_ter_enr-education-tertiary-enrollment
     (accessed 15 January 2014).

Hall, Kenneth & Benn, Dennis (Eds) (2000) *Contending With Destiny. The Caribbean in the 21st Century*. Kingston: Ian Randle.

Hanban News (2010) How Many Confucian Institutes Are There in the World?
     English.hanban.org/article 2010-07/02/content_153910.htm See also 'China's
     Confucius Institutes: rectification of statues', *The Economist*, 20 Jan 2011and
     'Soft Power Smackdown! Confucius Institute vs. Taiwan Academy,' *Wall Street
     Journal*, 12 August 2011.

Harris, R. (2009) Cuban Internationalism, Che Guevara, and the Survival of Cuba's
     Socialist Regime, *Latin American Perspectives*, 36(3), 27-42.

Hickling-Hudson, Anne (2000) Scholar-Activism for a New World: the future of the
     Caribbean university', in Sohail Inayatullah & Jennifer Gidley (Eds) *The
     University in Transformation. Global Perspectives on the Future of the University*, pp.
     149-159. Westport, CT: Bergin & Garvey.

Hickling-Hudson, Anne (2004) Towards Caribbean 'Knowledge Societies':
     dismantling neo-colonial barriers in the age of globalization, *Compare*, 34(3),
     293-300.

Hickling-Hudson, Anne (2012) Studying in Cuba, Returning Home to Work:
     experiences of graduates from the English-speaking Caribbean, in A. Hickling-
     Hudson, J. Corona Gonzalez & R. Preston (Eds) *The Capacity to Share. A Study
     of Cuba's International Cooperation in Educational Development*, pp. 107-126. New
     York: Palgrave Macmillan.

Hickling-Hudson, Anne, Corona Gonzalez, Jorge, Lehr, Sabine & Majoli, Marina
     (2012) The Cuban Revolution and Internationalism: structuring education and
     health, in A. Hickling-Hudson, J. Corona Gonzalez & R. Preston (Eds) *The
     Capacity to Share. A Study of Cuba's International Cooperation in Educational
     Development*, pp. 13-34. New York: Palgrave Macmillan.

Hickling-Hudson, Anne, Corona Gonzalez, Jorge & Preston, Rosemary (Eds) (2012)
     *The Capacity to Share. A Study of Cuba's International Cooperation in Educational
     Development*. New York: Palgrave Macmillan.

Hickling-Hudson, Anne & Springer, Melanie (2012) The International Film and
     Television School in Cuba: for a stronger media culture in the global South, in
     A. Hickling-Hudson, J. Corona Gonzalez & R. Preston (Eds) *The Capacity to
     Share. A Study of Cuba's International Cooperation in Educational Development*, pp.
     231-239. New York: Palgrave Macmillan.

Howe, Glenford (Ed.) (2000) *Higher Education in the Caribbean. Past, Present and
     Future Directions*. Kingston: The University of the West Indies Press.

Jaramillo, Isabel Cristina & de Wit, Hans (2009) Student Mobility Trends in Latin
     America.
     http://www.nxtbook.com/nxtbooks/naylor/IIEB0209/index.php?startid=16#/16

King, Kenneth (2007) China's Ambitious Training Aid for Africa. Implications for
     the Mainland – and for Hong Kong? Paper presented as Distinguished Visiting
     Professor to the Comparative Education Research Centre, University of Hong

Kong, 27 April. http://www.docsfiles.com/.../china-s-ambitious-training-aid-for-africa-1-

King, Kenneth (2010) China's Cooperation in Education and Training with Kenya: a different model? *International Journal of Educational Development*, 30, 488-496.

Lehr, Sabine (2008) Ethical Dilemmas in Individual and Collective Rights-Based Approaches to Tertiary Education Scholarships: the cases of Canada and Cuba, *Comparative Education*, 44(4), 425-444.

Lehr, Sabine (2012) The Children of the Isle of Youth: how Ghanaian students learned to cope with 'anything in life', in A. Hickling-Hudson, J. Corona Gonzalez & R. Preston (Eds) *The Capacity to Share. A Study of Cuba's International Cooperation in Educational Development*, pp. 83-105. New York: Palgrave Macmillan.

Li Wei (2011) China's Exchange and Scholarships With Africa: history, success, problems, *NORRAG News*, Special Issue, 'The Geopolitics of Overseas Scholarships and Awards: Old and New Providers, East & West, North & South', no. 45, April, 22-25.

Martin Sabina, Elvira, Corona Gonzalez, Jorge & Hickling-Hudson, Anne (2012) Cuba's Education System: a foundation for 'the capacity to share', in A. Hickling-Hudson, J. Corona Gonzalez & R. Preston (Eds) *The Capacity to Share. A Study of Cuba's International Cooperation in Educational Development*, pp. 53-72. New York: Palgrave Macmillan.

Martinez Perez, Francisco (2012) Cuban Higher Education Scholarships for International Students: an overview, in A. Hickling-Hudson, J. Corona Gonzalez & R. Preston (Eds) *The Capacity to Share. A Study of Cuba's International Cooperation in Educational Development*, pp. 73-82. New York: Palgrave Macmillan.

Mbeki, Thabo (1998) Quote from 'The African Renaissance Statement', SABC, Gallagher Estate, 13 August. http://ww.unisa.ac.za/contents/colleges/docs/1998/.../tm980813.pdf

Mishra, Prachi (2006) Emigration and Brain Drain. Evidence from the Caribbean. International Monetary Fund Working Paper, Western Hemisphere department (WP 06/25).

Mpinganjira, Mercy & Rugimbana, Robert (2009) Understanding International Student Mobility: what motivates African student choices? Unpublished paper, Australian and New Zealand Marketing Academy.

Özden, Çağla (2006) Brain Drain in Latin America. Population Division, Department of Economic and Social Affairs, United Nations Secretariat, Mexico City, 30 November-2 December 2005.

Sciencenet.cn. Chinese statistics cited in article on 'Brain Drain', *Wikipedia*. http://en.wikipedia.org/wiki/Brain_drain (accessed 11 January 2013).

UNESCO (1993) *World Education Report 1993*. Paris: UNESCO.

UNESCO, Institute for Statistics (2012) Global Flow of Tertiary-level Students: top 3 destinations by region. http://www.uis.unesco.org/Education/Pages/international-student-flow-viz.asp

CHAPTER 14

Empty Meeting Grounds: situating intercultural learning in US education abroad

ANTHONY C. OGDEN, BERNHARD STREITWIESER & EMILY R. CRAWFORD

ABSTRACT This chapter challenges MacCannell's view of the contact between hosts and guests as 'empty meeting grounds' by drawing upon insights gained from the larger body of existing research to critically examine the meeting grounds of education abroad. The authors critique the various programming components that have traditionally been lauded as intercultural spaces where transformative learning takes place (i.e. student accommodation, classroom settings, etc.) and challenge long-held notions about whether these meeting grounds deliver on their promises. They examine how the meeting grounds have changed in response to globalization and the internationalization of higher education and then present *positionality*, *reciprocity*, and *intentionality* as three new frontiers through which to better situate intercultural learning in education abroad.

In recent decades, education abroad programming has moved from the margins toward the center of the undergraduate curriculum. Once the purview of a small number of academic departments, education abroad today is acknowledged and integrated into curricula across most disciplines (Braskamp, 2008; Streitwieser et al, 2012). The popularity of education abroad programming has been driven largely by the ubiquitous public rhetoric around globalization, which poses major pressures and competing challenges for those who facilitate education abroad and seek to fully understand its impact. These include ensuring quality over quantity; fighting its perception as tourism over academic; ensuring a developmentally meaningful experience despite the trend toward ever shorter stays; producing rigorous evidence-based assessment and research that justifies the expense and effort; and keeping the profit motive and exploitative commercialization at bay.

During 2010-11, nationwide education abroad participation increased by 1.3% to a record total of 273,996 students who participated in education abroad programs (Institute of International Education [IIE], 2012). This marks nearly two decades of unprecedented growth in the number of students receiving credit for their international academic experiences, with an increase of nearly 175%, from under 100,000 in 1996-97 to well over a quarter of a million in 2010-11. Joining in the chorus of promoting education abroad is the federal government. In addition to funding national scholarship schemes like the Gilman and Boren scholarships, Congress is currently vetting *The Senator Paul Simon Study Abroad Foundation Act*, which calls for no less than one million undergraduates to study abroad annually. The US Department of State is advancing initiatives to increase the number of students studying abroad to certain regions of the world, including the *100,000 Strong in China*, *100,000 Strong in the Americas*, and *Passport to India*. The current numbers of students who engage in education abroad are actually more modest than the prevailing rhetoric on building education abroad capacity would suggest and, according to an American Council on Education report, it is more of a 'frustrated ideal' than a success as fewer than 5% of college students currently participate (2008, p. 1). Nevertheless, education abroad participants represent a segment of the undergraduate population taking part in arguably one of the more important 'high impact' activities of the undergraduate experience (Association of American Colleges and Universities, 2007; National Survey of Student Engagement, 2008; IIE, 2012).

Just as education abroad has taken on greater prominence in undergraduate education, so too have calls to understand what students learn as a result of these international experiences and how such knowledge is fostered. Pressure for exponential growth in participation rates over the last decade and at the same time continued criticism of the experience as more touristic than academic, coupled with the trend toward ever shorter periods of study, challenge the field to articulate uniform standards of excellence in both administration and assessment. While administrators grapple with pressure to expand and accommodate the numbers of students studying abroad and simultaneously strive to ensure quality, observers have grown more vocal over the years in their demands for less reliance on superficial program evaluations, mere tabulation of participation figures, and anecdotal narrative accounts as 'evidence' for meaningful education abroad, and more rigorous program assessment and research to provide a clearer understanding of the totality of the education abroad experience (Stimpfel & Engberg, 1997; Engle & Engle, 2003; Poole & Davis, 2006; Bolen, 2007, 2008; McLeod & Wainright, 2009; Stearns, 2009; Redden, 2013). There is no doubt as to the value of empirical research on education abroad outcomes (Steinberg, 2007;

Deardorff, 2009; Streitwieser, 2009; Streitweiser et al, 2012). Groups such as NAFSA: Association of International Educators, the Forum on Education Abroad, and others have developed committees and published handbooks devoted exclusively to assessing education abroad outcomes. However, a focus on assessing education abroad outcomes has only gained notable momentum among administrators in recent years.

Research on education abroad began to emerge during the 1950s, and by the end of the 1960s, a respectable literature base and focus was established (Weaver, 1989; Chao, 2001; Comp, 2005). Over time, education abroad outcomes assessment research has grown increasingly complex and sophisticated (Bolen, 2007; Vande Berg et al, 2012). Research informed by a growing body of work, supported by sound methodology and tested theoretical frameworks, is increasingly available for consumption. More panels and workshops that reflect critical analysis of issues in the field of education abroad are organized each year at the annual meetings of the Forum on Education Abroad, NAFSA: Association of International Educators, the Comparative and International Education Society, the American Educational Research Association, and the Council on International Educational Exchange, to name only the largest gatherings. Much of this discussion on US education abroad subsequently appears in publications such as *Inside Higher Ed* and the *Chronicle of Higher Education* and in respected, peer-reviewed journals, including the *Journal of Studies in International Education*, the *International Journal of Intercultural Relations*, and *Frontiers: The Interdisciplinary Journal of Study Abroad* among others. Yet, research on education abroad as one of the main themes in the internationalization of higher education remains surprisingly underrepresented in many of the leading comparative education journals (Streitwieser et al, 2012). However, the expansion of research on international education generally speaking and on education abroad in particular has facilitated continued attention to the purposes, values, goals, and outcomes associated with engaging students in education abroad experiences.

While early research sought to simply demonstrate acquisition of knowledge or skills while abroad, recent research explores student learning in domains such as intercultural competency development, second language acquisition, identity development, and disciplinary learning (Vande Berg, 2003; Ingraham & Peterson, 2004; Sutton & Rubin, 2004; Dolby, 2007; Paige et al, 2008; Deardorff, 2012; Streitwieser, 2012a). In recent years, several prominent and on-going studies have begun to challenge long-held assumptions about the value and impact of education abroad on student learning and development (Zemach-Bersin, 2008). The most notable of these studies are The Georgetown University Consortium Project (Vande Berg et al, 2004) and *Beyond Immediate Impact: study abroad for global engagement* (Paige et al, 2008). Both studies sought to examine the relationships between student learning and specific program features such as program type, duration, housing type, and student characteristics like gender and prior education abroad experience. No previous large-scale studies had attempted to correlate specific learning outcomes in this way by including key program and demographic variables.

These major contributions to education abroad research have not only begun the process of linking key programming features with targeted learning outcomes, but they also call attention to the growing need to better understand the dynamics of what is happening within specific program design features and how best to intervene to enhance student learning outcomes (Vande Berg et al, 2012). For example, it is out of vogue to make claims that simply living with a local family or having an internship while abroad automatically leads to intercultural learning. Rather, attention is shifting toward understanding *what it is that happens* within these intercultural spaces to enhance or impede student learning outcomes. Pratt (1992) has referred to these intersections between two cultures as *contact zones*, or 'the space in which peoples geographically and historically separated come into contact with each other and establish ongoing relations' (p. 8). We choose to refer to the intersections within education abroad settings as the *meeting grounds* of intercultural learning. It is in the meeting grounds that students and host community members confront cultural and individual differences. This intersection of cultures potentially leads to transformative intercultural learning, and it is with this perspective that we examine the symbolic and actual effects of the meeting grounds on both education abroad participants and the host culture.

This chapter challenges MacCannell's (1992) view of the contact between hosts and guests as 'empty meeting grounds' by drawing upon the insights gained from the larger body of existing research to critically examine the meeting grounds of education abroad. We begin with a critique of the meeting grounds that have traditionally been lauded as spaces where transformative intercultural learning takes place, and challenge whether these meeting grounds deliver on their promises. We argue that the next wave of education abroad outcomes assessment should focus on understanding these meeting grounds, and critique the learning that takes place at these points of cultural intersection. Education abroad literature has yet to fully recognize the changes an increasingly globalized and technologically advanced world has had on the meeting grounds of education abroad. Thus, we next contend that globalization, technology, and the internationalization of higher education have directly impacted the intercultural learning potential embedded within education abroad programming. We discuss the shifting nature of the meeting grounds and highlight key areas that demonstrate how the traditional junior year abroad model of education abroad is outdated. Our purpose is to suggest approaches for how international educators can better assist their students to successfully navigate contemporary meeting grounds.

Finally, we reframe the intercultural learning potential of an education abroad experience as an expression of *situated learning*. In a situated learning approach, new knowledge, skills, and attitudes are learned in contexts that reflect how knowledge is obtained and applied in everyday situations (Lave, 1988; Brown et al, 1989). We argue that it is the role of international educators to facilitate experiences that foster authentic conditions in which students can experience and reflect on the complexity and ambiguity associated with living and studying in a new culture. We present *positionality*, *reciprocity*, and *intentionality* as three frontiers through which international educators can better situate intercultural learning in education abroad and facilitate transformative student experiences abroad.

Meeting Grounds

In *Empty Meeting Grounds: The Tourist Papers*, Dean MacCannell (1992) builds on his earlier work to argue that tourism creates new grounds for interactions between people from which new forms of culture emerge. He argues that cultural boundaries are more permeable and are easily altered as people have more opportunity and ability to traverse the globe. However, MacCannell questions the conditions under which intercultural contact occurs between a guest and the host culture and is skeptical of these 'new cultural arrangements' (p. 2). He asserts that the spaces where people interact – the meeting grounds – where a guest encounters the host culture are not empty, but instead are 'vibrant with people and potential and tense with repression' (p. 2). Based on this premise, MacCannell challenges the quality of the encounters that take place on the meeting grounds and skewers the notion that people can develop a sense of community in the space whereby tourists come into contact with the host culture.

Pratt's (1992) concept of the 'contact zone' has similarly been used to understand the intercultural contact between peoples. Although Pratt's contact zone has been employed primarily to refer to the space of colonial encounters, the concept lends itself to furthering understanding of the nature of the meeting grounds within an education abroad setting. According to Pratt, a contact zone refers to 'the space in which peoples geographically and historically separated come into contact with each other and establish ongoing relations' (p. 2). She claims that these social spaces are 'often in highly asymmetrical relations of domination and subordination' (p. 2). Originally concerned with the relationship of the colonizer to the colonized, Pratt's contact zone can also be applied to an asymmetrical relationship between a student studying abroad and the host native, which, like MacCannell's meeting grounds, is similarly colored with notions of elitism and consumption.

Building on the work of MacCannell and Pratt, Ogden (2007) examines the student experience in education abroad by employing an analogy derived from a post-colonial paradigm, describing contemporary students as *colonial students*. To Ogden, students 'really want to be abroad and take full advantage of all the benefits studying abroad offers, but may not necessarily be open or ready to experience meaningful intercultural learning and engagement' (p. 37). Ogden contends that 'students are able to enter a new culture as consumer and proceed to linger within its pleasure periphery interacting only as needed and often in an objective and disassociated manner' (p. 47). He questions the extent to which the profession of education abroad is actually complicit in developing and perpetuating a *colonial system*. Rather than developing cultural activities and programming that target only the most ready and enthusiastic students, deeper understanding of what prevents and what motivates students to want to fully engage with the local culture is essential. Education abroad professionals need to acknowledge that students are likely best served when they are enabled and empowered to want to step outside of their comfort zones or move toward greater areas of novelty. What makes education abroad a truly transformative experience for students is their ability and willingness to engage the unknown.

By applying such conceptualizations to the meeting grounds where students encounter their host cultures, we gain a better understanding of how concepts and perceptions of the modern-day meeting grounds affect how social relationships are constructed and intercultural competence is developed. We concur with MacCannell, Pratt, and Ogden that the meeting grounds of education abroad can potentially reinforce asymmetrical relationships between the students and their hosts. However, we also see vast opportunities for international educators to proactively intervene in facilitating meaningful, respectful, and balanced interactions. It is not enough to merely get students to the meeting grounds – we also need to equip each student with the intercultural skills and knowledge necessary to successfully navigate these cultural intersections (Brubaker, 2006). Thus, we challenge those practices that offer student services in such a way that the outcomes work contrary to intercultural integration and in effect perpetuate the asymmetrical relationship in Pratt's contact zone, or at the very least reinforce an inherent division between the student and the host native. We question these practices not only because they run the risk of reinforcing unequal interactions, but also because the meeting grounds have expanded beyond the traditional spaces from student housing and campus life, for example, to include social media (Huesca, 2013) and service-learning programming. Evolving enrollment trends in education abroad programming have made it more difficult to define what constitutes genuine meeting grounds. This change necessitates a re-examination of modern-day meeting grounds and an interrogation of the assumptions of the learning that takes place there. With a reassessment of the meeting grounds, international educators will have new ways to think about how the meeting grounds can be utilized to foster targeted student learning outcomes.

Fortunately, research on education abroad is beginning to shift in response to the changing boundaries of the meeting grounds. First and foremost, the international educators are placing a sharper focus on looking at how education abroad programming leads to measurable student learning outcomes. Recent research is increasingly seeking to explain which elements of a program do or do not contribute to a student's growth in intercultural competency and language ability (Vande Berg et al, 2004, 2012), and which claims, such as acquisition of 'global citizenship', can be substantiated (Zemach-Bersin, 2009; Woolf, 2010; Streitwieser, 2012b). Research increasingly examines how program duration moderates student learning through program elements, on-going orientation and training, and other variables. Moreover, there are recent calls to not just measure this learning but to utilize new pedagogies to effectively intervene in the process to maximize learning outcomes (Vande Berg et al, 2012). While we have a better sense, supported by empirical studies, of the impact of education abroad on intercultural communication and competency, we still lack rigorously conducted large-scale and elegant smaller scale studies that deeply explore the meaning education abroad has for those who engage in this activity. Further research that interrogates widespread assumptions of the learning that takes place within the traditional meeting grounds of education abroad is also lacking.

This deficit of scholarship may be attributed to several possible factors, and we speculate at least five reasons as to why this could be so. First, there continues to be a divide between international education (the activity of education abroad and student exchange) and comparative education (the scholarly study of education systems and issues) that may keep practitioners and scholars apart from one another when, in reality, these twin pillars should be more smoothly bridged (Epstein, 1997; Streitwieser et al, 2012). Second, the field remains largely dominated by administrative practitioners whose workload and responsibility to facilitate the smooth logistics of sending and receiving students often leave them precious little time for critical, scholarly reflection. Third, while the assessment movement is generally alive and well in higher education, pressures for accreditation may not be reaching education abroad administrators or not demanding they provide rigorous data on the impact of their work, perhaps suggesting that simply reporting participation numbers and satisfaction results suffice. Fourth, administrators are usually not expected to produce research and publish, and their job security does not depend on it, thus it is not a natural part of their mission and expectations. Fifth, many current education abroad directors may be of a generation when rigorous assessment was not part of their training or paradigm, and as a result, they have little understanding of how to conduct or even consume assessment and evaluation studies.

No matter what the explanations may be for the deficit of scholarship, none of them are sufficient. The pool of students who study abroad today numbers in the hundreds of thousands, and yet we insufficiently understand what truly constitutes their learning. Without supportive data, platitudes about life-altering transformation or global citizenship mean little. The evidence is primarily speculative or anecdotal at this point in time, and it loses impact because it only has the power to suggest that a relationship exists between program participation and student learning. Research continues to rely heavily on student self-reports, confounded with self-selection bias, and seldom involves experimental methodology. It is interesting to note, however, that a significant body of empirically based literature is emerging in unpublished dissertations. This supports the notion that the field is in transition in terms of the kind of research that is deemed relevant (Sindt, 2007; Ogden, 2010; Barclay-Hamir, 2011).

Before discussing how forces of globalization are shaping the meeting grounds of education abroad, we must first take a brief, critical look at the evidence used to support the notion that the interactions taking place on the education abroad meeting grounds as traditionally viewed lead to direct student learning outcomes. The interactions taking place in these spaces where students have contact with members of the host culture have long been taken for granted as essential to transformative student learning. Yet, the available research does not support a clear link between student contact with the host culture on the meeting grounds and learning outcomes. This is not to say that transformative learning does not or cannot take place, but rather that the evidence is either lacking or remains inconclusive. We present gaps in the research literature to argue student learning outcomes necessitate a closer examination of the meeting grounds. The most common meeting grounds in education abroad programming that proposes to foster authentic intercultural integration include *student accommodation*, *academic programming*, *experiential learning*, and *student services*.

Student Accommodation

One traditional – and one of the most venerated – contact zones for students studying abroad to interact with the host culture is through a homestay with a local family. Although many education abroad programs proffer the homestay as an optimal living situation, the evidence to support student learning outcomes as a result of a homestay is inconclusive at best (Castiglioni, 2012). According to William P. Rivers (1998), the basic assumption behind the idea of the homestay is that if the student experiences continuous immersion with the local culture and language, it leads to greater gains in language acquisition than if the student were housed in a dormitory. Rivers found that students who stay in local homes make gains in reading a foreign language, but they have no significant advantage in terms of acquiring listening or speaking skills above and beyond students who stay in dormitories. These findings are counterintuitive, yet related studies have shown more encouraging results. For example, Iino (2006) found that students engage more linguistically in a homestay than in the classroom, and

Mancheno (2008) found that a family setting is more beneficial than an apartment setting because it creates more opportunities for the student to negotiate meaning. In an early study, Hansel (1986) found that living with a host family increases one's altruism, idealism, and emotional involvement with a different culture. On a positive note, Laar et al (2003) found that living with someone of another culture decreased prejudice.

It has become increasingly common for education abroad programs to provide students housing options in private apartments or in shared housing with local students who serve as roommates. Here again, evidence of student learning as a result of such housing options is inconclusive. While Mancheno (2008) found that language learners make greater gains when paired with those more proficient than themselves, Saidla and Parodi (1991) found no differences in roommate rapport and understanding between international/US and US/US pairs. Similarly, Minson (2000) found that living with international students does not promote higher levels of cultural activity among US college students. In a mixed-methods study of a roommate program offered in the course of an education abroad program in which 24 pairs of US university students and Japanese students from the host university in Japan shared apartments for the duration of the program, results indicated that students did not show any significant changes over time in any dimension of global citizenship (Morais & Ogden, 2011). While there were significant differences between the US and Japanese students in their level of global citizenship, sharing an apartment as roommates in of itself did not lead to significant learning over time (Ogden et al, 2011).

Perhaps one of the more robust studies on student accommodation in education abroad is The Georgetown University Consortium Project (Vande Berg et al, 2004, 2009). This large-scale, multi-institutional study found no correlation between types of housing and oral proficiency gains. However, students who spent more time with members of their host families showed significant gains in oral proficiency and intercultural learning, and those who lived with students from the host country also showed gains in their intercultural learning. The authors concluded that simply placing students in local housing options, for example, would not naturally result in their learning effectively, whether linguistically or interculturally. However, facilitating student learning with additional design interventions to motivate students to spend more of their free time with host family members was critical.

Academic Programming

The purpose and focus of academic programming also needs further attention and repositioning, particularly in light of the trend toward education abroad experiences of ever shorter durations. The academic learning environment of education abroad for students is changing, arguably impacting the foundation on which students have to develop intercultural competency and enhance their academic development. Although academic delivery modes have changed since the 1920s, when contemporary forms of US education abroad began (Hoffa, 2007; Hoffa & DePaul, 2010), students still generally choose among an array of courses offered by the host university, courses designed by third-party provider organizations exclusively for US students, or courses led by home school faculty members delivering instruction abroad for a cohort of their own students. In spite of the wide selection of program models available to students, international educators often prioritize directly enrolling in university taught courses, especially those courses taught in the host language that allow students to study alongside their host country peers. In spite of such preferences, evidence of student learning is inconclusive in part because scholarly research has yet to thoroughly and systematically examine variations in modes of academic delivery in education abroad.

The aforementioned Georgetown University Consortium Project investigated class composition, specifically looking at students who took courses alongside other US and international students compared with those who enrolled in courses made up entirely of host country students. Utilizing the Simulated Oral Proficiency Inventory and the Intercultural Development Inventory, they found that US students who took courses alongside other US students showed greater intercultural development gains than students who only studied in courses made up entirely of host country students. Students who took all of their courses at the host university made almost no advances in intercultural learning. In a similar study, Norris and Dwyer (2005) found that while students benefit from both direct enrollment programs and hybrid programming, in which students take a combination of in-house courses and courses offered by the host university, there were no statistically significant differences between the two groups. Here again these findings are counterintuitive and directly dispute professional prioritization of direct enrollment options.

The Georgetown study also examined the effect of students taking content-based area studies courses (e.g., history, business, etc.) taught in the target language compared with students who did not. Unsurprisingly, they found that students enrolled in content courses taught in the target language made greater gains in both oral proficiency and intercultural development. However, those students who enrolled in language instruction courses in the target language strangely did not make greater oral proficiency gains in the target language over those students who did not pursue instruction of the target language. This suggests that contact with the host language outside of the formal language classroom may be just as important in developing the oral proficiency of students abroad as taking formal in-class language instruction. That said, those students who did enroll in language study did make significantly greater intercultural development gains than those students who did not formally study the local language. In their discussion, the Georgetown study authors reflected on Nevitt Sanford's (1966) well-known challenge and support hypothesis to emphasize the need for educators to more actively support students in finding an ideal balance between formal classroom learning and meaningful host culture contact. They stressed that when students are challenged beyond their comfort zones and are not panicked, the results can be transformative. In an overly challenged situation, students may retreat to the foreign student bubble and close themselves off to future encounters with cultural difference.

Experiential Learning

Greater numbers of students today are either being given the opportunity by their university education abroad office, being encouraged by their home college or department, or simply articulating an interest in pursuing experiential learning opportunities abroad. Such opportunities increasingly include international internships, ethnographic field placements (Jurasek, 1995; Ogden, 2006), service-learning (Chisholm, 2005; Hartman & Kiely, 2013), and volunteerism. There has also been a growing interest in undergraduate research abroad (Streitwieser & Sobania, 2008) and student teaching abroad programming (Cushner & Brennan, 2007). National datasets such as the National Survey on Student Engagement suggest that students are coming to higher education with greater interest in internship and field experience opportunities as well as community service and volunteer work. The education abroad profession has responded with a proliferation of organizations that provide international internships, service-learning placements, and various other forms of experiential learning. Professional associations such as the National Society for Experiential Education, Campus Compact, the International Partnership on Service-Learning, and others have joined in a chorus calling for further integration of experiential learning into the undergraduate curricula (Chisholm, 2005).

While research on US students provides compelling evidence of the worth and value of experiential learning, available research on international experiential learning remains scant and does not yet support a clear link between these meeting grounds and student learning. Rather, the scholarly focus has been limited to topics such as experiential pedagogy (Citron & Kline, 2001; Lutterman-Aguilar & Gingerich, 2002; Steinberg, 2002), long-term career impact and employer expectations (Hannigan, 2001; Dwyer, 2004; Kruze et al, 2004; Curran, 2007; Trooboff et al, 2007-08; Paige et al, 2008; Franklin, 2010), workforce development (Tillman, 2005), and related national comparative analyses of student engagement schemes (Honigsblum, 2002). Research particular to international service-learning has been mixed, ranging from positions advocating service-learning as a laudable and creditworthy endeavor in education abroad (Steinberg, 2002; Chisholm, 2005) to intense criticism of misguided American students trying to soothe their troubled consciences by 'doing something nice' for the poor (Illich, 1968; Woolf, 2006, 2008). What is acutely absent in the scholarly literature is a focus on what students are actually learning through such programming and how this learning occurs, or of the impact our students have on the communities or organizations hosting them. Fortunately, emerging research has begun to focus more in this area, with studies examining global civic engagement and whether or not students demonstrate a greater predisposition toward volunteerism, political activism, and community participation as a result of having studied abroad (Paige et al, 2008; Braskamp et al, 2009; Ogden, 2010), curricular integration aspects of international service-learning (Haeckl & Manwell, 2010), and linking international service-learning to campus internationalization strategies (Chisholm, 2005; Hartman & Kiely, 2013). Unfortunately, this research stream has only begun to explicitly link experiential learning programming to student learning outcomes.

Student Services

The learning that takes place outside of the classroom can be among the most rewarding and empowering experiences that a student will have during an education abroad experience. Student services can be designed to further assist students to adapt to and explore aspects of the host culture that they may not be willing or able to do on their own, interact with persons of different backgrounds, and gain a better understanding and acceptance of their own values and capacities. For decades, student service professionals have venerated field trips and excursions, language exchanges, orientation programming, and related extracurricular activities. In recent years, third-party program providers such as Arcadia University and the Institute for Study Abroad at Butler University have codified extracurricular offerings to offer cross-cultural learning certificates. Unfortunately, there is still a dearth of literature on the impact of these many services on student learning. Although such activities are purportedly designed and facilitated as the authentic meeting grounds of education abroad, there is very little research to support them beyond student satisfaction surveys.

Almost all education abroad programs provide some type of field trip or excursion to important historical or touristic sites within the host country or region. Whether for a weekend or an extended period, academic or social, these field trips often lack well-articulated learning goals and are absent of any sort of accountability. Language or conversation exchanges, such as the Spanish *Intercambio* or the Italian *Spazio Conversazione*, are commonplace in education abroad programming in language destinations, yet there is no known research on the linguistic or intercultural effectiveness of such programs (Kinginger, 2009). Similarly, the common program requirement to have students sign language pledges has not been carefully investigated to show documented gains in oral foreign language proficiency. While program design interventions have begun to show intercultural development outcomes (Engle, 2012), there has been minimal research on the effect of on-going orientation programming, or on those sessions that are designed to guide and support students in the cultural adaptation process. In the aforementioned study by Ogden et al (2011), on-going orientation programming in a Japan-based education abroad program yielded no significant gains in any dimension of global citizenship (Morais & Ogden, 2011). Similarly, pre-departure and re-entry courses are thought to be essential for cultural preparation and reflection, yet there is little empirical data to show their usefulness in maximizing student learning. Although usually developed around well-crafted learning goals and/or competencies, there is no known published research to support the proliferation of intercultural learning certificates.

In summary, existing research on the traditional meeting grounds of education abroad simply does not fully support the many long-held assumptions on the value of education abroad programming. The evidence is inconclusive in part, because outcomes assessment research has yet to thoroughly and systematically examine these venerated programmatic components of the education abroad experience. We maintain the position that untested claims and casual assumptions need to be revisited, especially in light of the absence or inclusive nature of the existing research. Scholars must focus on understanding the meeting grounds of education abroad and critique the intercultural learning that takes place at these points of cultural intersection. Simply taking a student to the meeting grounds does not contribute to student integration into the host culture. Proximity does not breed intimacy, nor does it naturally lead to intercultural learning. In fact, Woolf (2001) states: 'It is an arrogant folly to assume that the US student can penetrate these structures simply by being there' (p. 28). However, the lack of a thorough examination of programming components may explain only part of the story. It may not be the act of visiting the meeting grounds that matters so much, but rather the time spent there and the nature of the interactions that occur (Vande Berg, 2003). Given the dramatic changes in the internationalization of higher education and increasing education abroad participation in recent decades, coupled with advances in technology, transportation, and communication, the dynamics of the traditional meeting grounds may be changing. Perhaps the spaces where students encounter and meaningfully interact with the host culture have changed – or perhaps are not what we thought they were.

Shifting Meeting Grounds

If education abroad is truly about international and intercultural learning, then more attention must be given to understanding the space in which learning occurs, how the boundaries of the meeting grounds have been shaped by forces of globalization to become more permeable, and how changes in education abroad programming have influenced learning. Consider, for example, that in recent years it has become possible through improved forms of transportation to move readily throughout the world. Where students once traveled via steamship for their junior year abroad experience (Hoffa, 2007), they are now able to choose destinations without much concern for the actual distance or travel time involved. The traditional junior year abroad has given way to short-term programming. In fact, nearly 60% of all students participate on programs of less than eight weeks' duration (IIE, 2012). By design, these programs are often itinerate and seldom do students reside for any significant amount of time in one location (Chieffo & Griffiths, 2009). John Urry speaks to the implications of improved communication flows and technological advances that allow for 'hugely enhanced capacities to simulate the spaces of nature and culture' (2002, p. 14). Social networking sites and communication media such as Facebook, Twitter, YouTube, Second Life, and Skype have reduced barriers to person-to-person contact by diminishing temporal and geographic boundaries. The emergence of new forms of distance learning and 'virtual classrooms' has greatly adjusted communication within the traditional meeting grounds of academia (Langran et al, 2009). Arguably, as global social and technological networks evolve, so will people's perceptions of cultural differences and their encounters within them.

Like MacCannell, we do not accept that these meeting grounds have been rendered empty. Rather, we recognize that noticeable shifts in student accommodation, academic programming, experiential learning, and student services have changed the conditions through which intercultural learning occurs. The growing popularity of short-term programming has directly reshaped the meeting grounds of student accommodation as exemplified by the fact that students are now more frequently staying in hotels, youth hostels, or other forms of temporary lodging. Perhaps due in part to enrollment growth and the need for greater cost efficiency, it is commonplace in longer programs to house multiple students in one homestay or apartment, which can buffer intercultural contact or enable US culture to dominate the learning potential within these spaces. In result of greater emphasis on safety and security, US students are often housed with more affluent families and in more upper-class environments at the risk of fostering a skewed understanding of local socioeconomic realities.

Although academic enrollment possibilities have greatly expanded in recent years, students are generally directed to or are drawn to classes taught in English or that have been designed exclusively for international students studying abroad. The demand for English-language courses has created a US-only space for academic learning, effectively shielding students from scholarly interaction with their hosts. When direct enrollment options in local universities are possible, students tend to group themselves together at the expense of interacting freely with local students or are met by many other international students for whom these courses have been developed. The dramatic expansion of faculty-directed programming in recent years has further contributed to academic isolation as these programs generally involve a faculty member (or members) from the home campus accompanying students abroad to deliver a home campus course. Instruction is generally delivered in transit and *in situ*, thus leaving little time for independent research or scholarly engagement.

Programs that offer experiential learning experiences are increasing in parallel with the trend toward shorter program durations. While internships were once integrated as an optional component within a general education abroad program, internship-only programs are now more frequently being offered, even without any requirements for proficiency in the local language. Moreover, the growing interest in non-English-speaking destinations, such as China, has resulted in more students being placed in internship settings where English is primarily spoken or with foreign-owned enterprises. These internship-only programs are less often tied to an academic course, language instruction, or requirements for on-going or critical reflection. Incidentally, the governments of France and the United Kingdom have begun to legally require more balance in internship programming and academic delivery.

The scope of student services available to education abroad participants has also changed. As students are in country for shorter durations, program coordinators or faculty directors often prioritize group travel to the most important cultural and historical sites where students could likely visit in their own if time allowed. For budgetary reasons or mere administrator convenience, these excursions seldom include local students or are structured to include any form of authentic community engagement. Orientation programming is similarly abbreviated in shorter programs to focus on only the main essentials of health, safety, and security at the expense of modeling appropriate intercultural communication or encouraging students to reflect on their own ethnocentric tendencies, values, and culturally laden ways of socialization. Perhaps in consequence of safety and security concerns, programs with their own center or offices for US students are actually off-limits to local students.

Consequently, all of these changes are a sign of the shifting nature of the contemporary meeting grounds of education abroad and consequently of the depth and extent of intercultural learning that may occur there. Yet, widespread and unchanging assertions about the transformative value of education abroad persist. In spite of inconclusive empirical evidence, many educators continue to argue that education abroad is the ideal way to gain intercultural competency, develop critical thinking skills, academic self-efficacy, personal growth, career skills, and civic engagement, to name only a few outcomes. According to Salisbury (2012), such claims are 'muddying the waters' on education abroad, and make it difficult to disentangle rhetoric from reality. We suggest that, without a better understanding of what happens in today's meeting grounds, we run the risk of potentially offering up false meeting grounds where our promises do not match programming realities. In other words, the modern-day meeting grounds of education abroad may be little more than *synthetic*, fabricated experiences that only faintly reflect or scratch the surface of what the local culture could teach our students. Education abroad programs may be making false promises by providing synthetic intercultural experiences in lieu of moving students toward meaningful intercultural learning and engagement. If so, then we must confront the probability that students arrive on the meeting grounds as strangers and leave the meeting grounds a short time later still as strangers who are likely only minimally more self-aware and acculturated to the host culture.

We need to ask how members of the host culture are entering the meeting grounds and what expectations are being placed upon them. How does education abroad programming determine who in the host culture is able to interact on the meeting grounds, to what extent, when, and how? Is it possible that students are selectively shielded from the more unsavory or complex aspects of the host culture or exposed to only the front stages of the culture, as MacCannell (1992) suggests? In response to the increasing demands of their student clientele, are educators unintentionally shaping the meeting grounds to exacerbate unequal relationships where the local culture must assume a consumed position? In other words, might local people enter the meeting grounds only to be confronted by an uninformed outsider who conveys the message to them that 'I am here, and I want you to be just like me'? Does the potential imbalance in financial resources contribute to the development of an artificial atmosphere, making it difficult for those on the meeting grounds to overcome barriers in distance and genuine human connection with one another (Ruder & Ogden, 2010)? Do the meeting grounds further marginalize those who are already living on the periphery, conceivably doing more harm than good? For example, Ivan Illich (1968) minces no words in his speech 'To Hell With Good Intentions', in his scathing condemnation of the bumbling, arrogant imposition of American do-gooders upon other cultures under the guise of voluntary service. Illich critiques Americans who venture overseas and announce their intention to 'help', despite the fact that they have little humility or insight into the host culture. These questions and other unintended consequences of education abroad programming must be recognized, debated, and addressed. We propose that reassessing education abroad programming from the perspectives of *positionality*, *reciprocity*, and *intentionality* offers a few strategic ways for international educators to utilize the meeting grounds to more effectively situate intercultural learning for both our students and those who host them.

Situating Intercultural Learning

Framing the intercultural learning potential of an education abroad experience as an expression of *situated learning* has useful implications for education abroad program design and implementation. In a situated learning approach, one enters a community on the periphery to begin with but then increasingly moves toward the innermost levels of the community. New knowledge, skills, and attitudes are learned in context through engagement within the community. In essence, situational learning requires authentic contexts, activities, and assessments that are coupled with guidance based on expert modeling, situated mentoring, and legitimate participation (Lave & Wenger, 1991). In education abroad, it is the role of educators to facilitate experiences that foster authentic conditions in which students can experience and reflect on the complexity associated with living and studying in a new culture. Through these experiences, students are encouraged to take the culture and its real-life challenges as a subject of study (Wagner & Magistrale, 1997) and in doing so, to see themselves as active agents in their learning process. Thus, learning becomes a social practice that places the student in the center of an instructional process that integrates *content*, *context*, *community*, and *participation* (Lave, 1988; Brown et al, 1989). Consider briefly four elements of situated learning and how each relates to student learning in education abroad.

1. *Content.* The student negotiates the meaning of new content, frames it in terms of real-life issues and concerns, investigates problem situations, and applies the content in ways that seek to better understand the host culture. The focus here is on content application rather than the acquisition of facts.
2. *Context.* Learning is in context of the host culture and focuses on the student's interaction with differing values, norms, and assumptions. Context provides the setting for examining experience; community provides the shaping of the learning.
3. *Community.* The host community provides the setting to engage in dialogue with others to explore various perspectives on a given issue. Community provides the opportunity for the interaction; participation provides the student with the meaning of the experience.
4. *Participation.* Participation describes the exchange of ideas, attempts at problem solving, and the active engagement of students within the host culture. It is through this process of interaction with others that new meaning systems are produced and established. Learning becomes a process of reflecting, interpreting, and negotiating meaning within the community.

These main elements of situated learning offer intriguing opportunities for international educators to engage students in novel and meaningful ways. As students begin their intercultural learning and adjustment process upon arrival to the new culture, their engagement is often hesitant and hovers on the cultural periphery. With experience and facilitated intervention, student engagement gradually deepens and their understanding of the new culture becomes more complex. As students interact with the new culture in an attempt to openly and actively understand it, they begin to learn in a reflexive way about their own core values, assumptions, and beliefs. In this way, students gradually develop cross-cultural empathy as they begin to recognize what things might look like from the viewpoint of those in the new culture. Slowly moving toward more equitable and respectful meeting grounds, the student develops the ability to deal more intelligently and sensitively with complex cultural issues (Ogden, 2006).

It is this idea of situating intercultural learning as the core focus of an international experience that has immediate relevance to education abroad. If a primary goal of education abroad is to support students in becoming more interculturally competent, then it is essential that intercultural learning be strategically situated within educational programming to make it possible. Though seldom discussed within education abroad contexts, the long-standing concepts of *positionality*, *reciprocity*, and *intentionality* can be reframed as three new frontiers through which to better situate intercultural learning in education (see Figure 1). These concepts suggest new approaches to facilitating student learning, promoting sustainable community engagement, and enhancing programming design and ongoing assessment. What follows is a brief description of each of these concepts and how each can theoretically be applied to an education abroad context.

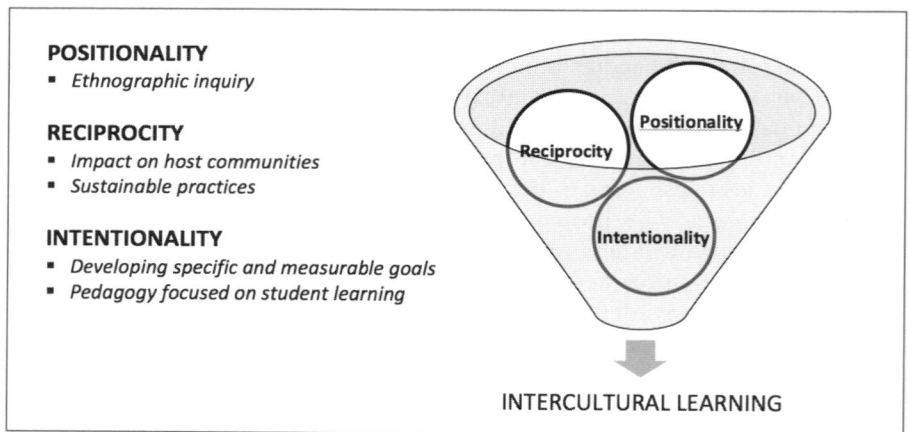

Figure 1. Situating intercultural learning.

Positionality

Although most widely understood in ethnographic research to refer to the nuanced status of a researcher, the concept of *positionality* has a direct application to understanding the shifting lines of *insider* and *outsider* in education abroad (Merriam et al, 2001; Peshkin, 2001). In conducting ethnographic research, a researcher must acknowledge the boundaries between the positions of insider and outsider and the advantages and disadvantages associated with each. As an insider, the researcher is perceived as belonging to the group under study. As an outsider, the researcher is considered more of an observer to the group. In practice, the boundary between the two positions is not so clearly delineated. It is important the researcher acknowledges his/her positionality, how it impacts the manner in which information is gathered, and how knowledge is situated within its cultural context.

In much the same way as an ethnographic researcher, education abroad students shift between insider and outsider status during an education abroad experience. This is particularly obvious in locations where a student's appearance can set him/her apart from the mainstream population (e.g. a white student studying in East Asia). However, the positionality of a student is often more subtle and shifts throughout a given day. For example, a student conducting an internship with a Japanese organization may be perceived as a foreign intern within the company offices, but this status shifts when the student joins a company outing where he/she may be regarded as an equal member of the company staff. A student may be perceived as an Asian-American within the education abroad program offices, but as an Asian person on his/her daily commute.

It is the awareness of one's ever-shifting status that holds potential for intercultural learning. At Beloit College in Wisconsin, the concept of positionality is already embedded within their education abroad programming. While on site, for example, students are asked to keep a journal in which they initially reflect on their identity as Americans and how the local culture perceives that identity. Over time, students learn to be more aware of how their mere physical presence and communication style impact their observations and interactions with the host culture, and how not doing so can potentially lead to inaccurate interpretations. As culturally based expectations of race and gender vary, for example, male and female students soon realize that they have different inroads of cultural accessibility. Students who are visible outsiders to the host culture may encounter differing degrees of acceptance, from exceptional privilege to outright discrimination. For instance, a monolingual Asian-American studying in Japan may initially be expected to speak Japanese based on appearance, and a bilingual European-American student may find few locals comfortable using the language with him/her. The Asian-American student may be considered rude or ignorant when not responding appropriately and the European-American, regardless of true linguistic skills and ability, may always be treated as a newly arrived tourist. Thus, it is essential for students to acknowledge their cultural lens, remain vigilant of their changing positionality, and be aware of how experiences and interpretations are shaped reflexively by one's interactions on the meeting grounds.

Reciprocity

Reconceptualizing international education in an era of globalization requires recognizing the need to learn with and from those within the host culture (Gillespie, 2003; Castiglioni, 2012). It means rethinking deep-seated notions of authority and control and inviting local hosts to participate in the planning and developing phases, as well as in the delivery of education abroad programming. For education abroad programs to be truly effective and sustainable, genuine reciprocity is essential. Although international educators certainly espouse respect for local people, places, and cultures, actual program development and implementation has not always led to the establishment of true reciprocity in which the local communities are both central to the viability of programs and also beneficiaries of their success (Johnson, 2009). The basic tenets of social exchange theory suggest that host communities are more likely to fully participate in such exchanges if they believe that they will enjoy benefits without incurring unacceptable costs (Gursoy & Rutherford, 2004). If the local community perceives the benefits of hosting international students, for example, they are inclined to be involved in the exchange and thus endorse future integration within their community (Allen et al, 1993). Simply put, the sustainability of most education abroad programming lies in the ability to provide opportunities for students and those in the host culture to live and learn alongside those from different cultures. To impose an American-ethnocentric educational philosophy or business model on host communities and then be concerned about issues of intercultural learning and integration is nothing short of hypocritical and does little to ensure that our students and local hosts approach intercultural meeting grounds on equal footing (MacCannell, 1992).

In recent years Bard College in New York has developed a number of collaborative ventures in Russia and South Africa with respect to principles of mutuality and equality among equal partners. As the mission statement of the Institute for International Liberal Education at Bard College states: 'The Institute does not seek to export an American model and methods. Rather, our aim is to create dynamic relationships though which we and our partner institutions learn from each other's ideas and experience' (2013).[1] Bard, like other institutions that employ principles of reciprocity in their international education programming, is beginning to explore what happens in the new intercultural meeting spaces they are creating (Gillespie, 2003).

Intentionality

The forces of globalization that have led to growing concerns of consumerism in higher education and the commodification of culture appear to have also sparked a number of disturbing trends in education abroad programming. According to the Council on International Educational Exchange (CIEE), there are trends that should be watched closely: namely the rampant commercialization of programming, the obsession with enrollment numbers, the lack of consistent program evaluation, and the emergence of an entrepreneurial spirit driven more by profits than with the collective enterprise and its impact on education and student learning (CIEE, 2008). CIEE emphasizes that there should be less focus on input and more focus on outcomes and delivery of quality learning experiences (CIEE, 2008).

CIEE and the American University Center of Provence (AUCP) (n.d.) have thus partnered to reintroduce notions of intentionality in education abroad programming (Engle, 2012). CIEE has called for greater dialogue on the need to establish clear and measurable program goals and objectives. It has also called for programs to implement end-of-program evaluations and related assessment measures to determine if the program objectives have been realized. AUCP has developed systems in which the students, faculty, staff, and community work together to determine what specific learning is intended as a result of the international experience and what program design interventions are essential for realizing these goals. These goals guide all aspects of AUCP programming and are the primary focus of program evaluations and outcomes assessment measures. Additionally, AUCP has developed a Certificate in Intercultural Competence, which specifies and highlights the skills developed in meeting program objectives for intercultural learning. The awarding of this certificate is based on the student's own self-evaluation, as well as on comments and testimonials solicited from the faculty, staff, and community hosts. Certainly, AUCP offers a good example of what is already being accomplished, yet also magnifies the importance of being purposeful and intentional in linking desired outcomes with design interventions and strategies for achieving them. When students and the local hosts share clarity of purpose and intention for what is to occur at the meeting grounds and a plan for how to best shape those meeting grounds accordingly, they are better able to position MacCannell's double movement toward intercultural learning, which is the respectful intercultural exchange of both host and guests.

In summary, it is essential that students first be appropriately situated on the meeting grounds of education abroad in ways that enable intercultural learning to occur. Educating students in the basic tenets of ethnographic inquiry, such as the concept of positionality, could better serve students in recognizing and negotiating their ever-changing roles, including being both guests and family members in the home stay or participating as both students and volunteers in service-learning placements. Reshaping the meeting grounds to embed notions of reciprocity can work to minimize the asymmetrical relationship between the student and the host culture and foster sustainable intercultural and intellectual exchange. Reframing meeting grounds with explicit goals and intentions will reduce uncertainty and, we believe, give those who enter these spaces more purpose and direction. The perspectives of *positionality*, *reciprocity*, and *intentionality* thus offer international educators new strategies through which to better situate students and hosts on meeting grounds that foster respectful intercultural learning.

Conclusion

This chapter has presented MacCannell's (1992) notion of the 'empty meeting grounds' between hosts and guests as an analogy in which to frame a discussion of the intercultural space in which students engage host cultures. The meeting grounds of education abroad are those intersections within which students and members of the host community confront cultural and individual differences. The meeting grounds of education abroad have typically been located within academic programming, student housing, experiential learning, and student services. We contend that it is the intersection of cultures that potentially leads to transformative intercultural learning. However, the existing empirical research on the traditional meeting grounds of education abroad programs simply does not fully support the many long-held assumptions of the learning associated with each. We hold the position that many untested claims and casual assumptions need to be challenged, especially in light of the shifting nature of contemporary meeting grounds. As other chapters in this volume have similarly noted, globalization, technology, and the internationalization of higher education have directly impacted the nature of contemporary student mobility and point to the need for international educators to reassess the learning potential of modern-day meeting grounds. Like MacCannell, we contend that these spaces have not been rendered empty but are still vibrant with people and potential. Recognizing that the meeting grounds are being continually reshaped and redefined by the ubiquitous and fluid forces of globalization, we presented *positionality*, *reciprocity*, and *intentionality* as three approaches which provide international educators with useful frameworks for structuring, facilitating, and assessing intercultural learning. So, as US education abroad programming continues to move toward the center of the undergraduate curriculum and is further acknowledged and integrated into curricula across all disciplines, international educators will need to continually survey the meeting grounds of education abroad to orient students and hosts to the vast intercultural learning potential awaiting them.

Questions for Discussion

As we face new frontiers of education abroad, we believe several questions present themselves as particularly important and include the following list to initiate and generate discussion.

1. What are the meeting grounds for intercultural contact between students and local host communities?

2. Have international educators been more concerned with getting students to these meeting grounds than with understanding the dynamics of what truly happens there?

3. These meeting grounds are highly valued by international educators for their role in promoting transformative intercultural learning (and the easy promise of global citizenship), but what evidence is there to support this position?

4. Is education abroad engaging students in false meeting grounds or *synthetic* experiences in the pretext of authentic intercultural encounters?

5. Long-held assumptions of education abroad programming may need to be revisited, especially in light of changes in contemporary higher education. Maybe all is not what it used to be or have we been asking the wrong questions?

6. What are the hidden or unintended consequences of contemporary education abroad?

Note

[1] http://iile.bard.edu.

References

Allen, L.R., Hafer, H.R., Long, P.T. & Perdue, R.R. (1993) Rural Residents' Attitudes Toward Recreation and Tourism Development, *Journal of Travel Research*, 31(4), 27-33.

American Council on Education (2008) *College-Bound Students' Interests in Study Abroad and Other International Learning Activities*. Washington, DC: American Council on Education, Art and Science Group, LLC and the College Board. http://www.acenet.edu/Content/NavigationMenu/ProgrammemesServices/cii/pubs/ace/StudentPoll.pdf.

American University Center of Provence (n.d.) International Careers. http://www.aucp.org/sous_pages/main/Careers.htm.

Association of American Colleges and Universities (2007) *College Learning for a New Global Century*. A Report by the National Leadership Council for Liberal Education and America's Promise. Washington, DC: AAC&U.

Barclay-Hamir, H. (2011) Go Abroad and Graduate On-Time: study abroad participation, degree completion, and time-to-degree. Unpublished doctoral dissertation, University of Texas at Austin.

Bolen, M.C. (2007) *A Guide to Outcomes Assessment in Education Abroad*. Carlisle, PA: Forum on Education Abroad.

Bolen, M.C. (2008) Basic Student Data and Outcomes Assessment in International Education. Forum on Education Abroad. http://www.forumea.org/documents/dataoutcome.pdf

Braskamp, L. (2008) Developing Global Citizens, *Journal of College and Character*, 10(1). http://www.collegevalues.org/pdfs/Braskampdeveloping.pdf (accessed February 24, 2010).

Braskamp, L., Braskamp, D.C. & Merrill, K.C. (2009) Assessing Progress in Global Learning and Development of Students With Education Abroad Experiences, *Frontiers*, 18, Fall, 101-118.

Brown, J.S., Collins, A. & Duguid, P. (1989) Situated Cognition and the Culture of Learning, *Education Researcher*, 18(1), 32-41.

Brubaker, C. (2006). Student Perceptions of Self-Identified Cultural Encounters During a Short-Term Study Abroad Program. Unpublished doctoral dissertation, Michigan State University.

Castiglioni, I. (2012) Intercultural Learning of Hosting Families, *Intercultura*, 65. Colle di Val d'Esa: Foundazione Intercultura.

Chao, M. (Ed.) (2001) *Research on US Students Abroad, Volume II, A Bibliography with Abstracts 1989-2000*. Washington, DC: NAFSA: Association of International Educators/SECUSSA (Section on US Students Abroad).

Chieffo, L. & Griffiths, L. (2009) Here to Stay: increasing acceptance of short-term study abroad programs, in R. Lewin (Ed.) *The Handbook of Practice and Research in Study Abroad: higher education and the quest for global citizenship*, pp. 365-380. New York: Routledge.

Chisholm, L. (Ed.) (2005) *Knowing and Doing: the theory and practice of service-learning*. New York: The International Partnership for Service-Learning and Leadership.

Citron, J.L. & Kline, R. (2001) From Experience to Experiential Education: taking study abroad outside the comfort zone, *International Educator*, 10(4), 18-26.

Comp, D. (2005) Underrepresentation in Education Abroad: comparative data on race and ethnicity, *Underrepresentation in Education Abroad Newsletter*, 1(2), 6. Washington, DC: NAFSA: Association of International Educators.

Council on International Educational Exchange (2008) Our View. http://www.ciee.org/home/research-publications/our-view.aspx.

Curran, S. (2007) The Career Value of Education Abroad, *International Educator*, November-December, 48-52. NAFSA: Association of International Educators.

Cushner, K. & Brennan, S. (2007) The Value of Learning to Teach in Another Culture, in K. Cushner & S. Brennan (Eds) *Intercultural Student Teaching: a bridge to global competence*, pp. 1-11. Lanham, MD: Rowman & Littlefield.

Deardorff, D.K. (2009) Understanding the Challenges of Assessing Global Citizenship, in R. Lewin (Ed.) *The Handbook of Practice and Research in Study Abroad: higher education and the quest for global citizenship*, pp. 346-364. New York: Routledge.

Deardorff, D.K. (2012) Intercultural Competence in the 21st Century: perspectives, issues, application, in B. Breninger & T. Kaltenbacher (Eds) *Creating Cultural Synergies: multidisciplinary perspectives on interculturality and interreligiosity*, pp. 7-23. Cambridge: Cambridge Scholars Publishing.

Dolby, N. (2007) Reflections on Nation: American undergraduates and education abroad, *Journal of Studies in International Education*, 11(2), 141-156.

Dwyer, M. (2004) Charting the Impact of Studying Abroad, *International Educator*, 13(1), 14-20.

Engle, L. (2012) Shifting Emphasis From Client to Student by Way of the Appropriate Qualitative Assessment Questionnaires, presentation at the Council on International Educational Exchange Annual Conference, Shanghai, China, November.

Engle, L. & Engle, J. (2003) Study Abroad Levels: toward a classification of program types, *Frontiers*, 9, Fall, 1-21.

Epstein, E.H. (1997) Comparative Education Review Annual Report for 1997. Comparative and International Education Society.

Franklin, K. (2010) Long-Term Career Impact and Professional Applicability of the Study Abroad Experience, *Frontiers*, 19, 169-190.

Gillespie, S. (2003) Toward 'Genuine' Reciprocity, *Liberal Education*, 89(1), 6.

Gursoy, D. & Rutherford, D.G. (2004) Host Attitudes Toward Tourism: an improved structural model, *Annals of Tourism Research*, 31(3), 495-516.

Haeckl, A.E. & Manwell, E. (2010) Kalamazoo and Carthage – the intersection of service-learning and intercultural learning, in E. Brewer & K. Cunningham (Eds) *Integrating Study Abroad into the Undergraduate Curriculum: theory and practice across the disciplines*, pp. 121-136. Sterling, VA: Stylus Publishing.

Hannigan, T.P. (2001) The Effect of Work Abroad Experiences on Career Development for US Undergraduates, *Frontiers*, 7, Fall, 1-23.

Hansel, B. (1986) The AFS Impact Study: final report. AFS Research Report 33.

Hartman, E. & Kiely, R. (2013) Interrogating Global Citizenship, in M. Johnson & P.M. Green (Eds) *Crossing Boundaries: tension and transformation in international service-learning*. Sterling, VA: Stylus Publishing.

Hoffa, W. (2007) *A History of US Study Abroad: beginnings to 1965*. A special publication of *Frontiers: The Interdisciplinary Journal of Study Abroad*. Carlisle, PA: Forum on Education Abroad.

Hoffa, W. & DePaul, S. (Eds) (2010) *A History of US Study Abroad: 1965 to the present*. Carlisle, PA: Forum on Education Abroad.

Honigsblum, G. (2002) Internships Abroad: the view from Paris, *Frontiers*, 8, Winter, 95-112.

Huesca, R. (2013) How Facebook Can Ruin Study Abroad, *The Chronicle of Higher Education*, 14 January. http://chronicle.com/article/How-Facebook-Can-Ruin-Study/136633/.

Iino, M. (2006) Norms of Interaction in a Japanese Homestay Setting: toward a two-way flow of a linguistic and cultural resources, in M. DuFon & E. Churchill (Eds) *Language Learners in Study Abroad Contexts*, pp. 151-176. Bristol: Multilingual Matters.

Illich, I. (1968) To Hell With Good Intentions. Presentation to the Conference on InterAmerican Student Projects (CIASP), Cuernavaca, Mexico, 20 April.

Ingraham, E.C. & Peterson, D.L. (2004) Assessing the Impact of Study Abroad on Student Learning at Michigan State University, *Frontiers*, 10, Fall, 83-100.

Institute of International Education (2012) Open Doors.
http://opendoors.iienetwork.org

Johnson, M. (2009) Post-Reciprocity: in defense of the 'post' perspective, *Frontiers*,
18, Fall, 181-186.

Jurasek, R. (1995) Using Ethnography to Bridge the Gap Between Study Abroad and
the On-Campus Language and Culture Curriculum, in C. Kramsch (Ed.)
Redefining the Boundaries of Language Study, pp. 221-251. Boston: Heinle &
Heinle.

Kinginger, C. (2009) *Language Learning and Study Abroad: a critical reading of research.*
New York: Palgrave MacMillan.

Kruze, L., Orahood, T. & Pearson, D.E. (2004) The Impact of Study Abroad on
Business Students' Career Goals, *Frontiers*, 10, Fall, 117-149.

Laar, C.V., Levin, S. & Sidanius, J. (2003) The Effect of University Roommate
Contact on Ethnic Attitudes and Behavior, *Journal of Experimental Social
Psychology*, 41(4), 329-345.

Langran, I., Langran, E. & Ozment, K. (2009) Transforming Today's Students Into
Tomorrow's Global Citizens: challenges for US educators, *New Global Studies*,
3(1), 1-20.

Lave, J. (1988) *Cognition in Practice.* Cambridge: Cambridge University Press.

Lave, J. & Wenger, E. (1991) *Situation Learning: legitimate peripheral participation.*
Cambridge: Cambridge University Press.

Lutterman-Aguilar, A. & Gingerich, O. (2002) Experiential Pedagogy for Study
Abroad: educating for global citizenship, *Frontiers*, 8, Winter, 41-82.

MacCannell, D. (1992) *Empty Meeting Grounds: the tourist papers.* New York:
Routledge.

Mancheno, A.A. (2008) A Study of the Effect of Study Abroad and the Homestay on
the Development of Linguistic and Interactional Practices by Spanish L2
Learners. Unpublished doctoral dissertation, University of Texas at Austin.

McLeod, M. & Wainright, P. (2009) Researching the Study Abroad Experience,
Journal of Studies in International Education, 13(1), 66-71.

Merriam, S., Johnson-Bailey, J., Lee, M., Kee, K., Ntseane, G. & Muhamad, M.
(2001) Power and Positionality: negotiating inside/outside status in multicultural
and cross-cultural research, *International Journal of Lifelong Education*, 20(5),
405-416.

Minson, H. (2000) Levels of Cultural Activity: differences by type of roommate.
Unpublished Master's thesis, Virginia Polytechnic Institute and State University.

Morais, D. & Ogden, A. (2011) Initial Development and Validation of the Global
Citizenship Scale, *Journal of Studies in International Education*, 20(10), 1-22.

National Survey of Student Engagement (2008) *Experiences That Matter: enhancing
student learning and success.* Bloomington: Indiana University Center for
Postsecondary Research. http://nsse.iub.edu/.

Norris, E. & Dwyer, M. (2005) Testing Assumptions: the impact of two study abroad
program models, *Frontiers*, 11, August, 121-142.

Ogden, A. (2006) Ethnographic Inquiry: reframing the learning core of education abroad, *Frontiers*, 13, Fall, 87-112.

Ogden, A. (2007) The View From the Veranda: understanding today's colonial student, *Frontiers*, 15, Winter, 35-56.

Ogden, A. (2010) *Education Abroad and the Making of Global Citizens: assessing learning outcomes of course-embedded, faculty-led international programming.* Saarbrucken: VDM Publishing.

Ogden, A., Dewey, D.P. & Kumai, T. (2011) Reframing Student Accommodation in Education Abroad. Reporting on a Cross-National Study of Learning Outcomes, presentation at the Council for the International Exchange of Students Annual Conference, New Orleans, LA, November.

Paige, R.M., Stallman, E. & Josić, J. (2008) Beyond Immediate Impact: Study Abroad for Global Engagement (SAGE). Report Submitted to the Title VI: International Research and Studies Program, US Department of Education.

a preliminary report on the SAGE research project, presentation at the NAFSA: Association of International Educators Conference, Washington, DC, 27 May.

Peshkin, A. (2001) Angles of Vision: enhancing perception in qualitative research, *Qualitative Inquiry*, 7(2), 238-253.

Poole, D. & Davis, T. (2006) Concept Mapping to Measure Outcomes in a Social Work Study Abroad Program, *Social Work Education*, 25, 61-77.

Pratt, M. (1992) *Imperial Eyes: travel writing and transculturation.* London: Routledge.

Redden, E. (2013) In Study Abroad, a Call for Greater Intentionality, and Ambition, *Inside Higher Ed*, 9 April. http://www.insidehighered.com.

Rivers, W.P. (1998) Is Being There Enough? The Effects of Homestay Placements on Language Gain During Study Abroad, *The Foreign Language Annals*, 31(4), 492-500.

Ruder, C. & Ogden, A. (2010) In Praise of Mortality, *Abroad View*, Spring, 50-53.

Saidla, D.D. & Parodi, R. (1991) International and American Roommate Relationships, *College Student Affairs Journal*, 10(3), 54-69.

Salisbury, M. (2012) We're Muddying the Message on Study Abroad, *The Chronicle of Higher Education*, 20 July. http://chronicle.com/article/Were-Muddying-the-Message-on/133211/.

Sanford, N. (1966) *Self and Society: social change and individual development.* New York: Atherton.

Sindt, P. (2007). Internationalization and Higher Education: understanding the impact of short-term study abroad. Unpublished doctoral dissertation, Arizona State University.

Stearns, P. (2009). *Educating Global Citizens in Colleges and Universities: challenges and opportunities.* New York: Routledge.

Steinberg, M. (2007) The Place of Outcomes Assessment in Higher Education Today and the Implications for Education Abroad, in M.C. Bolen (Ed.) *A Guide to Outcomes Assessment in Education Abroad*, pp. 7-22. Carlisle, PA: Forum on Education Abroad.

Steinberg, M. (2002) 'Involve Me and I Will Understand': academic quality in experiential programs abroad, *Frontiers*, 9, Winter, 207-229.

Stimpfel, J.R. & Engberg, D. (1997) What to Know Before You Go: creating a basis of comparison for research on study abroad programmes, *International Education Forum*, 17(1), 7-21.

Streitwieser, B. (2009) Undergraduate Research During Study Abroad: scope, meaning, and potential, in R. Lewin (Ed.) *The Handbook of Practice and Research in Study Abroad: higher education and the quest for global citizenship*, pp. 399-419. New York: Routledge.

Streitwieser, B. (2012a) Erasmus Mobility and Students' Conceptions of National, Regional and Global Citizenship Identity, in J. Beelen & H. De Wit (Eds) *Internationalisation Revisited: new dimensions in the internationalisation of higher education*, pp. 135-150. Amsterdam: Centre for Applied Research on Economics and Management, Amsterdam University of Applied Sciences.

Streitwieser, B. (2012b) Study Abroad and the Easy Promise of Global Citizenship: student conceptions of a contested notion. Working paper. Northwestern University Searle Center for Teaching Excellence.

Streitwieser, B., Le, E. & Rust, V. (2012) Research on Study Abroad, Mobility, and Student Exchange in Comparative Education Scholarship, *Research in International and Comparative Education*, 7(1), 1-4.

Streitwieser, B. & Sobania, N. (2008) Overseeing Study Abroad Research: challenges, responsibilities, and the institutional review board, *Frontiers*, 16, Spring, 1-16.

Sutton, R.C. & Rubin, D.L. (2004) The GLOSSARI Project: initial findings from a system-wide research initiative on study abroad learning outcomes, *Frontiers*, 10, Fall, 65-82.

Tillman, M. (Ed.) (2005) *Impact of Education Abroad on Career Development I.* Stamford, CT: American Institute for Foreign Study Publications.

Trooboff, S., Vande Berg, M. & Rayman, J. (2007-08) Employer Attitudes Toward Study Abroad, *Frontiers*, 15, Fall-Winter, 17-33.

Urry, J. (2002) *The Tourist Gaze.* London: Sage Publications.

Vande Berg, M.J. (2003) The Case for Assessing Educational Outcomes in Study Abroad, *Advances in International Marketing*, 13, 23-36.

Vande Berg, M.J., Balkcum, A., Scheid, M. & Whalen, B.J. (2004) The Georgetown University Consortium Project: a report at the halfway mark, *Frontiers*, 10, Fall, 101-116.

Vande Berg, M., Connor-Linton, J. & Paige, R. (2009) The Georgetown Consortium Project: interventions for student learning abroad, *Frontiers*, 18, 1-76.

Vande Berg, M.J., Paige, R.M. & Lou, K.H. (Eds) (2012) *Student Learning Abroad: what our students are learning, what they're not, and what we can do about it.* Sterling, VA: Stylus.

Wagner, K. & Magistrale, T. (1997) *Writing Across Culture: an introduction to study abroad and the writing process.* New York: Peter Lang.

Weaver, H.D. (Ed.) (1989) Research on US Students Abroad: a bibliography with abstracts. Council on International Educational Exchange; Education Abroad Program, University of California; Institute of International Education; and

National Association of Foreign Student Affairs.
http://globaledresearch.com/book_research_weaver.asp

Woolf, M. (2001) Not Waving But Drowning: arguments against immersion in education abroad, *International Educator*, 10(4), 28-34.

Woolf, M. (2006) Come and See the Poor People: the pursuit of exotica, *Frontiers*, 13, November, 136-146.

Woolf, M. (2008) Not Serious Stuff? Service-Learning in Context: an international perspective, *Frontiers*, 17, Fall, 21-32.

Woolf, M. (2010) Another Mishegas: global citizenship, *Frontiers*, 19, Fall-Winter, 24-60.

Zemach-Bersin, T. (2008) American Students Abroad Can't Be 'Global Citizens', *The Chronicle of Higher Education*, 54(26), 7 March, A34.

Zemach-Bersin, T. (2009) Selling the World: study abroad marketing and the privatization of global citizenship, in *The Handbook of Practice and Research in Study Abroad: higher education and the quest for global citizenship*, pp. 303-321. New York: Routledge.

APPENDIX. Empty Meeting Grounds: situating intercultural learning in US education abroad

MacCannell's (1992) notion of the 'empty meeting grounds' between hosts and guests provides an appropriate analogy in which to frame a discussion of the intercultural space in which students engage host cultures. The meeting grounds of education abroad are those intersections within which students and members of the host community confront cultural and individual differences. It is this intersection of cultures that potentially leads to transformative intercultural learning. The meeting grounds of education abroad have typically been located within academic programming, student housing, experiential learning, and student services.

Directions: Please consider these meeting grounds in the context of education abroad, namely summer and semester-length programming. For each, please suggest specific ways in which to enhance the intercultural learning potential within each.

	Academic Programming (*direct* enrollment, faculty-directed programs, etc.)	Student Housing (*hotel*, homestay, apartment, roommate, etc.)	Experiential Learning (*internships*, service-learning, field placement, etc.)	Student Services (*field* trips, language exchange, orientation, etc.)
Summer Program (≤ 8 weeks, 100% abroad, may be faculty-led)				
Semester Program (Lasting 12 to 17 weeks and occurring entirely or mostly during the academic year.)				

Enhancing Intercultural Learning in Education Abroad Programs

CHAPTER 15

The Erasmus Citizen: students' conceptions of citizenship identity in the Erasmus Mobility Programme in Germany

BERNHARD STREITWIESER[1] **&**
ZACHARY VAN WINKLE

ABSTRACT Since the Erasmus Mobility Programme was established in 1987, a primary goal has been to develop in participants a European citizenship identity. While establishing and strengthening this identity through Erasmus has long been a policy goal and is anecdotally presumed to occur, empirically determining a causal link has been challenging and controversial. Scholars debate whether students predisposed to supporting Europe self-select into the programme and thereby demonstrate European mindedness, or whether as a result of participating in the programme students develop a greater sense of European-mindedness. The research presented in this chapter pre-empts this debate by addressing a more fundamental question that must first be asked: How do Erasmus participants even interpret the notion of citizenship identity – be it local, national, regional, European or global – and are they convinced that participating in Erasmus can play an important role in developing their conception of identity? Based on a qualitative analysis of 1308 responses to open-ended items on a survey administered to Erasmus participants from 34 European countries at 14 institutions throughout Germany for a semester or a year, this study looks at the identity question within the German context. The findings are analysed with reference to Gaertner and Dovidio's Common Ingroup Identity Model and the discussion concludes with the suggested emergence of an 'Erasmus Citizen'.

Introduction

In the current landscape of developments challenging global higher education, some scholars have argued that unprecedentedly turbulent and indeed 'revolutionary' changes are shaping the current reality for institutions and students of higher education around the world (Knight, 2008; Altbach et al, 2009). This is no less so the case with one of the most visible trends in internationalisation, international student mobility, where we continue to witness major shifts in the movement of students, the locations they select or must migrate to and the sheer rising numbers who seek access to higher educational opportunity. As Altbach and Teichler (2001) pointed out well over a decade ago, understanding the meaning and implication of these developments is a deeply challenging task that will continue to engage researchers for years to come.

Shifts in global educational mobility and the substantial increase in student engagement in study abroad worldwide factor prominently in the political agendas of many countries today (Rivza & Teichler, 2007; Lewin, 2009; Stearns, 2009; Wuttig, 2009; European Parliament Directorate-General for Internal Policies, 2010; Wildavsky, 2010; Kandeko & Weyers, 2013; Choudaha & de Wit, 2014). These developments bring with them questions and challenges, ranging from who studies abroad for what purpose and to what ends, to how they experience their education elsewhere, to what benefits the experience should ideally bring back to its institutional and student stakeholders.

In the past years, researchers have studied and documented many significant intellectual and personal developments that students experience during the years of college or university study (Pascarella & Terenzini, 2005). For students who are able to also participate in study abroad during that time, even more significant developmental outcomes have been reported, many of them positive but some also negative (Teichler, 1996, 2004; Gmelch, 1997; Teichler & Maiworm, 1997; Hammer et al, 2003; Cushner & Karim, 2004; Bracht et al, 2006; Deardorff, 2006; European Commission, 2008; Ogden, 2007; Berghoff et al, 2012 ongoing). On the positive side, outcomes include greater intercultural sensitivity, increased confidence and independence, career clarity and wider professional contacts, to name just a few. On the more negative side, outcomes have included difficulty studying, binge drinking, superficially interacting with the host culture and withdrawing from friends back home. In the research on the impact of college more generally, some findings have also suggested that well-meaning institutional efforts to promote international education may have little impact on students if pre-college factors related to their social and cultural capital have already influenced them against studying abroad (Salisbury et al, 2009).

As part of the effort to entice students to study abroad, two assumptions alluded to in previous research can, arguably, help explain the increase in interest in study abroad in recent decades, particularly in the United States and Europe (Streitwieser & Light, 2011, 2012). On the US side, the simple promise that study abroad will develop students into global citizens (Lutterman-Aguilar & Gingerich, 2002; Woolf, 2009; Zemach-Bersin, 2009), and on the European side that study abroad through Erasmus should develop in participants a European citizenship identity (Papatsiba, 2005; European Commission 2008; Sigalas, 2009, 2010; Mitchell, 2012). Both of these noble aspirations – global citizenship and European identity – are rhetorically attractive and powerful arguments for education abroad, yet they are also contested and deeply complex notions whose use as an advertising hook cheapens their significance. Many programme developers may think they understand how students conceive of citizenship in relation to study abroad and so can evoke 'global citizenship' or 'European identity' without explanation. In fact, however, they are likely basing their assumptions on anecdotal 'evidence' that lacks any valid empirical support. Without carefully defining and appropriately contextualising these critical concepts as part of the argument for the supposed transformative potential of international education, these ideas ring hollow. Defining and problematising concepts related to citizenship and identity, and understanding the relationship between both notions, is an exceedingly difficult task. Notions of citizenship and identity have long histories of debate behind them because they are amorphous, diversely understood, multi-faceted and malleable social constructs (Everson & Preuss, 1995; Carter, 2001; Roman, 2003; Davies, 2006; Woolf, 2010).

One important arm of research under the general umbrella of citizenship studies consists of those concerned with understanding the meaning of national identity (Anderson, 1983;; Nussbaum, 1996; Duchesne & Frognier, 2008) and – for the purposes of the research presented in this chapter – European citizenship (Habermas, 1993; Bellamy, 2000; Carter, 2001; Eder & Giesen, 2001; Bruter, 2005; Frevert, 2008). Within the wide range of studies that researchers of international education have undertaken over the past decades, interest in the question of how students think about and further develop their sense of citizenship identity during an educational sojourn abroad has grown (Osler, 1998; Dolby, 2004; Stearns, 2009; Woolf, 2009; Zemach-Bersin, 2009; Knight, 2012, a, b). Although some of the concepts associated with European citizenship have already been explored in the scholarly literature (Habermas, 1993; Carter, 2001; Davies, 2006), how mobility students actually understand the notion of European citizenship has so far received little attention.

The Erasmus Mobility Programme

In Europe, the notion of citizenship development for university students is embodied foremost in the flagship mobility programme 'Erasmus' (European Community Action Scheme for the Mobility of University Students).[2] When it was first established by the European Community in 1987, primary goals included helping young Europeans forge links and gain knowledge throughout the continent, develop social and professional competencies, and diversify the general student population and thus make the educational system more open and competitive as a way to strengthen the Union as a more attractive place to study and work in the future (Everson & Preuss, 1995; Kritz, 2006; Commission of the European Communities, 2009; de Wit, 2009; Wuttig, 2009). As Sigalas (2010) has stated, 'it is clear that international student mobility and direct contact were meant to create a European identity' (p. 242).

As a taxpayer-funded initiative, the Erasmus Programme today represents the most expansive study abroad initiative of its kind in the world. Described as 'the single most successful component of EU policy' (Altbach & Teichler, 2001, p. 10), the programme has also been credited by many experts for being 'the single strongest driver for the attention paid to internationalization' in Europe (Teichler, 2010, p. 263). Between 1997 and 2008 nearly two-thirds of all mobile students in the European Union and over 2000 higher education institutions were engaged in Erasmus exchange opportunities (Kritz, 2006; Mitchell, 2012) and by now over three million students of all socio-economic levels have benefitted from competitive grants that have enabled them to work and study for 3-12 months in over 33 participating European countries. The programme has made continental European educational mobility, averaging close to 10%, more expansive than in most other regions or countries such as the USA or the United Kingdom (UK), where only 1-3% of students study abroad (Institute of International Education, 2012; UNESCO, 2012).

The Erasmus Mobility Programme

Within this unprecedented and by most accounts successful mobility experiment, the question of whether students develop a sense of European citizenship identity through participating in the Erasmus Mobility Programme remains largely unanswered. However, interest in being able to empirically document a link between Erasmus and European citizenship identity is growing. In addition to individual studies, collaborative research teams at institutions and universities are now also investigating these questions, such as through the current collaboration between the German Academic Exchange Service and researchers at the Group of Experts for Empirical Studies in Kassel, Germany.[3] Large-scale surveys such as the annual Eurobarometer studies,[4] the International Social Survey Programme on National Identity by Germany's Leibniz Institute for the Social Sciences [5] and the Erasmus Student Network [6] also routinely measure Europeans' attachment to and trust in a variety of aspects of the EU, including European identity.

While the belief at the European policy level is that the Erasmus Programme should 'strengthen in young people a sense of European identity' (Resolution of the Council of Ministers, 1987, p. 5), whether this actually happens is far from clear. The assertion made by researchers Jacobs and Maier well over a decade ago remains valid today: 'For over almost three decades supporters of European integration have been seeing the promotion of an European consciousness and the creation of an European identity as a crucial policy goal' (1998, p. 18). Researcher Michael Bruter has also argued that his study provides 'unprecedented evidence on the emergence of a mass European identity over the past 30 years' (Bruter, 2005, p. xvi). Yet, while numerous interview and survey studies discussed below have sought to investigate causal links between Erasmus experience and the development of European identity, their findings are contradictory.

By now the numbers of studies conducted between the late 1990s and late 2000s have grown in depth and variation. Studies have ranged from samples of only 100 students to those with 2000 participants; samples with diverse student populations; two-country comparative studies and also large-scale investigations including over 25 EU countries; and varied methodology, although so far primarily statistical and survey based. Within this corpus of data, the findings by research scholars differ noticeably. Mitchell's study in 2011 of 1041 Erasmus students from 25 EU countries and 970 non-mobile control group students argued that: 'The Erasmus experience increases participants' interest in Europe and the EU and that, as a direct result of the sojourn, students feel more European' (2012, p. 511). Michael Bruter's study of European citizenship in 15 pre-2004 EU member states did not investigate Erasmus directly but noted that: 'Traveling abroad regularly makes [Europeans] – logically – more likely to perceive concrete significance of a "People's Europe" whose citizens can travel without border control (within the Schengen area), and therefore increases their civic identity' (Bruter, 2005, p. 120).

Other researchers have been more hesitant. King and Ruiz-Gelices' 2000-01 survey of 261 University of Sussex students and graduates who had spent a year abroad suggested that 'YA [Year Abroad] graduates are more likely to see their identities as at least partially European' but warn that their findings are only suggestive and necessarily 'gloss over a number of complexities and alternative outcomes' (2003, p. 246).

A third group of researchers remains unconvinced. Kuhn's (2012) investigation of cross-national Eurobarometer data argues that: 'Educational exchange programmes are not as effective in promoting European identity as they could be: they mainly target the highly educated who already are more likely to interact transnationally and who are per se likely to develop a European identity' (p. 1007). And Wilson's study (2011) of 99 Erasmus and 145 control group students studying in the UK, France, Spain and Sweden found that: 'The Erasmus Programme has been founded partly on an assumption that Erasmus students will tend to become more pro-European as a result of their time abroad. The best evidence available is that this assumption is faulty' (p. 1134). In his 2003-04 longitudinal survey of 161 students from nine English universities studying abroad and 241 continental Europeans studying at the same nine universities in England, plus a control group of 60 English students, Immanuel Sigalas (2010) agreed that theoretically a 'conceptual link between Erasmus and European identity remains alive' (p. 242), but he was unable to find evidence supporting the Erasmus Programme itself strengthening participants' European identity. Although he found that increased socialisation among Europeans could potentially fortify feelings of identity, his sample of students who studied in the UK in fact declined in their level of European identity over their time abroad (Sigalas, 2010).

Kristine Mitchell's study (2012) – the most recently published investigation of Erasmus and European identity – suggests that future research needs to address exactly the question that motivated my study when I launched it in 2010.

> Existing studies, including this one, tend to take a rather one-dimensional approach to European identity. The survey instruments, for example, ask respondents whether, or how often, they 'feel European' without actually unpacking what that European feeling means to them. Qualitative methods – e.g. interviews, focus groups – might be more appropriate for teasing out precisely *what European identity actually signifies for its holders* but even surveys could incorporate questions that unpack the concept of European identity by asking those who 'feel European' follow up questions about *the circumstances that engender such a feeling*, how deeply-felt the identity is, and *how important European identity is* to the respondent, etc. (p. 510, my italics)

In addition to Mitchell's suggestion, a deficiency that was pointed out nearly two decades earlier by researchers Michelle Everson and Ulrich Preuss (1995) also served as early inspiration for the present study. In their work Everson and Preuss argued:

> It would be unwise to initially attempt to develop a monolithic 'European' definition of citizenship. Instead, any study of the emergent notion of Union citizenship should simply accept that the 'peoples of Europe' possess a great variety of understandings of the concept of citizenship. Future research should consequently *seek honestly to identify such conceptions*, and should only then assess their likely impact upon the emerging notion of Union Citizenship. (pp. 47-48, my italics)

In Europe in particular, most scholars acknowledge that any study of citizenship and identity must be sensitive to the tremendous diversity of the continent in terms of national, regional, linguistic, educational, political and socio-economic differences (Everson & Preuss, 1995; de Wit, 2006).

Purpose of the Study and Research Questions

Although I launched a funded, large-scale 'Erasmus Identity Study' in 2010 with aims similar to those of the studies discussed above, the qualitative findings presented in the remaining pages of this chapter can be seen as a direct response to the two suggestions for research noted above, each of which has not yet been addressed in the literature. The following questions have thus driven my analysis:

1. How do participants in the Erasmus Mobility Programme understand the notion of citizenship identity?
2. Do participants in the Erasmus Programme believe that the Erasmus experience can influence their perceptions of citizenship identity?

The Erasmus Identity Study

Data Collection and Sample

In 2010, with funding from the Fulbright Commission, I began a pilot study to investigate Erasmus experience in Germany and its link to the development of European identity. The study began with 45 interviews and 342 surveys that were collected from students from 29 European countries studying for a semester or year at one of two major universities in Berlin. The analysis of the interviews and survey data (Streitwieser, 2012) led to the development of a baseline understanding of the sample's general conceptions of citizenship identity. In 2011, with funding from the German Academic Exchange Service, I sent out an expanded survey [7] to 12 additional universities and technical colleges (*Hochschulen*) throughout Germany to create a larger sample of slightly over 3000 students from 34 participating Erasmus countries.[8] Data collection began in the fall of 2011 with newly arrived students. A second round of data was gathered in the spring of 2012 with incoming and outgoing students as well as those who had completed one of two semesters abroad. A third and last round of data was collected in the fall of 2012 from newly arrived students, departing one-semester students and students leaving Germany after a full year. The survey was sent out to students by each of the 14 participating higher education institution's Erasmus offices, administered online via SurveyMonkey, offered in either English or German, and addressed anonymously and voluntarily by students.

In each of the three panel rounds, the samples approximated the general demographics common to study abroad populations of university-age students from Europe and North America. Close to two-thirds were female; 85% were between the ages of 19-24; according to self-reporting more than 50% considered themselves to be in the middle of their country's socio-economic bracket; 50% came from the suburbs or larger cities; the majority were in language studies, the social sciences and humanities.

The qualitative results presented in this chapter are made up of two general analyses of data from the open-ended items in the survey: 593 responses were analysed from the first round of data collection (Fall 2011), in which students were asked, 'What does identity mean to you?' Another 715 responses were analysed from the second (Spring 2012) and third (Fall

2012) data collection rounds, in which students were asked, 'Do you think the Erasmus experience can influence how you feel about your identity and, if so, how?' In the second and third panel rounds, only students who had been in Germany for a semester or a year were asked to reflect on whether they felt Erasmus could influence their identity, since just-arrived students would not have had sufficient time to consider the programme's impact.

The survey included five sections and a total of 36 questions addressing: 1. students' feelings about the concepts of identity; 2. forms of citizenships (town/city/state; national; regional; European; and global); 3. levels of engagement with peers and German culture; 4. reasons for participating in Erasmus; and 5. demographic information. Answers from the open-ended items form the basis for the main analysis detailed in this chapter although some of the quantitative data are also presented. The two open-ended items in the survey were worded as follows:

Survey Item 5: What does identity mean to you?
Survey Item 11: Do you think the Erasmus experience can influence how you feel about your identity and, if so, how?

Data Analysis

The responses to the open-ended items were organised on an Excel sheet so that each person's written reflections could be understood in light of their full set of responses. The entire set of written responses were studied through a detailed thematic analysis that included iterative readings of the full scope of responses, the organisation into categories of repeated observations, and the gradual organising and culling of recurrent patterns of themes (Patton, 2002). Statistical tests on the close-ended questions included group mean comparisons of factor scores and regression analyses. I will refer mostly to the qualitative data and only to the quantitative data as it applies to the research questions stated above.

Definition of Terms

For an explanation of the various concepts of citizenship and identity I use in my analysis throughout this chapter, I refer to the interpretation I described in a previous discussion (Streitwieser, 2012). Important to note also is that my discussion of identity is circumscribed to only the concept of citizenship identity, not to gender, religious, political, sexual or any of the many other possible identities one could discuss in great detail. I use the concept of 'citizen' in reference to work by Willem Maass (2007) to mean 'a legal member of a politically defined state'. I interpret the concept of 'identity' with reference to the work of Duchesne and Frognier (2008) to mean 'the way citizens interpret their values within the citizen group to which they legally belong'. And I use the word 'conception' to mean 'understandings' or, as D.D. Pratt (1992) defines it: 'Specific meanings attached to phenomena which then mediate our response to situations involving those phenomena' (p. 205). In short, I see students going through the experience of study abroad aware of their status as legal citizens of a nation state, but how they interpret the experience and attach meaning to it is individual and idiosyncratic, including how they develop feelings about various notions of citizenship identity.

Findings

As Mitchell (2012) suggested in her paper, employing qualitative research methods to study Erasmus and European identity formation is important if we are to more adequately understand how participants interpret the concept of European identity, under what circumstances, how deeply and why it matters to them. Indeed, in this study these questions have been asked, first through interviews in the pilot study and then through open-ended items administered as part of a larger survey over three data collection phases.

As indicated earlier, analysis of the data collected in the pilot study asking students to explain their level of attachment to and understanding of identity choices along four main lines – 1. national, 2. European, 3. global and 4. 'other' citizenship – led to the establishment of a baseline understanding for our sample's conceptions of citizenship identity that a colleague and I initially developed.

Explanation of European citizenship identification types
Modern European Value Identification
My values, behaviour, even manners are typical for Europeans; Europe is where my friends are; Erasmus represents a new, young generation
Future Identification
My future lies in Europe; I belong to the EU, I trust in its institutions; if we make the EU succeed we all win; I am proud of the EU; I benefit from all of the administrative advantages of being an EU citizen
Travel Identification
I have travelled all over Europe, speak many languages and can participate everywhere; I feel tied to multiple EU countries and feel a strong regional identification
Negative Identification
I am ashamed of, or uncomfortable with, my own country; I prefer the 'loneliness' of EU anonymity over being identified to my nation

Table I. Citizenship identification types.

The initial European identity descriptions and explanations, detailed in Table I, were presented at the 2011 Comparative and International Education Society conference in Montreal, Canada, and then elaborated in a working paper (Streitwieser & Light, 2012, pp. 6-7). In this table, Erasmus students identify four distinct European citizenship identity types and the reasons for them.

This table was slightly revised and presented in a subsequent publication (Streitwieser, 2012) with a revised analysis of the categories of European citizenship identification simplified to three broad types:

1. Shared Identification;
2. Belonging Identification;
3. Dissociative Identification.

These three revised categories represent distinct ways students express their understanding of attachment to the notion of a European identity. While, as other researchers have also found, two or more citizenship types can certainly be represented within one person, these distinct types point to different values that students who express an attachment to European citizenship articulated.

Students with a *Shared Identification* conception base their attachment to European citizenship on feeling a special, shared bond with their fellow Europeans. Through their participation in Erasmus and their new membership in that group, these students are gratified that they have many points of common interest and understanding with other Europeans and deeply value that there can be diversity among differing perspectives but also enough common ground to share a mutual purpose. These students are convinced that the spirit of shared identity and openness represents the modern, youthful Europe they see as the best place to live and work in the future. These students combine identities 1 (modern) and 2 (future) from Table I.

Students with a *Belonging Identification*, on the other hand, are also those who share an excitement about the future of Europe, but they have built this feeling not only on their first eye-opening Erasmus experience but through previously collected mobility experiences and also a confidence in the ability to speak several foreign languages. The pride these students feel in Europe and the commitment they share to making Europe successful is built on their belief that national identification is only one type of belonging and in fact stretches out to a wider European identity, beyond national borders and perhaps even globally. This category expands identification 3 (travel) in Table I.

The third identification type, *Dissociative Identification*, repeats the fourth identification category (negative) in Table I and is characterised by students who reject their national identification altogether out of shame of association with their nation's history and stereotypes.

In light of the analysis of the pilot study findings and the development of initial baseline categories of citizenship identity, the larger survey developed for the three-panel study asked students to indicate their primary citizenship identity along six general lines – 1. local (town/city/state), 2.

national, 3. regional, 4. European, 5. global and 6. 'other' – and to provide
reasons for their choices in their own words in open-ended text boxes. The
analysis of students' written explanations for choosing European citizenship
were summarised as follows:

1. I am part of a new European generation shaping the modern future of
    Europe.
2. My values and behaviour are typically European and make me part of
    a group with common characteristics.
3. My future lies in Europe and I want the EU to succeed.
4. I have travelled all over Europe, speak several of its languages and
    could live and work comfortably anywhere there.
5. I am proud of being a European.

In panel rounds 2 and 3 students were presented with all of the summarised
reasons for choosing each type of citizenship. For those students who
selected European identification, the data came out as illustrated in Figure 1.

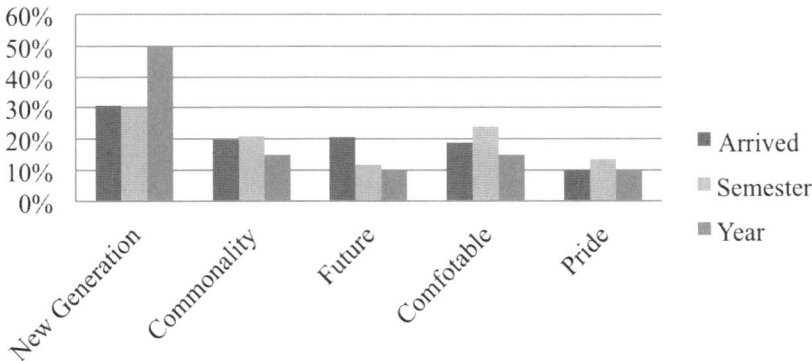

Figure 1. Reasons for choosing European
identification by program duration ($n = 188$).

The most frequently chosen explanation for the choice of European identity
was a feeling of being part of a new, forward-looking generation of youth
shaping the future of Europe. This feeling is particularly strong for students
who spent the whole year in Germany and, unlike the other four categories,
increased rather than declined with more time spent in Germany.

   The salience of these initial categories of European citizenship identity
is well represented in the comments from the second and third round of
panel data collection, in which students were asked to write in their own
words if and why Erasmus could play an important role in the development
of their identity. In those comments, detailed below, a major theme that
emerges is pride in being part of a new generation shaping Europe.

Research Question 1

How do participants in the Erasmus Mobility Programme understand the notion of citizenship identity?

In the first data collection phase (Panel 1, Fall 2011), one of the two open-ended items asked students to write their reflections on what the notion of identity means to them. This item was not repeated in the second and third panel surveys since analysis of the initial responses was deemed sufficient to form a baseline understanding for ways Erasmus students in Germany conceive of the notion of identity in general terms. The summary of the analysis of the 591 responses to this item follows below. As reflected in much of the literature discussing identity, in this study students' conceptions were no less complex and varied. Even when asking a relatively small and specific sample to explain how they interpret identity, no pithy or easily summarised definitions can capture the range of views. Erasmus students see the notion of identity as highly complex, constantly in flux, multiple in form and meaning, not mutually exclusive, often situation and/or context dependent and, in the end, both highly individual and also fundamentally social. One student called it, 'the sum of many parts' while another used the analogy of the 'melting pot' to capture its many facets. To simplify the long list of identity descriptors that emerged in the raw data, it is helpful to organise the two main characteristics of identity that students pointed out: identity for the individual, and identity for society.

At the individual level, Erasmus students see identity constituting personal characteristics, beliefs, habits and expectations that make up an idiosyncratic picture of each person individually. These factors make up one's personality or, as one student explained it, 'a person's stamp'. This stamp, however, includes any variety of character-forming elements that include nationality, religion, gender, values, sexuality, interests, lifestyle, habits, ways of understanding, ways of thinking and even 'how you eat'. At the level of society, on the other hand, the summarised data from students characterised identity as defined by individuals who belong to 'recognised groups', come from 'a known place', are 'shaped by the experiences' they have, and are formed by the people and groups with which they 'associate'. Within these conceptions it is not difficult to recognise the reference to Erasmus ('a recognised group' and 'the experiences one has'), their reference to nationality ('coming from a known place'), and the experience of meeting new people and being in a new place ('associate with other social groups'). All of these summarised perceptions of identity by the Erasmus students in this study [9] point to why many regard the Erasmus experience as being formative, developmental and a powerful vehicle for becoming more aware of the salience of the importance of identity. One male student from Poland studying for one semester in Hanover even used the word 'radicalise' to explain his perception of the impact of Erasmus on identity formation:

I think, that Erasmus experience in most cases radicalises people's feelings about identity. When someone identify strictly with his/her country or region, that person would after exchange identify stronger with his/her nation/region, and if someone identify him-/herself as an European or with certain region of Europe, that person after exchange would feel more as European, Western or even World citizen, and change in identifying oneself from local/national to more global (and vice versa) is not very common attitude.

Research Question 2

Do participants in Erasmus believe programme experience can influence their perception of citizenship identity?
To begin to understand the extent to which Erasmus students believe the programme experience can influence their perception of identity, first the number of 'yes' and 'no' responses was tabulated as part of the full list of responses downloaded onto Excel for analysis from SurveyMonkey. In most cases students clearly wrote 'yes' or 'no' and then went on to explain their answers – often very elaborately through long and passionate text passages – so tabulating was straightforward. The sum of 'yes' and 'no' responses in the combined second- and third-round panel data collection rounds for this open-ended item yielded a total of 715 responses, among which 87% (or 621 answers) were counted as 'yes' and 13% (or 94 answers) were counted as 'no'. While a simple tabulation only suggests the sample's convictions in a certain direction (i.e. well over two-thirds of the sample indicated that Erasmus is important for their identity development), analysis of the written responses provides greater clarity and specificity.

Reasons identified by students with a 'no' response were fairly similar in most cases. Answers ranged from students explaining they have had so much travel experience already they are unconvinced that Erasmus can add more nuance to their already formed conceptions of identity; that identity is deeply pre-determined and cannot be shaped by international experience or other extrinsic factors; or that the question itself is a trap for catching nationalistic tendencies and thus better addressed with a simple 'no'.

Analysis of the 'yes' responses, however, revealed a great deal of variation in how students thought about the value of Erasmus experience to help form or re-form their sense of citizenship identity. For the many 'yes' responses, students clearly engaged deeply with the issue of identity, what it means to them, and how and if they feel Erasmus might play an important role in its development. In that analysis, four main themes emerged, discussed below.

Theme I: It is Unavoidable That Identity Develops During Study Abroad

For some students the idea that Erasmus experience would impact their identity seemed obvious. As a female student from Spain studying for a year at the University in Freiburg wrote:

> Of course it does. When you live out of your country and meet people from different countries, your way of understanding the world changes. Also your feelings about citizenship and identity change.

This perception of the question as rhetorical may be due to the common lay assumption that study abroad is transformative and as such also challenges and changes one's personality and sense of identity. Along these lines, the assumption by many students was not only that confrontation with questions about identity were important, but also that it was a necessary thought process if a common identity is to be developed among Europeans. A male student from the Czech Republic studying for a semester in Bremen explained this:

> I'm sure that most of the students more or less change perception of their identity. The Erasmus stay provide you a unique opportunity to know about various European cultures, while not changing you own. From my point of view, that's the only way how to build-up our common European identity, (which surely exist) while not loosing our own nationality. It goes together very well. The European identity is reinforced by shared accommodation, joint cultural life during the stay and common school attendance.

Theme II: Erasmus Experience is Custom Made for Identity Development

Another theme that emerged was that students praised Erasmus as providing a sort of identity 'testing ground' for the development of their identity. As one female student from Spain studying for a year at the university in Hanover explained:

> Erasmus can be a 'gameboard' where you can test the ideas you had before about your identity, so some people may confirm their previous ideas and some people may find those were inaccurate. In any case, people in Erasmus often experiences a change of perspective at some level. For me, it didn't change my citizenship identity, if I ever had something like that, but it changed the way I feel about my identity in general.

To expand the respondent's analogy, on this identity gameboard students are given the opportunity to rethink their conceptions and either solidify previous beliefs or stereotypes or alter them based on new information. Another student, a female from Romania studying for a year in Constance, made a similar observation:

> I think that the Erasmus exchange may offer one the feeling of belonging to a larger community than a person's country or city. Therefore, the sense of identity is definitely transformed, whether the beneficiary of this experience reckons it or not. This programme also allows the students to better delimitate their identities. The concept of 'identity' is interrelated with the frame of a certain country/nationality and (worldwide) community. Thus, if while abroad one is identified as a citizen of his/her country, the perspective that people have on that nation will be projected on that individual. According to the perceptual typology, the international students will either take pride in their nationality or consider it a burden. Undoubtedly, this affects the perception of one's identity.

Theme III: Erasmus Helps Clarify What European Identity Means

One of the most important themes to emerge was the clear conviction by many respondents that if indeed Erasmus played an important role, it was to help them clarify what European citizenship more concretely means to them. As one female student explained:

> Surely the Erasmus experience influenced how I understand my identity. Although even before my Erasmus time I felt like a European, it was still an abstract concept for me. During the Erasmus experience I got to know other Europeans, their cultures and habits, the similarities and differences between us. In that way I came to concretely understand was Europe is, what the concept of 'Europe' means and how much feel like I'm part of that. (The student did not identify her country or institutional home in Germany.)

For some students the realisation – or 'revelation' in the words of one – of what Europe in a concrete experiential sense means was especially important and helped them to feel a stronger sense of belonging. Several comments pointed this important function out, for example a female student from Poland for one semester in Berlin:

> It just puts my citizenship in an European perspective. It doesn't make me feel embarrassed or overly excited about being from my country, but Erasmus experience made a different division: between people who come from Europe and other continents in the world. So in that sense it broadened my view on citizenship as not only belonging to just one country but also acknowledging that I come from Europe. That seemed like a revelation to me, although it seems obvious now that I write it.

For the following female student from Italy for one semester at the university in Freiburg, citing the EU motto 'unity in diversity', established in 2000, having the chance to experience first-hand the diversity behind this creed was particularly meaningful:

> I recognised in the motto 'unity in diversity' that sums up the European institutional vision, a tangible reality and I can say that I have had experience within Europe where for the first time, during my Erasmus I noticed its concreteness.

For another female student from France for a year at one of the Berlin universities, the Erasmus experience pointed out her generation's ability to transcend national boundaries. For her, Erasmus became the quintessential European experience, as she put it, because it helped her viscerally 'feel' European through the novelty of travel, new places and new friends.

> The Erasmus experience is an European experience. You can say I'm European but if you travel and discover the Europe you can really feel you're European. Study aboard, new friends, new city... you'll be more open minded than before and consequently it changes how you feel about your identity. Erasmus program shows how our generation can't have only one country's identity, we're a part of Europe. Theme IV: Erasmus Develops a Special European Youth Identity

Finally, the theme that came across most clearly in the data was that many students felt their Erasmus experience developed them as part of a new and exciting generation of Europeans who belong to a 'special' and in many cases lucky and potentially powerful group. Summarised, this group's distinctive character was defined by belonging to a unique and recognised demographic – sometimes simply characterised as 'something bigger'.

Many testimonials clarified this feeling in myriad different ways. One female student from Italy studying for a semester at a university in Berlin explained that for her the aspect of being part of something larger than herself but defined by being young and free to go anywhere and meet anyone gave her a new feeling of comfort that she had not experienced before.

> I feel a part of a big and new generation of young people who travel around the world, who meet other people from different countries, who share their own culture and traditions with others and I finally feel comfortable with myself because if I don't feel at home in Italy (with its laws and lifestyle) I can feel at home in other countries.

Another male student from Belgium and also in Berlin for a semester felt a similar pull of his generation during the Erasmus experience but expressed his feeling of belonging in terms of a liberation of thinking no longer based only on national attachment.

It gives you the feeling to be part of something bigger, you're more easily going to identify yourself as a generation, a way of thinking instead of a countries citizen.

A third student, a female from Bulgaria studying for a semester at the university in Cologne, explained that for her, the Erasmus experience made her both appreciative of where she came from but also glad to be part of something new and larger that had taken her out of her national framework.

The Erasmus program can be an eye-opening experience when it comes to identity: it can show you just how unique your culture is, and how unique you yourself are just because you are coming from this culture. It can make you appreciate your national identity in a way you have not appreciated it before. At the same time it can open doors to other cultures and make you relate to them yourself, make you part of something bigger and much more diverse.

Another important aspect of the theme of becoming part of a new and larger identity group was the focus on youth and the idea that they were now part of a new generation of people distinguished by similar values, less concerned with national identification and more focused on moving beyond stereotypes and imposed national and ethnic labels. Another female from Bulgaria, this time studying for one semester in Berlin, expressed this sentiment very elegantly:

Living abroad contributes to your understanding of other cultures and nationalities until the point where it no longer matters who is from where and you realised all the stereotypes you grew up with no longer hold where the new generation of young Europeans are concerned.

A male student from Italy for a year in Berlin also expressed the feeling of a shared, and over time strengthened, youth commonality among his fellow Europeans. For him, the camaraderie that grew out of the Erasmus experience came from sharing the challenges of intercultural adjustment and going through the ups and downs together.

Erasmus experience can change our perception of identity, strengthening our European identity. In almost no experience you can meet so many people from European countries as during the Erasmus staying. In this period you share with them moments of happiness and troubles. During and after the Erasmus experience I had the feeling that the European youth shares the same values.

This youth society developing in Europe is embodied by a feeling of truly belonging together and being united by the ability to comfortably and knowledgeably travel and live and work anywhere in Europe and be flexible and open to any possibilities that may come along. For the following student, a female from Estonia studying for a year at the university in Bremen, the openness and freedom she felt through Erasmus defined for her the very idea of what European identity is.

> It will only reinforce my feeling of belonging to one united European society. I felt myself as an European, before as well, but thanks to this Erasmus experience, I think I am even more attached to Europe as a continent. I am definitely planning to live and study/work in different countries of Europe. I come from Estonia, I study in France, right now I'm making my Erasmus year in Germany, and who knows where I will end up next year. That is the European identity for me.

The feeling of belonging to a special group – a 'special world' to use the words of one student – that is defined by youth, openness, opportunity, shared values and the ability to succeed in Europe is best captured in this final quotation by a female student from Italy who studied for a year at the university in Freiburg:

> The Erasmus experience helps the students understand they are part of the world. When you meet other people from other countries during this programme, you explain them where are you from, but it doesn't mean anything, because you are Erasmus. When you take part to this experience you are not Italian, or German or English anymore, you are simply International, you are part of all the world and you can be confronted with other cultures, people, and way of thinking. You just forget where you are from: you live there but you are part of a special world.

Discussion

The findings in this study at first glance present the researcher with a troublesome contradiction. In terms of the question about students' primary citizenship identification, when asked, 'How do you primarily characterise your identity?' students overwhelmingly chose national citizenship as their primary identity as illustrated in Figure 2.

Figure 2 shows that well over half (58-62%) of the Erasmus students in the sample expressed primary citizenship to their home nations. Only a much smaller percentage, 10-12%, identified first as European citizens, fewer even than those who identified as global citizens. However, when asked in the open-ended items about whether they believe Erasmus experience can affect their sense of citizenship identity, up to 83% are convinced it can, and in their comments students explain how the experience made them feel closer to 'something bigger' that is defined by being part of a definite group of young and influential European citizens. Thus, the two sets of data – the quantitative findings and the qualitative findings – at first appear to set up a contradiction between students' actual primary citizenship identification and whether or not they believe Erasmus can play an important identity-forming function.

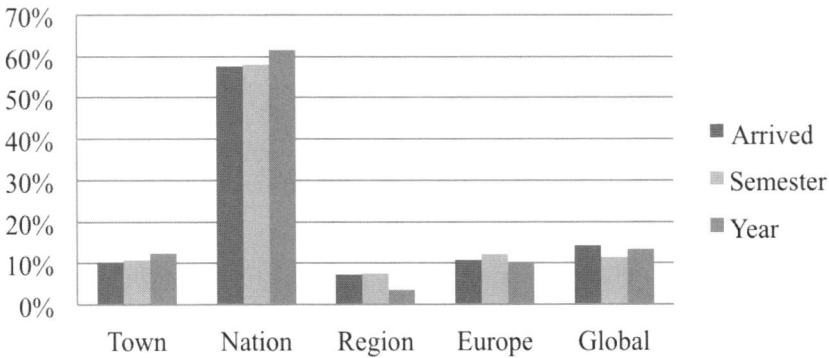

Figure 2. Citizenship identification by time spent in Germany.

However, this contradiction may mostly simply be due to how the questions are phrased and where they are placed in the survey and the difference between how closed and open-ended survey items are addressed. The apparent contradiction implies that national and European citizenship identification is exhaustive and cannot exist within the same person. However, when students are asked questions directed simply at the extent of their feelings about national or European belongingness, their answers indicate high levels of both. That is, strong identification as a citizen of one's nation or as a citizen of Europe does not seem to necessarily be associated with a weaker level of identification of the other. Indeed, given the complexity of the concept of identity and the desire to find an Erasmus Programme-to-identity development link, Mitchell's criticism (2012, p. 510) that the existing quantitative empirical studies on this matter can be 'rather one-dimensional' is entirely valid (Mitchell, 2012, p. 510). One female student from Sweden studying for a semester in Berlin makes this same argument:

> I think this survey is extremely limited because of this one-alternative-only-design. For me it's also very important what my secondary or tertiary identity is. Importantly it very much depends on the context. When living in another european city for a while, what sorts me out is not that i'm a european but that i'm not from the country i currently live in. in that way is my national identity rather strengthened. On the other hand, i feel more at home in other parts of europe than i did before and in that way i'm less from my country compared to just from europe in general.

Students need to be able to think more deeply about identity and have outlets beyond fairly crude survey choices that allow them to indicate their views on the complex questions of citizenship if, indeed, Erasmus policy-makers believe finding evidence of its development is important. Having a dual attachment to Nation and to Europe are not necessarily incompatible. In fact, it makes sense that students would hold on to their ties to their nation, especially after being away for a year, and at the same time also appreciate the wider identity they have formed through the Erasmus experience to a new European demographic, namely fellow Erasmus students. As the researchers who have studied European identity argue, and as studies attempting to document an Erasmus-to-European identity link often acknowledge, identity is not mutually exclusive. It is entirely compatible that one share several identities simultaneously and that through time and experience these identities shift and continue to develop.

What is rather more important in the findings produced by this study is that Erasmus students recognise the salience of identity as a construct with which they contend when they study abroad. The testimonials from this sample indicate that many participants felt the foreign study experience allowed them to become more open to altering their sense of identity and to letting their intercultural engagement experiences shape it. To contextualise the characteristic of this arguably 'special' group of European students formed through the common Erasmus experience, Gaertner and Dovidio's Common InGroup Identity Model (2012) – also alluded to in Mitchell's (2012) paper as a potentially fitting social theory – is instructive. The Common Ingroup Identity Theory

> … proposes that inducing people to recategorize ingroup and outgroup members within a common category boundary (a one-group representation based, for example, on common school, city, or national identity) redirects those motivational and cognitive processes that produce ingroup-favoring biases to increase positive feelings, beliefs, and behaviors toward others who were previously regarded primarily in terms of their outgroup membership. (p. 2)

Conclusion

The student testimonials in this chapter support many of the assumptions of the Common InGroup Identity Model (Gaertner et al, 1993; Gaertner & Dovidio, 2012) in terms of how Erasmus students conceive of their newly formed 'Erasmus Identity'. The theory 'emphasizes the fluidity of social categorization processes' (Gaertner & Dovidio, 2012, p. 4) just as Erasmus students through the experience come to accept shifted social categories. The theory points out 'the reality that people simultaneously can conceive of themselves as belonging to variety multiple groups that are hierarchically organized in terms of inclusiveness' (p. 4) and Erasmus students also come to accept more groups and their place within several of them simultaneously.

The theory holds that 'different goals, motives, expectations, or emphases in the immediate situation can shift the level of category inclusiveness that will be dominant' (p. 2) just as many Erasmus students attest to having shifted their former beliefs in line with new input and stimulation through meeting new people and engaging in new situations. And, finally, a Common Ingroup Identity can 'increase positive evaluations of others ... such as ethnic and racial groups that have extended histories of intergroup conflict' (pp. 1-3) and, indeed, many Erasmus students also spoke of becoming more open and inclusive through their foreign study experience.

Both Michael Bruter's conclusion that European identity allows for compatible allegiances to local and wider identities simultaneously (2005, p. 122), and Gaertner and Dovidio's Common Ingroup Identity Model support the idea that people can move 'memberships from "Us" and "Them" (two separate groups) to a more inclusive "we"' (Gaertner & Dovidio, 2012, p. 2). In a Europe that is increasingly, albeit slowly, populated by the so-called 'Erasmus Generation', the mentality of those leaving the programme allows for the existence of a broader view of identity that allows for dual identities and expressly mitigates against 'us–them' type thinking that has been so destructive in Europe's past.

The qualitative data from this study do not necessarily show that students as a group feel more European per se, but rather simply that they feel more attached to a particular group of Europeans: the group of Erasmus students they now call their friends. The open-ended items from this sample indicate that overwhelmingly students think deeply about the idea of identity and also that many are convinced the programme can play an important role in helping them think about their identity as Europeans – whether or not in fact they accept and use the label 'European citizen' or 'European identity' outright.

In exhibiting many of the characteristics of the Common Ingroup Identity, we feel this group of Erasmus students exemplifies what might be regarded as a new type of European citizen: an 'Erasmus Citizen'. This citizen is part of a demographic made up of primarily young, future-oriented Europeans who belong to a recognised group defined by a unique blend of cultures, backgrounds and new perspectives; whose identity is formed through a specific, shared experience; and who feel ownership of and the power to shape a defined European space in the future. The Erasmus experience has helped these students both dismantle stereotypes and also form new conceptions of their fellow Europeans, combining an appreciation of their own culture with the discovery of new cultures. These students not only embrace cultural diversity but have also come to identify and celebrate this diversity.

The implications of this new form of identity built out of Erasmus experience may lead to a larger, better networked group of highly educated European elites who migrate freely within the European labour market and further strengthen Erasmus-established contacts throughout the member states. For Europe and its future leaders this could be tremendously beneficial. 'Erasmus Citizenship' could enhance the Bologna Process, through coupling the standardisation of the European higher education system with a harmonious, yet diverse, culture of higher education. Erasmus students could become a driving force behind the European integration process as future leaders in the political, civic and economic institutions of the European Union. On the other hand, this 'special' group could also pose challenges: the process of European integration could become an elite project run by and only including the highly educated but not those who are unable to participate in the Erasmus Programme. For this reason, the inclusive nature of the 'Erasmus Citizen' needs to reach beyond that 'special' demographic and also be inclusive of Europeans much more widely if, indeed, the noble goals set by the Erasmus Programme over 25 years ago are to see continued fruition well into the future.

Whether the Erasmus Programme causally develops identification as a European citizen among participants is still a matter of debate. This study has produced strong qualitative evidence to support the argument that the notion of European citizenship identity is subjective and diversely understood among Erasmus participants, and that participants believe the programme can positively impact their identification as Europeans. While the quantitative data seem to contradict this belief to some extent, national and European citizenship identification do not inhibit one another. Rather, the Erasmus experience catalyses a group identity we refer to as the 'Erasmus Citizen' that we believe could prelude a growing sense of European citizenship identity.

Through the analysis of the qualitative data portion of our larger Erasmus Identity Study, we have shared findings that we believe are a convincing indication that the Erasmus experience can help form conceptions of citizenship identity among its participants and lead to the development of a specific type of European identity, an 'Erasmus Citizenship'. This argument is exploratory and intentionally provocative and based on suggestive though not yet conclusive or generalisable data. We hope our initial analysis, however, will encourage further research and studies on these questions that include samples and wider representation beyond Germany.

Notes

[1] The first author wishes to acknowledge the collaboration of Dr Gregory Light, Northwestern University, for his contribution to the original working draft paper of this chapter; and Tobias Ward for his help organising the survey data.

[2] See Norgaard's chapter in this volume for a broader discussion of the Erasmus Programme.

[3] The study, *Einstellungen ehemaliger und zukuenftiger Erasmus-Studierender zu Europa*, expects to release its findings in 2014.

[4] Eurobarometer Public Opinion Surveys are available at: http://ec.europa.eu/public_opinion/archives/eb_special_en.htm.

[5] See ISSP Research Group, International Social Survey Programme (ISSP): *National Identity II (ISSP 2003)*. GESIS Cologne Germany – Leibniz Institute for the Social Sciences, Cologne, Germany. Identification number: ZA3910.NSDstat. Data file version 2.0.0, 27.08.2007, doi:10.4232/1.10077

[6] See survey items from the Erasmus Student Network AISBL, Brussels. Authors: Alfranseder, E., Fellinger, J., Krzaklewska, E., Krupnik, S. & Taivere, M. for *The Experience of Studying Abroad for Exchange Students in Europe* (2005); *Exchange Students' Rights* (2006); *Generation Mobility* (2007); *Exchanging Cultures* (2008); and *Exchange, Employment and Added Value* (2011).

[7] Items in the survey funded by German Academic Exchange Service were both my own developed from the pilot study data, as well as some items adapted with permission from surveys created by Sigalas (2010), King and Ruiz-Gelices (2003), the International Social Survey Programme, the Erasmus Student Network and research reported by Teichler (2004) and Maiworm and Teichler (2002).

[8] Students represented Austria, Belgium, Bulgaria, *Croatia, Czech Republic, Denmark, England, Estonia, Finland, France, Germany, Greece, Hungary, Ireland, Italy, *Kazakhstan, Latvia, Netherlands, Norway, Poland, Portugal, *Russia, *Scotland, *Serbia, Slovak Republic, Slovenia, Spain, Sweden, Switzerland, Turkey. Note that countries marked with an asterisk do not have Erasmus 'National Agencies'.

[9] All of the student testimonials have been kept in their original form without any changes to structure of basic grammar, although some of the spelling has been corrected for the sake of coherence. Quotations originally in German have been translated for this chapter by the first author. Respondents are only identified by gender, how long they were in Germany and their home country.

References

Altbach, P., Reisberg, L. & Rumbley, L.E. (2009) *Trends in Global Higher Education: tracking an academic revolution. Executive Summary*. A Report prepared for the UNESCO 2009 World Conference on Higher Education. Paris: UNESCO.

Altbach, P. & Teicher, U. (2001) Internationalization and Exchanges in a Globalized University, *Journal of Studies in International Education*, 5(5), 5-25.

Anderson, B. (1983) *Imagined Communities: reflections on the origins and spread of nationalism*. London: Verso.

Bellamy, R. (2000) Citizenship beyond the Nation State: the case of Europe, in N. O'Sullivan (Ed.) *Political Theory in* Transition, pp. 91-112. London: Routledge.

Berghoff, S., Bischof, L., Brandenburg, U., Hachmeister, C. & Leichsenrihg, H. (2012, ongoing study) *Effects of ERASMUS Mobility*. Berlin: Centrum fuer Hochschulentwicklung.

Bracht, O., Engel, C., Janson, K., et al (2006) *The Professional Value of ERASMUS Mobility*. Kassel: INCHER.

Bruter, M. (Ed.) (2005) *Citizens of Europe? The Emergence of a Mass European Identity*. New York: Palgrave Macmillan.

Carter, A. (2001) European Citizenship: bridge or barrier to global citizenship? In A. Carter, *The Political Theory of Global Citizenship*, pp. 119-142. London: Routledge.

Choudaha, R. & de Wit, H. (2014) Challenges and Opportunities for Global Student Mobility in the Future: a comparative and critical analysis, in B. Streitwieser (Ed.) *Internationalization of Higher Education and Global Mobility*. Studies in Comparative Education. Oxford: Symposium Books.

Commission of the European Communities (2009) Green Paper: Promoting the Learning Mobility of Young People. http://ec.europa.eu/education/lifelong-learning-policy/doc/mobility/com329_en.pdf

Council of the European Communities (1987) Council Decision of 15 June, 1987, adopting the European Community Action Scheme for the Mobility of University Students (ERASMUS), *Official Journal of the European Communities*, L 166, 15.06.1987, 20-24.

Cushner, K. & Karim, A.U. (2004) Study Abroad at the University Level, in D. Landis, J.M. Bennett & M.J. Bennett (Eds) *Handbook of Intercultural Training*, 3rd edn, pp. 289-308. London: Sage.

Davies, L. (2006) Global Citizenship: abstraction or framework for action? *Educational Review*, 58(1), 5-25.

de Wit, H. (2009) Global Citizenship and Study Abroad: a European comparative perspective, in R. Lewin (Ed.) *The Handbook of Practice and Research in Study Abroad: higher education and the quest for global citizenship*, pp. 212-229. New York: Routledge.

Deardorff, D. (2006) Identification and Assessment of Intercultural Competence as a Student Outcome of Internationalization, *Journal of Studies in International Education*, 10(3), 241-266.

Dolby, N. (2004) Encountering an American Self: study abroad and national identity, *Comparative Education Review*, 48(2), 150-173.

Duchesne, S. & Frognier, A. (2008) National and European Identifications: a dual relationship, *Comparative European Politics*, 6, 143-168.

Eder, K. & Giesen, B. (Eds) (2001) *European Citizenship: national legacies and transnational projects*. Oxford: Oxford University Press.

European Commission (2008) The Impact of ERASMUS on European Higher Education: quality, openness and internationalisation. Directorate-General for Education and Culture. Lifelong Learning Programme.

European Parliament Directorate-General for Internal Policies (2010) Improving the Participation in the Erasmus Programme. Policy Department B: Structural and Cohesion Policies. IP/B/CULT/IC/2009-053

Everson, M.C. & Preuss, U.K. (1995) *Concepts, Foundations and Limits of European Citizenship*. Zentrum fuer Europaeische Rechtspolitik Diskussionspapier 2/95. Bremen: Universitaet Bremen.

Frevert, U. (2008) How to Become a Good European Citizen: present challenges and past experiences, in Viola B. Georgi (Ed.) *The Making of Citizens in Europe; New Perspectives on Citizenship Education*, pp. 37-51. Bonn: Bundeszentrale fuer Politische Bildung.

Gaertner, S.L. & Dovidio, J. (2012) Common Ingroup Identity Model, in D. Christie (Ed.) *The Encyclopedia of Peace Psychology*. Malden, MA: Wiley-Blackwell.

Gaertner, S.L., Dovidio, J.F., Anastasio, P.A., Bachman, B.A. & Rust, M.C. (1993) The Common Ingroup Identity Model: recategorization and the reduction of intergroup bias, *European Review of Social Psychology*, 4, 1-25.

Gmelch, G. (1997) Crossing Cultures: student travel and personal development, *International Journal of Intercultural Relations*, 21(4), 475-490.

Habermas, J. (1993) Citizenship and National Identity: some reflections on the future of Europe, in R. Robertson & K.E. White (Eds) *Critical Concepts in Sociology*, pp. 155-174. New York: Routledge.

Hammer, M.R., Bennett, M.J. & Wiseman, R. (2003) Measuring Intercultural Sensitivity: the intercultural inventory, *International Journal of Intercultural Relations*, Special Issue on intercultural development, 27(4), 421-443.

Institute of International Education (2012) *Open Doors Data 2012: US study abroad, fast facts*. Washington, DC: Office of Global Educational Programs, Bureau of Educational and Cultural Affairs of the US Department of State.

Jacobs, D. & Maier, R. (1998) European Identity: construct, fact and fiction, in M. Gastelaars & A. de Ruijter (Eds) *A United Europe. The Quest for a Multifaceted Identity*, pp. 13-34. Maastricht: Shaker Press.

Kandeko, C.B. & Weyers, M. (2013) *The Global Student Experience: an international and comparative analysis*. Abingdon: Routledge.

King, R. & Ruiz-Gelices, E. (2003) International Student Migration and the European 'Year Abroad': effects on European identity and subsequent migration behaviour, *International Journal of Population Geography*, 9, 229-252.

Knight, J. (2008) *Higher Education in Turmoil: the changing world of internationalization*. Rotterdam: Sense Publishers.

Knight, J. (2012a) Student Mobility and Internationalization: trends and tribulations, *Research in Comparative and International Education*, 7(1), 20-33.

Knight, J. (2012b) A Conceptual Framework for the Regionalization of Higher Education in Asia, in J.N. Hawkins, K.H. Mok & D.E. Neubauer (Eds) *Higher Education Regionalization in Asia Pacific: implications for governance, citizenship and university transformation*. New York: Palgrave Macmillan.

Kritz, M.M. (2006) Globalization and Internationalization of Tertiary Education. http://www.un.org/esa/population/migration/turin/Symposium_Turin_files/P02_K RITZ_Rev3_Augst21.pdf

Kuhn, T. (2012) Why Educational Exchange Programmes Miss their Mark: cross-border mobility, education and European identity, *Journal of Common Market Studies*, 50(6), 994-1010.

Lewin, R. (2009) Introduction: The Quest for Global Citizenship Through Study Abroad, in R. Lewin (Ed.) *The Handbook of Practice and Research in Study Abroad:*

higher education and the quest for global citizenship, pp. xiii-xxii. New York: Routledge.

Lutterman-Aguilar, A. & Gingerich, O. (2002) Experiential Pedagogy for Study Abroad: educating for global citizenship, *Frontiers*, 8, Winter, 41-82.

Maiworm, F. & Teichler, T. (2002) The Students' Experience, in U. Teichler (Ed.) *Erasmus in the Socrates Programme*, pp. 83-116. Bonn: Lemmens.

Maass, W. (2007) *Creating European Citizens*. Lanham, MD: Rowman & Littlefield.

Mitchell, K. (2012) Student Mobility and European Identity: Erasmus study as a civic experience, *Journal of Contemporary European Research*, 8(4), 490-518.

Nussbaum, M. (1996) Patriotism and Cosmopolitanism, in Joshua Cohen (Ed.) *For Love of Country: Debating the limits of patriotism*. Boston, MA: Beacon Press.

Ogden, A. (2007) The View from the Veranda: understanding today's colonial student, *Frontiers*, 15, 35-56.

Osler, A. (1998) European Citizenship and Study Abroad: student teachers' experiences and identities, *Cambridge Journal of Education*, 28(1), 77-96.

Papatsiba, V. (2005) Political and Individual Rationales of Student Mobility, *European Journal of Education*, 40(2), 173-188.

Pascarella, E.T. & Terenzini, P.T. (2005) *How College Affects Students*, vol. 2. San Francisco: Jossey-Bass.

Patton, M. (2002) *Qualitative Research & Evaluation Methods*. 3rd edn. Thousand Oaks, CA: Sage.

Pratt, D.D. (1992) Conceptions of Teaching, *Adult Education Quarterly*, 42(4), 203-220.

Rivza, B. & Teichler, U. (2007) The Changing Role of Student Mobility, *Higher Education Policy*, 20, 457-475.

Roman, L.G. (2003) Education and the Contested Leanings of 'Global Citizenship', *Journal of Educational Change*, 4, 269-293.

Salisbury, M.H., Umbach, P.D., Paulsen, M.B. & Pascarella, E.T. (2009) Going Global: understanding the choice process of the intent to study abroad, *Research in Higher Education*, 50(2), 119-143.

Sigalas, E. (2009) Does Erasmus Student Mobility Promote a European Identity? Constitutional Web Papers, ConWEB No. 2/2009. http://www.wiso.uni-hamburg.de/conweb

Sigalas, E. (2010) Cross-Border Mobility and European Identity: the effectiveness of intergroup contact during the ERASMUS year abroad, *European Union Politics*, 11(2), 241-265.

Stearns, P. (2009) *Educating Global Citizens in Colleges and Universities: challenges and opportunities*. New York: Routledge.

Streitwieser, B. (2012) Erasmus Mobility and Students' Conceptions of National, Regional and Global Citizenship Identity, in J. Beelen & H. de Wit (Eds) *Internationalisation Revisited: new dimensions in the internationalisation of higher education*, pp. 135-150. Amsterdam: Centre for Applied Research on Economics and Management, Amsterdam University of Applied Sciences.

http://www.carem.hva.nl/wp-content/uploads/2012/07/Internationalisation-Revisited-CAREM02012-def.pdf

Streitwieser, B. & Light, G. (2011) University Students and Conceptions of Global Citizenship: a case study. Working Paper No. 10-001. Available as a working paper at Northwestern University's Buffett Center for International and Comparative Studies website: http://www.cics.northwestern.edu/publications/workingpapers/cge.html

Streitwieser, B. & Light, G. (2012) Study Abroad and the Easy Promise of Global Citizenship: student conceptions of a contested notion. Working paper, Searle Center for Advancing Learning and Teaching, Northwestern University.

The Erasmus Citizen: student conceptions of citizenship in the Erasmus Mobility Programme. Also available as a working paper at Northwestern University's Searle Center for Advancing Teaching and Learning website: http://www.northwestern.edu/searle/research/publications-and-presentations/working-papers.html

Streitwieser, B. & Light, G. (2012) Study Abroad and the Easy Promise of Global Citizenship: student conceptions of a contested notion. Available as a working paper at Northwestern University's Searle Center for Advancing Teaching and Learning website: http://www.northwestern.edu/searle/research/publications-and-presentations/working-papers.html

Teichler, U. (1996) Student Mobility in the Framework of ERASMUS: findings of an evaluation study, *European Journal of Education*, 31(2), 153-179.

Teichler, U. (2004) Temporary Study Abroad: the life of Erasmus students, *European Journal of Education*, 39(4), 395-408.

Teichler, U. (2010) Internationalising Higher Education: debates and changes in Europe, in D. Mattheou (Ed.) *Changing Educational Landscapes: educational policies, schooling systems and higher education – a comparative perspective.* Dordrecht: Springer.

Teichler, U. & Maiworm, F. (1997) The ERASMUS Experience: major findings of the ERASMUS evaluation research project. Wissenschaftliches Zentrum für Berufs-und-Hochschulforschung der Universität Gesamthochschule Kassel.

UNESCO (2012) Institute for Statistics, Global Flow of Tertiary-Level Students. http://www.uis.unesco.org/Education/Pages/international-student-flow-viz.aspx

Wildavsky, B. (2010) *The Great Brain Race: how global universities are reshaping the world.* Princeton, NJ: Princeton University Press.

Wilson, I. (2011) What Should We Expect of 'Erasmus Generations'? *Journal of Common Market Studies*, 49(5), 1113-1140.

Woolf, M. (2009) Study Abroad Changed My Life and Other Problems, paper presented at the Annual Forum on Education Abroad Meeting, Portland, OR, 18-20 February.

Woolf, M. (2010) Another Mishegas: global citizenship, *Frontiers*, 19, Fall-Winter, 47-60.

Wuttig, S. (2009) Understanding Mobility and Recognition, in K. Lauridsen, K.K. Zethsen, D. Leonhard, S. Wuttig & A. Timofei (Eds) *Developing Mobility and Ensuring Recognition*. Best of the Bologna Handbook Series. Berlin: Raabe Fachverlag fuer Wissenschaftsinformation.

Zemach-Bersin, T. (2009) Selling the World: study abroad marketing and the privatization of global citizenship, in R. Lewin (Ed.) *The Handbook of Practice and Research in Study Abroad: higher education and the quest for global citizenship*, pp. 303-320. New York: Routledge.

CHAPTER 16

The Other Side of Mobility: the impact of incoming students on home students

JOS BEELEN

ABSTRACT This chapter explores the role and value of incoming student mobility for Internationalisation at Home. I present two projects from the United Kingdom and Australia, countries with a long tradition in recruiting international students, and three from the Netherlands, where a growing number of programmes are delivered in English. The comparison shows that, while the underlying aim may be to internationalise the curriculum for all students, priority is given to accommodating international students and home students become marginalised. The author argues that incoming student mobility will not have an impact on the receiving institution as a whole and that traditional (physical) incoming mobility has limited value for Internationalisation at Home. New forms of mobility, combining physical with virtual and outgoing with incoming, may better serve to provide the international experience for all students that traditional incoming mobility fails to deliver, but that a new generation of students may expect.

Introduction

Clifford (2011, p. 555) states that: 'The idea of internationalising university curricula for all students, rather than just with a focus on international students, has received little attention since the flurry of activity following Nilsson's coining of the term "internationalisation at home" (IaH) in 1999.' Considering the fact that the concept of IaH has steadily grown in popularity since its introduction and is now considered to be one of the two main streams in internationalisation, next to the more traditional internationalisation abroad (Knight, 2008, pp. 22-24), it is worthwhile to investigate if, indeed, the focus on internationalising all students has become less important. Clifford's quote is from her editorial to a special issue on

287

internationalising the home student, with contributors all coming from English-speaking countries, mainly the United Kingdom (UK) and Australia. We will therefore contrast examples from recent projects in those countries with developments in the Netherlands, which delivers an increasing number of programmes in English, to see if similar developments can be distinguished there.

In order to do this, we will first see what the concept of IaH represents, how it has evolved since its introduction in 1999 and how it is related to both internationalisation for all students and incoming student mobility.

Internationalisation at Home

The term 'Internationalisation at Home' originated in 1999 in Malmö, where the newly established university had as yet no bilateral agreements and therefore no opportunities to send students abroad. The definition of Internationalisation at Home as it was presented at the time (Crowther et al, 2001, p. 8) therefore excluded all forms of outgoing mobility. For the same reason, the university did not have incoming mobility. Internationalisation at Home in Malmö had to rely on integrating the international and intercultural aspects of the city into the learning experiences of all students. The focus on all students is an essential one and explains much of the conceptual confusion with regard to Internationalisation at Home.

Internationalisation at Home has become the most prominent term for internationalisation of the curriculum (formal, informal and hidden) in Europe, but it shares many of its characteristics with similar concepts in other parts of the world, notably Australia and the United States (Beelen & Leask, 2011). In her discussion of key concepts, elements and rationales for the 2005 International Association of Universities Global Survey Report, Knight (2006, p. 25) distinguishes Internationalisation at Home as one of the two streams in internationalisation.

Knight stresses that the two streams are interdependent rather than independent. She broadens Nilsson's original concept of Internationalisation at Home and distinguishes a 'diversity of activities' that constitute Internationalisation at Home: curriculum and programmes, teaching/learning processes, extra-curricular activities, liaison with local cultural/ethnic groups and research or scholarly activity (Knight, 2006, p. 27, Figure 1.5). In the analysis of the 2005 Global Survey, Knight describes that it addresses a number of 'Internationalisation at Home-related factors': the 'international/intercultural dimension of the curriculum', 'research collaboration' and 'area and foreign language studies' (Knight, 2006, p. 128). As we will see below, new forms of mobility may integrate Internationalisation at Home and abroad and show the interdependency of both types of activities more than ever before.

During the Nineties, the concept of IaH evolved and became connected with student competencies. International and intercultural skills were now included in the competences of all graduates, hence the term 'Internationalisation for all'. It was stressed that IaH should bring an international experience to all students and that electives would not suffice if all students were to acquire the intercultural competencies that were required by society and the world of work.

This led to formulating the following characteristics of Internationalisation at Home:

– Internationalisation at Home is aimed at all students and is therefore part of the compulsory programme.
– Internationalisation at Home is a set of instruments and activities 'at home' that focus on developing international and intercultural competences in all students.
– Internationalisation at Home is based on the assumption that, while students will travel for personal reasons, the majority will not travel for study-related purposes, although the latter option is not entirely excluded.
– Internationalisation at Home may include short-term outgoing mobility in the form of study visits or research assignments that are a component of the compulsory curriculum.
– Internationalisation at Home only includes the individual experiences of students undertaken during study and placement abroad if these are integrated into the home institution's standard assessment tools (such as the portfolio for all students). (Beelen & Leask, 2011, p. 5)

The UK and Australia

The UK and Australia have a long tradition in the recruitment of degree-seeking international students and occupied second and third position, respectively, on the list of top host countries with 11% and 8% global market share in 2009 (Banks & Bhandari, 2012, p. 388). In Australia, the strong focus on student recruitment contributed to development of the concept of Internationalisation of the Curriculum, which focuses on learning outcomes of both home and international students. This did not, however, lead to the desired results, which led universities to try and improve the international learning outcomes of domestic students (Brewer & Leask, 2012, p. 245). At least at national level however, international students continue to remain the dominant focus. This is illustrated by the two cases of government-initiated projects presented below, one from the UK and one from Australia.

The Higher Education Academy and the United Kingdom Council for International Student Affairs coordinated the project 'Teaching International Students' (TIS). The project was grounded in the assumption that 'increasing student mobility and successful national policies to recruit international students have led to more culturally diverse higher education landscapes around the world'.[1] This suggests that the approach of the UK has been followed everywhere and that the cultural diversity in higher education is a consequence of student mobility rather than of migration. The TIS project, while primarily focused on international students, does not lose sight of the value that incoming mobility can have for the home students:

> The project therefore focuses on the ways that lecturers and other teaching staff can maintain and improve the quality of teaching and learning for international students through providing guidance and information about how to meet the diverse learning needs of international students, and, importantly, in ways that will benefit all students.[2]

The Australian Government's Office for Learning & Teaching Project 'Internationalisation at Home' 'aims to internationalise the learning and teaching practices of teachers, placement supervisors, international students, and domestic students in the Business and Health higher education sectors'.[3]

This demonstrates that, although the project aims to achieve international learning outcomes for all students, the focus is first on international students, with home students coming in second. As the presentation of the project shows (Mak, 2011), it takes place in a setting in which 28% of Australian higher education students are from overseas, but with an overrepresentation (83.3%) of enrolments from Asian countries (2010) and these unevenly distributed over disciplines (Austrade, 2011).

Lawley (2009) concludes, from an Australian perspective, that many sources for internationalisation of the curriculum 'focus on the perspective of international students and ignore domestic students albeit with an emerging consensus that internationalisation of the curriculum should involve more than international students and sending domestic students abroad'.

We now contrast these developments in Australia and the UK with those in the Netherlands, a country that does not have a long-standing tradition of international student recruitment but that offers an increasing number of programmes in English, in order to see if similar processes can be identified.

Incoming Student Mobility in the Netherlands

Countries with widely spoken languages such as English, French, German, Russian and Spanish are leading destinations for foreign students (Organisation for Economic Co-operation and Development [OECD], 2012, p. 363). Yet, the market share of English-speaking countries in the provision of international education is diminishing. The percentage of students that chose to study in English-speaking destination countries declined from 49% in 2000 to 42% in 2009 (Banks & Bhandari, 2012, p. 388). In Europe, Denmark, the Netherlands, Sweden and Finland capture a share of this by offering the largest number or programmes in English outside the English-speaking countries (OECD, 2012, p. 365). The main consideration for this is not income generation, like in the UK and Australia, but ultimately to attract better-quality students from abroad. With a stay rate of 27%, international students also act as skilled migrants. The introduction of full tuition fees for non-EU/European Economic Area students aims to 'ease the financial burden on domestic taxpayers' in the process (de Wit et al, 2013, p. 20).

The delivery of an increasing number of programmes in English has allowed the global market share of the Netherlands to rise from 0.6% in 2000 to 1.3% in 2007 (de Wit, 2012, p. 431). The Netherlands are exceptional in that 51.6% of its international students come from neighbouring countries (OECD, 2012, p. 382). In Germany this is 15.3%, Sweden 19.5%, Finland 20.6% and Denmark 36.9%. Part of this is due to the success of Dutch government policies that, since the 1990s, have been advocating cooperation between Dutch universities and universities across the border in Germany and Belgium. This policy is usually referred to as 'Internationalisation on a bike'. The strange situation now exists that programmes offering content in English as a way to attract international students are attracting German students who in fact could follow the curriculum in Dutch.

Although limited in market share, the relatively large number of English-medium programmes in the Netherlands leads to increased possibilities for international recruitment and it is therefore relevant to see if there are similar shifts in focus from domestic to international students as we have seen in Australia and the UK. A characteristic difference is that in the Netherlands projects aimed at teaching international students are initiated by the universities themselves rather than by the government. Three examples from the Netherlands follow.

The 'Acculturatieproject', run by Surf, E-Merge and Nuffic between 2008 and 2010, involved five research universities and five universities of applied sciences. The project aimed to have international students make a more informed choice for a programme in the Netherlands and improve their preparation, thereby reducing dropout rates. Within the project, a number of online preparation courses for international students were developed. The project aims were focused only on international students and there was no mention of any effects of incoming mobility on domestic students. As such, the project had a remarkably strong business focus for the Dutch context. Delft University of Technology and University of Twente were among the participants in the project and both universities had embarked on their own attempts to accommodate international students.

Delft University of Technology, ranked 51 in the *Times Higher Education* World Reputation Rankings 2013, has been delivering all its Masters programmes in English since 2005 and enrols on average 30% of international students in those programmes. The university started the 'Thousand Flower Project' to stimulate lecturers to make the international dimension in their courses more explicit. One of the aims of the project was to contribute to Internationalisation at Home 'in which local students are prepared for the international environment at the university itself and acquire competencies for the international labour market' (Brummelink et al, 2009, p. 2). However, the subtitle of an article on the project is: 'a bottom up approach to improve teaching international students' (Brummelink et al, 2009). Apparently, the original aim of the university was to internationalise curricula, but the focus shifted and narrowed to teaching international students somewhere in the process.

University of Twente, in the extreme east of the Netherlands, also delivers all its Masters programmes in English, increasingly to German students. The university aims to enrol 35% of its students from abroad. It runs the 'Acculturation Project', attempting to integrate international students into student life at the self-styled 'only campus university in the Netherlands' (most Dutch universities are inner city universities). The student unions have played a prominent role in the project, which was initiated from the International Office and therefore focuses on an area that the International Office traditionally controls: the informal curriculum. Only in the final stages of the Acculturation Project have the Internationalisation at Home aspects present in the original plan resurfaced and a number of pilot projects been defined that aim to internationalise curricula for all students, starting with Dutch-language Bachelor's programmes.

Problems and Obstacles:
an analysis of terminological confusion

The Australian, UK and Dutch projects described above have in common that they focus on international students while, tacitly or explicitly, assuming that domestic students will somehow benefit from their presence. When faced with the challenges and opportunities of recruiting international students, domestic students apparently move into the background.

This may be partly due to lack of conceptualisation for internationalisation of the curriculum. Definitions tend to be confusing, such as one by OECD (1996): 'A curriculum with an international orientation in content and/or form, aimed at preparing students for performing (professionally/socially) in an international and multicultural context and designed for domestic and/or foreign students' (p. 6). This definition leaves the ultimate aim of an internationalised curriculum up in the air when it mentions acquiring professional or personal skills (or both), for domestic 'or foreign students' (or both). This allows the overall purpose of an internationalised curriculum to change from domestic students acquiring international competences to accommodating international students. Rizvi (2007) therefore criticised it as lacking specificity and being too abstract as it gives little guidance on implementation or interpretation. Even so, it still continues to be widely used (Brewer & Leask, 2012, p. 246). The more recent definition by Leask (2009, p. 246) mentions outcomes of student learning through 'incorporation of an international and intercultural dimension into the content of the curriculum as well as the teaching and learning arrangements and support services of a program of study'. This makes it clear that an internationalised curriculum should address the learning outcomes of all students.

Also, in the absence of business considerations, for example when it comes to student exchange through the Erasmus Programme, the conceptualisation of the value of incoming mobility remains problematic. Receiving international students is an element of strategies of European universities but it is not always clear what the expected impact would be. Some scholars have therefore concluded that student mobility, outgoing or incoming, will 'significantly influence the learning outcomes for the majority of students' (Brewer & Leask, 2012, p. 249). The general notion that incoming student mobility – degree seeking or exchange – has highly positive results is still widespread and mostly unchallenged, being associated with 'academically-enhancing diversity for receiving institutions' (Rumbley, 2012, p. 125).

The Numbers Game

The circumstances under which incoming student mobility takes place determine if there will be effects on domestic students, what they will be and how they can be demonstrated. There are a range of factors that need to be taken into consideration before there can be any controlled impact of incoming mobility on (a segment of) the domestic student body.

It is difficult to imagine that the relatively small number of incoming international students at most continental European universities will contribute significantly to student learning across the whole university. Their effect will only be felt by those domestic students that study with them in international (Masters) programmes. This means that disciplines with a national focus and delivered in the local language, such as teacher education, will not easily attract enough international students, except maybe in some elective modules delivered in English. Therefore, incoming student mobility in those programmes alone will not serve to internationalise the curriculum of all domestic students. The domestic student, by the way, is no better off when the opposite happens. In the Anglo-Saxon countries, some programmes attract an overwhelming majority of international students, sometimes as many as 80-90% and from a narrow range of countries.

At universities where most programmes are delivered in the local language, it is tempting to place international exchange students in a separate group for the duration of their stay. This makes such a programme easy to run since this can be done detached from the main teaching and learning processes but it isolates international students almost completely. Accommodating international students in minor or elective programmes delivered in English to domestic and international students is better, but still limits an international learning experience to a minority of domestic students.

Only in the informal curriculum, for example through buddy systems, will students mix. The effects of this can be significant (Leask, 2009) but at the same time also limited to a minority of domestic students.

Getting the International Classroom Right

Even if we look at the micro-level of the international classroom, the effects of international students on domestic students are not evident. Both a low and a high percentage of international students may affect the learning experience of the domestic student.

Apart from the numbers, the domination of certain nations may influence the learning experience and may also be less than ideal for the discipline. Rather than working with just the students who happen to come in, there will be an 'ideal' composition which is based on the discipline and determines which perspectives from which countries should be represented in the classroom to make it into a truly international learning environment that allows for a comparison of different perspectives within the discipline. This implies that the choice of partner institutions should depend on discipline-based considerations. The Dutch Ministry of Education, Culture and Science (2012) urges the universities to aim for balanced international classrooms, by 'in principle' discouraging overrepresentation of specific groups of foreign students. This could apply to German students at universities in the east of the Netherlands (where they may commute) but not in the rest of the country. Overrepresentation may not only differ between universities, but may also vary considerably between programmes within the same university. Using incoming exchange mobility to compensate for overrepresentation in diploma mobility is an option but requires individual departments to develop elaborate mobility plans.

The Role of Academic Staff

Lecturers may be aware of the international aspects of their discipline and even have international research collaboration but this not the same as designing and facilitating an international learning environment for domestic and international students. It is remarkable that while this is identified as one of the main obstacles in the 3rd Global Survey (Egron-Polak & Hudson, 2010), professional development programmes at universities hardly offer courses that address internationalisation skills. Although the Global Survey focuses on obstacles to internationalisation in general, many obstacles apply to internationalisation of the curriculum in particular (Beelen, 2011). Many universities limit their efforts to offering courses in English language proficiency, confusing the international dimension of education with the language in which it is delivered and ignoring the importance of didactics and methodology, which are a condition for intercultural and international learning (Leask, 2010; Leask & Carroll, 2011). In addition to skills for internationalisation, the Global Survey identifies lack of foreign language proficiency of academic staff as a main obstacle (Egron-Polak & Hudson, 2010). Universities in mainland Europe recognise this and encourage lecturers to improve their language proficiency in English.

Among them is Delft University of Technology, which undertook an extensive project to assess the English language proficiency of all its non-native-speaking staff teaching in English-medium Masters programmes (Klaassen & Bos, 2010). The assessment took place because of students' complaints, but the Klaassen and Bos article does not specify whether these were domestic or international students or both and to what extent the complaints addressed pronunciation or other aspects. After academic staff improved their English language proficiency, the complaints diminished temporarily only to resurface later, which leads to the question of whether the English language proficiency level of the students should have been assessed as well.

Another issue is that a better command of English will not automatically lead to more effective teaching in English without a command of the pedagogy of teaching in one's second language to students who use their second language to learn.

Problems and Obstacles: assessment

Another issue is to what extent learning outcomes of the international classroom are assessed. It is clear that learning does not take place automatically as soon as students from different countries or cultures share a learning environment. An international classroom is – as internationalisation itself – not an aim but a tool for learning. The assessment of learning outcomes in the international classroom requires much from the educational skills of the lecturer. How international and intercultural competences of all students in an international classroom can be assessed is a topic that will require much debate in the coming years.

New Forms of Mobility

The discussion above makes it clear that traditional incoming mobility, either diploma mobility or in the framework of exchange, does not provide a quick and clear tool to internationalise the curriculum of all students. A number of tools for IaH that do not require incoming student mobility, such as incoming guest lecturers or study of international literature and cases, may achieve the same aim. But there are forms of mobility that may contribute.

Virtual mobility enables students to study at a university abroad without physically leaving their domestic institution. Lecturers can teach to an international audience, supervise students and collaborate with colleagues, all without leaving their office. These possibilities may profoundly change educational practice as students now have the opportunity to enrol in global online higher education through Massive Open Online Courses or MOOCs. European students now follow these at eminent higher education institutions in the USA and have started demanding recognition of the credits at their domestic institutions.

Interestingly, virtual mobility in Europe is leading to a revival of traditional mobility. Students from different European countries, working together virtually, enhance their collaboration with short-term physical mobility. The availability of low-cost flights between cities is becoming a determining factor in forming institutional partnerships. Existing short-term mobility is made more effective by complementing it with longer term virtual collaboration between students and lecturers. In this way, students may study together online as well as during short-term study visits. This combines incoming mobility with outgoing mobility and the virtual with the physical, thus stressing the interconnection between them.

As this type of short-term mobility is part of the formal curriculum and its outcomes are being assessed within the curriculum, they can be considered elements of Internationalisation at Home. That they fall outside the original definition of IaH (Crowther et al, 2001) demonstrates that definitions are shifting too.

The New Student

We should take care to avoid the impression that the domestic students are always national in outlook and international students always represent an international mindset. In Western European countries, the domestic student body has become quite diverse. In addition, Dutch students will increasingly have international experiences before they enter higher education. Students in European secondary education participate in international projects, such as Comenius. In the new Erasmus Programme, the possibilities for individual mobility in secondary education have been extended, which will enable students to have an individual pre-university mobility experience. The increasing popularity of the gap year may positively influence outgoing mobility. Preliminary research in the Netherlands shows that 47% of students who have spent (part of) their gap year abroad choose a more internationally oriented programme (Posthumus & Heuts, 2012). It is also assumed that these students are more likely to go abroad during their programme, but no results on this issue are known yet. Finally, there are now more than 125 schools in the Netherlands that offer part of the secondary education programme in English, which trains students to study school subjects in English. This may help to change the domestic student into a more internationally focused one. However, this will not take the responsibility away from universities and academic staff to design and facilitate appropriate international learning environments for all their students.

Conclusion

In this chapter I have argued that the focus on international students in the UK and Australia distracts from the focus on domestic students. With expanding opportunities to recruit international students for English-medium programmes in the Netherlands, the same seems to be happening there.

One of the reasons for this is an unclear conceptualisation of what internationalisation in fact is, which leads to the assumption that the mere presence of international students at the university or in a limited number of international programmes or classrooms will have beneficial effects on the entire university.

Another reason is one of scale: at most continental European universities, the number of incoming students is simply not large enough to provide a meaningful international experience for all domestic students.

In individual international classrooms, the composition of the student body and the lack of skills of academic staff with regard to English language proficiency, didactic and methodical issues and assessment present obstacles to learning, both for domestic and international students.

We can therefore not rely on incoming student mobility, whether it be diploma mobility or exchange, as the only or even the most prominent tool to internationalise the (entire) domestic student body. Yet, this does not suffice to conclude that the domestic student has disappeared from the picture. In the Netherlands, most Bachelor's programmes are taught in Dutch, both at research universities and at universities of applied sciences. Without international students in those programmes, the international dimension is entirely focused on the domestic students. All Dutch universities of applied sciences are attempting, albeit with varying degrees of success, to implement such international dimensions. This partly explains why new forms of mobility combining virtual and physical are developing. They extend beyond traditional mobility and may, together with teaching staff mobility and a range of other tools for Internationalisation at Home, eventually become instrumental in providing an international experience to all students.

Notes

[1] http://www.heacademy.ac.uk/teaching-international-students.

[2] http://www.heacademy.ac.uk/teaching-international-students.

[3] https://sites.google.com/site/internationalisationathome/home.

References

Austrade (2011) International Student Data for 2010. http://www.austrade.gov.au

Banks, M. & Bhandari, R. (2012) Global Student Mobility, in D. Deardorff, H. de Wit, J. Heyl & T. Adams (Eds) *The Sage Handbook of International Higher Education*, pp. 379-397. Thousand Oaks, CA: Sage.

Beelen, J. (2011) Internationalisation at Home in a Global Perspective: a critical survey of the 3rd Global Survey Report of IAU, *Globalization and Internationalisation of Higher Education* [online monograph], *Universities and Knowledge Society Journal/Revista de Universidad y Sociedad del Conocimiento*, 8(2), 249-264. http://rusc.uoc.edu/ojs/index.php/rusc/article/view/v8n2-beelen

Beelen, J. & Leask, B. (2011) Internationalisation at Home on the Move. In *Handbook Internationalisation*. Berlin: Dr Josef Raabe Verlag. http://www.raabe.de

Brewer, E., & Leask, B. (2012). Internationalization of the Curriculum, in D. Deardorff, H. de Wit, J. Heyl & T. Adams (Eds) *The Sage Handbook of International Higher Education*, pp. 245-266. Thousand Oaks, CA: Sage.

Brummelink, M.L., Frantzeskaki, N., Klaassen, R.G., Blom, E.M., Kooij, R.E., Kroesen, J.O., Stadler, D.I. & Van den Boogaard, M.E.D. (2009) One Thousand Flowers in Delft: a bottom up approach to improve teaching international students, paper presented at Edulearn 09 Conference, Barcelona, 6-8 July.

Clifford, V. (2011) Editorial: Internationalising the Home Student, *Higher Education Research & Development*, 30(5), 555-557.

Crowther, P., Joris, M., Otten, M., Nilsson, B., Teekens, H. & Wächter, B. (2001) *Internationalisation at Home: a position paper*. Amsterdam: EAIE.

de Wit, H. (2012) The Netherlands: constructing the policy framework – but will they stay? In D. Deardorff, H. de Wit, J. Heyl & T. Adams (Eds) *The Sage Handbook of International Higher Education*, pp. 430-431. Thousand Oaks, CA: Sage.

de Wit, H., Ferencz, I. & Rumbley, L. (2013) International Student Mobility: European and US perspectives, *Perspectives*, 13(1), 17-23.

Egron-Polak, E. & Hudson, R. (2010) *Internationalization of Higher Education: global trends, regional perspectives* (International Association of Universities 3rd Global Survey Report). Paris: IAU.

Klaassen, R. & Bos, M. (2010) English Language Screening for Scientific Staff at Delft University of Technology, *Hermes*, 45, 51-60.

Knight, J. (2006) *Internationalization of Higher Education: new directions, new challenges* (2005 International Association of Universities Global Survey Report). Paris: IAU.

Knight, J. (2008) *Higher Education in Turmoil; the changing landscape of internationalization*. Rotterdam: Sense Publishers.

Lawley, M. (2009) Internationalising the Curriculum: an exploratory study, in D. Tojib (Ed.) *Proceedings of the ANZMAC 2009 Conference*. Melbourne: Australian and New Zealand Marketing Academy. http://pandora.nla.gov.au

Leask, B. (2009) Using Formal and Informal Curricula to Improve Interactions Between Home and International Students, *Journal of Studies in International Education*, 13(2), 205-211.

Leask, B. (2010) 'Beside Me is An Empty Chair'; the student experience of internationalization, in E. Jones (Ed.) *Internationalisation and the Student Voice*, pp. 3-17. New York: Routledge.

Leask, B. & Carroll, J. (2011) Moving Beyond 'Wishing and Hoping': internationalisation and student experiences of inclusion and engagement, *Higher Education Research & Development*, 30(5), 647-661.

Mak, A. (2011) Internationalisation at Home: project overview. https://sites.google.com/site/internationalisationathome

Ministry of Education, Culture and Science (2012) *Kosten en baten van internationalisering in het hoger onderwijs* [Costs and benefits of internationalisation in higher education]. Letter by the State Secretary of Education to the House of Representatives, 16 May. http://www.rijksoverheid.nl/ministeries/ocw

Organisation for Economic Cooperation and Development (OECD) (1996) *Internationalising the Curriculum in Higher Education.* Paris: OECD.

Organisation for Economic Cooperation and Development (OECD) (2012) *Education at a Glance 2012.* Paris: OECD.

Posthumus, A. & Heuts, E. (2012) Aanjager voor internationale mobiliteit [Engine for international mobility], *Transfer*, 20, December, 16-18.

Rizvi, F. (2007) Internationalization of Curriculum: a critical perspective, in M. Hayden, J. Levy & J. Thompson, *The Sage Handbook of Research in International Education.* London: Sage.

Rumbley, L. (2012) So Many Data, So Little Clarity... the ongoing challenges of making sense of academic mobility in Europe, in J. Beelen & H. de Wit (Eds) *Internationalisation Revisited: new dimensions in the internationalisation of higher education*, pp. 125-134. Amsterdam: Centre for Applied Research on Economics and Management, Amsterdam University of Applied Sciences.

CHAPTER 17

Key Factors of Participation in Study Abroad: perspectives of study abroad professionals

LISA LOBERG & VAL D. RUST

ABSTRACT Despite the many demonstrated benefits of a study abroad experience, trends in campus internationalization, and initiatives to promote international education, participation in study abroad by US college students remains at 1-2%. Low participation, however, is not due to lack of student interest. Previous research has compared intent, motivation, and characteristics of participants versus non-participants, and a number of barriers, both real and perceived, have been shown to impact student mobility. The current study seeks to identify ways to overcome barriers by exploring factors that lead to participation in study abroad. While previous studies have focused on the student, the current study gathers the unique perspectives of professionals who work in the field of international education and have experience at successful institutions. Findings indicate that faculty support and curriculum/academic integration are key factors that lead to student participation in study abroad. The current study suggests that rather than targeting the many barriers that prevent participation, outreach efforts to garner faculty support may be more effective. Furthermore, working towards curriculum/academic integration of study abroad can create an institutional culture that supports study abroad, thereby eliminating barriers and ultimately leading to greater participation rates for US students.

Despite the many demonstrated benefits of a study abroad experience and large-scale government initiatives to promote participation, just 1-2% of US college students studied abroad in 2010-11 (Institute of International Education [IIE], 2012). Low participation, however, is not due to lack of student interest. A study by the American Council on Education, Art & Science Group and the College Board (2008) found that 50% of college-bound high school students plan to participate in a study abroad program in college. With only 1-2% of enrolled college students participating each year in programs of all durations, there remains a considerable disparity between the percentage of students who indicate initial interest in study abroad and the percentage of students who actually end up participating. The goal of the current study is to explore factors that lead to student participation in study abroad by gathering the unique perspective of professionals who work in the field of international education – specifically those who have experience working directly with or at institutions with consistently high or increasing participation rates.

Previous studies on choice and intent have sought to explain the discrepancy between high rates of interest and low rates of participation by investigating characteristics of students. Rust et al (2007) found that college freshmen who were active in high school government and other school activities were more likely to study abroad in college. In an analysis of Cooperative Institutional Research Program data at a large, public university in the northeast, Stroud (2010) discovered a correlation between participation in study abroad and attendance of university more than 100 miles from home. In looking at several nationally administered surveys, BaileyShea (2009) found that intent and participation in study abroad was affected by students' background, college involvement, and institutional factors, as well as parents' level of education.

Salisbury et al (2009) contend that there is still very little known about what makes a student decide to study abroad but note many similarities between the process of choosing college and the intent to study abroad. Salisbury et al (2010) also call into question national and institutional efforts to promote international education, pointing to studies that indicate that students are already shaped when they enter college. Their findings suggest that pre-college marketing and outreach might be most effective (Salisbury et al, 2010); Doyle et al (2010) also identified early understanding of opportunities as a positive factor of student participation. While exposure and early planning are factors to consider, these studies do not fully explain the substantial figure of 50% of graduating high school seniors who are already indicating plans to study abroad during college (American Council on Education et al, 2008) but who ultimately do not participate.

Barriers to Participation

Researchers have examined factors that impact a student's decision to study abroad; they have also identified a number of barriers that prevent more students from participating. These barriers include: students' perceptions of finances, concerns about graduating on time, cultural background, and level of family support (Goldstein & Kim, 2006; Sánchez et al, 2006; Salisbury et al, 2009). Barriers also exist at many levels within an institution (Heisel & Stableski, 2009) and include limited staffing and resources, lack of support from faculty and administration, and the need for curricular integration and financial support. When study abroad professionals were polled for a 2010 international education survey ($n = 219$), the majority of respondents (80%) who gave a reason for declining participation rates cited financial constraints and limited resources (IIE & The Forum on Education Abroad, 2011). The importance placed on finances, however, may be more a matter of perception than reality, as quantitative analysis of survey variables revealed only a weak correlation between change in budget and change in participation (Loberg, 2012).

Salisbury et al (2009) agree that finances are not the only issue but state that many students with financial concerns do not inquire about study abroad in the first place. The ability to navigate and overcome these identified barriers may be a result of having sufficient social and cultural capital, as defined by Bourdieu (1996), as well as an environment that has shaped choice, as discussed by McDonough (1994); in the way that students with college-educated parents are more likely to successfully navigate the college process, students whose parents did not study abroad may not be as aware of the opportunities or see the value. Students of color continue to be underrepresented in study abroad (Penn & Tanner, 2009; McClure et al, 2010), as do males and students in science, technology, engineering, and mathematics disciplines (Shirley, 2006). The typical profile of a study abroad student is still a Caucasian female whose chosen major of study is in the humanities (Stroud, 2010; IIE, 2012).

Communicating Information to Students

Several studies have examined how students find out about the study abroad opportunities available to them and whether there is a direct impact of certain communication strategies on student participation. In conducting a content analysis of the prospective student viewbooks of various colleges and universities, Hartley and Morphew (2008) saw that study abroad was a featured item under the category of academics, though they did not examine whether this marketing placement encouraged students to participate. Bolen's (2001) examination of informational materials found an element of consumerism in study abroad marketing that seemed to portray the experience as less academic in nature. Shirley (2006) contends that marketing messages about study abroad often leave out male students, which further perpetuates the gender imbalance in eventual participation. Salisbury et al (2010) found distinct differences in the way that pre- and in-college experiences impact men's and women's decisions to study abroad and recommend that marketing strategies take into account gender differences.

Need for the Study

While much is known about the characteristics of students who study abroad and the barriers that prevent more students from participating, very little is known about the strategies of the institutions that seem to have navigated the barriers and regularly send high numbers of students abroad each year. Certain US institutions already have an international focus, a reputation likely cultivated over decades. At these institutions students arrive on campus with an expectation that they will study abroad at some point during their college career. Study abroad participation is high, and allocated resources and staffing typically reflect a true commitment to campus internationalization. Institutions at the other end of the spectrum send few students abroad; they struggle with limited resources and often have one-person study abroad offices, or in the case of some institutions and community colleges, zero staff members dedicated to study abroad. They may lack support from administration, and investing in international education is not an institutional priority. Still some colleges and universities have dramatically increased student participation in a span of a few short years. Few studies have examined these trends or analyzed correlations between institutional variables. For institutions with goals of sending more of their students abroad, information about effective best practices is critical.

Previous research has provided insight as to how participation in study abroad may relate to intent, motivation, or other characteristics; however, studies have focused primarily on the student. An overlooked constituent in the literature is the study abroad professional, an individual who works for a college/university, or for a third-party provider that administers study abroad programs – also known as an International Education Organization (IEO). Collecting data from study abroad professionals as to what has led to consistently high or increased rates of student participation could be tremendously helpful to strategic planning efforts of an institution and to the field of international education as a whole. Study abroad professionals typically have experience working on or with various kinds of campuses, they work directly with students, and many are advocates and champions of international education. They are often the ones shaping institutional policy, and in many cases, experimenting with strategies in order to make study abroad accessible to more students. Study abroad professionals have a wealth of knowledge and experience to contribute to the discussion about which factors lead to student participation.

Research Design

The current study sought to capture the perspectives of professionals who work in the field of study abroad and to discover what factors may be leading to the success of institutions that are sending consistently high or increasing numbers of students abroad. The study was guided by the following research questions:

1. What do study abroad professionals view as factors that lead to student participation in study abroad?
2. To what extent are these identified factors prevalent at institutions with consistently high or increasing rates of student participation in study abroad programs between the years 2006-11?

Data were gathered from a focus group and semi-structured interviews conducted with a total of 17 individuals who work in study abroad – eight who worked for a college or university and nine who worked for a third-party provider. All of the participants had experience working at or with institutions with consistently high or increasing rates of student participation in study abroad. The range of experience of these individuals was 3 to 20 years working in international education, and they resided in the west, southwest, central, northeast, and southeast regions of the USA, representing 11 states. Table I offers a description of the interview and focus group participants by institution type.

Associate		Baccalaureate		Masters		Doctorate		IEO	
n	*%*	*n*	*%*	*n*	*%*	*n*	*%*	*n*	*%*
0	0	3	17.6	4	23.5	1	5.8	9	52.9

Table I. Study participants by institution type.

Representatives of third-party program providers, or IEOs, were specifically included in the sample as they spend a great deal of time recruiting students on college campuses for study abroad programs. Because the nature of their work involves visits to many different institutions, these study abroad professionals are in a unique position to compare what they have observed about the study abroad operations, campus climate, and student population of the campuses they visit. As a result of their travels and institutional connections, they have insight as to the overall feel of one campus as compared to another with regards to student interest and general awareness of study abroad. Consequently, these international education professionals are a tremendous resource in study abroad research; the current study sought to acquire and highlight their perspectives.

Data on participation factors were captured through the focus group, which consisted of four participants, and interviews conducted in person and by telephone, each lasting a range of 30 minutes to one hour. Access to participants was made possible by several international education conferences: the November 2011 Council on International Educational Exchange conference in New Orleans, Louisiana; the February 2012 Lessons From Abroad returnee conference in San Diego, California; and the March 2012 Forum on Education Abroad conference in Denver, Colorado. The protocol for the focus group and interviews was based on the IIE and Forum Snapshot survey (2011) yet was semi-structured in nature. Rather than selecting from a pre-determined list, participants were asked to generate factors in their responses. Prompts included: 'In your experience, what do you think moves a student to study abroad? Is there anything that an institution can do to overcome barriers and encourage more students to participate? Can an institution create a climate that encourages study abroad participation? If so, how?' The discussions were digitally recorded, transcribed, and coded for themes.

Findings

What emerged from these discussions was a clear prioritization of faculty support and curricular/academic integration as key factors that lead to student participation in study abroad. Not only were these key factors identified as leading to participation, they were seen as effective in overcoming obstacles. Study participants brought up and acknowledged the barriers to participation that exist in the literature, such as concerns about finances and on-time graduation, but they did not see the need to counter these barriers with discrete strategies. Instead, they saw the presence of faculty support and the academic integration of study abroad as part of a holistic approach that effectively removed the barriers altogether.

In explaining the concept of 'faculty' as a key factor of student participation, there was a general consensus among participants that if a faculty member talks about study abroad and says directly to a student, 'This is something you should do', that conversation with a faculty member will 'carry more weight than if a student hears the same thing from someone who works in the study abroad office'. When discussing the influence of faculty, one IEO professional summarized, 'They have a lot of power.' Another interviewee commented, 'There has to be 100 percent buy-in from the faculty, or it's never going to happen.' This participant characterized faculty support as flexibility in approving coursework taken abroad, allowing courses to fulfill requirements on the home campus, and permitting classroom presentations about study abroad. 'The key piece is having faculty members that are supporters of it,' one interviewee declared. Faculty members were seen by all participants as highly influential advisors that could either encourage or discourage students about study abroad. 'You have to have faculty recommending it,' said a participant. Working with academic departments was seen to be 'effective' regardless of institution size; a respondent from a comprehensive university explained, 'At such a big institution, it really comes down to the individual faculty member.' A respondent from a small institution stated that students are 'influenced by faculty', and especially, by 'faculty in their major'.

Not having the support of faculty was seen by all focus group and interview participants as a factor that contributes greatly to the disparity between student interest and rates of participation. As one participant summarized, 'Faculty can stop students from studying abroad.' When it comes to courses in a particular discipline, participants reported that some faculty members maintain the stance that 'those classes can only be taught here' at the home institution, not anywhere abroad.

All participants in the focus group and interviews linked faculty support to the concept of curriculum/academic integration. It is important to note here that curriculum/academic integration connotes several potential concepts: study abroad as a graduation or general education requirement, as a required part of a major, or as one of several ways to fulfill an experiential or cultural requirement. One professional at an institution with increasing participation rates explained how the college had redesigned its core curriculum so that courses taken abroad now fulfilled an international/cultural requirement and had a specific place in the curriculum.

All of the IEO professionals recognized their unique position to make observations and comparisons between the various campuses they visit and with which they work and drew on their observations and experience and often gave examples from specific campuses in their discussions. One participant noted specifically, 'Because we go to so many different campuses I see all the time that campuses are asking, "How do they structure it financially over there [at that other institution]? Could I try that?"'

In all of the discussions, the identified factors of faculty support and curricular/academic integration were seen as characteristic of successful institutions. A participant from a campus with recent increases in participation in all program types explained the factors of change in more detail, specifying that the increase was due to a 'confluence of events'. These events included: a change in 'institutional mission' to a more international focus, a 'structural change' in administration, and 'revisions to curriculum' that provided a place for courses taken abroad to count towards a 'global requirement'. This participant also noted that there were 'tremendous growing pains' at the institution during this process, but the outcome of these concentrated efforts is that participation in study abroad continues to increase. Another participant acknowledged that international education endeavors are most effective when 'coming from [within] the institution'.

Two participants raised the point that study abroad professionals could benefit from more training and experience in higher education administration in order to better advocate for study abroad initiatives on the home campus. One of the participants said, 'We need to have a better professional understanding of the institutions that we are part of.' Using budget models and reporting to the governing boards as examples, this participant also noted, 'The path to leading study abroad at a university is also diverse ... I have a degree in international education; I had never considered what a discount rate meant', referring to institution models of financial aid packaging. As a result, many of those concepts unique to higher education administration and institutional budgets are 'learned on the fly'. The participant went on to say: 'Not that the Business Office has any clue about what we do in the study abroad office ... but if we want to start building the institutional relationships, we need to start to educate ourselves better about that.' The other participant described large institutions as operating in 'silos' and emphasized the need for study abroad professionals to effectively communicate the right data in order to get administrative departments, as well as faculty, 'on board'.

The mission statement of an institution was seen by study participants as an important indicator of support, but it was the 'intentional integration' of a study abroad experience into the academics that focus group and interview participants felt actually led to student participation. As one professional explained of the institutional integration of study abroad: 'You know it's going to be part of the experience' at the university. 'It's part of the culture of the institution,' said two participants from institutions with traditionally high rates of study abroad participation. It was agreed by all participants in the focus group and interviews that student participation in study abroad was also influenced by institutional factors such as whether courses abroad would fulfill campus requirements. All participants mentioned that they often heard students express concern that studying abroad would affect progress in their major and/or have the potential to delay graduation. Focus group and interview participants brought up and acknowledged other factors of participation including: funding, concern for on-time graduation, peer influence, marketing and outreach, institutional partnerships, level of family support for study abroad, previous experience abroad, connection to career, level of faculty support, and institutional culture, many of which are already featured prominently in the literature. All participants discussed student concerns about the cost of studying abroad, and all agreed that in many cases funding was a barrier because of student perception; however, cost was unanimously seen as something that could often be worked out – with advising, program selection, financial aid packaging, and greater awareness of available scholarships.

What emerged in the findings was surprising, because with all of the talk about barriers and financial constraints in the field of international education, these 17 study abroad professionals had a very different approach that pushed to the side traditional efforts to increase marketing, to garner more funding, or to combat each individual obstacle that students encounter. They acknowledged many of the barriers identified in the literature, such as concerns about finances and on-time graduation, but categorized them as an issue of 'student perception', not as true, insurmountable barriers. They discussed other potential factors such as campus climate, peer influence, and the need for advocacy, but not with the same frequency. Drawing upon their experience working at or with successful institutions, these study participants identified and prioritized faculty support and curriculum/academic integration as key factors that lead to higher rates of student participation in study abroad.

Discussion

While the concepts of faculty support and curriculum/academic integration are not new to the field of international education, their prioritization over funding represents a potential new area of focus. Efforts to address low student participation often involve increased marketing to students and requests to the institution for more funding and staffing. The current study suggests that, given the role of faculty support in encouraging higher rates of student participation at successful institutions, outreach efforts aimed directly at faculty may be more effective than trying to convince students to study abroad or trying to target the many barriers. Working towards curriculum/academic integration of study abroad can more effectively build an institutional culture that supports study abroad and eliminates barriers, ultimately leading to greater rates of student participation.

Recommendations and Areas for Future Research

The current study creates many opportunities for additional follow-up and for future research. Because the exploratory nature of the interview protocol allowed for factors to be generated organically by the participants, the participation factors that were identified merit further study to see if they would be the same factors identified by professionals at other institutions. As discussed earlier, a future research project could list the factors that were identified in the current study and ask more study abroad professionals, as well as other constituents such as faculty and administrators, to rank their level of impact on student participation.

The current study focused on professionals who worked at or with successful institutions. A more rounded picture might be accomplished by interviewing professionals from institutions that are struggling to send students abroad. What factors are identified by those professionals? Are the barriers they identify viewed differently? What, if any, strategies are being employed at those institutions to counteract barriers and to what level of success?

The current study considered international education experiences in the most general sense and did not distinguish between year-long, semester, summer, and short-term programming. A follow-up project might seek to identify factors that might be specific to program types. Institutional factors could also be further explored: is there a correlation between characteristics of institution (such as location, region, type of city, institution size, age) and participation in study abroad?

When considering the findings of the current study, many more questions come to mind. What is it about faculty support and curriculum/academic integration specifically that leads to higher participation rates? Do the same principles apply to community colleges and to institutions outside the USA? How can a campus strategically forge partnerships with faculty in order to promote study abroad and how can academic departments be persuaded to see study abroad as an essential facet of the major? An action research study could follow an institution that was intentional about building a study abroad-going culture to see if it moved through similar stages of development and to see how student participation rates corresponded to strategic changes made on the campus.

So much of the prior research has focused on the barriers to participation and on the student, but more needs to be known about the professionals and the institutions that are successfully navigating the barriers if we are serious as a profession and as a nation about increasing student participation in study abroad.

References

American Council on Education (ACE), Art & Science Group LLC & the College Board (2008) *College-Bound Students' Interest in Study Abroad and Other International Learning Activities.* Baltimore: Art & Science Group.

BaileyShea, C. (2009) Factors That Affect American College Students' Participation in Study Abroad. Doctoral dissertation, University of Rochester, NY.

Bolen, M. (2001) Consumerism and US Study Abroad, *Journal of Studies in International Education*, 5(3), 182-200.

Bourdieu, P. (1996) *The State Nobility: elite schools in the field of power*, trans. L. Clough. Stanford: Stanford University Press.

Doyle, S., Gendall, P., Meyer, L.H., Hoek, J., Tait, C., McKenzie, L. & Loorparg, A. (2010) An Investigation of Factors Associated With Student Participation in Study Abroad, *Journal of Studies in International Education*, 14(5), 471-490.

Goldstein, S.B. & Kim, R.I. (2006) Predictors of US College Students' Participation in Study Abroad Programs: a longitudinal study, *International Journal of Intercultural Relations*, 30(4), 507-521.

Hartley, M. & Morphew, C.C. (2008) What's Being Sold and to What End? A Content Analysis of College Viewbooks, *The Journal of Higher Education*, 79(6), 671-691.

Heisel, M. & Stableski, R. (2009) Expanding Study Abroad: where there's a will, there's a way, in P. Blumenthal & R. Gutierrez (Eds) *Expanding Study Abroad Capacity at US Colleges and Universities*, pp. 28-37. New York: Institute of International Education.

Institute of International Education (IIE) (2012) *Open Doors: 2011 report on international education exchange*. New York: IIE.

Institute of International Education (IIE) & The Forum on Education Abroad (2011) IIE-Forum Snapshot Survey 2010 and Data Set.

Loberg, L. (2012) Exploring Factors That Lead to Participation in Study Abroad. Doctoral dissertation, University of California, Los Angeles.

McClure, K.R., Szelényi, K., Niehaus, E., Anderson, A.A. & Reed, J. (2010) 'We Just Don't Have the Possibility Yet': US Latina/o narratives on study abroad, *Journal of Student Affairs Research and Practice*, 47(3), 367-386.

McDonough, P.M. (1994) Buying and Selling Higher Education: the social construction of the college applicant, *Journal of Higher Education*, 65(4), 427-446.

Penn, E.B. & Tanner, J. (2009) Black Students and International Education: an assessment, *Journal of Black Studies*, 40(2), 266-282.

Rust, V., Dhanatya, C., Furuto, L.H.L. & Kheiltash, O. (2007) Student Involvement as Predictive of College Freshmen Plans to Study Abroad, *Frontiers*, 15, Fall, 1-16.

Salisbury, M.H., Paulsen, M.B. & Pascarella, E.T. (2010) To See the World or Stay at Home: applying an integrated student choice model to explore the gender gap in the intent to study abroad, *Research in Higher Education*, 51(7), 615-640.

Salisbury, M.H., Umbach, P.D., Paulsen, M.B. & Pascarella, E.T. (2009) Going Global: understanding the choice process of the intent to study abroad, *Research in Higher Education*, 50(2), 119-143.

Sánchez, C.M., Fornerino, M. & Zhang, M. (2006) Motivations and the Intent to Study Abroad Among U.S., French, and Chinese Students, *Journal of Teaching in International Business*, 18(1), 27-52.

Shirley, S.W. (2006) The Gender Gap in Post-Secondary Study Abroad: understanding and marketing to male students. Doctoral dissertation. Proquest No. 3233968.

Stroud, A.H. (2010) Who Plans (Not) to Study Abroad? An Examination of US Student Intent, *Journal of Studies in International Education*, 14(5), 491-507.

Notes on Contributors

Rose Amazan is a lecturer in the Faculty of Education and Social Work, University of Sydney. Her research and teaching is in the area of comparative education and development studies. She has conducted research on the Ethiopian skilled diaspora with a strong focus on skilled female diasporas. Her research experience spreads across themes of education and belonging, skilled migration, diaspora mobility, knowledge transfer, female skilled migration/mobility and knowledge. She is currently working on a research project looking into the impact of AusAID scholarships on development in sub-Saharan Africa.

Robert F. Arnove works in the field of comparative and international education. He has been the lead co-editor of major textbooks in this field over the past 30 years. A major focus of much of his scholarship has been on educational and social change. His most recent single-authored book, *Talent Abounds*, explores the role of master teachers in cultivating peak performance in the arts and athletics. Although his principal region of interest has been Latin America and the Caribbean, he also has worked in China, India and Africa, as well as in several European countries.

Angeline M. Barrett is a lecturer in education in the Graduate School of Education, University of Bristol. She has conducted research in sub-Saharan Africa on teacher professionalism, social justice perspectives on education quality, capacity-building in higher education, and language and teaching. She is currently associate editor of the *International Journal of Educational Development*.

Jos Beelen is a researcher and consultant on internationalisation of the curriculum at the Centre for Applied Research on Economics and Management at the Amsterdam University of Applied Sciences. He is chair of the Special Interest Group Internationalisation at Home of the European Association for International Education and Visiting Fellow at Leeds Metropolitan University's Centre for Academic Practice and Research in Internationalisation. He is currently doing research into the implementation of the international dimension into higher education curricula, in cooperation with researchers from Europe and Australia.

Rahul Choudaha is Director of Research and Strategic Development at World Education Services (WES) in New York. At WES, a non-profit with over 40 years' expertise in international education research and evaluation, he leads advisory services for higher education institutions (wes.org/RAS) and international students (WESStudentAdvisor.org). Dr Choudaha is passionate about leveraging research to uncover strategic insights that can help institutions develop and implement internationalisation plans in an inherently complex, competitive and changing environment of global higher education. He specialises in student mobility trends with implications for enrolment management and transnational education strategies. Dr Choudaha is an Editorial Board member of the *Journal of Studies in International Education* and a recipient of the Tony Adams Award for Excellence in Research by the European Association of International Education. He has presented in nearly 75 sessions at professional conferences. He earned a doctorate in higher education from the University of Denver, a Master's degree in management and a Bachelor of Engineering degree from India. He also blogs as DrEducation.com and tweets @DrEducationBlog.

Emily Crawford is an Assistant Professor in Educational Leadership and Policy Analysis. She earned her doctorate in educational theory and policy with a minor in comparative and international education from Penn State University, where she focused on issues affecting educational equity for undocumented students. Her research interests include international immigration and education policy, looking at how educational leaders and teachers advocate for vulnerable students' access to education, and how education policy intersects with educators' professional and personal ethical codes.

Michael Crossley, AcSS, is Professor of Comparative and International Education, Director of the Research Centre for International and Comparative Studies at the Graduate School of Education, Director of the Doctor of Education Programme and Director of the Education in Small States Research Group (www.smallstates.net), University of Bristol, UK. He is a former editor of the journal *Comparative Education* and former chair of the British Association for International and Comparative Education. Key research interests relate to: theoretical and methodological scholarship on the future of comparative and international education; the international transfer of educational policy and practice; educational research capacity and international development cooperation: and educational development in small states.

Joan Dassin was the founding Executive Director of the Ford Foundation International Fellowships Program (IFP), responsible for developing IFP's original design and guiding its implementation in 22 participating countries from 2000-13. In June 2011, she received the Marita Houlihan Award for

Distinguished Contributions to International Education (NAFSA: Association of International Educators). She currently holds positions as Senior Associate Member, St Antony's College, and Visiting Research Associate, Centre for Latin American Studies, University of Oxford. Her research interests include access and equity in international higher and education reform and social mobility in Latin America. She has published articles in the *Academic Cooperation Association Papers on International Cooperation*, the *Chronicle of Higher Education* and *Inside Higher Education*. She recently collaborated on an edited volume entitled *Origins, Journeys and Returns: social justice in international higher education* (Social Science Research Council, 2009). She holds a PhD from Stanford University in modern thought and literature.

Darla K. Deardorff is a research scholar at Duke University, as well as Executive Director of the Association of International Education Administrators, a national professional organisation headquartered at Duke University. Founder of ICC Global, a global research network on intercultural competence, she has lived, taught and worked in Germany, Japan and Switzerland and has taught at numerous universities including Harvard University's Future of Learning Institute. She has published widely on intercultural and international education topics, including as editor of *The SAGE Handbook of Intercultural Competence* (Sage, 2009), and is regularly invited to speak and consult around the world on these topics. Other recent books include lead editor of *The Sage Handbook of International Higher Education* (Sage, 2012) and co-author of *Building Cultural Competence* (Stylus, 2012).

Hans De Wit is Director of the Centre for Higher Education Internationalisation (CHEI) at the Università Cattolica Sacro Cuore in Milan, Italy, and Professor of Internationalisation of Higher Education at the School of Economics and Management of the Hogeschool van Amsterdam, University of Applied Sciences. He is also Research Associate at Nelson Mandela Metropolitan University, Port Elizabeth, South Africa. He is the founding editor of the *Journal of Studies in International Education* (Association for Studies in International Education/SAGE publishers). His latest book is Darla Deardorff, Hans de Wit, John D. Heyl and Tony Adams (Eds) (2012) *The SAGE Handbook on International Higher Education*. He publishes a monthly blog in *University World News* on internationalisation of higher education (http://www.universityworldnews.com). He has (co-)written several other books and articles on international education and is actively involved in assessment and consultancy in international education for organisations like the European Commission, UNESCO, World Bank and IMHE/OECD. In 2005-06, he was a New Century Scholar of the Fulbright Program Higher Education in the 21st Century, and in 1995 and 2006 a visiting scholar in the USA and in 2002 in Australia. Hans de Wit is founding member and past president of the European Association for International Education (EAIE). Currently, he is a member of the Board of Trustees of World Education Services (New York), member of the ESL TOEFL Board. He is also a jury member for several awards, such as the Tony Adams Scholarship Awards, the Internationalization through Technology Award of the American Council on Education and SUNY COIL, and the IEASA Awards Committee for Excellence in Internationalisation.

Jürgen Enders is Professor at the School of Education at the University of Southampton, UK, having previously worked as the Director of the Center for Higher Education Policy Studies in the Netherlands. His research interests are in the areas of the political sociology of higher education, research and innovation; the governance and management of higher education; organisational change in higher education; the student experience, employability and graduate careers; and the academic profession. He is elected member of the Academia Europaea and of the German Academe of Science and Engineering; and member of advisory committees to the Higher Education Funding Council in England and the German Ministries for Education. He has written and (co)-edited 14 books and published more than 100 articles in books and journals on higher education.

Titanji Peter Fon is Associate Professor in Leadership in Schooling and presently serving as Vice-Dean in charge of Studies and Students' Affairs in the Faculty of Education, University of Buea, Cameroon. His research interests are in educational policy and implementation, institutional leadership, school culture, governance and equity issues in education. He is also interested in the changing environments of educational organisations and leadership implications. He teaches in the areas of sociology of education and educational administration, planning and policy.

Jonathan Z. Friedman is a PhD candidate in international education in the Steinhardt School of Culture, Education and Human Development at New York University. His research interests include the sociologies of education, knowledge, nationalism and globalisation. Since 2010, Jonathan has served as a research assistant on a multi-year project looking at the production of knowledge on world regions in the American university, housed at the US Social Science Research Council. He is currently focusing on a comparative study of university administrators' perspectives on internationalization at elite and mass institutions in the US and Britain.

Jürgen Henze has been Professor of Comparative Education at Humboldt University of Berlin since 1993. His research expertise is in Asian education with special reference to Chinese education. His main interest in teaching and research is on modernisation and educational developments in East Asia, the theory and practice of cultural sensitivity (training), as well as non-

Western approaches of intercultural communication and competence formation.

Anne Hickling-Hudson specialises in cross-cultural, comparative and international education in Australia's Queensland University of Technology. Now retired, she continues as Professor of Education in an adjunct capacity. Born and raised in Jamaica, Anne was educated at the Universities of the West Indies and of Hong Kong, and gained her PhD at the University of Queensland in Australia. Her career as a teacher, teacher educator, researcher, education planner and community activist spans the Caribbean, the UK, the USA, Hong Kong and Australia. A Rockefeller Fellow, her publications include analysis of education for development and decolonisation, of race relations in schools and texts and of intercultural and postcolonial approaches. She co-edits a book series and an online journal focusing on postcolonial studies in education. She is past president of several scholarly associations including the World Council of Comparative Education Societies and the British Association for International and Comparative Education.

Jane Knight, Ontario Institute for Studies in Education, University of Toronto, focuses her research on the international dimension of higher education at the institutional, national, regional and international levels. Her work in over 65 countries with universities, governments and UN agencies helps to bring a comparative, development and international perspective to her research, teaching and policy work. She is the author of numerous publications on internationalisation concepts and strategies, quality assurance, institutional management, trade, education hubs and crossborder education. She is the co-founder of the African Network for Internationalization of Education and sits on the advisory boards of several international organisations, universities and journals. In 2010 the University of Exeter awarded her an Honorary LLD, in 2011 she was the recipient of the Outstanding Researcher Award from the European Association for Institutional Research and in 2013 she was awarded the Gilbert Medal from Universitas 21 for her contribution to higher education internationalisation.

Andrea Kottmann is a Senior Researcher at the Center for Higher Education Policy Studies at the University of Twente in the Netherlands. In her work she has been specialising on the evaluation of fellowship or funding programmes for postgraduate education. Andrea has also been doing research on the development of higher education professionals in teaching and learning in European universities. Currently she is involved in research on the reform of doctoral training across Europe. In addition she is interested in the later careers of the highly qualified and their transitions to the labour market.

Lisa Loberg is Director of Study Abroad and a senior lecturer of French at California Lutheran University, where she has overseen the creation of a study abroad centre and the expansion of international programmes and partnerships. She serves on the advisory board for the American Institute for Foreign Study and International Studies Abroad, and is a founding member of the Lessons From Abroad organisation, which provides programming and resources for study abroad returnees. She received her EdD from the University of California, Los Angeles and her MA in French from Boston College.

Simon Marginson is Professor of International Higher Education at the Institute of Education, University of London, UK, where he has worked since October 2013. Previously he worked as Professor of Higher Education at the University of Melbourne, Australia (2006-13). He is joint editor-in-chief of the journal *Higher Education* and a commissioning editor for *Thesis Eleven*. A widely published and cited scholar, he focuses primarily on globalisation and comparative and international higher education, including international students, the effects of university ranking systems, policy approaches to STEM, and higher education and science in East Asia. His current research includes a comparison of the 'public good' or social role of universities in seven countries. His books include *Markets in Education* (1997), the co-authored *The Enterprise University* (2000), *Global Creation* (2010), *Imagination* (2010), *International Student Security* (2010) and the edited and co-edited *Prospects of Higher Education* (2007), *Handbook of Higher Education and Globalization* (2011), *Higher Education in the Asia-Pacific* (2011), *Tertiary Education Policy in Australia* (2013) and *The Dawkins Revolution 25 Years on* (2013).

Cynthia Miller-Idriss is Associate Professor and Program Director of the International Training and Education Program at American University and is also a research associate at the Social Science Research Council in New York. A sociologist by training, Miller-Idriss works on nationalism and extremism in contemporary Europe and on the internationalisation of higher education in the United States. Prior to her arrival at American University in 2013, she spent 10 years on the faculty at New York University and is in residence in 2013-14 at the Morphomata Center for Advanced Studies at the Universität zu Köln.

Thomas Nørgaard received a DPhil in philosophy from Oxford in 2002. Since then he has been a faculty member at the European College of Liberal Arts (ECLA), now Bard College Berlin. For a decade he was also a part of ECLA's administration, first as Programme Director, then as Co-Dean of the College and Academic Affairs/Managing Director. In 2013-14, he will be a Visiting Professor at the Artes Liberales Faculty at Warsaw University and a Research Fellow at the Remarque Institute at New York University. His primary interests are ethics, value theory and the philosophy of education. He is currently working on a book about liberal education in Europe.

Anthony C. Ogden is Executive Director of Education Abroad and Exchanges and an adjunct Assistant Professor in Educational Policy and Evaluation Studies at the University of Kentucky. Ogden earned his Bachelor's degree from Berea College and his Master's degree in international and intercultural management at the SIT Graduate Institute. He completed his PhD at Pennsylvania State University in educational theory and policy with a dual title in comparative and international education. A career international educator, Ogden's research interests and scholarly work have focused on education abroad outcomes assessment, global citizenship and academic development.

Justin J.W. Powell, PhD, Freie Universität Berlin, is Professor of Sociology of Education at the University of Luxembourg. His main fields of interest are sociology of education, special and inclusive education, higher education and science systems, social inequality and disability studies. Recent publications include *Barriers to Inclusion: special education in the United States and Germany* (Paradigm Publishers, 2011), *Soziale Ungleichheit: Klassische Texte zur Sozialstrukturanalyse* (Campus Verlag, 2009; co-edited with Heike Solga & Peter A. Berger) and *Comparing Special Education: origins to contemporary paradoxes* (Stanford University Press, 2011; co-authored with John G. Richardson), which received an AERA Outstanding Book Award (2012).

Val D. Rust is Professor of Education at the University of California, Los Angeles (UCLA). He received his PhD from the University of Michigan in education studies. He recently served as the faculty chair of the Graduate School of Education and Information Studies and served for many years as the Director of the International Education Office at UCLA, which houses the Education Abroad Program, the Travel Study Program, non-University of California study abroad providers and other student exchange programmes. He is also Director of the Center for International and Development Education in the Department of Education, which deals extensively with higher educational mapping around the world, international educational leadership and teacher training.

Bernhard Streitwieser is an International Research Fellow of Northwestern University's Center for Advancing Learning and Teaching. From 2010-13 he was a Visiting Professor at Berlin's Humboldt Universität and served as acting co-chair for the Department of Comparative Education in 2012-13 and lectured on the internationalisation of higher education, student identity development and global mobility. From 2010-14 he conducted a study on the Erasmus Mobility Programme and student identity development, which was funded by grants from the Fulbright Commission and the German Academic Exchange Service. In 2012 he guest-edited a special issue (Volume 7) on comparative education and educational mobility for the journal *Research in International and Comparative Education*, and his publications have appeared in books by Routledge, Teachers College Press, Symposium Books and Schneider Verlag and in *The International Journal of Teaching and Learning in Higher Education*; *Research in International and Comparative Education*; *Change: The Magazine of Higher Learning*; *European Education*; *Educational Research & Evaluation*; the *American Journal of Evaluation*; and the *Journal of Innovative Higher Education*.

Bernd Wächter is the Chief Executive Officer of ACA, a think-tank on European and international higher education focusing on internationalisation. Together with the Board of ACA, Bernd is in charge of setting the policy directions of ACA. He is also in charge of ACA's research agenda.

Anthony Welch is Professor of Education at the University of Sydney. He has substantial national and international project experience, and has published widely on themes such as multiculturalism, schooling and work, indigenous minorities, international students, higher education and the academic profession, and the internationalisation of (higher) education. With an MA and PhD from the University of London, he has significant experience in working abroad, including having taught and/or researched at universities in the USA, Japan, Germany, China and Vietnam. He speaks, reads and writes German, holds a Visiting Professor position at Tianjin University, China, and is author and editor of 10 books, and around 200 articles and chapters. He is currently part of an international team conducting the Comprehensive Education Sector Review for the Ministry of Education, Myanmar.

Zachary Van Winkle is a master's student in the social sciences at Berlin's Humboldt University and works as a student employee at the Institute for Social Sciences (Department of Empirical Social Research and the Department of Demography).